SHARE
the
Music
McGRAW-HILL

**AUTHORS**
Michael Jothen, Vincent Lawrence,
Barbara Staton, Merrill Staton

**CONTRIBUTING AUTHOR**
Jeanne Ruviella (Knorr)

## McGraw-Hill School Division

*A Division of The McGraw·Hill Companies*

McGraw-Hill School Division
Two Penn Plaza
New York, NY 10121

Printed in the United States of America

ISBN 0-02-295382-5

3 4 5 6 7 8 9 058 03 02 01 00 99

McGraw-Hill
School Division
New York          Farmington

# $\mathcal{C}$ONTENTS

## $\mathcal{M}$EET THE MUSICIAN

Recorded interviews with composers, arrangers, performers, producers, and engineers—a career motivator.

## T E C H N O L O G Y

- **Music with MIDI** allows students to play, improvise, create, and analyze music with the MIDI sequencer. Builds upon musical concepts and skills presented in the *Share the Music* program.

- **Videos** make music come alive through movement, signing, and authentic performances.

## KEYBOARD AND GUITAR

Hands-on activities that build keyboard and guitar performance skills in group and individual instruction.

## AMERICAN POPULAR MUSIC

Engaging exploration of the development of ragtime, blues, rock, and other popular styles from 1900 to the present. Abundant keyboard and guitar playalong accompaniments foster active student involvement.

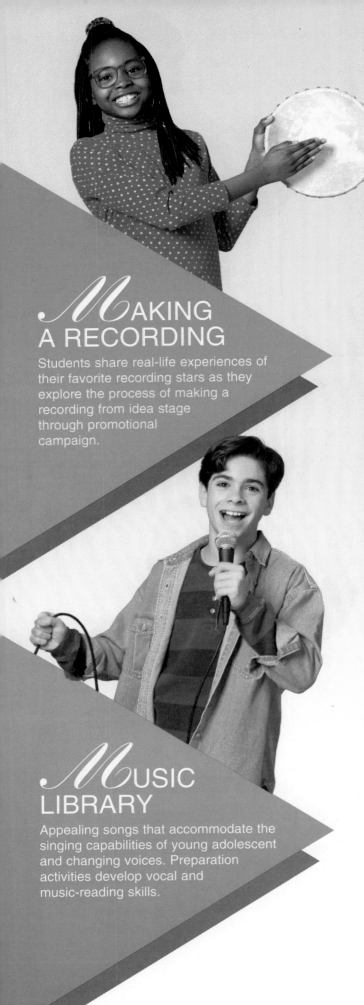

# MAKING A RECORDING

Students share real-life experiences of their favorite recording stars as they explore the process of making a recording from idea stage through promotional campaign.

# MUSIC LIBRARY

Appealing songs that accommodate the singing capabilities of young adolescent and changing voices. Preparation activities develop vocal and music-reading skills.

# OUR AUTHORS
## SHARING A UNITY OF PURPOSE AND A DIVERSITY OF TALENTS

### Dr. Michael Jothen

Michael is an Associate Professor of Music and Coordinator of the Graduate Program in Music Education at Towson State University in Maryland. He is a nationally-known music educator, choral clinician, and conductor. Michael has received many commissions for choral compositions and has been recognized by ASCAP for his contributions as a composer of choral music. He has served as President of the National Board of Directors of Choristers Guild. Michael is an author of *Music and You* and of *Share the Music* (Grades K-6).

### Barbara Staton

During her eight years as a music television teacher for the State of Georgia, Barbara pioneered the teaching of music through movement on television. Her diverse teaching experience spans pre-kindergarten through graduate courses. Barbara is the author of the *Move Into Music* series and is a recognized ASCAP composer. A popular clinician, she has conducted music and movement workshops for teachers throughout the U.S. and Canada. Barbara is a senior author of *Music and You.*

### Dr. Vincent Lawrence

Vincent is widely recognized as an expert in secondary general music education. For 21 years he was Professor of Music at Towson State University in Maryland, where he was the chairperson of Music Education and directed the University Chorale. During that time he was actively involved in teaching general music in the middle school. Vincent is an author of *Music and You,* a coordinating author of *Share the Music* (Grades K-6), and an author of the leading high school text *Music! Its Role and Importance in Our Lives.*

### Dr. Merrill Staton

Merrill is nationally known as a music educator, choral conductor, singer, ASCAP composer and producer of recordings. He has been music director of and has conducted the Merrill Staton Voices on many network TV series and recordings. A leader in the field of music education recordings for over thirty years, Merrill pioneered the separation of instrumental and vocal tracks and the use of children's voices on recordings. He is a senior author of *Music and You.*

### Jeanne Ruviella (Knorr)

Jeanne teaches music education and theory at Towson State University in Maryland. She has taught vocal and instrumental music at all levels and is a noted teacher trainer in the Orff, Kodály, and Dalcroze approaches. Jeanne holds a Dalcroze-Orff-Kodály Certificate from the Manhattan School of Music and a Dalcroze Certificate from the Longy School of Music. She is a contributing author of *Music and You.*

# A PHILOSOPHY

## SHARING YOUR COMMITMENT FOR SUCCESSFUL LEARNING

**SHARE THE MUSIC** is an activity-centered program that involves students of all learning styles. Sequenced and thematic activities develop the cognitive, affective, and psychomotor domains of learners.

**SHARE THE MUSIC** helps you address the issues of today and tomorrow. Here's how!

---

**OUTSTANDING SONGS, LISTENINGS, AND NEW SONG RECORDINGS**

- Present the highest-quality materials in a variety of musical styles.
- Highlight the natural sound of young adolescent voices recorded with artistic and captivating accompaniments.

---

**CULTURALLY AUTHENTIC MUSIC**

- Celebrates cultural diversity and similarity through motivating multicultural materials and recordings.
- Broadens the students' experiences with diverse vocal techniques used around the world while building vocal skills.

---

**SEQUENCED LEARNING PROCESS**

- Helps students to understand the different elements of music and analyze the reasons they enjoy their favorite musical styles.
- Integrates Kodály, Orff, Dalcroze, and traditional music approaches.
- Builds music literacy and understanding through singing, listening, moving, creating, music reading, critical thinking, and meaningful assessment.

---

**ACTIVE STUDENT INVOLVEMENT**

- Engages students' interest through composition, creative movement, critical listening, and instrumental playalongs.
- Encourages students to become musically independent.

---

**FLEXIBLE ORGANIZATION FOR DIVERSE NEEDS**

- Presents multiple options to fit 6-week, 9-week, full-semester, or full-year course offerings.
- Provides a wide range of activities and materials to meet the varied interests, needs, and skill abilities of the young adolescent student.

---

# AN ORGANIZATION

## DEDICATED TO MEETING DIVERSE TEACHING NEEDS

- FLEXIBLE FORMAT TO ACCOMMODATE 6-WEEK, 9-WEEK, FULL-SEMESTER, OR FULL-YEAR COURSE

- 8 UNITS OF GENERAL MUSIC INSTRUCTION AND SUPPLEMENTARY SECTIONS

### GENERAL MUSIC

- Unit 1, the "core" unit, forms the basic structure for all other units. Designed to be taught first.

- Listening lessons, songs, motivational music topics, concepts, music reading, and playalong accompaniments are integrated throughout.

- Unit reviews assess student content and skill mastery.

### SPECIAL STUDY SECTIONS

**Grade 7**
- American Popular Music
- Making a Recording

**Grade 8**
- Western Musical Styles
- Music of the World's Cultures
- Music in Your Life

### INSTRUMENTAL SECTIONS

**Grade 7**
- Keyboard and Guitar
- Accompaniments and Lyrics to Songs in *American Popular Music*

**Grade 8**
- Keyboards of Today
- Playing the Guitar

### MUSIC LIBRARY

**Grades 7 and 8**
- Song Anthology
- Choral Anthology

# THE LESSON PLAN *DESIGNED FOR CREATIVE*

**SHARE THE MUSIC** builds on our tradition of sequential instruction.

Each lesson outlines specific objectives, step-by-step teaching procedures, and appraisals that save you time in reaching and teaching your students.

Teaching suggestions are easily organized by color coding and placement on the teacher's page.

> **Lesson preparation information**

> **Basic teaching plan**

> **Extended activities for in-depth study**

**LESSON PLANNER**
A quick outline of the lesson.

**1 SETTING THE STAGE**
A creative "lesson starter."

**2 TEACHING THE LESSON**
Sequenced lesson steps.

CD1

## LESSON 3

**Focus: Unity and Variety**
**Objectives**
To recognize how changes in musical sound (instruments, voices, sections, dynamics) contribute to unity and variety in a musical composition
To identify a simple form (introduction A B A B A coda)

**Materials**
Recordings: "Do You Hear the People Sing?"
Sticks, drums, tambourines, and triangles
(See More Music Teaching Ideas.)

**Vocabulary**
Form

**1 SETTING THE STAGE**
Tell the students that unity and variety can be found in everyday life.

**2 TEACHING THE LESSON**
1. Introduce visual unity, variety, and repetition and contrast in pictures. Have the students:
• Examine the pictures to identify examples of repetition or contrast.
• Identify unity or variety in each picture.

## LESSON 3

3. Introduce the form of "Do You Hear the People Sing?" Have the students:
• Read page 14.
• Listen to the recording again.
• Identify the form of the melody. (introduction A B A B A coda)

• Listen again to the recording of "Do You Hear the People Sing?" Notice the repetition of words and music and the changes in the different voices and instruments.

Repetition and contrast help to give music its form. **Form** is the way a composition is organized. When form is described, letters are used to represent different sections. The form of "Do You Hear the People Sing?" can be outlined as:
Introduction, A B A B A, coda.

*Les Misérables*

*The Phantom of the Opera*

*Ragtime*

Am...
The F...
arts...
of the...
comb...
roma...
come...
and e...
bases...
as Co...
in Y...
De...
develo...
and e...
Oklah...
1950s...

## EXTENSION

**EXTENSION**
Optional resources for meeting individual needs. Includes more music teaching ideas, biographies, curriculum connections, cooperative learning, suggestions for special learners, critical thinking strategies, and additional background information.

**THE MUSICAL**
**Les Misérables**
Victor Hugo's monumental novel is the basis of this musical. The setting of the musical is nineteenth-century France. The characters suffer from oppression and are struggling to survive. The show was originally written in 1979 and presented on a small scale in Paris. It was then developed into a large-scale musical and opened in London in 1985. The music is by Claude-Michel Schönberg. The original French lyrics are by Alain Boublil and the English lyrics are by Herbert Kretzmer.

**MORE MUSIC TEACHING IDEAS**
Have the students play the steady beat on classroom instruments to accompany each section of "Do You Hear the People Sing?" to emphasize and clarify different sections. For example—introduction: sticks; A sections: drums; B sections: tambourines; coda: triangles.

**TE...**
Sh...
wh...
dev...

**Piano Accompaniments**
Conveniently bound in a separate booklet for each grade.

14 UNIT 1

# INSTRUCTION AND MANAGEABILITY

**D VARIETY**

**ay Life**

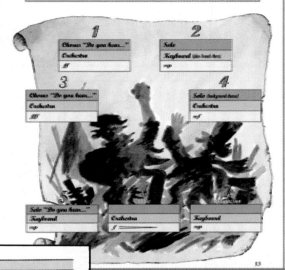

• Listen to "Do You Hear the People Sing?" from the musical *Les Misérables*. Notice the changes in the voices, instruments, and dynamics.

CD1:7

Which sections are similar? Which are different? The order of the sections is scrambled on this page. Arrange the sections in the order in which you hear them. 7, 5, 2, 1, 4, 3, 6

🎵 "Do You Hear the People Sing?" from *Les Misérables*
by Claude-Michel Schönberg and Alain Boublil

13

## LESSON 3

2. Introduce unity and variety in "Do You Hear the People Sing?" Have the students:
• Identify and name the content of each picture, focusing on the voices, instruments, and dynamic levels. Identify which pictures are similar. (1, 3, 5; 2, 4; 6, 7) Identify the differences among them. (Review the meaning of the dynamic symbols if needed.)
• Listen to the recording of "Do You Hear the People Sing?" Notice the combination of voices, instruments, and dynamic levels. Write down the order of the pictures. (You may wish to signal when each section starts. Play the recording several times if needed.)
• Analyze and discuss the answers. (7, intro; 5 *Do you hear*; 2, *Will you join*; 1, *Do you hear*; 4, *Will you give*; 3, *Do you hear*; 6, coda)
• Identify voices heard. (solo, chorus)
• Identify instruments heard. (keyboard, orchestra)
• Identify dynamic levels heard. (*mp*, *mf*, *f*, *ff*–*fff*, decrescendo)
• Discuss how "Do You Hear the People Sing?" has both unity and variety. (Unity is provided by repetition of words, voices, instruments, and sections. Variety is provided by changing voices, instruments, dynamic levels, and sections.)

## LESSON 3

4. Introduce American musical theater. Have the students:
• Read and discuss the background information on American musical theater. You may wish to use some of the following items as a basis for extended discussion.
1. Music in the theater has many functions. Music can set a mood, announce an event, or describe a character. Name some specific examples of each of these uses of music in the theater. (In "Summer Days" from *Grease*, a boy and girl tell their respective friends about their summer romance. In "Memory" from *Cats*, an old, tattered alley cat recalls her youth and beauty and wishes those happy days would come again.)
2. Name some musical compositions from the American musical theater whose popularity has outlasted that of the shows from which they came. ("Tomorrow" from *Annie*; "Hello, Dolly!" from the musical of the same name; "The Impossible Dream" from *Man of La Mancha*.) Discuss some reasons why some songs might remain popular longer than the musicals. (Answers will vary.)

### Reinforcing the Lesson

Review the features that contribute unity and variety to the song. (Repetition of the words, voices, instruments, and sections contributes to the unity of the song. Variety is provided through contrasts in voices, instruments, sections, and dynamic levels.)

**3 APPRAISAL**

The students should be able to:
1. Verbally identify at least two features that contribute to unity, and at least two features that provide variety in "Do You Hear the People Sing?"
2. Verbally identify the form of "Do You Hear the People Sing?" as introduction A B A B A coda.

... Listening Map can ... help guide the students ... section.

UNIT 1   13

**REINFORCING THE LESSON**
Lesson strategies for application, reinforcement, and synthesis of concepts.

**3 APPRAISAL**
A check for student understanding and accomplishment of each objective.

**COMPREHENSIVE EVALUATIONS**
• *Review* and *Just Checking* at the end of each unit of the Pupil Book.
• Unit written/recorded evaluations in the Teacher's Resource Masters.

**TEACHER'S RESOURCE MASTERS**
• Blackline masters to extend and evaluate learning.

UNIT 1   15

# ᴁCTIVE PARTICIPATION

Special study sections focus on high-interest topics that help students link music learning with their everyday lives.

**Grade 7**
- American Popular Music
- Keyboard and Guitar
- Making a Recording

**Grade 8**
- Western Musical Styles
- Music of the World's Cultures
- Keyboards of Today
- Playing the Guitar
- Music in Your Life

## AMERICAN POPULAR MUSIC

Engaging exploration of the development of ragtime, blues, rock, and other popular styles from 1900 to the present. Abundant keyboard and guitar playalong accompaniments foster active student involvement.

## MAKING A RECORDING

Students share real-life experiences of their favorite recording stars as they explore the process of making a recording from idea stage through promotional campaign.

## MEET THE MUSICIAN

Recorded interviews with composers, arrangers, performers, producers, and engineers serve as a career motivator for students.

# MUSIC LIBRARY

Appealing songs that accommodate the singing capabilities of young adolescent and changing voices. Preparation activities develop vocal and music-reading skills.

## SONG ANTHOLOGY

The **Song Anthology** contains lively arrangements of folk and recreational songs.

## CHORAL ANTHOLOGY

The **Choral Anthology** contains vocal arrangements suitable for performance.

# NEW RECORDINGS

## OUTSTANDING SOUNDS AND INNOVATIVE CHOICES

### SONG RECORDINGS

- Teen and young adult voices that provide exemplary and motivating vocal models.

- Rich, contemporary instrumental arrangements that inspire participation.

- The warm sound of analog recordings mixed and mastered with state-of-the-art digital technology.

- **Divided Tracks** allow students to hear the vocal and instrumental tracks separately by adjusting the balance control on the CD player.

- **Divided Vocal Parts** in part songs allow students to hear selected vocal parts over a stereo accompaniment by adjusting the balance control.

### PERFORMANCE MIXES

- Stereo accompaniments without vocals for selected songs and choral arrangements.

### RECORDED INTERVIEWS

- Recorded interviews, entitled MEET, bring the voices and music of famous musicians into the classroom to help motivate and inform young people about musical careers.

### MUSIC ACROSS CULTURES

Open a new world of understanding and a rich heritage for your students with song recordings representing many American cultures.

- Pronunciation guides by native speakers.

- Variety of ethnic instruments.

- Native singers, speakers, and instrumentalists provide authentic regional music and cultural background.

**PERFORMING GROUPS** selected from around the country.

# Integrated Arts

## VISUAL ARTS • DANCE • THEATER • MUSIC

Motivating materials invite students to explore connections among the visual arts, dance, theater, and music.

ETITION
H VARIATION

at is the original idea in each
ure?

at has been changed in each
cture to provide visual interest
d contrast?

ation results when an idea is
anged or altered.

*I Saw the Figure 5 in Gold,*
by Charles Demuth

*Teke,*
by Victor Vasarely

153

### Mixing Musical Cultures

In this first section you will listen to music that mixes the characteristics of music of the United States with characteristics of the music of another culture. Some ways musicians do this are to combine instruments, rhythm, melodies, or harmonies of both cultures.

*Kogoklaras* (kō-gō-klä´räs) is one example of this mix. It combines characteristics of Indonesian music and music of the United States.

Right and below, dancers from the island of Bali, Indonesia. The dancers must practice for years to master these difficult techniques.

• Listen and identify musical characteristics of Indonesia and the United States.

*Kogoklaras,* by Vincent McDermott

211

xiii

A consistent Teaching Plan focuses on concepts and skills that are first experienced, then identified and labeled, creatively reinforced, and finally evaluated.

Boldface type indicates a *basic concept or skill* is measured.

Concepts and skills are measured informally in the Pupil books at the end of each unit.

Written Unit Evaluations are provided in *Teacher's Copying Masters*.

| ELEMENTS OF MUSIC | UNIT 1 YOU AND MUSIC Objectives | UNIT 2 RHYTHM AROUND US Objectives | UNIT 3 RHYTHM EVERYWHERE Objectives |
|---|---|---|---|
| Dynamics | Identify dynamic changes **Identify piano and forte Identify and perform accents** | | **Identify dynamic contrasts and changes Identify *crescendo*** |
| Tone Color | **Perform on percussion, pitched instruments** Identify solo and chorus Listen to electronic sounds Identify voice qualities **Review orchestral families** | Perform on Orff instruments Listen to folk instruments, ragtime ensemble | Identify sounds of orchestral and folk instruments Perform on guitar Listen to electronic sounds |
| Tempo | **Perform slow tempo** | Sing in slow tempo **Identify tempo change** | **Identify *ritardando* and *a tempo*** |
| Duration/ Rhythm | **Identify and perform quarter, eighths, quarter rest, duple and triple meter** Perform rhythm patterns, steady beat | **Perform steady beat Identify meter signature Identify and perform quarter, eighth, sixteenth notes, and quarter rests** Perform melodic rhythm **Identify syncopation** | **Identify, distinguish, and perform equal and dotted rhythms, triplets Identify and perform syncopation and augmentation** |
| Pitch | **Perform melodic patterns using G A C** | | **Perform melodic accompaniments using G A B D** |
| Texture | **Identify homophonic, polyphonic, and monophonic textures** | Perform polyphony, harmonic accompaniment, two-part harmony | Perform homophonic and polyphonic textures **Perform homophonic textures** Hear harmonic repetition Perform harmonic and melodic accompaniments |
| Form | Identify unity and variety Identify ABABA **Identify a round** Experience fugue **Identify ternary (ABA) form** | **Identify verse-refrain form (AB) Identify phrase lengths** | Identify and perform phrases of equal and unequal length Perform songs in ABA and AB form |
| Style | Discuss, listen to, and identify pop, musical, folk song, spoken music, romantic period | **Identify ragtime** Perform song in Spanish | Perform folk-rock song and spiritual Listen to the operatic music of the romantic period |

| UNIT 4 | UNIT 5 | UNIT 6 | UNIT 7 | UNIT 8 |
|---|---|---|---|---|
| MELODY | HARMONY | REPETITION: THE BASIS OF FORM | FORM: REPETITION AND CONTRAST | TONE COLOR |
| Objectives | Objectives | Objectives | Objectives | Objectives |
| **Identify dynamics** | **Listen to and identify changing dynamics** | **Hear dynamic changes** | **Listen to and identify repetition and contrast in dynamics** | Identify dynamic changes |
| **Listen to and identify vocal and instrumental tone color** | **Perform instrumental accompaniments** Listen to early blues ensemble, synthesizer, folk instruments | Hear string bass, orchestra, tone color variations **Perform accompaniment on classroom instruments** Perform spoken music | Perform on pitched and unpitched instruments Listen to Renaissance ensemble | **Identify marching band, orchestra, families of instruments, blend and contrast Identify decisions about tone color and tone colors in scores** Create a composition with various tone colors |
| **Perform in slow and fast tempo** | Distinguish and perform slow and fast tempos | **Identify accelerando, tempo changes** | Listen to tempo contrasts | **Perform rhythms in steady tempo** |
| **Identify an ostinato** | Perform syncopated rhythm pattern **Perform rhythmic ostinato Identify** *legato* **and** *staccato* **articulation** | **Identify repeated patterns** Identify syncopation Hear meter changes, augmentation | **Perform** *legato* **and** *staccato* **articulation** | Listen to and perform beat and beat subdivisions Listen to and perform in duple meter |
| Identify stepwise motion **Identify major scale** Perform a five-tone scale **Perform minor pentaton, music in minor mode Identify melodic contour** Identify sharp symbol **Perform melody using C-E$^{\mathrm{I}}$** | Create melodic patterns **Identify or perform Dorian and Mixolydian modes Identify blues scale, major, minor** Follow melodic sequence and melodic contour **Listen to and identify tonal and atonal music** | **Perform melodic ostinato using G Em C D chords or roots** Identify upper and lower registers | Review Dorian mode Perform vocal improvisations **Perform melodic accompaniment using C-D$^{\mathrm{I}}$** | **Perform G A B C D on recorder, bells, or keyboard** Sing four partner songs |
| **Identify homophonic, polyphonic, and monophonic textures** Listen to thin and thick textures **Define ostinato** | **Identify and perform homophonic texture Listen to, identify, and perform I, IV, V chords and roots** Perform thin/thick textures | Listen to, identify, and perform homophonic and polyphonic textures **Perform homophonic and polyphonic textures** | Listen to and perform homophonic and polyphonic textures | Identify thin and thick textures Perform in polyphonic texture |
| Identify and perform AABA form, round, AB form, phrases **Identify and define phrases** | Perform music in AB form Perform twelve-bar blues | **Identify theme and variations Identify subject and episode** | **Listen to and identify sections of equal and unequal length Identify contrasting sections, repetitions Review ternary form Identify rondo and suite** | **Identify march form** Improvise rondo form Perform four-part quodlibet |
| Listen to music of the baroque and romantic periods Perform an American folk song Listen to music of classical period | Listen to and perform Spanish folk music, blues, American folk song Listen to and accompany film music | Listen to American popular music, romantic style, minimalist style, baroque style in 20th-century orchestration, American nationalistic music, jazz | Listen to Renaissance, American and English folk music, orchestral music | Listen to and perform American march, baroque music, film music |

# UNIT 1 ● OVERVIEW

| ELEMENTS OF MUSIC | UNIT 1 OBJECTIVES | Lesson 1 Focus: Steady Beat, Accent | Lesson 2 Focus: Steady Beat, Accent, Eighth Notes | Lesson 3 Focus: Unity and Variety | Lesson 4 Focus: Duple and Triple Meter |
|---|---|---|---|---|---|
| Dynamics | **Identify *piano* and *forte* Perform accents** | Identify, define, and perform accents | Identify and perform accents | | Identify *piano* and *forte* |
| Tone Color | **Perform on percussion and pitched instruments** Identify solo and chorus Listen to electronic sounds Identify voice qualities **Review orchestral families** | Perform on percussion instruments | Perform on percussion instruments | Listen to and identify instruments and solo/chorus in Broadway-style music | Hear electronic sounds (synthesizer) |
| Tempo | **Perform slow tempo** | | | | |
| Duration/ Rhythm | **Identify and perform quarter, eighths, quarter rest, duple and triple meter** Perform rhythm patterns Perform steady beat | Identify steady beat Perform rhythms Experience duple meter Identify, define, and perform quarter notes and quarter rests  Create rhythm patterns | Perform rhythmic accompaniment with accents, steady beat Move to duple meter Perform and identify quarter and eighth notes Identify rhythmic patterns  Create rhythm patterns | Experience duple meter  Play steady beat on classroom instruments | Identify and move to duple and triple meter Perform conducting patterns, body percussion in duple and triple meter |
| Pitch | **Perform melodic patterns using G A B** | ♪ | | Hear a melody | |
| Texture | Identify unity and variety Identify ABABA **Identify a round** | | | Experience homophonic texture | |
| Form | Experience fugue **Identify ternary (ABA) form** Discuss and listen to pop, musical, folk, spoken music, romantic period | | | Identify unity and variety Identify a simple form (intro ABABA coda) Define form | Identify unity and variety in a composition |
| Style | Discuss and listen to disco, musical, popular, folk, spoken music, romantic period | Listen to different styles of music Experience contemporary pop style | Listen to, discuss, and perform Latin-influenced pop | Listen to, discuss, and perform music from American musical theater | |
| Reading | | Read sticking patterns, ♩ , ♩ , > , ‖: :‖ , 4/4 | Read ♩ , ♫ , ♩ , ‾ , 4/4 D.S., Fine. | | Read and identify duple and triple meter, *piano*, *forte* |

## PURPOSE Unit 1: You and Music

In this unit the students will review and/or experience rhythm, pitch, tone color, meter, texture, and form. They will gain an understanding of musical concepts through listening and performance.

## SUGGESTED TIME FRAME

| September | October |
|---|---|
| | |

## FOCUS

- Steady beat
- Accent
- Eighth notes
- Unity and variety
- Duple and triple meter
- Texture
- Voice quality and register
- Vocal and instrumental tone color
- Reading melodic notation
- Pitch memory
- Major scale

| Lesson 5<br>Focus: Texture–Monophonic, Homophonic, Polyphonic | Lesson 6<br>Focus: Voice Quality, Vocal Tone Color, Register | Lesson 7<br>Focus: Instrumental Tone Color–Strings, Woodwinds, Brass, Percussion | Lesson 8<br>Focus: Reading Melodic Notation | Lesson 9<br>Focus: Pitch Memory, Major Scale |
|---|---|---|---|---|
| | | Identify dynamic change within form | | |
| Emphasis on diction in performance | Listen to and identify voice quality and register<br>Identify tone color of speaking and singing voices | Listen to and identify tone color of orchestral families | Play recorder, bells, or keyboard | Perform accompaniment on Orff instruments |
| | | | Experience and perform in slow tempo | |
| Keep the steady beat by singing and patting<br>Review duple and triple meter<br>Perform body percussion in triple meter<br><br>**Create rhythmic patterns** | | Perform steady beat | Identify and perform rhythm patterns<br>Identify half rest | Experience legato |
| Sing a song with range from c-d¹<br><br>**Play melodic ostinato**<br>**Sing song on pitch syllables** | Identify high and low range<br>Sing a melody with a range from C#-D¹ | | Perform melodic accompaniment with pitches G A C<br>Identify the range of a melody<br><br>**Create melodies with G A C**<br>**Sing a melody** | Identify interval, stepwise and skipwise motion, melodic direction<br>Create tunes using a tone ladder<br>Identify mystery tune<br>Experience interval relationships<br>Experience and perform the major scale |
| Identify homophonic, polyphonic, and monophonic texture | Listen to polyphonic music<br>Sing in two parts | | | |
| Perform polyphonic music by singing round | Experience fugue | Identify ternary form (ABA)<br><br>**Create compositions in ternary form** | | Perform a song in unison and/or as a round |
| Perform folk song | Listen to 20th-century spoken music | Listen to descriptive music of the romantic period | Listen to and perform a popular 20th-century ballad | |
| Read body percussion notation | \|1.          \|\|2.          \|<br>                :\|\| | Following listening map | Read melodic notation G A C, ♩ , ♩ , − in 4/4 | Read notation intervals c-c¹ |

# TECHNOLOGY

## MUSIC WITH *MIDI*

MIDI technology allows students to manipulate musical elements and make musical decisions.
- Lesson 2, page 8: Create a **Pop Song**
- Lesson 6, page 24: Analyze a **Fugue:** *"Little Fugue in G Minor"* by J. S. Bach

## VIDEO RESOURCES

Use video resources to reinforce, extend, and enrich learning in this unit.

## WORLD WIDE WEB

Visit Macmillan/McGraw-Hill's Web site at **http://mhschool.com**

# LESSON 1

UNIT **1**

YOU
AND
MUSIC

# LESSON 1

**Focus: Steady Beat, Accent**

**Objectives**
To identify and define accent
To play unaccented and accented beats in a one-line rhythmic accompaniment with quarter notes and quarter rests

**Materials**
Recordings: "Still Reflections"
            "Studio 21"
            "Classics Montage"
Drumsticks or substitutes (two for each student)

**Vocabulary**
Beat, steady beat, quarter note, quarter rest, accent, repeat signs

**1 SETTING THE STAGE**
Tell the students that most of the music they are familiar with has a steady beat.

1

# LESSON 1

**AND THE BEAT GOES ON**

In music, the **beat** is the basic unit of time.

## ② TEACHING THE LESSON

**1. Experience the steady beat.** Have the students:
• Snap, pat, or clap the steady beat while listening to "Still Reflections."
**2. Introduce steady beat and accent.** Have the students:
• Perform lines 1–9 by clapping the quarter notes and using a silent hand gesture (hands out, palms up) for the quarter rests while counting the beats out loud.
• Perform lines 1–9 twice with the recording of "Still Reflections." (The recording has a sixteen-beat introduction.)
• Repeat the rhythm activity, beginning with line 9 and ending with line 1.

• Show the **steady beat** by snapping, clapping, or patting with the music.

> "Still Reflections'" by Greg Hansen

## Clapping the Beat

• Clap once for each **quarter note** (♩). Make a silent, palms-up motion for each **quarter rest** (𝄽).

• Perform lines 1 through 9 without stopping. Practice first without the music. Then perform lines 1 through 9 twice as you listen to "Studio 21."

> "Studio 21"
> by Greg Hansen

Phil Collin

• Perform the pattern by beginning with line 9 and ending on line 1.

2

---

## Accenting the Steady Beat

Beats that are stressed or emphasized are called *accented* beats.

- Perform these patterns by clapping on each quarter note marked with an **accent** ( > ). Snap your fingers on all other beats.

- Perform these patterns as you listen to "Studio 21." Play the notes between the **repeat** signs ( ‖: :‖ ) again.

- Practice the patterns below with drumsticks. Use your right (R) and left (L) hands as indicated.

- Find each pattern on pages 4 and 5.

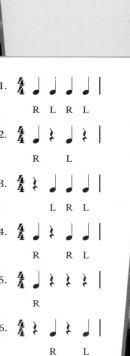

Simon Phillips

- Discuss the definition of accent.
- Perform accented patterns 1–4 by clapping the accented beats and snapping their fingers on all other beats while counting out loud. Repeat each line as needed.
- Perform lines 1–4 while listening to "Studio 21." (There is a sixteen-beat introduction. Repeat each line emphasizing the accents. Do the routine again. There is a seventeen-beat ending that they do not play.)

3. **Introduce the rhythmic accompaniment to "Classics Montage," which uses quarter notes and quarter rests.** Have the students:
- Prepare to play the rhythmic accompaniment by clapping the six rhythm patterns.
- Pat the patterns as marked. (L = left hand, R = right hand)
- Learn the matched-grip drumstick position. (The matched grip is a method of holding drumsticks for snare drum playing. The fingers and thumb wrap around the stick loosely near the balance point of the stick. The thumb touches the side of the first joint of the index finger. The palms are down. The sticks should rebound off the drumhead.)
- Play the rhythm patterns, using drumsticks.
- Find the six patterns in the rhythmic accompaniment on pages 4–5. (1: *The Stars and Stripes Forever*; 2: *Maple Leaf Rag*; 3: Beethoven, Symphony No. 5; 4: Schubert, "Trout" Quintet; 5 and 6: Bach, "Little Fugue in G Minor")

### EXTRA HELP

You may want to have the students pat the rhythms on the thighs, using left and right hands. This procedure is called *patschen*. If the students have difficulty playing the rhythm patterns, review the patting procedure or use motivational strategies. For example, have volunteers play three of the patterns for the class to identify, or have all the students perform the patterns in different orders.

# LESSON 1

- Read and play the rhythmic accompaniment. Practice with drumsticks.
- Perform the accompaniment with "Classics Montage."
- Discuss the definitions of beat and accent.
- Read and play the rhythmic accompaniment with accents along with the recording.

**Drumming the Accented Beat**

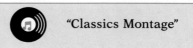
"Classics Montage"

- Perform this rhythmic accompaniment to "Classics Montage."

Introduction         Sousa, *The Stars and Stripes Forever*     *(4 times)*

Joplin, *Maple Leaf Rag*           *(4 times)*

J. S. Bach, "Little Fugue in G Minor"

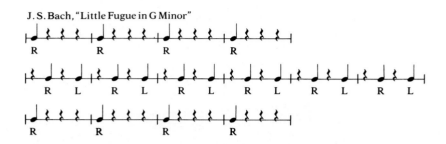

Handel, "Hallelujah" Chorus from *Messiah*

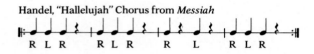

Tchaikovsky, "Dance of the Reed Pipes" from the *Nutcracker Suite*

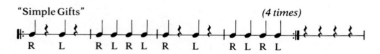

"Simple Gifts"           *(4 times)*

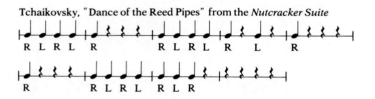

Mussorgsky, "The Great Gate of Kiev" from *Pictures at an Exhibition*
*(4 times)*

4

---

# E X T E N S I O N

## SPECIAL LEARNERS

If your class includes mainstreamed retarded or learning-disabled students with reading deficiencies, or students who are visually impaired, prepare a transparency of pupil pages 4 and 5. Use six different marking pens to premark the beginning of each pattern. Divide the class into six groups, with some mainstreamed students in each group. Teach one pattern to each group. As each pattern comes up in the "Classics Montage," point to that part of the accompaniment and to that group. Each group should perform its pattern until you indicate another section in the score and another group.

## MORE MUSIC TEACHING IDEAS

Have the students:
1. Create and notate additional rhythm patterns to perform with "Classics Montage," using quarter notes and quarter rests.
2. Compose rhythmic accompaniments to recordings of their choice, using quarter notes and quarter rests.

Beethoven, Symphony No. 5, 1st movement

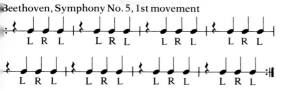

```
L R L     L R L     L R L     L R L
L R L     L R L     L R L     L R L
```

Beethoven, Symphony No. 9, 4th movement ("Ode to Joy")

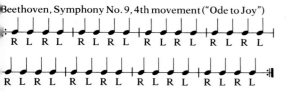

```
R L R L   R L R L   R L R L   R L R L
R L R L   R L R L   R L R L   R L R L
```

Schubert, Quintet in A Major ("Trout"), 4th movement

```
R   R L R   R L R   R L R   R L
```

J. S. Bach, Brandenburg Concerto No. 2, 3rd movement

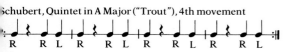

```
R   L   R   L   R   L   R   L
R   L   R   L   R   L   R   L
```

Armstrong, "West End Blues"

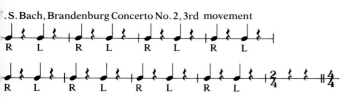

```
4/4
    R L R L   R L R L   R L R L   R L R L
R L R L   R L R L   R L R L   R L R L
```

Sousa, The Stars and Stripes Forever          (3 times)

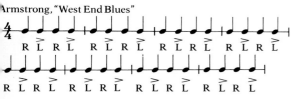

```
R L R L   R L R L   R L R L   R L R L
R L R L   R L R L   R L R L   R   L
```

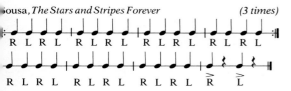

When you performed "Classics Montage," you experienced a *steady* unchanging *beat*. The *accents* you performed placed emphasis or stress on certain beats.

• Play the rhythmic accompaniment with and without accents. Which version sounds more interesting? Why?   version with accents; more variety

## LESSON 1

### Reinforcing the Lesson

Have the students play at least part of the rhythmic accompaniment without accents and compare the sound of "Classics Montage" with and without accents. (The version with accents has more rhythmic interest.)

### 3 APPRAISAL

The students should be able to:
1. Identify and verbally define *accent* as stress or emphasis on a beat.
2. Using drumsticks, perform accented and unaccented beats in the rhythmic accompaniment to "Classics Montage."

# LESSON 2

**Focus: Steady Beat, Accent, Eighth Notes**

**Objectives**
To perform quarter notes and eighth notes through movement and instrumental performance
To identify rhythm patterns and accents in a two-line percussion score

**Materials**
Recordings: "Rhythm Montage 1"
"Rhythm Montage 2"
"Seal Our Fate"
Drumsticks or substitutes (two for each student), drums

**Vocabulary**
Eighth note, whole rest

## 1 SETTING THE STAGE

Tell the students that people react and move differently to different types of music.

## 2 TEACHING THE LESSON

**1. Introduce styles of music.** Have the students:
• Discuss the pictures of people moving to music.
• Listen to "Rhythm Montage 1" and match the pictures with the music.

## Moving to Rhythm

People move differently to different styles of music.
• Match the pictures with the music as you listen. marching band; Olympics; American Indian; ballet

 "Rhythm Montage 1"

6

# You Move to Music

Marching bands step to the steady beat.

- Pat a steady quarter-note beat ( ♩ ).
- Clap two even sounds or **eighth notes** ( ♫ ) for each beat.

As you listen to "Rhythm Montage 2,"

- Step when you hear quarter notes ( ♩ ).
- Stand still and clap when you hear eighth notes ( ♫ ).

 "Rhythm Montage 2"

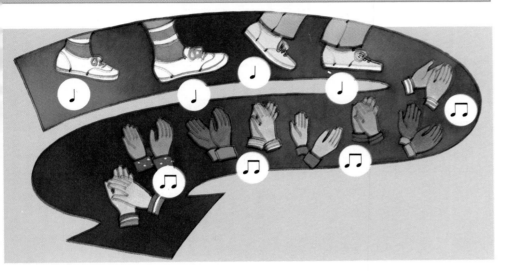

- Practice these patterns with drumsticks. When you see a **whole rest** (–), be silent for four beats.

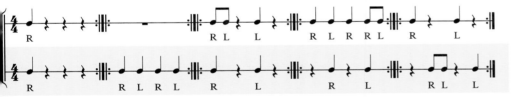

- Find these two-line patterns in the percussion score to "Seal Our Fate" on pages 8 and 9.

7

# LESSON 2

**2. Introduce quarter notes and eighth notes.** Have the students:
- Pat a steady quarter-note beat.
- Clap two even sounds (eighth notes) for each steady beat. (Be sure students understand that the quarter note is equal in duration to two eighth notes.)
- Listen to "Rhythm Montage 2." Step (or pat) when they hear quarter notes. Stop and clap when they hear eighth notes.

**3. Introduce rhythm patterns.** Have the students:
- Review the matched-grip drumstick position. (See *Teacher's Edition* page 3.)
- Play the patterns at the bottom of the page, observing the repeat signs. (You may wish to have students use two percussion tone colors for variety, such as Part 1 on snare drum and Part 2 on a lower drum or hand drum.)
- Examine the score of "Seal Our Fate" on pages 8 and 9 to find the rhythm patterns shown on page 7. (pattern 1: mm. 3–6; pattern 2: m. 30; pattern 3: mm. 10, 14, 18; pattern 4, mm. 32, 34, 36, 38; pattern 5: mm. 9, 13, 17, 21)
- Identify which line uses only quarter notes and quarter rests. (line 1)
- Identify which lines have accented notes. (lines 1, 5)

# LESSON 2

- Find the introduction, verse, and refrain in the score. (Explain that *D.S.* stands for *del segno*, which means to go back to the sign 𝄋 in this case, measure 7.)
- Listen to the song and follow the score. (Call attention to the order of the song: introduction, verse 1, refrain, D.S. to verse 2, refrain, D.S. to verse 3, refrain, refrain—ending on a fermata at the *Fine*.)
- Play the score, first without the song and then with the song.

Follow this rhythmic accompaniment.

- Play the accompaniment as you listen again.

 "Seal Our Fate" by Gloria Estefan

8

# EXTENSION

## EXTRA HELP

If students are having difficulty, have them practice sections of the score before trying to play it all the way through.

Unless otherwise noted, the following procedure will be used throughout the book for performing note values: Pat-slide-slide-slide whole notes (pat desk or lap with hands and slide them forward); pat-slide half notes; pat quarter notes; clap eighth notes; tap sixteenth notes on the back of the hand; snap triplets with alternating hands.

## MORE MUSIC TEACHING IDEAS

Have the students create and notate additional rhythm patterns to perform with "Seal Our Fate" using quarter notes, quarter rests, eighth notes, and accents.

9

## SPECIAL LEARNERS

Prepare a transparency of pupil pages 8 and 9 for this lesson. Color code the transparency in the same manner as the pages. Some students also may require a color code or visual prompt at the beginning of each line of the rhythm score. If students are unable to track the score visually and perform the rhythms, teach each rhythm pattern separately (page 7 of the pupil edition). Give each pattern a name, and call and point each out on the transparency as the students perform from the score.

# LESSON 2

• Read page 10 and discuss the background information on Gloria Estefan. You may wish to use some of the following items as a basis for extended discussion.

1. Some popular artists or groups have crossed over from one style to another. Their music became popular in two or more styles. Miami Sound Machine produced hits that crossed from Latino to American popular music. Name other musicians whose music has crossed over into other styles. (For example, Aretha Franklin has crossed over from gospel to rhythm and blues to soul and other styles.)

2. Gloria Estefan used real-life experiences as the basis for some of her songs. Name other composers who have done this. (For example, "Tears in Heaven" by Eric Clapton, "My Hometown" by Bruce Springsteen," "It Ain't Easy" by John Lennon, "The Star-Spangled Banner" by Francis Scott Key.)

3. Gloria Estefan progressed from singing in a group to singing as a solo artist. Name other performers who have progressed this way. (For example, Diana Ross sang with the Supremes. Michael Jackson started out with the Jackson Five. Barry McGuire sang with The New Christy Minstrels. Sting sang with The Police, Peter Gabriel sang with Genesis.)

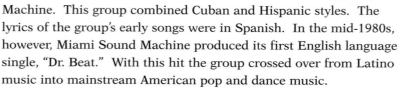

## Gloria Estefan

Gloria Estefan is a dynamic singer whose inspiring life is reflected in her music. She was born in Cuba and moved to Miami when she was a young child. In 1974 she became the lead singer for Miami Sound Machine. This group combined Cuban and Hispanic styles. The lyrics of the group's early songs were in Spanish. In the mid-1980s, however, Miami Sound Machine produced its first English language single, "Dr. Beat." With this hit the group crossed over from Latino music into mainstream American pop and dance music.

The driving Latin rhythms of the group's music enhanced Gloria's powerful vocals and energetic stage performance. Gloria Estefan and Miami Sound Machine made a strong impact on American popular music. Their successful combination of Latino styles with mainstream pop helped make people more aware of the musical contributions of Hispanic cultures.

In the late 1980s Gloria started her solo career. She demonstrated her vocal diversity with successful ballads like "Anything for You" and "Don't Wanna Lose You." In 1990 Gloria was severely injured in a near-fatal automobile accident. She made a remarkable recovery and put this experience into her music with songs such as "Coming Out of the Dark," in which she sings of the love and support of her friends. Her song "Seal Our Fate" deals with accepting responsibility for one's decisions. Gloria has remained loyal to her Cuban roots and has produced many songs in Spanish as well as English.

10

# Seal Our Fate

Words and music by Gloria Estefan

1. They say it's never too late, and though that might be the case, sometimes
   The sad truth of it is, opportunity won't knock twice.
   You can put off until tomorrow, but tomorrow might never come.
   Gotta think about the future, 'cause today soon will be long gone.
   Where will you be a few years down the line?
   Will it be everything you've dreamed of?
   It's always harder to do what is right.
   Sometimes one bad decision can mess up your life.

*Refrain*

   We seal our fate with the choices we make
   But don't give a second thought to all the chances we take.
   Could come up anytime, better be wide awake, 'cause we
   Seal our fate with the choices we make,
   Seal our fate, seal our fate, seal our fate,
   Seal our fate with the choices we make.

2. Surely, you say, it's not as bad as you make it sound.
   If we make a mistake, we can always turn it back around.
   Get back on the straight and narrow when I'm through having all my fun,
   After all it's my decision, I'm not really hurting anyone.
   ✳ Before you know it's gotten way out of hand
   In ways that you had never dreamed of.
   Never worth the price you pay in the end,
   Instead of being ahead, you're starting over again. *(Refrain)*

3. *(Instrumental, then go to ✳)*

11

# LESSON 2

- Listen to "Seal Our Fate," following the lyrics.
- Sing along with the recording of "Seal Our Fate."
- Discuss the meaning of the lyrics.

**Reinforcing the Lesson**

Review steady beat and accent on pages 2 and 3 to help students perform the score to "Seal Our Fate."

## 3 APPRAISAL

The students should be able to:
1. Perform quarter and eighth notes by stepping or patting the quarter notes and clapping the eighth notes in quarter-note and eighth-note rhythm patterns.
2. Play accurately on drums a two-line rhythmic accompaniment with quarter notes, quarter rests, and eighth notes and accents.

# LESSON 3

**Focus: Unity and Variety**

**Objectives**

To recognize how changes in musical sound (instruments, voices, sections, dynamics) contribute to unity and variety in a musical composition

To identify a simple form (introduction A B A B A coda)

**Materials**

Recordings: "Do You Hear the People Sing?"

Sticks, drums, tambourines, and triangles (See *More Music Teaching Ideas.*)

**Vocabulary**

Form

## 1 SETTING THE STAGE

Tell the students that unity and variety can be found in everyday life.

## 2 TEACHING THE LESSON

1. **Introduce visual unity, variety, and repetition and contrast in pictures.** Have the students:
• Examine the pictures to identify examples of repetition or contrast.
• Identify unity or variety in each picture.

## Unity and Variety in Everyday Life

- Which pictures illustrate unity through repetition? those on the left
- Which pictures illustrate variety through contrast? those on the right
- Describe how each picture shows unity or variety. Answers may vary.

12

- Listen to "Do You Hear the People Sing?" from the musical *Les Misérables*. Notice the changes in the voices, instruments, and dynamics.

Which sections are similar? Which are different? The order of the sections is scrambled on this page. Arrange the sections in the order in which you hear them.  7, 5, 2, 1, 4, 3, 6

 "Do You Hear the People Sing?" from *Les Misérables* by Claude-Michel Schönberg and Alain Boublil

**1**

| Chorus "Do you hear..." |
| Orchestra |
| *ff* |

**2**

| Solo |
| Keyboard (plus French Horn) |
| *mp* |

**3**

| Chorus "Do you hear..." |
| Orchestra |
| *fff* |

**4**

| Solo (background chorus) |
| Orchestra |
| *mf* |

**5**

| Solo "Do you hear..." |
| Keyboard |
| *mp* |

**6** Coda

| Orchestra |
| *f* ——————— |

**7** Introduction

| Keyboard |
| *mp* |

# LESSON 3

**2. Introduce unity and variety in "Do You Hear the People Sing?"** Have the students:

• Identify and name the content of each picture, focusing on the voices, instruments, and dynamic levels. Identify which pictures are similar. (1, 3, 5; 2, 4; 6, 7) Identify the differences among them. (Review the meaning of the dynamic symbols if needed.)

• Listen to the recording of "Do You Hear the People Sing?" Notice the combination of voices, instruments, and dynamic levels. Write down the order of the pictures. (You may wish to signal when each section starts. Play the recording several times if needed.)

• Analyze and discuss the answers. (7, intro; 5 *Do you hear*; 2, *Will you join*; 1, *Do you hear*; 4, *Will you give*; 3, *Do you hear*; 6, coda)

• Identify voices heard. (solo, chorus)

• Identify instruments heard. (keyboard, orchestra)

• Identify dynamic levels heard. (*mp*, *mf*, *f*, *ff*, *fff*, decrescendo)

• Discuss how "Do You Hear the People Sing?" has both unity and variety. (Unity is provided by repetition of words, voices, instruments, and sections. Variety is provided by changing voices, instruments, dynamic levels, and sections.)

13

**LISTENING**

You may wish to use the Listening Map overhead transparency to help guide the students through the listening selection.

# LESSON 3

**3. Introduce the form of "Do You Hear the People Sing?"** Have the students:
• Read page 14.
• Listen to the recording again.
• Identify the form of the melody. (introduction A B A B A coda)

• Listen again to the recording of "Do You Hear the People Sing?" Notice the repetition of words and music and the changes in the different voices and instruments.

Repetition and contrast help to give music its form. **Form** is the way a composition is organized. When form is described, letters are used to represent different sections. The form of "Do You Hear the People Sing?" can be outlined as:
Introduction, A B A B A, coda.

*Les Misérables*

*The Phantom of the Opera*

*Ragtime*

## THE MUSICAL
### Les Misérables
Victor Hugo's monumental novel is the basis of this musical. The setting of the musical is nineteenth-century France. The characters suffer from oppression and are struggling to survive. The show was originally written in 1979 and presented on a small scale in Paris. It was then developed into a large-scale musical and opened in London in 1985. The music is by Claude-Michel Schönberg. The original French lyrics are by Alain Boublil and the English lyrics are by Herbert Kretzmer.

## MORE MUSIC TEACHING IDEAS
Have the students play the steady beat on classroom instruments to accompany each section of "Do You Hear the People Sing?" to emphasize and clarify different sections. For example—introduction: sticks; A sections: drums; B sections: tambourines; coda: triangles.

# American Musical Theater

The Broadway musical is a uniquely American contribution to the arts. Early American musical plays, those popular at the beginning of the 1900s, were based on European musical styles. These plays combined singing, dancing, and acting, and usually had light-hearted, romantic plots. In the early decades of the 1900s, American musical comedy was born in the works of George M. Cohan, Jerome Kern, and George Gershwin. These composers began to write musicals based on current topics. Many songs from these early musicals, such as Cohan's "Give My Regards to Broadway" and Kern's "Smoke Gets in Your Eyes," are still sung today.

During and after World War II, musicals began to have more fully developed plots and serious messages. The team of Richard Rodgers and Oscar Hammerstein II produced such famous musicals as *Oklahoma!*, *The King and I*, and *The Sound of Music* in the 1940s and 1950s. In the late 1950s Leonard Bernstein and Stephen Sondheim's *West Side Story* brought a new standard of real-life drama to the musical. *West Side Story* is a retelling of *Romeo and Juliet* that depicts urban tensions in the New York City of the 1950s.

During the 1960s musicals continued to develop and expand their range of musical styles. The first rock musical, *Hair*, reflected social issues and the rock sounds of the late 1960s. *The Wiz*, a retelling of *The Wizard of Oz*, incorporated the African American musical styles of the mid-1970s. During the 1980s and 1990s, the musicals of British composer Andrew Lloyd Webber have dominated the Broadway scene. His works such as *Cats*, based on poems by T. S. Eliot, and *The Phantom of the Opera* have enchanted American audiences with their elaborate staging and lavish melodies. The French team of Claude-Michel Schönberg and Alain Boublil had similar successes with *Les Misérables*, based on the Victor Hugo novel of the same name, and *Miss Saigon*, a retelling of Puccini's opera *Madame Butterfly*, set in Vietnam.

Musical theater continues to be a popular form of entertainment. Tourists flock to Broadway to see revivals such as *The Sound of Music* (1959 original; 1998 revival) and lavish new shows such as *The Lion King* and *Footloose*. Through movies, videos, recordings, and performances in schools and regional theaters, musicals can be enjoyed everywhere.

15

**4. Introduce American musical theater.** Have the students:
• Read and discuss the background information on American musical theater. You may wish to use some of the following items as a basis for extended discussion.
1. Music in the theater has many functions. Music can set a mood, announce an event, or describe a character. Name some specific examples of each of these uses of music in the theater. (In "Summer Days" from *Grease*, a boy and girl tell their respective friends about their summer romance. In "Memory" from *Cats*, an old, tattered alley cat recalls her youth and beauty and wishes those happy days would come again.)
2. Name some musical compositions from the American musical theater whose popularity has outlasted that of the shows from which they came. ("Tomorrow" from *Annie*; "Hello, Dolly!" from the musical of the same name; "The Impossible Dream" from *Man of La Mancha*) Discuss some reasons why some songs might remain popular longer than the musicals. (Answers will vary.)

## Reinforcing the Lesson

Review the features that contribute unity and variety to the song. (Repetition of the words, voices, instruments, and sections contributes to the unity of the song. Variety is provided through contrasts in voices, instruments, sections, and dynamic levels.)

### 3 APPRAISAL

The students should be able to:
1. Verbally identify at least two features that contribute to unity and at least two features that provide variety in "Do You Hear the People Sing?"
2. Verbally identify the form of "Do You Hear the People Sing?" as introduction A B A B A coda.

## TEACHER INFORMATION

*Share the Music* use the term *African American* when referring to Americans of African descent.

# LESSON 4

## Focus: Duple and Triple Meter

### Objectives
To distinguish between duple and triple meter
To introduce conducting patterns for duple and triple meter
To identify dynamic contrasts between forte and piano
To describe elements of unity and variety in a composition

### Materials
Recordings: "Music in Twos"
             "Music in Threes"
             "Shifting Meters"
Tennis balls (one for each student)

### Vocabulary
Duple meter, triple meter, measure, bar line, dynamics, forte, piano

## 1 SETTING THE STAGE
Tell the students that beats can be grouped into sets.

## 2 TEACHING THE LESSON

**1. Introduce duple and triple meter.**
Have the students:
• Discuss the information about grouping beats in sets of two.
• Perform the body percussion in duple meter as shown, first without, then with, "Music in Twos."
• Perform the body percussion in triple meter as shown, first without, then with, "Music in Threes."
• Listen to "Shifting Meters" and identify the sections in duple and triple meter. Perform the appropriate body percussion with the music.
• Decide which example shows the way the meters are organized.

# DUPLE AND TRIPLE METER

Beats can be grouped in sets. The first beat of each group is emphasized.

Beats that are grouped in sets of two are in **duple meter**.

• Perform the following rhythm pattern as you listen to the music.

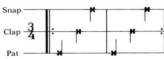

 "Music in Twos"

Beats that are grouped in sets of three are in **triple meter**.

• Perform the following rhythm pattern as you listen to the recording.

 "Music in Threes"

• As you listen to "Shifting Meters," identify when the piece is in duple meter or triple meter by performing the appropriate rhythm pattern.

 "Shifting Meters"

• Listen again and decide which of the following shows the order of the meters.

| | | | |
|---|---|---|---|
| 1. | triple | duple | triple |
| 2. | duple | duple | triple |
| 3. | duple | triple | duple |

3: duple, triple, duple

16

# E X T E N S I O N

## SPECIAL LEARNERS
A visual cue on each downbeat will enable some exceptional learners to participate in this activity. If they have difficulty coordinating the duple and triple meters, divide the class into two groups, each with some mainstreamed students. Have each group perform a pattern. As each meter comes up, say its name and point to that group. After both groups have played their patterns successfully, have them switch patterns. After the class has played both parts successfully, have everyone perform both meters.

## COOPERATIVE LEARNING
After they listen to "Shifting Meters," have the students work in cooperative groups to show ABA form and practice the two contrasting meters. First draw a chart on the board showing the form of the piece and the meter of each section:

A           B           A
duple     triple     duple

Now assign the students to cooperative groups of three. Once in groups, the students in each group should assign themselves the numbers 1, 2, and 3. (There should be one of each number in each group.) Number 1 chooses a two-syllable word for the group to say during the A sections. Number 2 chooses a three-syllable word for the group to say during

the B section. The group together decides on a body percussion pattern for each of these words. Number 3 writes both patterns in graphic or traditional notation, with help from numbers 1 and 2. The group practices their spoken and body percussion accompaniments, then performs them with "Shifting Meters." Another day you may have the groups reassemble, then distribute each set of notation cards to a different group than originated it. Have the groups try to decipher and perform the notation they receive.

- Practice sensing meters by bouncing a tennis ball on the first beat of each set. In triple meter, change hands on the third beat.

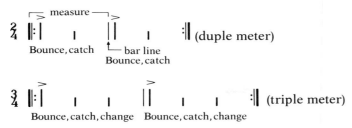

A set of beats becomes a **measure** when it is placed between two **bar lines**. Repeat signs also are used as bar lines.

- Bounce the tennis ball in duple or triple meters as you listen again.

- Follow the diagrams to conduct in duple and triple meter. The photographs show how the patterns look when a conductor faces you.

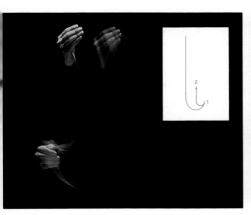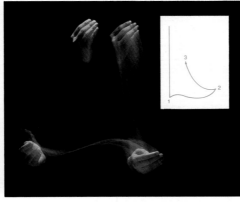

- Listen to "Shifting Meters" again and conduct in duple meter and triple meter.

The changes of meter give contrast to "Shifting Meters."
Varying the *dynamics* is another way to provide contrast. **Dynamics** refer to the softness or loudness of sound. Musicians use the Italian words **forte** (fôr′ tā, "loud") and **piano** (pyä′ nō, "soft"). They are written as *f* and *p*.

- Listen to "Shifting Meters" again. Which of the following best describes the dynamics? Explain your answer. 3: A, forte; B, piano

1. *f  f  p*    2. *p  f  p*    3. *f  p  f*

17

# LESSON 4

**2. Introduce the tennis ball activity to reinforce duple and triple meter.** Have the students:
- Practice duple and triple meters by bouncing a tennis ball on the first beat of each measure. (Duple meter is performed as "bounce, catch." Triple meter is performed as "bounce, catch, change" [change hands].)
- Identify a measure as a set of beats between two bar lines.
- Listen to "Shifting Meters" again. Bounce the tennis ball in duple or triple meter with the music.
- Practice each conducting pattern. (You may wish to encourage the students to use both hands in a mirror image when conducting.)
- Listen to "Shifting Meters" again and conduct in duple or triple meter.
- Discuss the information on dynamics.
- Listen to "Shifting Meters" again and determine which example describes the dynamics.

## Reinforcing the Lesson
Review unity and variety from pages 12–15 and discuss how the meter and dynamics give unity and variety to "Shifting Meters."

## 3 APPRAISAL
The students should be able to:
1. Listen to "Shifting Meters" and identify duple and triple meter by responding to meter changes through body percussion and conducting.
2. Listen to "Shifting Meters" and use the terms *forte* and *piano* to identify verbally the contrasting dynamic levels of the sections.
3. Describe how the form (ABA) and dynamic levels (forte, piano) give "Shifting Meters" unity and variety.

## MORE MUSIC TEACHING IDEAS
Have the students:
1. Identify words with two syllables (*U-tah* or *base-ball*), and three syllables (*Ar-kan-sas* or *bas-ket-ball*) to be spoken as an accompaniment to the A and B sections of "Shifting Meters."
2. Create their own body percussion patterns to accompany speech rhythms.
3. Choose partners and bounce a tennis ball in duple and triple meter.

## SPECIAL LEARNERS
If your class includes students who are physically handicapped, preplan an alternative to the tennis ball activity. A small group, including those who cannot bounce tennis balls, can play the first beat of each measure on a rhythm instrument.

## EXTRA HELP
For beginning experiences with the tennis balls, select two or three students to demonstrate. Gradually add more students to the group, or have half the class use tennis balls while the others observe, and then alternate.

# LESSON 5

**Focus: Texture—Monophonic, Homophonic, Polyphonic**

**Objectives**
To identify and describe monophonic, homophonic, and polyphonic textures
To review duple and triple meter

**Materials**
Recordings: "Bottletop Song" (unison version)
"Bottletop Song" (as a round)
Bells, keyboard (see *More Music Teaching Ideas*)
Copying Master 1-1 (optional; see *More Music Teaching Ideas*)

**Vocabulary**
Texture, unison, polyphonic, monophonic, homophonic

## 1 SETTING THE STAGE

Review duple and triple meter patterns on page 16, and listen to the "Bottletop Song" to determine if the song is in duple or triple meter. (triple meter)

## 2 TEACHING THE LESSON

**1. Experience texture in the "Bottletop Song."** Have the students:
• Sing the song in unison. (Changing voices can sing part 1 only and/or play the melodic ostinato in *More Music Teaching Ideas*.)
• Sing the song as a round, using the body percussion.

## MUSICAL TEXTURE

• Learn to sing the "Bottletop Song" in unison and as a round.

**Bottletop Song**

• Experiment with using these patterns as an accompaniment to the song. Which part of the "Bottletop Song" goes best with pattern 3?[3]

 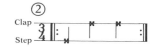 

• Create your own patterns to go with this song.

18

---

**VOCAL DEVELOPMENT**
Have the students emphasize diction (consonant articulation) for rhythmic precision and vitality.

**MORE MUSIC TEACHING IDEAS**
Have the students:
1. Play the following melodic ostinato to the "Bottletop Song" on bells or keyboard.

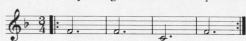

2. Sing the "Bottletop Song," using pitch syllables. (You may wish to use Copying Master 1-1 at this time.)
3. Create and notate other body percussion patterns for this song.

**Texture** in music refers to the way layers of sound are combined. When you sang the "Bottletop Song" the first time, without accompaniment, you sang in *unison*. Two or more voices singing the same melody is called **unison**.

Unison singing is a texture known as **monophonic** (mo-no-fo' nik), meaning "one sound."

When you sang the "Bottletop Song" as a round, you created a texture known as **polyphonic** (po-lē-fo' nik), meaning "many voices sounding together." In polyphonic texture, each melody is independent and can stand alone.

- Which diagram represents the "Bottletop Song" sung as a round?
- Which of the following shows the texture of the "Bottletop Song" sung in unison?

1.

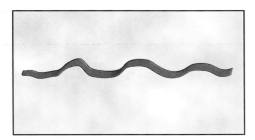

2.

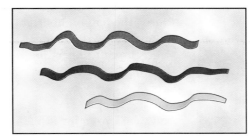

When you sang the "Bottletop Song" with the patterns, the melody was in the foreground with accompaniment in the background. This texture is called **homophonic** (ho-mo-fo' nik) and can be shown like this:

3.

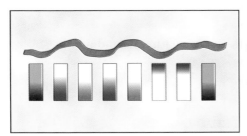

melody

accompaniment

19

**2. Introduce musical texture.** Have the students:
- Analyze the musical texture of the "Bottletop Song" when it is sung in unison and decide which diagram shows monophonic texture.
- Discuss and identify the texture of the "Bottletop Song" when it is sung as a round.
- Identify the texture of the "Bottletop Song" with body percussion as homophonic.

## Reinforcing the Lesson

Review the description and definition of musical texture.

### 3 APPRAISAL

The students should be able to:
1. Verbally define monophonic, polyphonic, and homophonic texture.
2. Sing the "Bottletop Song" while performing the body percussion and verbally describe it as having homophonic texture since the melody is in the foreground with accompaniment in the background.
3. Use body percussion to show triple meter in the "Bottletop Song."

## EXTRA HELP

If all three textures seem difficult for students to grasp at once, teach monophony and polyphony in one session and homophony another time.

# LESSON 6

**Focus: Voice Quality, Vocal Tone Color, Register**

### Objectives
To identify the unique characteristics of voice quality and register in speaking and singing voices
To identify tone quality as tone color

### Materials
Recordings: "Foul Shot"
"Ridiculous Rose"
"The Termite"
"Geographical Fugue"
"Trav'ler" (with call numbers)
"Trav'ler"
"Trav'ler" (performance mix)

### Vocabulary
Tone color, register

## 1 SETTING THE STAGE
Tell the students that everyone's speaking and singing voice has its own distinctive sound, or tone color.

## 2 TEACHING THE LESSON
**1. Introduce voice quality (tone color) of speaking voices.** Have the students:
• Follow the text as they listen to the recording of the reading of "Foul Shot" by people with different voice qualities.

## SOUNDS OF SPEAKING VOICES

CD1:13 **Tone Color**

Every person's voice has its own unique sound. Listen to the sounds of voices as different people read portions of the poem "Foul Shot."

 "Foul Shot"

# FOUL SHOT

Reader 1　With two 60's stuck on the scoreboard
　　　　　And two seconds hanging on the clock,
　　　　　The solemn boy in the center of eyes,
　　　　　Squeezed by silence,
　　　　　Seeks out the line with his feet,
　　　　　Soothes his hands along his uniform,
　　　　　Gently drums the ball against the floor,
Reader 2　Then measures the waiting net,
　　　　　Raises the ball on his right hand,
　　　　　Balances it with his left,
　　　　　Calms it with fingertips,
Reader 3　Breathes,
　　　　　Crouches,
　　　　　Waits,
　　　　　And then through a stretching of stillness,
　　　　　Nudges it upward.
Reader 4　The ball
　　　　　Slides up and out,
　　　　　Lands,
　　　　　Leans,
Reader 5　Wobbles,
　　　　　Wavers,
　　　　　Hesitates,
　　　　　Exasperates,
Reader 6　Plays it coy
　　　　　Until every face begs with unsounding
　　　　　　　screams—
Reader 7　And then
　　　　　　　And then
　　　　　　　　　And then,
　　　　　Right before ROAR-UP
　　　　　Dives down and through.
　　　　　　　　—Edwin A. Hoey

20

# EXTENSION

### CURRICULUM CONNECTION: LANGUAGE ARTS

An action verb is a word that names an action. Have the students read "Foul Shot" and make a list of the action verbs. (stuck, hanging, squeezed, seeks, soothes, drums, measures, raises, balances, calms, breathes, crouches, waits, nudges, slides, lands, leans, wobbles, wavers, hesitates, exasperates, plays, begs, dives) Have the students announce the events of a basketball game as if they were sports reporters in a press box. Each student, in turn, is to create one sentence using a verb from the list of action verbs. Continue until all of the action verbs from the list have been used.

When you identify someone by his or her speaking voice, your decision is based on the **tone color** of the voice. Some terms used to describe vocal tone color are:

heavy ←→ light          nasal ←→ clear

dark ←→ bright          thick ←→ thin

 "Ridiculous Rose"; "The Termite"

• Listen to these poems read by people whose voices have different tone colors.

## Ridiculous Rose

Her mama said, "Don't eat with your fingers."
"O.K." said Ridiculous Rose,
So she ate with her toes!

—*Shel Silverstein*

## THE TERMITE

Some primal termite knocked on wood
And tasted it, and found it good,
And that is why your cousin May
Fell through the parlor floor today.

—*Ogden Nash*

• Read the poems and experiment with different vocal tone colors.

21

# LESSON 6

• Discuss the terms used to describe qualities (vocal tone color) of speaking voices.
• Listen to "Ridiculous Rose" and "The Termite" read by people demonstrating specific vocal tone colors.
• Read the poems in the text, experimenting with various vocal tone colors.

**CURRICULUM CONNECTION: READING**

**Shel Silverstein** has written and illustrated many books for children. **Ogden Nash** (1902–1971) was famous for his humorous verse. His poems use puns and comparisons of apparently unrelated topics to make serious points about society and our behavior. Nash believed people should use humor to help them cope with the complexities of modern life.

# LESSON 6

22

## EXTENSION

### CURRICULUM CONNECTION: LANGUAGE ARTS

**Vocabulary**—You may wish to explain the phrase "mad as a hatter." In the 1800s, mercury was used to soften felt for hats, which were made by hand. Prolonged exposure to the mercury caused brain damage, which made the hatmakers behave as though they were insane.

### SPECIAL LEARNERS

If some students are reading below grade level, prepare a transparency of "The Naming of Cats." Point to the beginning of every other line so these learners will be able to follow the text and participate in the activity.

• Read this poem and experiment with vocal tone color.

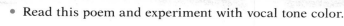

# THE NAMING OF CATS

The Naming of Cats is a difficult matter
   It isn't just one of your holiday games;
You may think at first I'm as mad as a hatter
When I tell you, a cat must have THREE DIFFERENT NAMES.
First of all, there's the name that the family use daily,
   Such as Peter, Augustus, Alonzo or James,
Such as Victor or Jonathan, George or Bill Bailey—
   All of them sensible everyday names.
There are fancier names if you think they sound sweeter,
   Some for the gentlemen, some for the dames:
Such as Plato, Admetus, Electra, Demeter—
   But all of them sensible everyday names.
But I tell you, a cat needs a name that's particular,
   A name that's peculiar, and more dignified,
Else how can he keep up his tail perpendicular,
   Or spread out his whiskers, or cherish his pride?
Of names of this kind, I can give you a quorum
   Such as Munkustrap, Quaxo, or Coricopat,
Such as Bombalurina, or else Jellylorum—
   Names that never belong to more than one cat.
But above and beyond there's still one name left over,
   And that is the name that you never will guess;
The name that no human research can discover—
   But THE CAT HIMSELF knows, and will never confess.
When you notice a cat in profound meditation,
   The reason, I tell you, is always the same:
His mind is engaged in a rapt contemplation
   Of the thought, of the thought, of the thought of his name:
     His ineffable effable
     Effanineffable
Deep and inscrutable singular Name.

                    —T.S. Eliot

23

• Read ''The Naming of Cats,'' experimenting with and listening to each other's voice qualities.

## CURRICULUM CONNECTION: LANGUAGE ARTS

Have the students list the specific names given to cats in T.S. Eliot's ''The Naming of Cats.'' Have them decide which names are more universal and more familiar, and which names seem archaic or are unfamiliar. Ask the students to research the origins of the unfamiliar names. Have them determine which names may have been ''created'' by T.S. Eliot. Ask them why a poet may wish to create ''new'' names. (Guide them to explore some of the aspects of creating poetry, such as rhyming, rhythm, and so on.) Then have them create unique names for cats and substitute them for those in the T.S. Eliot poem.

## CURRICULUM CONNECTION: READING

**T. S. (Thomas Stearns) Eliot** (1888–1965) was born in St. Louis, Missouri, but lived most of his life in England. His writings, mainly poetry, were quite different from those of his time and helped change the style of modern literature. Besides poetry, he wrote literary criticism and verse plays. ''The Naming of Cats'' is from his book of verse titled *Old Possum's Book of Practical Cats*. This book later formed the basis of the musical *Cats* (see page 15). Eliot was granted the Nobel Prize for literature in 1948.

# LESSON 6

**2. Introduce voice register.** Have the students:

• Discuss the information on register.

• Listen to "Geographical Fugue" and identify the number of registers and the order in which they appear. (There are two registers, higher and lower. Voices enter in this order: lower, higher, higher, lower.) (You may wish to explain that a fugue is a polyphonic composition. It begins with a single line that states the main theme, called the subject. The subject is repeated by the rest of the voices, one at a time.)

## Voice Registers

Every person's voice has its own tone color and *register*. **Register** describes the general low or high pitch range of a sound. Women's and children's voices usually are in a higher register than men's.

The print of the sound of a person's voice, or *voice print*, is as individual as a fingerprint. Below are pictures of two voice prints. The two people were saying the same words, but the pictures of their voices are very different.

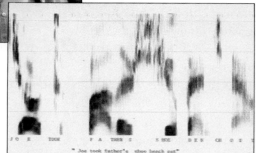
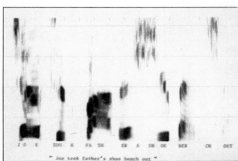

• Think of the voices of two people you know. How would you describe the difference between their voices? The similarities?

• Listen to how composer Ernst Toch uses the higher and lower registers in his composition for speaking chorus.
Follow this listening guide. It will help you identify the number of registers and the order in which they appear.
The word *Trinidad* marks the entrance of each voice.

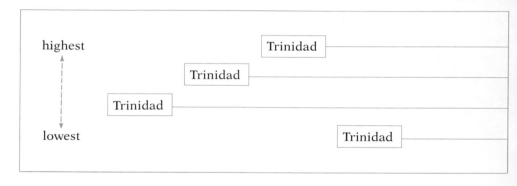

highest

Trinidad

Trinidad

Trinidad

lowest

Trinidad

 "Geographical Fugue" by Ernst Toch (ernst tôкн)

24

E X T E N S I O N

## THE COMPOSER

**Ernst Toch** (1887–1964)—Austrian-American composer, was born in Vienna. At first he taught himself music as a hobby. After winning the Mozart prize awarded by the city of Frankfurt, he moved to Germany to study piano and composition. He taught these subjects in Berlin until the Nazis came to power in 1933. Then he moved to the U.S., where he wrote film scores. Toch's other works include operas, symphonies, chamber music, and music for radio. The "Geographical Fugue," from his suite *Spoken Music*, is one of his frequently performed works.

## MORE MUSIC TEACHING IDEAS

Have the students identify the tone color and registers of two girls and two boys in the class.

## CURRICULUM CONNECTION: SCIENCE

Have students research and examine a picture of the vocal mechanism. You may wish to have them make a drawing and label it. The enlarged upper end of the trachea is called the larynx, or Adam's apple. The larynx, which is also called the voice box, contains flexible vocal cords. Air passes through these cords and causes them to vibrate. The vibrating air, shaped by the mouth and tongue, produces the sounds. Have the students identify instruments that produce sounds by vibration of cords (instruments with strings, such as violin or guitar). Have

them identify and describe those aspects of these instruments that "shape" the sound (body of violin, body of guitar, and so on).

Have the students place their fingers on their voice boxes. Ask them to describe the movement of the larynx while breathing (none) and while talking (up and down). Ask the students whether sound is produced as air moves into or out of the lungs (out). Point out that the faster the air is forced past the vocal cords, the louder is the sound.

## Singing Voices

- Listen to "Trav'ler" sung in four different registers and four
17 different tone colors. Each time you hear a number, decide which
terms best describe the singer's register and tone color.

Possible answers—
1: male, low, dark;
2: male, high, clear;
3: female, low, nasal;
4: female, high, light

**3. Introduce register and tone color of singing voices.** Have the students listen to the recording of "Trav'ler" (with call numbers). Look at the descriptions of registers and tone colors. List the answers on a separate sheet of paper.

| Register | Tone Color |
|---|---|
| lower ←→ higher | heavy ←→ light |
| male ←→ female | nasal ←→ clear |
| | dark ←→ bright |
| | thick ←→ thin |

 "Trav'ler," by Jane Foster Knox and Mark Wilson

Wailua Falls on the island of Maui, Hawaii

25

---

## MORE MUSIC TEACHING IDEAS

Have the students identify and label the tone color and registers of the current top five popular singers.

# LESSON 6

- Find the first and second endings in "Trav'ler." (measures 36, 37. Review their meanings as needed.)
- Sing "Trav'ler" focusing attention on register and vocal tone color. (The melody is in Part I. Add the other parts when the students are ready.)

### Reinforcing the Lesson
Review register and descriptive terms used to classify vocal tone color (voice quality).

## 3 APPRAISAL

The students should be able to:
1. Verbally define vocal tone color as voice quality and list the eight adjectives from the lesson that can be used to describe vocal tone color.
2. Listen to examples of male and female speaking and solo singing voices and classify and describe accurately their vocal tone color and register, using adjectives from the lesson.

CD1:18, • CD7:19 Sing "Trav'ler." Be aware of the tone color and register of your own voice.

## Trav'ler

Music by Mark Wilson
Words by Jane Foster Knox

Piano Accompaniment on page PA 2

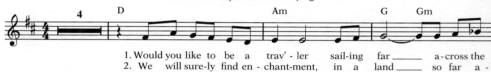

1. Would you like to be a trav'-ler sail-ing far_____ a-cross the
2. We will sure-ly find en-chant-ment, in a land_____ so far a-

sea? I can take you on a jour-ney, to a place where you have longed to
way. But we fail to see the splen-dor that sur-rounds us ev'-ry

be, For oth-er lands seem so much more ex-cit-ing! ___ Our spir-its
day. For beau-ty blooms where it is plant-ed! ___ It

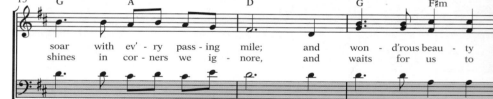

soar with ev'-ry pass-ing mile; and won-d'rous beau-ty
shines in cor-ners we ig-nore, and waits for us to

**Scale Tones:** *ti₁ do re mi fa so lo la ti do¹*

26

# EXTENSION

## CRITICAL THINKING

What far-away places seem exciting to you? Why? What is beautiful in the area where you live? What types of scenery seem to inspire poetry and songs? Why?

## MORE MUSIC TEACHING IDEAS

Have the students determine the rhyme scheme of the lyrics of "Trav'ler." (Verse 1: aa bb aa cc; Verse 2: dd ee aa fff) Have them create a poem using pairs of rhymed lines about some place of beauty. You may wish to choose one of the poems and add a melody to it.

# LESSON 7

**Focus: Instrumental Tone Color—Strings, Woodwinds, Brass, Percussion**

### Objectives
To review and identify tone color of brass, woodwind, string, and percussion instrument families
To identify ternary (ABA) form
To recognize how changes in orchestral tone color and dynamics contribute to unity and variety in a composition

### Materials
Recordings: "Procession of the Nobles"
"Orchestral Montage"
"Procession of the Nobles" (with call numbers)
"Shifting Meters"
Sticks, drums, tambourines, triangles (for *More Music Teaching Ideas*)

### Vocabulary
Brass, woodwinds, strings, percussion, ternary

## 1 SETTING THE STAGE
Have the students listen to "Procession of the Nobles" (without call numbers) as they enter the classroom.

## 2 TEACHING THE LESSON
**1. Introduce tone color of orchestral families.** Have the students:
• Discuss the pictures of the four families of orchestral instruments.
• Discuss the information on orchestral instruments and tone color.

# SOUNDS OF THE ORCHESTRA

You find tone color not only in voices but also in the instruments of the orchestra. Orchestral instruments are divided into four families, or sections. The tone color of each section is different and depends on how the sound is produced.

The sound of **brass** instruments is produced when the player buzzes the lips against the mouthpiece. The sound of **woodwinds** is produced by the vibration of a reed in the mouthpiece (as on the clarinet), or two reeds vibrating together (as on the oboe), or through a mouthpiece (as on the flute). The sound of **stringed** instruments results from the vibration of the strings, which are set in motion when a bow is drawn across them or when they are plucked with the fingers. The sound of **percussion** is produced when the player strikes the instruments with mallets or sticks, or the hands

28

You have heard the four families of instruments in the orchestra many times. Examine the pictures of each family and the individual instruments. As you listen to the "Orchestral Montage," match the tone color you hear with the correct instrument family. strings, percussion, brass, woodwinds

 "Orchestral Montage"

| Strings | Woodwinds |
|---|---|
| violin    cello | clarinet    oboe |
| viola    harp | piccolo    flute |
| string bass | bassoon |
|  | English horn |

| Brasses | Percussion |
|---|---|
| trumpet    tuba | cymbals    chimes |
| French horn | timpani    gong |
| trombone | bass drum |
| baritone horn | snare drum |

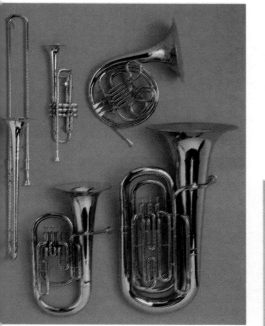

• Listen to "Orchestral Montage" and match the tone colors they hear with the correct pictures. (Excerpts are from: Concerto in F for Strings, by Tommaso Albinoni; *Ionisation*, by Edgar Varèse; Canzona por Sonare, No. 28, by Giovanni Gabrieli; and *The Young Person's Guide to the Orchestra*, by Benjamin Britten.) You may wish to use some of the following items as a basis for extended discussion.

1. A family can be defined as a group of closely related individuals. Name the orchestral families and list several instruments in each family. Name the largest and the smallest instruments in each family. What determines the family of an instrument? (Consider how instruments are constructed, how tones are produced, how the instruments are played.) Discuss ways in which the different orchestral families fit the criterion of being closely related.

2. The orchestral families (brass, strings, woodwinds, percussion) are part of another, larger family—the orchestra. Do the musicians in these orchestral families have a responsibility to each other and to the group as a whole? Relate this discussion to the different peoples of the world.

29

# LESSON 7

**2. Introduce instrumental tone color in "Procession of the Nobles."** Have the students listen to the recording of "Procession of the Nobles" (with call numbers). When numbers 1–6 and 11–15 are called, write on a sheet of paper which of the four orchestral families they hear. (1: brass, percussion; 2: brass, percussion; 3: strings, woodwinds, brass, percussion; 4: strings, woodwinds, brass, percussion; 5: strings, woodwinds, brass; 6: brass, percussion; 11: brass, percussion; 12: brass, percussion; 13: strings, woodwinds, brass, percussion; 14: strings, woodwinds, brass, percussion; 15: brass, percussion) Listen and read the description when numbers 7–10 are called.

## Listening for Orchestral Tone Color

CD1:21 "Procession of the Nobles" features the four families of orchestral instruments. When numbers 1 to 6 and 11 to 15 are called, identify which instruments you hear: strings, woodwinds, brass, or percussion. Listen and read the description when numbers 7 to 10 are called. *See Teaching the Lesson.*

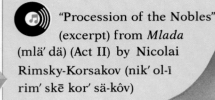

"Procession of the Nobles" (excerpt) from *Mlada* (mlä′ dä) (Act II) by Nicolai Rimsky-Korsakov (nik′ ol-ī rim′ skē kor′ sä-kôv)

1
Strings/Woodwinds
Brass/Percussion

2
Strings/Woodwinds
Brass/Percussion

3
Strings/Woodwinds
Brass/Percussion

4
Strings/Woodwinds
Brass/Percussion

5
Strings/Woodwinds
Brass/Percussion

6
Strings/Woodwinds
Brass/Percussion

7
Strings/woodwinds
with soft
background

8
Solo trumpet
melody and snare
drum added to
strings/woodwinds

9
Strings/woodwinds
continue

10
High woodwinds
and tambourine
join trumpet melody
as strings and other
woodwinds continue

11
Strings/Woodwinds
Brass/Percussion

12
Strings/Woodwinds
Brass/Percussion

13
Strings/Woodwinds
Brass/Percussion

14
Strings/Woodwinds
Brass/Percussion

15
Strings/Woodwinds
Brass/Percussion

30

# EXTENSION

## LISTENING

You may wish to use the Listening Map overhead transparency to help guide the students through the listening selection.

Rimsky-Korsakov used orchestral tone color as the basis for the form of "Procession of the Nobles." Which families of instruments do you hear most often in the first part? The second part? The third part? The repetition of melody and tone quality after a contrast creates an ABA form as in the picture on page 30. The second A section is shorter than the first. brass and percussion; strings and woodwinds; brass and percussion

**Ternary** (tur' nə-rē) ("having three parts") describes ABA form.

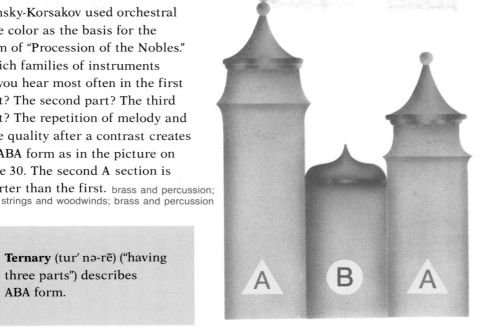

# NICOLAI RIMSKY-KORSAKOV

Nicolai Rimsky-Korsakov (1844-1908), Russian composer, showed his musical talent at a very young age. Although he followed his parents' wishes and joined the Russian navy, he eventually left it to devote himself to music, his real love. He did not have much formal training in music, but he became a brilliant writer for orchestra and a famous teacher of composition. In composing for orchestra, Rimsky-Korsakov paid special attention to combinations of instrumental sounds. He was one of the great orchestrators of the nineteenth century. "Procession of the Nobles" is an example of his unusual selection and mixing of tone colors.

31

# LESSON 7

**3. Introduce ternary form.** Have the students:
• Discuss the illustration (on page 30) of the form of this excerpt from "Procession of the Nobles." (The two towers and bridge illustrate ABA form: repetition after one contrast. The second A section is shorter than the first A section, and the B section is the shortest of the three.)
• Discuss how the orchestration and dynamics reinforce the ternary form of the composition. (The A sections are mostly brass and percussion, while the B section is mostly woodwinds and strings. The B section is soft [piano] and is a marked dynamic contrast to the A section which is loud [forte].)
• Define ternary (ABA) form.
• Discuss the information on Rimsky-Korsakov.

## Reinforcing the Lesson
Review "Shifting Meters" (page 16), which also is in ternary form.

### 3 APPRAISAL
The students should be able to:
1. Define tone color as the unique sound of a voice or instrument.
2. Identify accurately brass, woodwind, string, and percussion instrument families in "Procession of the Nobles."
3. Identify ternary form as repetition after one contrast (ABA).
4. Describe how orchestration and dynamics reinforce the ternary form of "Procession of the Nobles."

## MORE MUSIC TEACHING IDEAS
Have the students:
1. Play the steady beat on classroom instruments, accompanying each section of "Procession of the Nobles," to emphasize and clarify the A and B sections. (A: nos. 1–6, sticks, drums, tambourine; B: nos. 7–10, triangle; A: nos. 11–15, sticks, drums, tambourine.)
2. Create their own ABA compositions using classroom instruments, quarter and eighth notes, and quarter rests. The A and B sections should contrast with each other.

# LESSON 8

**Focus: Reading Melodic Notation**

## Objectives
To develop aural discrimination and reading skills involving the pitches G A C on recorder, bells, keyboard, or C instruments
To identify repeated pitches and rhythm patterns in a melodic accompaniment
To identify and define the range of a melody

## Materials
Recording: "Colour My World"
Recorders, bells, keyboard, or other C instruments

## Vocabulary
Half note, half rest, range

## 1 SETTING THE STAGE

Tell the students that they will be learning to play an accompaniment to "Colour My World," a song by the jazz-rock group Chicago.

## 2 TEACHING THE LESSON

**1. Introduce the pitches G A C on the recorder.** Have the students:
• Learn to play G A C on recorder or bells by lightly touching, then playing, each note. Repeat each pitch as many times as necessary at first, then play each pitch four times.
• Echo you and without looking at the notes, play several patterns on G A C.
• Identify the staff, treble clef, and notation of G A C.
• Play G A C as you point to staff notation on the chalkboard.

# LEARNING A MELODIC ACCOMPANIMENT

• Learn to play the pitches G, A, and C on bells, recorder, keyboard, or other instruments.

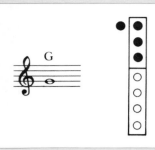

Play G by covering the thumb hole with the thumb, and the first, second, and third holes with the first, second and third fingers of the left hand.

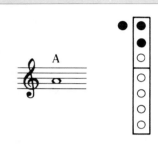

Play A by covering the thumb hole with the thumb, and the first and second holes with the first and second fingers of the left hand.

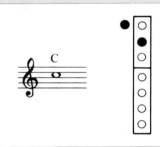

Play C by covering the thumb hole with the thumb, and the second hole with the second finger of the left hand.

• Repeat each pitch, using quarter notes.

G G G G     A A A A     C C C C

32

---

# E X T E N S I O N

**MORE MUSIC TEACHING IDEAS**
Have the students create their own melodies on G A C.

The **half note** ( ♩ ) sounds as long as two quarter notes.

- Perform this pattern on G, A, and C.

- Find the rhythm pattern ♩ ♩ ♩ in this melodic accompaniment to "Colour My World." all measures except last

(3 times)

(Play after third repeat)

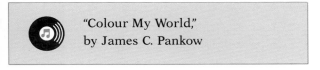

The **half rest** ( ➖ ) in the final measure lasts for two silent beats.

- As you listen to "Colour My World," touch the notes lightly on your recorder without playing them.

> "Colour My World,"
> by James C. Pankow

- Play the melodic accompaniment three times on recorder, bells, or keyboard while you listen to the song again.

The highest and lowest pitches in a song indicate the **range** of that melody.

- Find the range of the melodic accompaniment above. G–C

33

# LESSON 8

- Learn the half-note rhythm.
- Find the rhythm in the melodic accompaniment.

**2. Introduce the melodic accompaniment to "Colour My World," emphasizing pitch notation.** Have the students:
- Read the notation of the melodic accompaniment, saying the letter names of the notes while touching them lightly on the instruments but not playing them.
- Discuss the definition of the half rest.
- Practice the melodic accompaniment on recorder, bells, keyboard, or C instrument.
- Play the melodic accompaniment with the recording.
- Identify the repeated rhythm, repeated pitches (mm. 1-2, 3-4, 5-6, 8-9), highest pitch (C), and lowest pitch (G).
- Define range as the pitch distance between the highest and lowest notes, and identify the narrow range of the melodic accompaniment.

## Reinforcing the Lesson

Have the students summarize how the melodic accompaniment is unified. (repeated pitches and rhythm)

### 3 APPRAISAL

The students should be able to:
1. Hear, read, and play accurately the pitches G A C in a melodic accompaniment on recorder, bells, keyboard, or other C instruments.
2. Identify the repeated rhythm and repeated pitches within the melodic accompaniment.
3. Identify and define the narrow range of the melodic accompaniment.

## MORE MUSIC TEACHING IDEAS

Have the students sing the words to "Colour My World" with the recording.

As time goes on
I realize
just what you mean
to me.

And now,
now that you're near,
promise your love
that I've waited to share
and dreams of our moments together.
Colour my world with hope of loving
you.

—James C. Pankow

# LESSON 9

**Focus: Pitch Memory, Major Scale**

### Objectives
To develop pitch memory
To perform the major scale with numbers and/or syllables
To reinforce interval relationships through the use of hand levels, numbers, and syllables

### Materials
Recordings: "Go Now in Peace"
    "Go Now in Peace" (performance mix)
    "Go Now in Peace" (Orff accompaniment)
Orff instruments or substitutes (resonator bells, hand bells, or keyboard instruments)
Copying Master 1-2 (optional)

### Vocabulary
Tone ladder, major scale, interval, stepwise, skipwise, staff, notation

---

### 1 SETTING THE STAGE

Have the students sing "Go Now in Peace" in unison as a preparation for the activities in this lesson. (Changing voices can sing Part 1 and/or Part 3.)

### 2 TEACHING THE LESSON

**1. Prepare the tone ladder and pitch memory.** Have the students:
• Sing "Go Now in Peace" as a round.
• Learn the instrument parts for the song by practicing the rhythms, then practicing the parts before playing them with the song. (You may wish to use Copying Master 1-2 at this time.)

---

## THE TONE LADDER

CD1:23–24, CD7:20  Key: C major  Starting Pitch: G  Scale Tones: *do re mi fa so do*

• Sing "Go Now in Peace" in unison or as a round.

### Go Now in Peace

Words and music by Natalie Sleeth
Copyright © 1976 by Hinshaw Music, Inc.
Used by Permission.

① Go now in peace, go now in peace,

② may the love of God sur - round you

③ ev - 'ry-where, ev - 'ry-where you may go.

• Learn instrumental parts for this song.

N.F.

Sop. Gl. or Alto Gl.
Alto Met.
Susp. Cymbal or Triangle
Wood block
Bass Xyl. or Bass Met.

34

---

# E X T E N S I O N

## VOCAL DEVELOPMENT

Encourage students to breathe deeply and sit or stand up straight to support the voice. Dropping the jaw on the words *go, now, love,* and *God* will make the sound more resonant.

# Singing Up and Down the Tone Ladder

The eight pitches on this **tone ladder** represent a **major scale**.

- See, hear, and try to sense the musical distance between pitches as you sing up and down the tone ladder. The musical distance between two pitches is called an **interval**.
- As you sing use your left arm to show pitches going up. Use your right arm to show pitches going down. When you sing two numbered pitches that are next to each other, for example 1 to 2 or 3 to 2, the melody is said to move **stepwise**.

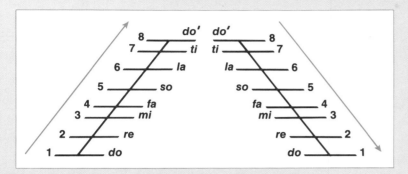

- Sing tone ladders *a*, *b*, and *c*. Omit the pitches that are blue. Remember to think and sense *all* pitches, even the ones you do not sing. When you omit pitches, for instance sing 1 to 3 or 5 to 1, the melody is said to move **skipwise**.

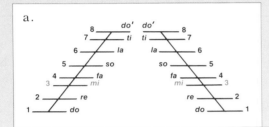

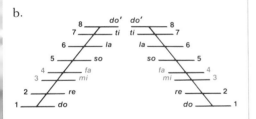

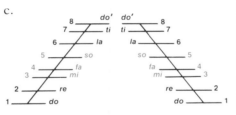

35

**2. Introduce the tone ladder (major scale).** Have the students:

- Sing up and down the tone ladder (major scale) on numbers or syllables. (The major scale will be defined in Unit 4.)
- Follow the directions in the text, using arm levels to show the pitches moving up and down as they sing the tone ladder.
- Identify the tone ladder as a major scale, the distances between pitches as intervals, and stepwise motion.

**3. Develop pitch memory.** Have the students:

- Sing the tone ladder and omit pitches that are circled, in the order presented. The students should leave space for each silent pitch, thinking the pitch sound. Use arm levels to reinforce melodic direction and pitch levels.
- Identify skipwise motion.

## SPECIAL LEARNERS

Use a transparency of the first tone ladder on pupil page 35. When students are directed to sing up and down the tone ladder, point to each syllable on the transparency. When students are to sing the ladder and omit pitches, circle the omitted pitches on the transparency with a colored marker.

# LESSON 9

**4. Assigning pitch numbers or syllables.** Have the students:
- Sing the scale with all pitches, using numbers or syllables, referring to the notation on the staff.
- Sing the third phrase of "Go Now in Peace" on numbers or syllables, using arm levels to sense the musical distance between the pitches.
- Identify the numbers or syllables for the first two phrases of "Go Now in Peace."
- Sing the entire song with numbers or syllables, using arm levels.

When the tone ladder, or major scale, is placed on the **staff**, it can be **notated** like this:

1 2 3 4 5 6 7 8 | 8 7 6 5 4 3 2 1
do re mi fa so la ti do' | do' ti la so fa mi re do

- Sing the third line of "Go Now in Peace" with numbers. Use arm levels for each pitch.

1 1 5 1 1 5 3 2 1
do do so do do so mi re do

- Find the skips between pitches in this example. *do–so, so–mi*

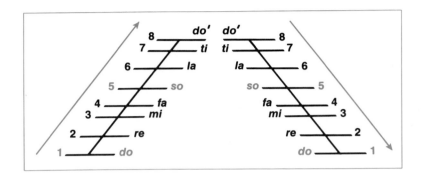

- Identify the pitches by number for the first two lines of "Go Now in Peace." 5 5 4 5 5 5 4 5 8 5 8 5 8 5 4 3 2

- Sing the whole song with numbers or using arm levels.

E X T E N S I O N

- Sing the tone ladder again, omitting pitches 1 and 8.
- Sing "Go Now in Peace," using numbers. Omit the pitches that are blue.

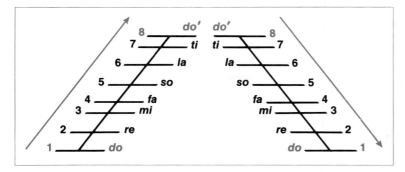

- Sing "Go Now in Peace" again. Omit the pitches that are blue.

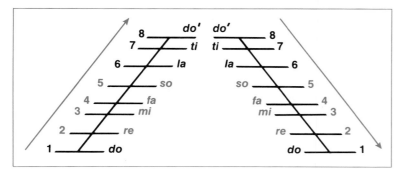

- Look at the tone ladder. Sing the pitches and identify the song. "Are You Sleeping?"

**CHALLENGE**
Create your own mystery tunes and sing them with pitch syllables.

37

# LESSON 9

- Repeat the tone ladder, omitting pitches 1 and 8.
- Repeat "Go Now in Peace," omitting pitches 1 and 8. Use arm levels to show pitch relationships.
- Repeat the song again, omitting pitches 5, 4, 3, and 2, and identify the pitches they sing. (1 and 8)

**5. Introduce the "mystery tune."**
Have the students:
- Identify the mystery tune by singing the pitches as you point to one side of the tone ladder on an overhead transparency or the chalkboard. ("Are You Sleeping?")
- Sing the "mystery tune," using numbers or syllables with arm levels.
- Create their own tunes using given pitches, or pitches of the pentatonic scale (C D E G A), or pitches of the major scale. (Encourage students to begin on 1, 3, or 5 [*do, mi, so*] and end on 1 [*do*].)

## Reinforcing the Lesson

Have the students:
1. Practice, notate, and play the "mystery tune" on bells or keyboard.
2. Assign numbers and/or syllables to other familiar tunes.

**3 APPRAISAL**

The students should be able to:
1. Sing the major scale up and down, with correct pitches, using numbers or syllables.
2. Sing the correct pitches, using numbers or syllables as you point to numbers or syllables on the tone ladder.
3. Assign numbers or syllables to given phrases of a familiar song and, using hand levels, identify upward or downward movement of pitches.
4. Give the name of a "mystery tune" after observing you point to the numbers or syllables of the tune on the tone ladder.

## MORE MUSIC TEACHING IDEAS

Have the students sing the "mystery tune," pointing to the pitches on the tone ladder or the scale in the book.

# REVIEW AND EVALUATION

## JUST CHECKING

### Objective
To review and test the skills and concepts taught in Unit 1

### Materials
Recordings: Just Checking Unit 1
Unit 1 Evaluation (question 4)
*For Extra Credit* recordings (optional)
Recorder or bells
Copying Master 1-3 (optional)
Evaluation Unit 1 Copying Master

## TEACHING THE LESSON

**Review the skills and concepts taught in Unit 1.** Have the students:
• Follow the recorded review with pages 38–39, perform the activities, and answer the questions.
• Review their answers.
(You may wish to use Copying Master 1-3 at this time.)

## JUST CHECKING

See how much you remember.

1. Listen to the steady beat and perform these rhythm patterns by patting the quarter notes and clapping the eighth notes. Make a hands-up, palms-out motion on the quarter rests.

2. Play this melody on recorder or bells with the recorded accompaniment.

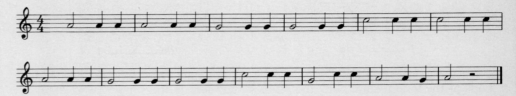

3. Listen to "Shifting Meters" and show when the meter is duple or triple by conducting.

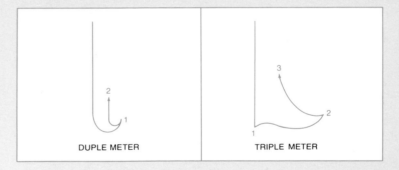

DUPLE METER          TRIPLE METER

38

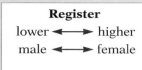

4. Listen and decide which term best describes the singer's register and tone color.  lower, male, dark

| Register | Tone Color |
|----------|-----------|
| lower ⟷ higher | heavy ⟷ light |
| male ⟷ female | nasal ⟷ clear |
| | dark ⟷ bright |

5. Listen and decide if the musical texture of each of these examples is monophonic, polyphonic, or homophonic.
    a. "Bottletop Song" (version 1)  monophonic
    b. "Bottletop Song" (version 2)  polyphonic
    c. "Do You Hear the People Sing?"  homophonic

6. Listen and identify the instrument families you hear in this excerpt from "Procession of the Nobles."  1, 3

1.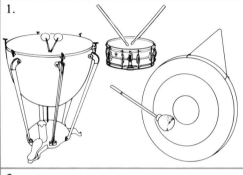
2.
3.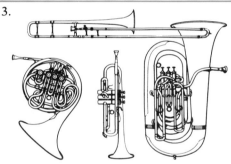
4.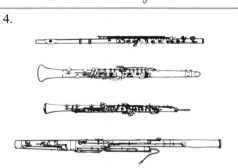

7. As you listen to this excerpt from "Do You Hear the People Sing?" name two features that provide unity through repetition.  melody and words are repeated

39

# REVIEW AND EVALUATION

## GIVING THE EVALUATION

Evaluation Unit 1 Copying Master can be found in the *Teacher's Copying Masters* book along with full directions for giving the evaluation and checking the answers.

## FOR EXTRA CREDIT

You may want to have the students do one of the following activities.

1. Listen to the two compositions you have focused on most in this unit. Write a short paragraph describing the compositions and giving reasons why they like or do not like them.

2. Answer one of the following:

a. How do tone color, sections, and dynamic levels give unity and variety to "Do You Hear the People Sing?" (Different tone colors, sections, and dynamic levels occur in the piece, giving variety. Some tone colors, sections, and dynamic levels repeat, giving unity.)

b. "Shifting Meters" and "Procession of the Nobles" are both in ABA (ternary) form. In what other ways are they similar? How are they different? Compare them in terms of length and tone colors used. ("Procession of the Nobles" is longer, has varied orchestral tone colors; "Shifting Meters" has rock style, same tone colors throughout. (You may wish to play these recordings to refresh students' memories.)

# UNIT 2 • OVERVIEW

| ELEMENTS OF MUSIC | UNIT 2 OBJECTIVES | Lesson 1<br>Focus: Meter Signature, AB Form | Lesson 2<br>Focus: Rhythm of the Words, Phrase |
|---|---|---|---|
| Dynamics | | | |
| Tone Color | Perform on Orff instruments<br>Listen to folk instruments, ragtime ensemble | Listen to folk instruments | Read and perform melodic accompaniments<br>Learn to sustain the phrase on the vowel |
| Tempo | Sing in slow tempo<br>**Identify tempo change** | Identify changes in tempo | |
| Duration/ Rhythm | **Perform steady beat**<br>**Identify meter signature**<br>**Identify and perform quarter, eighth, sixteenth notes, and quarter rests**<br>Perform melodic rhythm<br>**Identify syncopation** | Review steady beat<br>Identify and discuss meter signature<br>Identify and perform rhythm patterns<br>Review duple meter, eighth notes | Identify, read, and perform steady beat<br>Perform a rhythm while listening to a melody<br>Perform one, two, and four sounds to the beat<br>Say or clap melodic rhythm<br>Identify and perform rhythm patterns on Orff instruments<br>Play rhythms against a steady beat<br><br>Play melodic rhythms of popular songs against the steady beat |
| Pitch | | Sing a song with a range of A-dˡ | Sing a song with range of d-cˡ or A-a |
| Texture | Perform polyphony, harmonic accompaniment, two-part harmony | | Sing a song in two parts<br>Perform a harmonic accompaniment |
| Form | **Identify verse-refrain form (AB)**<br>**Identify phrase lengths** | Sing a song with verse and refrain (AB)<br>Sing a song with antecedent/consequent phrase structure<br><br>Create compositions in AB form with classroom instruments | Sing a song with six verses<br>Perform and identify phrases of a song<br>Identify phrase lengths |
| Style | **Identify ragtime**<br>Perform song in Spanish | Listen to, sing, and discuss folk music | Listen to, sing, and discuss the spiritual |
| Reading | | Read ♫ , ♩ , ♩ , ♩ ─ , ²⁄₂ | Read 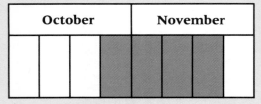 , ²⁄₄ |

## PURPOSE Unit 2: Rhythm Around Us

In this unit the students will explore complex rhythms against a steady beat, as well as the relationships between note values. They will gain an awareness of phrase structure by identifying the number and length of phrases. They will listen to and perform syncopated and nonsyncopated patterns.

## SUGGESTED TIME FRAME

| October | | | | November | | | |
|---|---|---|---|---|---|---|---|
| | | | ▓ | ▓ | ▓ | ▓ | |

### FOCUS
- Meter signature
- AB form
- Rhythm of the words
- Phrase structure
- Quarter, eighth, sixteenth notes
- Syncopation

| Lesson 3<br>Focus: Quarter, Eighth, Sixteenth Notes | Lesson 4<br>Focus: Syncopation | Lesson 5<br>Focus: Phrase Beginning with a Quarter Rest |
|---|---|---|
| Listen to and identify instruments in ragtime ensemble | Perform accompaniment on bells, keyboard, or Orff instruments | |
| | | Sing a song in a slow tempo |
| Identify and perform steady beat<br>Identify and perform one, two, and four sounds to a beat<br>Locate rhythm patterns in a composition<br>Experience syncopation<br>Read and perform a rhythm accompaniment<br>Create patterns with quarter, eighth, and sixteenth notes | Hear, read, sing, and perform syncopation<br>Perform rhythmic ostinato<br>Create a two-part composition with steady beat and syncopation | Identify and perform syncopated patterns<br>Perform rhythmic body ostinati<br>Identify quarter rest at the beginning of a phrase<br>Work for rhythmic precision in singing |
| | Sing melodies with a range of c-d¹ and f-f¹ | Sing a melody with a range of B-e¹ |
| | Experience harmony by performing two-part nonimitative polyphony (partner songs) | Sing a two-part song |
| | | Identify and perform body motions according to phrase structure<br>Compare phrase length |
| Listen to, perform, and discuss ragtime<br>Discuss Scott Joplin | Perform a spiritual and folk song | Sing a Puerto Rican folk song in Spanish |
| Read ♫♫, ♫♪, ♫♪♫ , ♪,♩, 3, tie | Read body percussion score<br>Read ♪♩  ♪♩ | Read ♫ , ♩, ‡, ‒, ♩ in 2/2<br>Find and clap ♩. ♪♩ |

# TECHNOLOGY

## MUSIC WITH *MIDI*

MIDI technology allows students to manipulate musical elements and make musical decisions.
- Lesson 1, page 42: *"Cripple Creek"*; Create a **Country Song**
- Lesson 2, page 44: *"Oh, Sinner Man"*
- Lesson 3, page 48: Tutorial: *"The Entertainer" by S. Joplin*

## VIDEO RESOURCES

Use video resources to reinforce, extend, and enrich learning in this unit.

# LESSON 1

# UNIT 2

## RHYTHM AROUND US

Standing Violin. Arman. MARISA DEL. RE GALLERY, NY

# LESSON 1

**Focus: Meter Signature, AB Form**

### Objectives
To identify and discuss meter signature
To identify and perform a song in AB form
To identify changes in tempo

### Materials
Recordings: "Cripple Creek"
            (sung version)
           "Cripple Creek"
            (performance mix)
           "Cripple Creek"
            (bluegrass version)
           "Bottletop Song" (optional)
           "Trav'ler" (optional)
Drumsticks or substitutes (one for each student)

### Vocabulary
AB form, meter signature, tempo

### 1 SETTING THE STAGE
Review steady beat, duple meter, and eighth notes on pages 1-3.

41

## LESSON 1

### 2 TEACHING THE LESSON

**1. Introduce "Cripple Creek."** Have the students:
• Discuss the information on "Cripple Creek."
• Pat-slide the duple-meter pattern as they listen to the sung version.

**2. Introduce AB form.** Have the students:
• Follow the score and sing the song with the recording. (Changing voices can sing measures 3, 4, 7, and 8 of the verse, and the entire refrain, marked in the score.)
• Review and rehearse phrases or sections as necessary.
• Find the verse and refrain and designate them as A and B. Identify this form as AB form.

## A TWO-PART SONG

CD1:39, CD7:21    Key: D major    Starting Pitch: D    Scale Tones: *so, ti, do re mi fa so la do'*

"Cripple Creek" is a popular song from the western United States. It takes its name from the town of Cripple Creek, Colorado.

• Pat-slide the steady beat on your desk while you listen to "Cripple Creek."

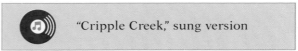

"Cripple Creek," sung version

### Cripple Creek

Piano Accompaniment on page PA 10

Traditional (arr. V.L.)

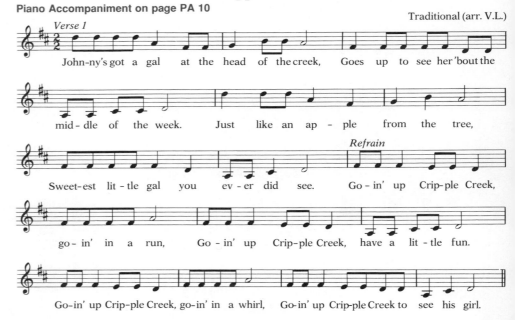

*Verse 1*
John-ny's got a gal at the head of the creek, Goes up to see her 'bout the mid-dle of the week. Just like an ap-ple from the tree, Sweet-est lit-tle gal you ev-er did see. *Refrain* Go-in' up Crip-ple Creek, go-in' in a run, Go-in' up Crip-ple Creek, have a lit-tle fun. Go-in' up Crip-ple Creek, go-in' in a whirl, Go-in' up Crip-ple Creek to see his girl.

*Verse 2*
Cripple Creek's wide and Cripple Creek's deep,
He'll wade Cripple Creek before he sleeps.
Rolls up his britches to his knees,
He'll wade Cripple Creek whenever he please.

*Verse 3*
Halfway there he stops to rest,
Thinks about the gal that he loves best.
Picks him a watermelon from the vine,
Pickin' them seeds sure takes some time.

*Coda* (ending section)

Go-in' up Crip-ple Creek to see his girl!

The form of "Cripple Creek" is created by alternating the verse and refrain. This can be described as **AB form**.

42

---

## E X T E N S I O N

### VOCAL DEVELOPMENT

Have the students sing the following five-note pattern on an *oo* vowel on descending scale tones. (Changing voices can sing an octave lower.)

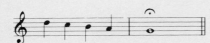

# The Meter Signature

When you performed the steady beat to "Cripple Creek," you performed two beats in a measure. The $\frac{2}{2}$ at the beginning of "Cripple Creek" is called the **meter signature**. It indicates that there are two beats in a measure and that a half note represents the steady beat.

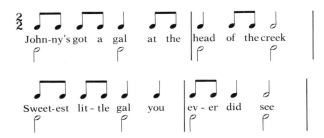

> 2 ←—— number of beats in a measure
> 2 ←—— half note represents the steady beat

• Say these patterns from "Cripple Creek" and pat the steady half-note beat.

John-ny's got a gal    at the | head  of the creek

Sweet-est lit - tle gal    you | ev - er did    see

• Tap this rhythm pattern to the verses of "Cripple Creek." Hold a drumstick in your right hand and tap to the right and left as you say "right, left," keeping the steady beat.

right  left  right  left  right  left  right  left

• Perform this pattern to the refrain of "Cripple Creek." Keep the stick in your right hand. As you say "right" or "left," tap the stick in front of you.

right    right left right    right left right    right left right    right left

• Perform both parts of the pattern as you listen to "Cripple Creek."

> "Cripple Creek," bluegrass version

• How does the **tempo**, the speed of the beat, change? It becomes faster.

43

---

# LESSON 1

**3. Introduce meter signature.** Have the students:
• Discuss the information on meter signature.
• Say the patterns from the song while playing the steady half-note beat.

**4. Introduce the stick pattern.** Have the students:
• Practice the first part of the stick pattern while saying "right, left," then saying the verses, then singing them.
• Practice the second part of the stick pattern while saying "right, left," then saying the refrain, then singing it.
• Play the complete stick pattern while singing the verses and refrain of the song.
• Play the complete stick pattern to the bluegrass version of "Cripple Creek" and identify the change in tempo.

## Reinforcing the Lesson

Review meter signatures of other songs, such as "Bottletop Song" in $\frac{3}{4}$, page 18, and "Trav'ler" in $\frac{4}{4}$, page 26.

**3 APPRAISAL**

The students should be able to:
1. Identify and define the meter signature of "Cripple Creek."
2. Identify the verse and refrain structure of "Cripple Creek" as AB form by playing contrasting drumstick patterns on the verses and refrain.
3. Sing "Cripple Creek" with rhythmic and melodic accuracy.
4. Identify changes in tempo in the recording of "Cripple Creek."

---

## MORE MUSIC TEACHING IDEAS

Have the students use classroom instruments to create their own compositions in AB form.

# LESSON 2

**Focus: Rhythm of the Words, Phrase**

**Objectives**
To play the rhythm of the words of a song against the steady beat
To identify and perform phrase structure
To sing a spiritual in unison or two parts with harmonic accompaniment

**Materials**
Recordings: "Oh, Sinner Man"
  "Oh, Sinner Man" (performance mix)
  "Oh, Sinner Man" (Orff accompaniment)
  "Go Now in Peace" (optional)
  "Bottletop Song" (optional)
Orff instruments or resonator bells
Copying Master 2-1 (optional)

**Vocabulary**
Phrase, spiritual

## 1 SETTING THE STAGE

Have the students perform the following rhythm pattern softly to "Oh, Sinner Man":

## 2 TEACHING THE LESSON

**1. Introduce the rhythm of the words and duple meter.** Have the students:
• Sing the song. (Changing voices can sing the lower part.)
• Focus on the rhythm score of "Oh, Sinner Man," tap the beat, and say or clap the rhythm of the words while following the top line of the rhythm score. (This experience will prepare the students for sixteenth notes.)

# PERFORM THE RHYTHM OF THE WORDS

**Key: D minor     Starting Pitch: A     Scale Tones:** *mi, so, la, ti, do re mi so*

Piano Accompaniment on page PA 15  **Oh, Sinner Man**

CD1:41, CD7:22

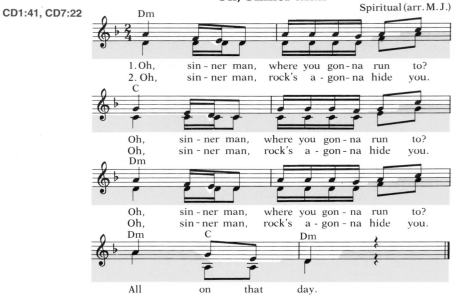

1. Oh, sin-ner man, where you gon-na run to?
2. Oh, sin-ner man, rock's a-gon-na hide you.

Oh, sin-ner man, where you gon-na run to?
Oh, sin-ner man, rock's a-gon-na hide you.

Oh, sin-ner man, where you gon-na run to?
Oh, sin-ner man, rock's a-gon-na hide you.

All on that day.

3. Run to the sea, sea will be a-boiling. *(3 times)*
   All on that day.
4. Run to the Lord, Lord won't you hide me? *(3 times)*
   All on that day.
5. Oh, sinner man, you ought to be a-praying. *(3 times)*
   All on that day.
6. Oh, sinner man, where you gonna run to? *(3 times)*
   All on that day.

• Tap the steady beat (the bottom line) with your foot as you say or clap the rhythm of the words (top line).

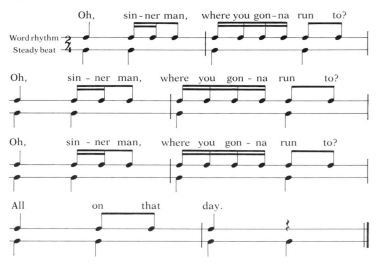

Oh, sin-ner man, where you gon-na run to?

Oh, sin-ner man, where you gon-na run to?

Oh, sin-ner man, where you gon-na run to?

All on that day.

44

---

# E X T E N S I O N

**SPECIAL LEARNERS**

Prepare a transparency of the rhythm score at the bottom of the pupil page. If a class includes several exceptional students, first rehearse the rhythm score with two groups, one group performing each line. This practice will provide these students with a visual and sound model before they are to perform both lines simultaneously.

**MORE MUSIC TEACHING IDEAS**

Have the students select other familiar songs and tap or step the steady beat while playing or clapping the rhythm of the words. Notate the rhythm of the words if they are able.

**VOCAL DEVELOPMENT**

Have the students sing the melody of "Oh, Sinner Man" on a long *oo* vowel to develop good singing tone while learning how to sustain the phrase.

# Recognizing Phrases

• Move your hands in an arc from left to right as you sing each line of "Oh, Sinner Man."  CD1:42

Oh, sin-ner man, where you gon-na run to?

Your movements correspond to the phrases of "Oh, Sinner Man."
A **phrase** is a complete musical idea.

How many phrases does this song have? four
Are the phrases equal or unequal in length? equal
Which phrases have the same rhythm of the words? 1,2, and 3

• Learn these instrumental parts to accompany "Oh, Sinner Man."
• Practice the rhythm of each part. Then play the parts with the song.

## Accompaniment to "Oh, Sinner Man"

N.F.

45

• Compare the meter signatures of "Oh, Sinner Man" and "Cripple Creek," page 42.
(In "Oh, Sinner Man," the quarter note represents the steady beat; in "Cripple Creek," the half note represents the steady beat.)

**2. Introduce the phrase.** Have the students:
• Move their hands in an arc from left to right as they sing each line of the text.
• Identify and define the arc movement as corresponding to a musical phrase, and discuss the definition.
• Answer the analysis questions about phrase and phrase structure.

**3. Introduce the following optional movement activity.** Have the students reinforce their understanding of the phrase structure by clapping the rhythm of the words and stepping the steady beat, changing direction on each new phrase. (You can structure this activity by having the class form two lines. Have students step four beats in and four beats out as shown.)

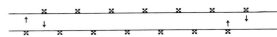

**4. Introduce the harmonic accompaniment.** Have the students:
• Practice the rhythm of each part by patting as they sing the melody.
• Use Orff instruments or bells to accompany the song. (You may wish to use Copying Master 2-1 at this time.)
• Play the rhythms on instruments as they sing the song. Take turns playing the instrumental parts.

# LESSON 2

## EXTRA HELP

If the students are having trouble with phrase length, have them count the number of beats in each phrase. Timpani pitches D and C can be played easily on the string bass by retuning the D string down to C. The student plays C by plucking the open string. D can be played by placing the first finger on the retuned string in first position.

# LESSON 2

**5. Introduce background on spirituals.** Have the students discuss the background information on spirituals and "Oh, Sinner Man."
You may wish to use the following item as a basis for extended discussion.
*Musical heritage* is a term that describes tonal sounds and rhythm patterns that frequently are characteristic of a particular group of people or a geographical area. (For example, banjos and fiddles are associated with bluegrass; and electric guitars and synthesizers are associated with rock.)

## Spirituals

The African American spiritual, a unique kind of song, grew from the experience of Africans brought to America in slavery. Music became a way of adapting to a new language, a new religion, and a new, difficult way of life. The songs were a means for them to communicate with each other and expressed their troubles and hope for a better life.

As the name suggests, spirituals have a religious or "spiritual" meaning. The oldest spirituals had no known composers and were not written down. They passed from generation to generation of singers, and are still sung today.

Some spirituals are slow and full of emotion. Others are lively, with strong rhythms emphasized by hand clapping. Spirituals can be sung by one person alone, or in call-response form, like many African songs. Examples of well-known spirituals are "He's Got the Whole World in His Hands," "Joshua Fought the Battle of Jericho," and "Wade in the Water."

"Oh, Sinner Man" is also a classic spiritual. The words are a warning about Judgment Day.

Ruby Green Singing, James Chapin, NORTON GALLERY AND SCHOOL OF ART, West Palm Beach, FL

James Chapin painted this portrait of Ruby Green, a young singer, in 1928.

46

# E X T E N S I O N

## COOPERATIVE LEARNING

Before dividing the class into groups, have the students read together the information on page 46. Then read from the board a definition of *musical heritage*. (Musical heritage: the sounds and rhythms that are characteristic of a group of people or a geographic location) The students should discuss together the musical characteristics that describe spirituals, based on what they read. (They have a religious or spiritual meaning, they may be slow and full of emotion or lively with strong rhythms, they may be sung by one person alone or by call and response, and they may have a hand-clapping accompaniment.)
Now randomly assign the students to cooperative groups of four. Each group will follow these directions:

1. Choose a particular group of people or a geographic region, for example: Native Americans, the Appalachian Mountain region, or the inner city.
2. Discuss what characteristics they would expect to find in the music of the group or region.
3. Make a list of these characteristics, along with reasons why they think they might exist, for example: Native American music would use natural materials to produce sounds; Appalachian music might use homemade instruments; inner city music might be fast and hard because life is hard there and many people are bustling around in a small space.

4. Optional: Do research to find out whether their speculations are accurate, and find examples of recorded music to use as evidence that their information is accurate.
5. All group members should sign the list before handing it in.

This poem recognizes the contributions of the unknown composers of African American spirituals.

O black and unknown bards of long ago,
How came your lips to touch the sacred fire?
How, in your darkness, did you come to know
The power and beauty of the minstrel's lyre?
Who first from midst his bonds lifted his eyes?
Who first from out the still watch, lone and long,
Feeling the ancient faith of prophets rise
Within his dark-kept soul, burst into song?

Heart of what slave poured out such melody
As "Steal away to Jesus"? On its strains
His spirit must have nightly floated free,
Though still about his hands he felt his chains.
Who heard great "Jordan roll"? Whose starward eye
Saw chariot "swing low"? And who was he
That breathed that comforting, melodic sigh,
"Nobody knows de trouble I see"?

What merely living clod, what captive thing,
Could up toward God through all its darkness grope,
And find within its deadened heart to sing
These songs of sorrow, love and faith, and hope?
How did it catch that subtle undertone,
That note in music heard not with the ears?
How sound the elusive reed so seldom blown,
Which stirs the soul or melts the heart to tears.

—from "O Black and Unknown Bards,"
*by James Weldon Johnson*

47

# LESSON 2

**6. Introduce the excerpt from "O Black and Unknown Bards" by James Weldon Johnson.** Have the students discuss the poem as it relates to the development of spirituals. (The poet wants to acknowledge the unknown composers of this music.)

### Reinforcing the Lesson

Have the students identify the rhythm of the words and the steady beat of familiar songs such as "Go Now in Peace," page 34, or the "Bottletop Song," page 18.

## 3 APPRAISAL

The students should be able to:
1. Perform the rhythm of the words against the steady beat by stepping the beat and simultaneously clapping and/or saying the rhythm of the words.
2. While listening to or singing "Oh, Sinner Man," use arm movements and changes in movement directions to identify the number and length of phrases.
3. Sing "Oh, Sinner Man" in unison or parts with the harmonic accompaniment.

### CURRICULUM CONNECTION: READING

**James Weldon Johnson** (1871–1938) was educated at Atlanta and Columbia universities. His career covered many fields, including teaching, the law, composing songs (including "Lift Every Voice and Sing"), and diplomacy. He also served as field secretary and later secretary for the NAACP. Some of his publications are *The Autobiography of an Ex-Colored Man, Black Manhattan, God's Trombones,* and *Saint Peter Relates an Incident,* from which "O Black and Unknown Bards" is taken.

# LESSON 3

**Focus: Quarter, Eighth, Sixteenth Notes**

## Objectives
To perform and move to examples of quarter, eighth, and sixteenth notes
To perform a one-line rhythmic accompaniment containing quarter, eighth, and sixteenth notes

## Materials
Recordings: *The Entertainer*
(instrumental version)
*The Entertainer*
(complete piano version)
Drumsticks (two for each student)
Copying Master 2-2 (optional)

## Vocabulary
Melodic rhythm, sixteenth note, tie, ragtime

---

**1 SETTING THE STAGE**

You may wish to play *The Entertainer* while the students enter the room.

**2 TEACHING THE LESSON**

**1. Introduce melodic rhythm in *The Entertainer*.** Have the students:
• Follow the steady beat as they listen to the instrumental version of *The Entertainer*.
• Listen again to the instrumental version of *The Entertainer*, and tap the melodic rhythm.
• Identify which instruments perform the upper and lower parts.
• Discuss the information on sixteenth notes.
• Discuss the information on the tie.
• Perform the Challenge! activity by tapping both the melodic rhythm and the steady beat while listening to *The Entertainer*.

---

# E X T E N S I O N

## SPECIAL LEARNERS

If your class includes exceptional learners, prepare a transparency of pupil page 48. Use the transparency of the full rhythm score to point to the beginning of each line when students are directed to tap the lower part and then the upper part.

---

# A LITTLE RAGTIME

 **Tapping Rhythms**

• Listen to *The Entertainer* and tap the steady beat.
Which instrument plays the steady beat? tuba (percussion doubles)

 *The Entertainer* by Scott Joplin

• Listen to *The Entertainer* again. This time, tap the rhythm of the melody, also called the **melodic rhythm.** Which instrument plays the melody? clarinet (piano doubles)

Most of the notes in the first phrase of *The Entertainer* are **sixteenth notes** (  ).

Each eighth note can be divided into two sixteenth notes.

In the rhythm pattern some notes are connected by curved lines called **ties**. The tied notes are added together to make one longer sound.

**CHALLENGE** Tap both parts at the same time while you listen to *The Entertainer*.

Robert Redford gets a haircut and manicure while Paul Newman looks on in this scene from *The Sting*.

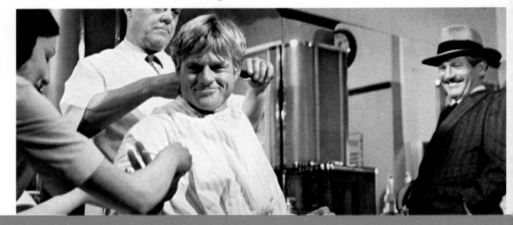

# Ragtime and Scott Joplin

Ragtime was one of the first truly American styles of popular music. Ragtime began in the African American communities of St. Louis and Sedalia, Missouri. It reached the height of its popularity in the late 1890s and faded by 1920.

Ragtime is exciting to hear because the melody has complex, off-the-beat ("ragged") rhythms against a simple, steady beat in the accompaniment. Most ragtime was written for piano.

Scott Joplin (1868-1917) was called the "King of Ragtime." He was born into a musical family in Texarkana, Texas. His father played the violin. His mother played the banjo and encouraged Scott to study music. When he was a teenager, he was earning money by playing the piano in churches and restaurants. Later, he studied classical music at the George R. Smith College in Sedalia, Missouri. *Maple Leaf Rag*, published in 1899, was his first great success. Some of his other works are *The Easy Winners, The Cascades,* and *The Entertainer.*

Joplin wrote over fifty works, including a ballet and two operas, most in ragtime style. His music expresses his belief that ragtime could be as complex and as expressive as "classical" music.

In 1907, Joplin went to New York City and composed his second opera, *Treemonisha.* He could not find anyone to provide the money to stage it, because most people would not accept the idea of a ragtime opera. He produced a concert version himself (without scenery or special costumes) in 1915. It got poor reviews, and Joplin was heartbroken. By the time he died, two years later, ragtime no longer was popular.

Since the 1970s, ragtime has regained much of its popularity. Joplin's collected works were published in 1972, and his music has been recorded many times. In 1975, the motion picture *The Sting* won an Academy Award for its soundtrack, which included *The Entertainer* and other Joplin works. The same year, *Treemonisha* opened on Broadway. It was shown on national public television in 1986. Ragtime is now a permanent part of American music.

49

**2. Introduce Scott Joplin and ragtime.** Have the students discuss the information on ragtime and Scott Joplin.
You may wish to use the following items as a basis for extended discussion.
1. What historical events of the 1890s would have influenced behavior, attitudes, and music? (Antonin Dvořák, arriving in the U.S. in 1892 to teach for three years, pressured young American composers to look to their native heritage for inspiration, rather than copy European models. Flat phonograph discs were invented by Emil Berliner in 1894. The ease of mass producing these on presses led to the widespread availability of the latest music.) Did Scott Joplin's music reflect the public mood of the time? (Scott Joplin's *Maple Leaf Rag* and later works were very successful from 1899 on, but his operas and ballets were not. So the answer to the public mood question is yes and no. People were in the mood for light, carefree music, not weighty works with social messages.)
2. *The Entertainer* became popular again after it was reintroduced in the motion picture *The Sting.* Name some other compositions that have had similar success. (The second movement, Andante, from Mozart's Piano Concerto No. 21 in C major gained fame in the film *Elvira Madigan.* The opening of Beethoven's Symphony No. 5 in C minor became a symbol of victory in World War II, because its four opening notes have the same rhythm pattern as the Morse code for the letter *V.* )

# LESSON 3

**3. Introduce rhythm patterns containing quarter, eighth, and sixteenth notes.** Have the students:

• Pat the beat as they say each rhythm pattern. Repeat each pattern to extend it. (Point out that rhythm pattern 1 has one sound per beat; pattern 2 has two even sounds per beat; and pattern 3 has four even sounds per beat.)

• Combine patterns, and repeat in succession, such as nos. 2 and 4, or 3 and 7.

• Assign specific patterns to different groups. Pat the beat while tapping and saying patterns simultaneously, changing patterns on signal.

• Tap a steady beat with the foot as they clap and say each pattern at the bottom of the page while listening to the music.

• Pat the beat while saying the patterns in the rhythm accompaniment to *The Entertainer* as they listen to the music again.

**4. Introduce movement activity.** Have the students tap the quarter-note beat and clap the rhythm of the melody as they listen again to the music.

**5. Introduce the rhythmic accompaniment.** Have the students:

• Read out loud, in rhythm, each of the seven rhythm patterns, using the words *right* and *left* alternately.

## Ragtime Rhythms

• Pat the steady beat as you say each rhythm.

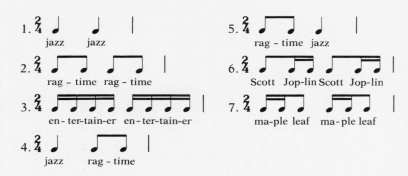

• Create your own patterns by combining two or more rhythms.

The rhythmic accompaniment to *The Entertainer* uses the rhythm patterns below.

• Tap the steady beat with your foot as you clap each pattern and say the words with the recording.

50

### SPECIAL LEARNERS

Prepare a transparency of the bottom of this page in the pupil edition. As you direct students to clap and say a pattern with the recording, cover the patterns that are not being used. This will eliminate visual distraction and will help exceptional learners focus on each pattern.

### COOPERATIVE LEARNING

Copy patterns 1, 2, and 3 from the *top* of pupil page 50 on the board. Have the students read the notation and word rhythms from the board, patting the steady beat and repeating each pattern at least four times. (Point out that the first pattern has one sound per beat, pattern 2 has two even sounds per beat, and pattern 3 has four even sounds per beat.)

Assign the students randomly to cooperative groups of four to create new words for the rhythm patterns and create an improvised piece, following these directions:

1. One group member writes the three rhythms on a piece of paper, leaving room below each for a word.

2. A second group member chooses the category to which the group's words will belong, for example: names of states, countries of the world, sports teams, and so on.

3. Group members choose together the three words from the category to be used, and a third group member writes the words under the rhythms.

4. The last group member will act as the conductor, pointing to the rhythm patterns as the rest of the group says each word once on each beat until the conductor points to a different rhythm. The conductor should try to achieve interesting repeated patterns, and occasionally stop pointing to give the speakers time to breathe.

5. Have successful groups perform their improvised speech pieces for the class.

- Using the percussion matched grip, play the rhythm accompaniment to *The Entertainer*.

Use your right and left hands as marked in the score. The ⊢³⌐ at the beginning means that you should listen and count for three measures before you start to play the accompaniment. These three measures are called the *introduction*.

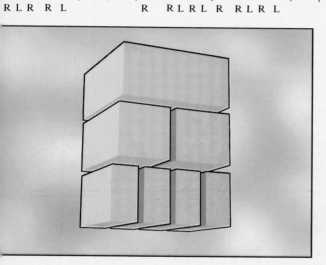

This computer image represents the ratios among quarter, eighth, and sixteenth notes: a quarter note is equal to two eighth notes and to four sixteenth notes.

51

# LESSON 3

- Review the matched-grip drumstick position (page 3).
- Read and practice each of the patterns on page 50 separately, using drumsticks, while listening to the piano version of *The Entertainer*.
- Using the percussion matched grip, play the rhythmic accompaniment to *The Entertainer*. (measures 1–52; 5–52; 1–20; 17–20) (You may wish to use Copying Master 2–2 at this time.)

## MORE MUSIC TEACHING IDEAS

Have the students tap the steady beat of *The Entertainer* with one hand and the melodic rhythm with the other.

# LESSON 3

**6. Introduce the Challenge! activity.**
Have the students perform the Challenge! rhythm activity. (Example: You or a student will perform a pattern by patting quarter notes, clapping eighth notes, and tapping sixteenth notes on the back of the hand. The class repeats it. Then challenge the class to identify by square number the rhythm values used, for example, 5, 6, 7, 8, or 1, 6, 11, 16.)

## Reinforcing the Lesson

• Draw the Challenge! grid on the chalkboard. Have the students perform all the way through. Erase two connecting squares, such as 5 and 6, or 7 and 8. Challenge students to perform, remembering the missing note values. (Students may clap or pat the beat while saying the rhythms.) Gradually erase all squares and have students perform entire Challenge! grid without written notation.

## 3 APPRAISAL

The students should be able to:
1. Listen to *The Entertainer* and tap the beat in twos while clapping the rhythm pattern of the lower part.
2. Demonstrate by stepping, clapping, and tapping their understanding of the relationship of the quarter note to eighth and sixteenth notes.
3. Read and perform accurately the patterns in the rhythmic accompaniment and the Challenge!.

Create your own rhythm patterns. Connect the notes in two or more squares that are next to each other (across, down, up, or diagonal). Perform the patterns by patting the quarter notes ♩, clapping the eighth notes ♫, and tapping the sixteenth notes ♬ on the back of your hand. Make a palms-up motion on the quarter rests ♩.

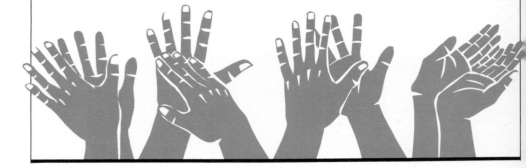

# E X T E N S I O N

## MORE MUSIC TEACHING IDEAS

Have the students:
1. Create rhythm patterns using combinations of patting (quarter notes), clapping (eighth notes), and tapping on the backs of their hands (sixteenth notes). Have individual students perform these patterns for the rest of the class to identify, notate, and play. (Encourage students to vary the body percussion.)
2. Form two groups and perform the Challenge! grid. One group can perform the squares in reverse order (nos. 16–13, 12–9, and so on) while the other group performs the squares in the normal order. Other directions can be used.

# CREATING HARMONY

These songs, which can be sung together in **harmony,** are called **partner songs.**

CD1:45–47

Key: F major    Starting Pitch: C    Scale Tones: *so, la, do re mi so la*

### I Saw the Light

Spiritual

I saw the light, I saw the light,

No more dark-ness, no more night.

Now I'm so hap-py, no sor-row in sight,

Praise the Lord, I saw the light.

Key: F major

Starting Pitch: A    Scale Tones: *do re mi so la do¹*

### Don't Let the Wind

St. Helena Island song

Don't let the wind, don't let the wind,

Don't let the wind stir here no more.

Oh, don't let the wind,

Don't let the wind stir here no more.

53

---

# LESSON 4

**Focus: Syncopation**

**Objective**
To read, play, and compare syncopated and unsyncopated patterns

**Materials**
Recordings: "I Saw the Light" and "Don't Let the Wind" (separate and combined)
*American Quodlibet* (optional)
Bells, keyboard, or Orff instruments

**Vocabulary**
Harmony, partner songs, syncopation

## 1 SETTING THE STAGE

Explain to students that they can create harmony just by singing songs at the same time that "go together."

## 2 TEACHING THE LESSON

**1. Introduce harmony using partner songs.** Have the students:
• Echo the following body percussion pattern as modeled by you or by a student. (You may wish to notate this on the chalkboard or on an overhead transparency.)

snap
clap
pat

• Perform the body percussion lightly while listening to "I Saw the Light" and "Don't Let the Wind" (separately).
• Follow the score and sing the songs with the recordings, first separately, then together. (Changing voices should sing the lower part in "I Saw the Light.")
• Review and rehearse phrases or sections as necessary.

---

# EXTENSION

## VOCAL DEVELOPMENT

Work for rhythmic accuracy and expression when combining "I Saw the Light" and "Don't Let the Wind."

## CURRICULUM CONNECTION: SOCIAL STUDIES

St. Helena Island is off the coast of South Carolina, near Parris Island.

# LESSON 4

## 2. Introduce the syncopated pattern.

Have the students:

• Find rhythm patterns 1 and 2 in "I Saw the Light." (pattern 1, m. 3; pattern 2, mm. 1, 2, 6, 8)
• Clap each pattern as they recite the text in rhythm.
• Compare and contrast the two patterns.
• Define syncopation.
• Form two groups. While listening to "I Saw the Light," one group should clap and say the words to rhythm pattern 1; the other group should clap and say the words to rhythm pattern 2.
• Respond to the Challenge! by tapping both patterns at the same time.

---

# A New Kind of Rhythm

• Think the rhythm patterns in "I Saw the Light." Which words match these patterns? no more darkness; I saw the light; sorrow in sight

• Clap each pattern as you say the words. Which feels catchy and uneven?

This off-the-beat rhythm is called **syncopation**. It emphasizes beats or parts of the beat that are not normally accented.

• Find different ways of saying the syncopated pattern as you clap.

|   I   |  SAW  |  the  |
|-------|-------|-------|
|  □    |  ▭    |   □   |
| don't |  LET  |  the  |
| short | LONG  | short |
| syn–  |  CO–  |  pah  |

**CHALLENGE** Tap rhythm pattern 1 with one hand while you tap rhythm pattern 2 with the other hand. Repeat, this time changing hands.

These computer images represent on-the-beat rhythms and syncopation.

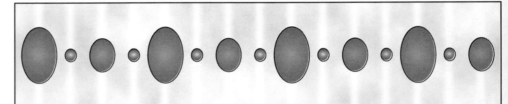

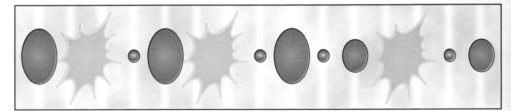

54

---

## MORE MUSIC TEACHING IDEAS

Have the students create a two-part composition with classroom instruments, with one group of students playing the syncopated pattern in this lesson and another group playing simpler patterns.

**d an Accompaniment**

ay this instrumental part on keyboard as you sing "I Saw the ght," and then "Don't Let the Wind."

### I Saw the Light — Don't Let the Wind

Instrumental part (arr. N.F.)

# LESSON 4

**3. Introduce the instrumental accompaniment.** Have the students:
• Find rhythm pattern 2 in the instrumental part (m. 8).
• Sing the songs together as they play the instrumental part on bells, keyboard, or Orff instruments. (You can divide the class into two groups, with each group playing one line of the instrumental part.)

### Reinforcing the Lesson

Encourage the students to sing other songs together to create harmony, for example, "When the Saints Go Marching In" and "Swing Low, Sweet Chariot," both of which are in *American Quodlibet* on page 197.

### 3 APPRAISAL

The students should be able to:
1. Listen to and accurately label syncopated and unsyncopated rhythms.
2. Listen to a steady beat and perform at least two different syncopated rhythm patterns by stepping, clapping, speaking, or singing.
3. Sing "I Saw the Light" and "Don't Let the Wind" with rhythmic and melodic accuracy.
4. Play the instrumental accompaniment to "I Saw the Light" and "Don't Let the Wind" with rhythmic precision.
5. Verbally define syncopation as emphasizing beats or parts of beats that are not normally accented.

# LESSON 5

**Focus: Phrase Beginning with a Quarter Rest**

### Objectives

To experience a quarter rest at the beginning of each phrase of a song
To identify and perform phrase structure
To identify and perform syncopated patterns

### Materials

Recordings: "Las Flores"
            "Las Flores" (performance mix)
            "When the Saints Go Marching In"
            "Go Now in Peace"
Drumsticks (two for each student)

## 1 SETTING THE STAGE

Tell the students that "Las Flores" is a folk song in Spanish from Puerto Rico.

## 2 TEACHING THE LESSON

**1. Introduce phrases beginning with a quarter rest.** Have the students:

• Pat the half-note beat while listening to the recording.
• Listen to "Las Flores" again, performing the pattern.
• Listen to the song again, performing the same pattern and moving both hands in an arc on each phrase.
• Sing the refrain and verse 1 of "Las Flores" in Spanish as they pat each quarter rest and show the phrases with an arc.
• Decide if the phrases are equal or unequal in length. (Phrases 3 and 6 are twice as long as phrases 1, 2, 4, and 5.)
• Discuss the information and compare the phrase beginnings in "Oh, Sinner Man" (page 44) and "Las Flores." (The phrases in "Oh, Sinner Man" begin on the first beat of the measure.)

# START WITH A REST

Key: E minor    Starting Pitch: E    Scale Tones: *mi, so, si, la, ti, do re mi fa so la*

• Pat the half-note beat as you listen to "Las Flores" ("The Flowers"), a folk song from Puerto Rico.

CD2:1–2, CD7:23
Piano Accompaniment on page PA 16   **Las Flores**

Puerto Rican folk song
(arr. V.L., M.J., and J.K.

• Perform this pattern of silence and sound as you listen to "Las Flores" again. Open your hands and make no sound on the rest, and snap your fingers on the remaining beats for each phrase.

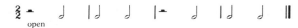

EXTENSION

### SPECIAL LEARNERS

Prepare a transparency of "Las Flores" and add color overlay to measures 8, 10, 12, and 16. This visual cue will enable exceptional learners to play the stick pattern and simultaneously find the syncopated patterns.

### VOCAL DEVELOPMENT

Encourage the students to end the last word of each phrase on the first beat of the next measure. This will insure rhythmic precision in performing the rest at the beginning of each phrase.

### PRONUNCIATION

*Refrain*
Hermoso "bouquet" aquí te traemos
er-mo' sô bōō-ka' a-kē' te trä-ä' môs
Here we bring you a beautiful bouquet,

bellísimas flores del jardín riqueño
be-yē' sē-mäs flô' res del här-dēn'
rrē-ken' yô
gorgeous flowers from a Puerto Rican garden.
1. De todas las flores yo te traigo un ramo;
de tô' däs läs flô' res yô te trī' gô ōōn rrä' mô
I bring you a bouquet of all the flowers;

recíbelo bien, que éste es tu aguinaldo.
rre-sē' be-lô b' yen ke es' te es too
a-gē-näl' dô
accept it well, because it is a gift for you.

### CURRICULUM CONNECTION: SOCIAL STUDIES

The people of Puerto Rico do not sing traditional seasonal songs such as "White Christmas" or "Jingle Bells" at Christmastime, because the weather is warm. In December, the flowers are in full bloom on this Caribbean island. Beautiful blossoms are collected and arranged in patterns at Christmastime. Nativity scenes are decorated with blossoms. "Las Flores," a song about flowers, is often sung during the Christmas season.

- Perform the same pattern and move your hands in an arc from left to right as you listen to "Las Flores" again.
- Sing the song as you pat each quarter rest and show the phrases with arcs.
- Notice that each phrase of "Las Flores" begins with this rhythm pattern: ‡ ♫ ♩ ♩ |
- Sing "Oh, Sinner Man" again and compare the phrase beginnings with those in "Las Flores."
- Find, then clap, the repeated syncopated pattern ♩. ♪♩ in "Las Flores." How many times does this pattern occur? four

**CHALLENGE** Listen to "Las Flores" again. Pat the steady beat ♩ and clap the syncopated pattern ♩. ♪♩ When you can do this easily, choose a partner and perform these rhythms with a drumstick in each hand.

1. Tap your drumsticks in front of you on the steady beat.
2. Tap your drumsticks together with your partner's on the syncopated pattern.

57

# LESSON 5

- Find the repeated syncopated pattern and clap it by rote. Identify how many times the pattern occurs in "Las Flores." (four times, in mm. 8, 10, 12, and 16)

**2. Introduce the stick pattern.** Have the students:

- Prepare to play the stick pattern by patting the steady beat and clapping the syncopated pattern.
- Take two drumsticks each and sit on the floor or at their desks, facing partners.
- Play the stick pattern by tapping the floor (or desk tops) on the steady beat and tapping their drumsticks together with their partner's on the syncopated pattern.

## Reinforcing the Lesson

Have the students step the beat and clap the rhythm of the melody while they sing "When the Saints Go Marching In," page 251, and "Go Now in Peace," page 34. ("When the Saints Go Marching In" begins with a rest; "Go Now in Peace" begins on the first beat of the measure.)

## 3 APPRAISAL

The students should be able to:

1. Perform rhythm patterns with rests on the first beat by opening their hands silently on the quarter rests and clapping or tapping the remaining beats of each phrase.
2. Listen to "Las Flores" and with eyes closed demonstrate equal and unequal phrases by moving their hands in an arc from left to right.
3. Verbally identify written examples of syncopated patterns and play the syncopated patterns by clapping or by tapping drumsticks.
4. Sing "Las Flores" with rhythmic and melodic accuracy.

## MORE MUSIC TEACHING IDEAS

Have the students learn the rest of the verses to "Las Flores."

2. Traigo el clavel blanco, también la azucena,
Trī′gô el klä-vel′ blän′ kö täm-byen′ lä ä-zōō-se′ nä
I bring the white carnation, also the white lily.

la dama de noche, flor de yerba buena.
lä dä′ mä de nô′ che flôr de yer′ bä bwe′nä
the night jasmine, the flower of mint.

3. Entre tantas flores hoy te saludamos
en′ tre tän′ tas flô′ res oi te sä-lōō-dä′ môs
Among so many flowers today we greet you

como se saludan el lirio y el nardo.
kô′ mô se sä-lōō′ dän el lē′ re-ô ē el när′ dô
as the iris and the spikenard greet one another.

4. Entre tantas flores ya nos despedimos
en′ tre tän′ täs flô′ res yä nôs des-pe-dē′ môs
Among so many flowers we say goodbye already

como se despiden el nardo y el lirio.
kô′ mô se des-pē′ den el när′ dô ē el lē′ re-ô
As the spikenard and the iris say goodbye.

# REVIEW AND EVALUATION

## JUST CHECKING

### Objective
To review and test the skills and concepts taught in Unit 2

### Materials
Recordings: Just Checking Unit 2 (questions 2 and 5)
"Cripple Creek" (sung version)
"Cripple Creek" (bluegrass version)
*The Entertainer* (complete piano version)
"I Saw the Light"
"Oh, Sinner Man"
Unit 2 Evaluation (question 2)
*For Extra Credit* recordings (optional)
Drumsticks (two for each student)
Copying Master 2-3 (optional)
Evaluation Unit 2 Copying Master

## TEACHING THE LESSON

**Review the skills and concepts taught in Unit 2.** Have the students:
• Perform the activities and answer the questions on pages 58–59. (For this review, examples for questions 2 and 5 are included in the "Just Checking Unit 2" recording. Have the students answer these questions first. Then have them answer the other questions in the review, using the recordings in the unit where necessary.)
• Review their answers.
(You may wish to use Copying Master 2-3 at this time.)

---

## JUST CHECKING

See how much you remember.

1. Listen to the two versions of "Cripple Creek" and pat-slide the steady beat with your hand. Which version changes tempo, version 1 or version 2? version 2

2. Listen and tap the steady beat with your hand as you say the following rhythm patterns.

a.
jazz   jazz   rag-time jazz

b.
rag-time rag-time   rag-time jazz

c.
ma-ple leaf rag-time   ma-ple leaf  jazz

d.
Scott Jop-lin rag-time Scott Jop-lin jazz

e.
en-ter-tain-er rag-time   en-ter-tain-er jazz

f.
jazz   en-ter-tain-er   rag-time jazz

g.
ma-ple leaf ma-ple leaf   ma-ple leaf rag-time

58

3. Perform this rhythmic accompaniment for *The Entertainer* using the percussion matched grip.

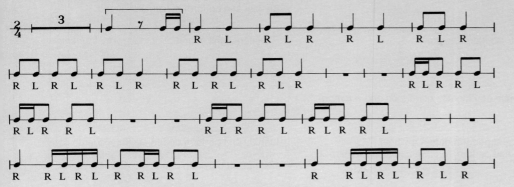

4. As you listen to "I Saw the Light" clap the syncopated rhythm pattern ♪ ♩ ♪ . Which words of the text fit this syncopated pattern? "I saw the," "now I'm so," etc.

5. Listen to two different versions of "I Saw the Light." Does version 1 or version 2 contain syncopation? version 2

6. Show the phrase structure of "Oh, Sinner Man" by moving your hands in an arc from left to right. How many phrases does the song have? Are the phrases of equal or unequal length? four; equal

7. Listen to "Cripple Creek" and show when you hear the refrain by raising your hand. Snap the steady beat when you hear a verse.

8. Ragtime piano music has a steady beat in the left hand with syncopated rhythms in the melodies played by the right hand. As you listen to *The Entertainer:*

    a. Tap the steady beat.
    b. Tap the rhythm of the melody.

59

# REVIEW AND EVALUATION

## GIVING THE EVALUATION

Evaluation Unit 2 Copying Master can be found in the *Teacher's Copying Masters* book along with full directions for giving the evaluation and checking the answers.

## FOR EXTRA CREDIT

You may want the students to do one of the following activities.
1. Perform the following rhythm pattern:

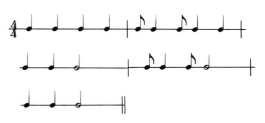

2. Answer one of the following instead:
a. What gives spirituals their special sound and expressiveness? (can be slow and full of emotion or fast and lively, sung by one person or as call-response, expressed troubles of slaves and hope for better life)
b. What are some of the musical qualities shared by ragtime and today's popular music? (emphasis on steady beat in bass, syncopated rhythms in melody, use of keyboard instruments) You may wish to play the recordings of "Oh, Sinner Man" (or "Joshua Fought the Battle of Jericho," page 85) and *The Entertainer* to refresh students' memories.

| ELEMENTS OF MUSIC | UNIT 3 OBJECTIVES | Lesson 1 Focus: Dotted Rhythm Patterns | Lesson 2 Focus: Dotted Rhythm Pattern |
|---|---|---|---|
| Dynamics | **Identify dynamic contrasts and changes** **Identify *crescendo*** | | Identify *crescendo* and dynamic contrasts Identify and perform dynamic changes |
| Tone Color | Identify sounds of orchestral and folk instruments Perform on guitar Listen to electronic sounds | Listen to electronic sounds | Experience the sound of orchestral instruments |
| Tempo | **Identify *ritardando* and *a tempo*** | Experience and identify *ritardando* and *a tempo* | |
| Duration/ Rhythm | **Identify, distinguish, and perform equal and dotted rhythms, triplets** **Identify and perform syncopation and augmentation** | Identify and perform dotted rhythms Identify and perform augmentation of a rhythm pattern | Identify and perform dotted eighth-sixteenth note rhythm Distinguish between equal and dotted rhythms |
| Pitch | **Perform melodic accompaniments using G A B D** | Sing melody with a range of C#-D' | Sing a song with a range of A♭-e♭' |
| Texture | Perform homophonic and polyphonic textures **Perform homophonic textures** Hear harmonic repetition Perform harmonic and melodic accompaniments | Combine a song with descant to create homophonic texture by singing with accompaniment | |
| Form | Identify and perform phrases of equal and unequal length Perform songs in ABA and AB form | Sing phrases of equal and unequal length | |
| Style | Perform folk-rock song and spiritual Listen to the operatic music of the romantic period | | Listen to and discuss music of the romantic period |
| Reading | | Read ♪, ♩, ♩., ♩♪, ♩ ♩, ○, ⁓, #, ⁴⁄₄, ⌣, tempo marks, recorder notes G A B C# | Read [rhythm notation], *p*, *f*, |1. |2. |

## PURPOSE Unit 3: Rhythm Everywhere

This unit involves further exploration of rhythm, with identification and performance of patterns using dotted, augmented, triplet, syncopated, and nonsyncopated rhythms. The students will listen to and perform compositions that use these new rhythm patterns.

## SUGGESTED TIME FRAME

| November | December |
|---|---|
| | |

## FOCUS

- Dotted rhythm patterns
- Triplets
- Syncopation

| Lesson 3<br>Focus: Rhythm Patterns | Lesson 4<br>Focus: Triplet | Lesson 5<br>Focus: Syncopation |
|---|---|---|
| Listen to and perform folk-rock accompaniment<br>Experience playing the guitar | Listen to electronic sounds | Perform body percussion accompaniment<br>Work on consonant articulation in singing |
| Listen to and perform whole, half, dotted half, quarter, eighth notes, and dotted eighth and sixteenth<br>Perform rhythm patterns on recorder and guitar<br><br>Create strum patterns on guitar | Listen to and perform one and three sounds to a beat<br>Perform rhythm patterns using triplets<br><br>Create triplet rhythm patterns | Listen to and perform dotted and syncopated rhythms<br>Experience syncopation<br>Identify and perform syncopated rhythm patterns<br><br>Identify popular songs with syncopation |
| Perform melodic accompaniment with the pitches G A B D | Perform melodic accompaniment with triplets<br>Perform a melodic accompaniment using the pitches G A C D | Sing a melody with a range of d-e' |
| Perform a harmonic accompaniment of two chords<br>Hear harmonic repetition | Perform a melodic accompaniment with repeated rhythm pattern | Sing a song in nonimitative polyphonic texture<br>Sing a song in two parts |
| Play a song with equal phrase lengths | Identify and perform a melodic accompaniment with equal and unequal phrase lengths, ABA form<br>Identify repetition and contrast in phrases | Sing a song with verse and refrain |
| Listen to, perform, and discuss folk-rock music<br><br>Identify folk-rock groups | Listen to and perform film music | Listen to, perform, and discuss the spiritual |
| Read ♩. ♫ , ♫ ♩, ♩, ♩, ♩, ♩, ♩, o<br>4/4 meter, guitar strum notation, chord symbols | Read ♪♪♪ ,♩, ♩, ♩, ▬ , o , ▭² in 4/4 | Read ♩. ♫ , ♩, ♩, ♪ , ♪♪ ♩, > in 4/4 |

# TECHNOLOGY

## MUSIC WITH *MIDI*

MIDI technology allows students to manipulate musical elements and make musical decisions.

• Lesson 2, page 73: Create a **Rap**

## VIDEO RESOURCES

Use video resources to reinforce, extend, and enrich learning in this unit.

# LESSON 1

## UNIT 3

### RHYTHM EVERYWHERE

The Old Guitarist, Pablo Picasso, THE ART INSTITUTE OF CHICAGO

61

# LESSON 1

**Focus: Dotted Rhythm Patterns**

**Objectives**
To identify and play dotted rhythm patterns
To identify and play augmentation of a rhythm pattern
To read and play a melodic descant with dotted quarter and eighth notes and with dotted half and quarter notes
To identify and perform *ritardando* and *a tempo*

**Materials**
Recording: "Trav'ler"
Recorders, bells, keyboard, or other C instrument

**Vocabulary**
Dotted quarter note, dotted half note, augmentation, *ritardando (rit.), a tempo*

**1 SETTING THE STAGE**
Review beat and beat subdivisions on pages 50-52.

## THE ARTIST

**Pablo Picasso** (pa'blō pē-käs' sō) (1881–1973)—was born in Spain but worked in France. He was a pioneer in many styles of painting during his lifetime, and was one of the most famous painters of the twentieth century. His early style is called the *Blue Period* because, as in *The Old Guitarist*, he mostly used shades of blue and focused on the themes of loneliness and despair. He expressed these emotions in this painting by showing an old man, alone, tired, and forgotten.

# LESSON 1

**2** TEACHING THE LESSON

**1. Introduce "Trav'ler" and the dotted quarter-eighth and dotted half-quarter note rhythm patterns.** Have the students:

• Find the dotted quarter-eighth and dotted half-quarter note rhythm patterns as they listen to "Trav'ler" (see pp. 26-27).

• Sing the song to sense the difference between the patterns.

CD1:18 **As you listen to "Trav'ler" look for these rhythms:** ♩. ♪ **and** ♩. ♩
**Remember that a whole rest (–) lasts for four beats.**

Key: D major   Starting Pitch F♯
Scale Tones: *ti, do re mi fa so lo la ti do*

# Trav'ler

Music by Mark Wilson
Words by Jane Foster Knox

Piano Accompaniment on page PA 2

1. Would you like to be a trav'-ler sail-ing far _____ a-cross the
2. We will sure-ly find en-chant-ment, in a land _____ so far a-

sea?   I can take you on a jour-ney, to a place where you have longed to
way.   But we fail to see the splen-dor that sur-rounds us ev'-ry

62

# EXTENSION

## SIGNING FOR "TRAV'LER"

In sign language the meaning of the words is signed. For example, in the first phrase, "Would you," we simply sign "question." The words in parentheses are the actual words being signed. Feel free to sign only part of the song, or drop signs that become difficult due to tempo or placement. The objective should be to enjoy the added dimension that signing can bring to music.

Would You (question)

Draw a question mark in the air.

Travel

With a downturned "V" make circles in the air.

Sailing

Move the cupped hands forward together.

Can

The closed fists, palms down, move downward.

Take (Bring)

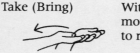

With open palms up, move hands from left to right in an arc.

Place

With the letter "P" and middle fingers touching, draw a circle to include the space in front of you, coming to rest close to your body.

Longed (Wished)

With the palm facing the body in letter "C" position, move the hand down the body.

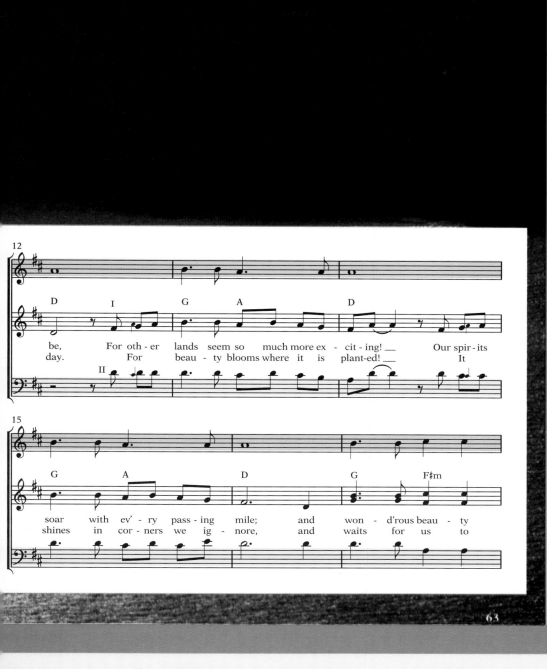

12

D · I · G · A · D

be, For oth - er lands seem so much more ex - cit - ing! ___ Our spir - its
day. For beau - ty blooms where it is plant - ed! ___ It

II

15

G · A · D · G · F♯m

soar with ev' - ry pass - ing mile; and won - d'rous beau - ty
shines in cor - ners we ig - nore, and waits for us to

63

**For (Because)** The index finger touches the forehead and then moves up into an "A" position.

**Lands** With palms down, one hand outlines a circle.

**Exciting/Soar** The middle fingers alternately strike the heart.

**Spirits** The right hand is above the left hand, with palms facing and fingers spread. The right hand moves upward as both thumbs and index fingers close.

**With Every Passing Mile (Moving Along)** With palms facing, move bent hands forward.

**Wondrous/Splendor** With palms out, open hands move forward and up one or two times.

**Beauty** The "O" hand starts at the chin, opens while circling the face, coming to rest again at the chin.

**Calls** Tap the back of the hand.

# EXTENSION

**Rest/Pause**
With hands in "R" position, cross the arms against the chest.

**Close Eyes**
Close index fingers and thumbs of both hands, which are next to the eye corners.

**Dream**
The index finger touches the forehead and outlines a wavy line as it moves from the body.

**Heart**
The index fingers outline a heart on the chest.

**End (Finish)**
Both upright "5" hands move from palms inward and facing the body to palms outward.

**Home**
The closed right hand touches the lips, then opens to the flat palm on the cheek—a place to eat and sleep.

**Know/Aware**
Touch the forehead.

**Surround (Around)**
The right index finger outlines a circle around the closed fingers of the left hand.

**Find**
With palm down, index finger and thumb open and close, as in picking up something.

**Enchantment (Fascinate)**
Open index finger and thumb touch the chest, pull away, and close.

30 Recorders

A  G  Gm  D

jour - ney,  we'll come home to pla - ces we know  More a - ware of all the

we'll come  home to pla - ces we know.

34

1  2

Am  G  A7  D  D

1  2

beau - ty  that sur - rounds us ev' - ry-where we  go.  go,  that sur -

1  2

beau - ty sur - rounds us ev' - ry-where we  go.  go,  that sur -

38

G  A7  D

rounds  us  ev' - ry - where  we  go.

rounds  us  ev' - ry - where  we  go.

65

| Far Away | 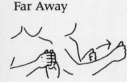 | Palms are facing, fists closed together with thumbs up. Move one hand forward in an arc away from the body. | Blooms (Plant)  | Sign "to plant" first, to show the natural order of events. The right hand puts imaginary seeds into the cupped left hand. | Ignore 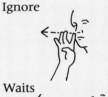 | The tip of the index finger touches the nose and the "4"-position hand moves away from the body. |

**Fail (Not)**
Open palms face down, with wrists crossed. Move hands apart, like "safe" in baseball.

**Planted (Blooms)**
The right hand emerges from the cupped left hand and extends upward while opening.

**Waits**
With right hand behind left hand and palms up, wiggle fingers.

**Slow**
The right hand moves down the back of the left hand from fingers to wrist.

**See**
"V"-position hand moves away from the eyes.

**Shines**
Move index or middle fingers in a wavy line while moving hands up and apart.

**Explore**
With palms facing left, the "C" hand circles the face.

# LESSON 1

**2. Prepare and introduce the dotted quarter note and dotted half note.** Have the students:
• Clap each eighth-note pattern to discover that the dotted quarter note has the same durational value as the three tied eighth notes, or the tied quarter and eighth notes.
• Clap each quarter-note pattern to discover that the dotted half note has the same durational value as the three tied quarter notes, or the tied half and quarter notes.
• Clap the example from "Trav'ler."

## Clapping Dotted Patterns

• Clap the following patterns. Two eighth notes sound as long as one quarter note.

• Now clap these patterns. The **dotted quarter note** sounds as long as the three eighth notes tied together. It also sounds as long as the quarter note and the eighth note tied together.

• Clap the following example from "Trav'ler":

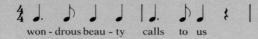

won - drous beau - ty    calls    to us

• Clap these patterns. Two quarter notes sound as long as one half note.

• Now clap these patterns. The **dotted half note** sounds as long as the three quarter notes tied together. It also sounds as long as the half note and the quarter note tied together.

• Now clap this example from "Trav'ler":

Close    your    eyes    and  dream    with    me.

66

# Expanding a Rhythm Pattern

Expanding note values to longer durations is called **augmentation.**
In "Trav'ler," the rhythm pattern ♩ ♪ is augmented to ♩. ♩
The notes in the ♩. ♩ pattern are twice as long as those in the
♩ ♪ pattern.

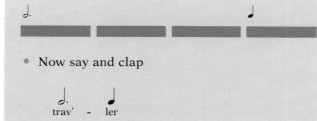

Say and clap

trav' - ler

Now say and clap

trav' - ler

Say and clap the two patterns together:

say    trav'- ler  trav' - ler

clap

Notice that clapping ♩. ♩ takes twice as long as saying

trav' - ler

Sing "Trav'ler." Look for the ♩ ♪ and ♩. ♩ patterns as you sing.

Examples of augmentation occur all around us.

## CURRICULUM CONNECTION: ART

The photograph of the interior of the Guggenheim Museum in New York City shows the use of repetition of a pattern to create unity. The main visual interest lies in the relationship and size of the circular balconies. Unity in music can be created also by the use of repeated patterns. One way of providing interest is by repeating a pattern of pitches while doubling, or augmenting, the note values.

**3. Introduce augmentation.** Have the students:
• Focus on the illustration of augmentation. (The boxes on the right are twice as long as the boxes on the left.)
• Tap the augmented pattern ♩. ♩ while clapping in a circular motion.
• Say speech patterns to accompany the rhythm.
• Sing "Trav'ler." (Add Parts II and III if students are ready for them.)
**4. Prepare and introduce the melodic accompaniment to "Trav'ler."** Have the students:
• Review the pitches G and A (page 32) on recorder, bells, or keyboard. Learn the new pitches B and C♯.

# LESSON 1

- Practice the melodic patterns.
- Discuss the tempo information.
- Play a body-percussion pattern of quarter notes (clap, snap, snap, snap) in a circular motion while listening to "Trav'ler" to focus on the gradual slowing of the beat (*ritardando*) at the end.
- Sing "Trav'ler" without the recording, adding *ritardandos* and *a tempos* in various places.
- Play the melodic accompaniment to "Trav'ler" with rhythmic and melodic accuracy.

## Reinforcing the Lesson

Have the students say the rhythm patterns on page 67 while clapping in a counterclockwise circular motion.

## 3 APPRAISAL

The students should be able to:
1. Identify visually all measures in "Trav'ler" with the dotted quarter-eighth note pattern and the dotted half-quarter note pattern.
2. Play the recorder melodies with dotted half-quarter note and the dotted quarter-eighth note patterns.
3. Verbally define augmentation as expanding the duration of a note.
4. Sing "Trav'ler" demonstrating *ritardando* and *a tempo*.
5. Verbally define *ritardando* as the gradual slowing of the beat and *a tempo* as return to the original tempo.

## Play an Accompaniment

- Review the pitches G and A. Add the new pitches B and C#.

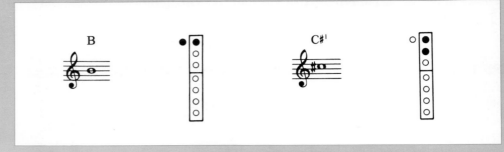

- To learn the accompaniment for "Trav'ler," first practice these melodic patterns.

- Listen to "Trav'ler" to sense the tempo. The speed of the beat is steady except for a gradual slowing of the beat (**ritardando, or rit.**) at the end. If there is a ritardando in the middle of a piece, it is often followed by a return to the original tempo (**a tempo**).

68

## MORE MUSIC TEACHING IDEAS

Have the students play the descending scale passages in the melodic descant to "Trav'ler" on bells or keyboard. Have some students perform the recorder and bell parts as others sing the song.

# ONE RHYTHM IN THREE STYLES

What musical selection would you be likely to hear at these events?

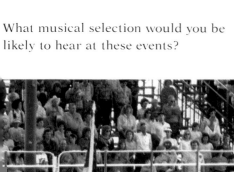

# LESSON 2

**Focus: Dotted Rhythm Pattern**

## Objectives
To distinguish the dotted eighth-sixteenth pattern from the equal eighth-note pattern.
To read and play rhythm notation using equal and dotted rhythms
To identify compositions using equal and dotted rhythm patterns by listening to and reading rhythm notation
To identify *cresendo*

## Materials
Recordings: "The Star-Spangled Banner"
"The Star-Spangled Banner" (performance mix)
"Rhythm Montage 3"
"Zudio"
"Zudio" (performance mix)
Prelude to Act I of *Carmen* (with call numbers)

## Vocabulary
Dotted rhythm, crescendo, opera

## 1 SETTING THE STAGE

Have the students discuss the pictures to determine the musical selection heard at the events illustrated.

69

# LESSON 2

TEACHING THE LESSON

**1. Introduce "The Star-Spangled Banner."** Have the students:

• Discuss how the words describe the battle.

• Listen to and sing the song with the recording. (You may wish to remind students to stand when the anthem is played or sung at official events. Boys should take off their hats, if they are wearing them. The national anthem should never be applauded.)

## Our National Anthem

• Listen to the first verse of "The Star-Spangled Banner." How do the words describe the battle?

 "The Star-Spangled Banner"

Key: A♭ major     Starting Pitch: E♭     Scale Tones: *do, mi, fi, so, la, ti, do re mi fa so*

### The Star-Spangled Banner

Words by Francis Scott Key
Music attributed to J. S. Smith

Piano Accompaniment on page PA 18

70

# The Story of "The Star-Spangled Banner"

The words to our national anthem were written in 1814 when England and the United States were at war. Francis Scott Key and John S. Skinner had boarded a British warship in Chesapeake Bay to negotiate for the release of an American prisoner. While they were on board, the British began their attack on Fort McHenry, so Key and Skinner were detained overnight. Fort McHenry protected Baltimore, Maryland, and Key knew that the fort was poorly fortified. All night he watched the shore closely. He could not see what was happening because thick smoke and haze surrounded the fort. Shortly after dawn the mist cleared, and Key saw that the American flag was still flying above the fort. Overjoyed, he took out an envelope and quickly wrote some poetry on it.

When Key returned to Baltimore, he finished the poem. It was published soon after and was an immediate success. Later the poem was adapted to the old English tune "To Anacreon in Heaven." In 1931 Congress named "The Star-Spangled Banner" the official national anthem of the United States.

Our Flag Was Still There, Edward Percy Moran, PEALE MUSEUM, Baltimore

This picture illustrates the event in history that inspired the creation of "The Star-Spangled Banner." The artist shows Francis Scott Key gazing at the clearing mist.

★ ★ ★ ★ ★ ★ ★ ★ ★ ★ ★ ★

• Discuss the historical information about "The Star-Spangled Banner." You may wish to use the following item as a basis for extended discussion.

Francis Scott Key was inspired to write "The Star-Spangled Banner" by seeing the attack on Fort McHenry. Name some artists, scientists, athletes, or musicians who have been inspired to be creative "on the spot." (for example, Isaac Newton)

# LESSON 2

**2. Introduce the dotted eighth-sixteenth note rhythm.** Have the students:
• Read and clap the rhythms, emphasizing the difference between the equal eighth-note rhythm and the dotted rhythm. (Suggest that they think the first two words of "The Star-Spangled Banner.")
• Describe how the two rhythms are different. (The eighth-note pattern is equal; in the dotted rhythm pattern the first note is held longer.)
• Which rhythm is at the beginning of "The Star-Spangled Banner"? (the dotted rhythm)
• Find the even and dotted rhythms in "The Star-Spangled Banner." (The even rhythms are tinted pink, the dotted rhythms are tinted blue.)
• Read and sing "The Star-Spangled Banner," emphasizing the differences between the even and dotted rhythms.

**3. Practice learning dotted rhythms.** Have the students:
• Listen to "Rhythm Montage 3" and respond to the Challenge! by reading each line of rhythm notation to decide which one matches the rhythm they hear.
• Discuss the answers. (The rhythm patterns are: 1. "Are You Sleeping"; 2. "Old Joe Clark"; 3. "Battle Hymn of the Republic.")
• Read and clap the rhythm of each example.

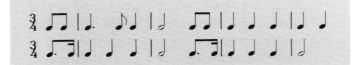

CD2:9 Which of these two rhythm patterns appears at the *beginning* of "The Star-Spangled Banner"? the second pattern

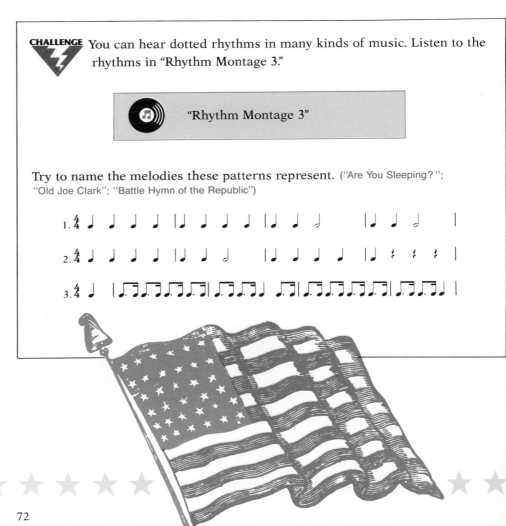

The rhythm [dotted eighth-sixteenth] is called a **dotted rhythm**.

• Sing "The Star-Spangled Banner." Emphasize the difference between the equal ( [eighth notes] ) and unequal dotted ( [dotted rhythm] ) rhythms.

**CHALLENGE** You can hear dotted rhythms in many kinds of music. Listen to the rhythms in "Rhythm Montage 3."

"Rhythm Montage 3"

Try to name the melodies these patterns represent. ("Are You Sleeping?"; "Old Joe Clark"; "Battle Hymn of the Republic")

72

---

## COOPERATIVE LEARNING

Have the students review rhythms and terms from the first two lessons in this unit in cooperative groups. Place the following rhythms and terms on the board:

[rhythm symbols]    ritardando

   augmentation

   a tempo

Randomly assign the students to groups of four and divide each group into two pairs. Assign each pair one of the above rhythms

or terms to research, define, and then teach to the other pair in their group. Then they should teach their term or rhythm to the entire class. Both group and class members should be encouraged to ask clarifying questions during the presentations when definitions and teaching examples are unclear. The presenters should be encouraged to listen to questions and thoughtfully give answers that clarify the information they are sharing.

Key: C major    Starting Pitch: C    Scale Tones: *do re ri mi so la do¹*

"Zudio" is a street game that is popular in many cities in the United    CD2:10, CD7:23
States. Notice the dotted rhythm ♪♫.

• Sing all three parts of the refrain (A) before singing each verse.

### Zudio

Piano Accompaniment on page PA 20

Traditional (arr. V. L.)

73

# LESSON 2

**4. Introduce "Zudio," which uses the dotted rhythm.** Have the students:
• Become familiar with "Zudio" in preparation for the line-dance game.
• Follow the score and sing the song with the recording. (Changing voices can sing parts A and C.)
• Review and rehearse phrases or sections as necessary.
• Learn the "Zudio" game, which corresponds to the sections of the music as follows:

A1 Form two lines facing each other, with the head couple at the front of the room. Take four steps forward and four steps back on the steady beat. Clap the steady beat while stepping. On fourth clap, clap partner's hand.

A2 One member of the head couple struts "down the avenue" between the two lines.

A3 The other member of the head couple follows, imitating the strut of first partner. They then face each other at the foot of the line.

B1 All students create pantomimes illustrating the first two phrases.

C All students take one step to the front (in), one step to the back (out), three steps to the side; repeat. Change direction when moving to the side.

Sing all three lines of A before singing and pantomiming each new verse of B; sing C after each verse of B.

## SPECIAL LEARNERS

Preplan alternative activities for children who are physically unable to participate in the line dance for "Zudio." The dotted eighth-sixteenth pattern could be reintroduced by rhythm instruments. The form of the song could be reintroduced by adding contrasting instrument sounds to the refrain and the verse. The dance could be slightly changed so the students who are unable to move can create the pantomimes.

UNIT 3    **73**

# LESSON 2

**5. Introduce the dotted eighth-sixteenth rhythm in the Prelude to Act I of *Carmen*.** Have the students:
- Clap rhythm patterns a, b, and c.
- Find the pattern with dotted rhythms. (b)
- Discuss the information on dynamics, with emphasis on *crescendo*.
- Listen to the recording. As each number is called, write on a sheet of paper the letter of the example that shows the correct rhythms and dynamic indication heard.
- Analyze and discuss the answers.

## Find the Dotted Rhythm

CD2:11 • Clap the rhythm patterns below.
Which example features the dotted rhythm (  )? b

Escamillo (Samuel Ramey) sings the "Toreador Song" (rhythm b).
Carmen (Agnes Baltsa), sitting at right, pretends not to be interested.

• Listen to the Prelude to Act I of *Carmen*. When you hear a number called, identify which of the rhythm patterns above you hear.   c, c, a, c, b, c

The dynamic markings *p* and *f* will help you identify each section of the music. The dynamic marking ——— means a gradual increase in the amount of sound from soft to loud. It is called a **crescendo** (kre-shen' dō).

> 🎵  Prelude to Act I of *Carmen* by Georges Bizet (zhorzh bē-zā')

74

E X T E N S I O N

## Carmen

An **opera** is a play in which all or most of the words are sung to the accompaniment of an orchestra. The opera *Carmen*, by Georges Bizet (1838–1875), was first performed in Paris in 1875 and was based on a true story.

Set in nineteenth-century Spain, this opera is about a gypsy woman, Carmen; a soldier, Don José (dôn zhō-sā′); and a famous bullfighter, Escamillo (es-kä-mē′ yo). As the story unfolds, Carmen is arrested for attacking another woman with a knife, and Don José is ordered to take her to prison. Carmen flirts with him, hoping he will set her free, which he does. For this he is jailed. When he is released, of course he meets Carmen again. By this time she is working for a group of smugglers. Don José is so obsessed with her that he deserts from the army and joins the smugglers, but already Carmen's love for him is waning.

Carmen has fallen in love with the bullfighter Escamillo and soon leaves Don José. She knows that Don José is wildly jealous, but ignores all warnings of doom. She believes that nothing she can do will change her destiny.

Don José finds Carmen waiting for Escamillo outside the bullring. He pleads with her to come back to him, but she refuses. She taunts him, declaring her love for Escamillo. In a jealous rage Don José fatally stabs her. Escamillo enters, victorious, from the bullring to find Carmen dead with Don José confessing his crime at her side.

At first the opera was not an immediate success. People could not accept the realism of the opera and criticized Bizet harshly. They thought the story too violent and the characters, especially Carmen, too earthy. However, over the years *Carmen* has grown in popularity. Today it is one of the most famous operas in the repertoire.

75

# LESSON 2

**6. Introduce Georges Bizet.** Have the students discuss the information on *Carmen* and composer Georges Bizet.

You may wish to use the following as a basis for extended discussion.

Carmen flirted with Don José to get him to help her escape from prison. Because he helped her, Don José himself was put in jail. Describe the feelings Don José might have had when he realized that he had been used. (anger conflicting with his fascination with Carmen)

### Reinforcing the Lesson

Encourage the students to think of popular songs with even and dotted rhythms.

## 3 APPRAISAL

The students should be able to:
1. View several equal and dotted rhythms taken from the Prelude to Act I of *Carmen* and clap the patterns accurately.
2. Listen to the clapping of several measures of dotted rhythms taken from familiar compositions and accurately name the compositions.
3. Identify the visual dynamic marking as *crescendo* and define it as a gradual increase in the loudness of sound.

## CURRICULUM CONNECTION: FINE ARTS (DRAMA)

List several adjectives on the chalkboard that describe the personal qualities and the character of Carmen and Don José, such as:

| (for Carmen) | (for Don José) |
|---|---|
| ruthless | trusting |
| uncaring | very caring |
| not loyal | very loyal |
| controlled | uncontrolled (at |
| earthy | end of opera) |
| | naive |

Have the students decide which statements fit which character. Ask which one goes through a significant change in personal qualities and character (Don José), and which one remains more constant (Carmen).

# LESSON 3

**Focus: Rhythm Patterns**

**Objectives**
To read and play a melodic accompaniment with equal and dotted rhythms
To develop performance skills on the guitar
To read and play a harmonic accompaniment with even and dotted rhythms

**Materials**
Recording: "A Horse with No Name"
Recorders, bells (handbells or Orff), keyboard
Guitars

**Vocabulary**
Chord

**1 SETTING THE STAGE**

Introduce folk rock by playing "A Horse with No Name" as the students enter the classroom.

**2 TEACHING THE LESSON**

1. **Introduce the style of folk rock.** Have the students:
- Read about the history of folk rock and the group America.
- Discuss information on folk rock and the group America. (You may wish to tell the students that the members of America were sons of American servicemen stationed in England. Dewey Bunnell, the composer, wrote the song to express his homesickness for the desert country of southern California, which he had once visited.)
- Listen to "A Horse with No Name."
- Read about the influence of folk rock on later musicians.

CD2:12 **Folk Rock**

Many traditional folk songs were created long ago. However, new folk songs are still emerging. During the 1960s many musicians used the folk style to write songs that dealt with important social issues, such as civil rights, social injustice, and the war in Vietnam. The simplicity and directness of folk music (often using just a single guitar to accompany the vocals) allowed musicians like Bob Dylan and Joan Baez to emphasize lyrics that had greater depth and meaning than those of early rock-and-roll music.

In the 1960s an interesting crossover happened between rock and folk. Bob Dylan, an important folk musician, shocked his audiences when he started playing an electric "rock-and-roll" guitar. Meanwhile, rock-and-roll groups like The Beatles began writing lyrics that had the depth and social significance of the current folk music. These lyrics dealt with more complicated themes than the simple love songs of their earlier works. This blending of folk with rock and roll created a style called folk rock. The songs of groups such as The Byrds; Buffalo Springfield; and Crosby, Stills and Nash are examples of this style.

One popular folk-rock group of the early 1970s was called America. Their folk-rock sound featured high, close vocal harmonies and acoustic guitars. They produced their first and most important hit "A Horse With No Name" in 1972. Composer Dewey Bunnell was inspired by homesickness for the desert country of southern California.

The Byrd

 "A Horse With No Name"

76

## E X T E N S I O N

**MORE MUSIC TEACHING IDEAS**

Have the students identify other folk-rock groups that used to be popular or may be currently popular.

Folk rock still influences many current rock musicians, such as John Mellencamp, Bruce Springsteen, Tracy Chapman, and Neil Young. In the 1990s folk rock also merged with alternative rock music. Both styles often deal with social issues and emphasize the personal quality of a song's lyrics. Folk instruments, such as the mandolin, have made a comeback in recent music. Among the modern artists who use folk elements in their music are R.E.M., Hootie and the Blowfish, Jewel, Blues Travelers, Beck, and Natalie Merchant.

John Mellencamp

America

Natalie Merchant

You may wish to use the following items as a basis for extended discussion.
1. Discuss the reasons for combining folk and rock music. What features did the new style gain?
2. The folk-rock group America began to create and perform their music while they were high school students. Relate this beginning to local bands trying to work in the field of music. What are some problems these groups might encounter?
3. Name two styles of music. Would it be possible to combine these two styles of music? What features would exist in this new style?

77

# LESSON 3

**2. Introduce and prepare the melodic accompaniment to "A Horse with No Name."** Have the students:

• Review/learn G A B D on recorder, bells, or keyboard.

• Sight-read and clap the rhythm of the seven melodic patterns.

• Sight-read in rhythm and name the notes in each melodic pattern while touching them lightly on the recorder or bells.

• Read and play the seven melodic patterns, first practicing each line separately, then playing them consecutively or in combinations.

• Read and play the melodic accompaniment to "A Horse with No Name."

Learn to play the pitch D on the recorder. You have already learned G A B.

Play D by covering the second hole with the second finger of the left hand. All of the other holes are open.

• Play the patterns in order, one after another, or form groups
and play two or more of them together along with "A Horse with No Name."

78

# Learning to Play the Guitar

- Hold the guitar as shown. The fingers of your left hand should be above the open strings.

- Strum the following rhythm with your right hand on open strings as shown. Your fingernails should brush the strings with a downward motion. The symbol ⊓ means to strum downward.

- Now strum this rhythm:

79

**3. Introduce playing the guitar.** Have the students:
- Note the playing position for the guitar.
- Examine the picture of left-hand position with fingers lifted off the strings.
- Practice strumming downward on open strings, and note the symbol for strumming downward.
- Play the open-string strum on the two notated rhythm patterns, using a downward motion.

## SPECIAL LEARNERS

Prepare an overhead transparency of pupil pages 79 and 81 to use as visual reinforcements if a class includes different learners who have difficulty tracking visual symbols. When following the teaching directions on page 81, cover the lines on the transparency that are not being practiced. Instead of guitar, have the physically disabled students play the root of each chord (E and D) on bells in the different rhythms.

# LESSON 3

**4. Introduce the E minor and D 6/9 chords.** Have the students:
• Form and practice playing the E minor chord, strumming downward with the fingernails. (You can use the autoharp if you retune the E major chord to E minor and substitute the D major chord for the D 6/9.)
• Play the two rhythm patterns on page 79, using the E minor chord.
• Form and practice playing the D 6/9 chord, strumming downward with the fingernails. (You may wish to have the students turn their books sideways so the grids look like guitar tablature.)
• Play the two rhythm patterns on page 79, using the D 6/9 chord.
• Practice the chord changes at the bottom of this page.

• Learn to play the E minor (Em) and D6/9 chords. A **chord** consists of three or more pitches sounding together.

Notice where to place your fingers on the strings to form each of these chords. The fingers are numbered from the index finger (1) to the little finger (4).

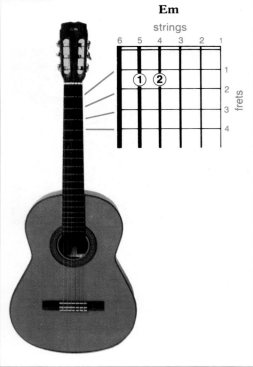

**Em**

**D 6/9**

• Practice these chord changes:

80

EXTENSION

# Strumming to the Music

The symbol v stands for an *up* strum with the fingers of your right hand.

- Practice rhythms 1-4, playing only the E minor chord, then both the E minor and D6/9 chords.
- Play rhythms 1-6, changing chords between measures.
- Choose one line of the rhythms to play as an accompaniment to "A Horse with No Name."

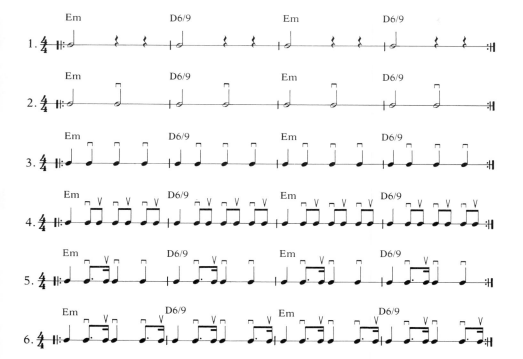

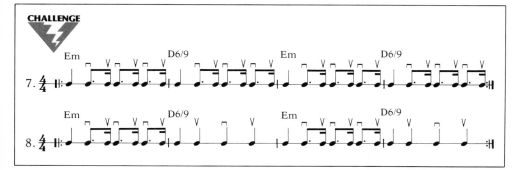

81

**5. Introduce strumming technique.** Have the students:
- Learn the symbol and playing technique for upward strum patterns.
- Sight-read and clap the rhythms of the harmonic accompaniment.
- Practice the strum patterns in lines 1-4, using only the E minor chord, then both the E minor and D 6/9 chords.
- Play lines 1–6, changing chords between measures and concentrating on the strum markings. (If the students are having difficulty, divide them into two groups. Assign Group 1 the E minor chord, Group 2 the D 6/9 chord.)
- Play one line of the rhythms with the recording of "A Horse with No Name."
- Form two groups. Group 1 will play the melodic accompaniment on page 78 while Group 2 plays the harmonic accompaniment. (Some students may wish to respond to the Challenge! of rhythms 7 and 8.)

## Reinforcing the Lesson

Have the students create their own melodic patterns using the pitches G A B, and rhythm patterns using half, quarter, dotted eighth, and sixteenth notes to accompany "A Horse with No Name."

## 3 APPRAISAL

The students should be able to:
1. Play accurately on recorder, bells, or keyboard the rhythms and pitches found in the melodic accompaniment to "A Horse with No Name."
2. Play downward and upward guitar strum patterns as indicated by markings.
3. Play the E minor and D 6/9 chords on the guitar.
4. Play accurately on the guitar the rhythms in the harmonic accompaniment to "A Horse with No Name."

## MORE MUSIC TEACHING IDEAS

Have the students create their own rhythm strum patterns to accompany "A Horse with No Name."

# LESSON 4

**Focus: Triplet**

**Objectives**
To play and move to examples of steady beat and triplets
To develop skills in reading and playing a melodic accompaniment with triplets

**Materials**
Recording: Theme from *Star Wars*
Bells, recorder, or keyboard instruments
Copying Master 3-1 (optional)

**Vocabulary**
Triplet

---

**1 SETTING THE STAGE**

Tell students that just as beats can be divided into two or four equal parts, they can also be divided into three equal parts called triplets.

**2 TEACHING THE LESSON**

**1. Introduce the triplet.** Have the students:
• Clap the quarter-note beats in a circle as they listen to the recording of the theme from *Star Wars*.
• Practice tapping the quarter-note beat and snapping the triplets while listening to the recording.
• Perform the two rhythm patterns as indicated.

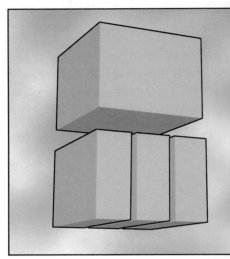

CD2:13 • Listen to the theme from *Star Wars* and clap a steady quarter-note beat in a circle.

 Theme from *Star Wars*, by John Williams

A quarter note can be divided evenly into a group of three notes called a **triplet**.

• Listen to the theme from *Star Wars* again. Tap your foot to the steady quarter-note beat as you snap your fingers, alternating hands, on the triplets.

R L R L R L R L R L R L

• Perform the following rhythm pattern by patting the quarter-note beat with both hands and snapping the triplets with alternating hands.

p  p   s s s s s s   p  p   s s s s s s   p  p   s s s s s s   p  p   s s s s s s

• Perform this rhythm by snapping the triplets with alternating hands and patting the half notes on your desk with a pat-slide motion.

p-sl   s s s s s s   p-sl   s s s s s s   p-sl   p-sl   s s s s s s   p-sl

82

- Review playing the pitches G A B C D on recorder, bells, or keyboard.

Remember that ⌐2¬ at the beginning of the score means that the music will start two measures before you begin to play the melodic accompaniment.

### Melodic Accompaniment to the Theme from *Star Wars*

V.L. and J.K.

- Find this phrase in the music above.

How many times does this phrase repeat? Find a different phrase.

4 (mm. 3-7, 7-11, 20-24, 24-28); 12-20

- Notice the repetition and contrast of phrases. What is the form of this accompaniment? ABA

83

**2. Introduce the melodic accompaniment to the theme from *Star Wars*.** Have the students:
- Review/learn G A B C and D on recorder, bells, or keyboard by echoing the patterns and reading the melodic notation (see pages 32, 68, and 78).
- Examine the melodic accompaniment to the theme from *Star Wars* and identify the rhythm values. (triplet, quarter note, half note, dotted half note, and whole note; quarter rest, half rest)
- Lightly touch the notes on recorder, bells, or keyboard while singing or saying the pitch names in rhythm.
- Play the melodic accompaniment with the recording, concentrating on accurate performance of all rhythm values.
- Find the opening phrase of the melodic accompaniment in the score. (mm. 3–7, 7–11, 20–24, 24–28 with two-measure coda)
- Find a contrasting phrase. (mm. 12–20. Note that this phrase is not in triplets.)
- Determine the form of the melodic accompaniment, based on repetition and contrast of phrases.

# LESSON 4

**3. Introduce composer John Williams.** Have the students discuss the information on film music and John Williams.

You may wish to use the following item as a basis for extended discussion.

John Williams took over as director of the Boston Pops Orchestra after Arthur Fiedler died. Arthur Fiedler had led this orchestra for fifty years, and he was loved by the people of Boston. What problems might John Williams have encountered as he began that job? (Some of the orchestra players might have felt Fiedler was irreplaceable or a "hard act to follow.") Do you think Keith Lockhart (John Williams' replacement) might have encountered similar problems?

## Reinforcing the Lesson

Have the students perform the patterns on page 82 while listening to the theme from *Star Wars*.

### 3  APPRAISAL

The students should be able to:
1. Tap a steady beat and simultaneously snap triplets to each beat.
2. Play triplets as they occur in several rhythm patterns.
3. Play accurately the melodic accompaniment to the theme from *Star Wars* on recorder, bells, or keyboard.
4. Verbally define *triplet* as the division of the beat into three sounds of equal duration.

John Williams was born in New York City in 1932 and studied piano at The Juilliard School. He later moved to Los Angeles and studied with many famous composers of movie scores.

During the 1960s Williams wrote music for television and won two Emmy Awards. He also has been music director and composer for over 75 motion pictures, including *Jaws*, all three *Star Wars* films, *Superman*, the three *Indiana Jones* films, *Jurassic Park*, and *E.T. (The Extra-Terrestrial)*. He has won many awards for his music, including five Oscars and 16 Grammies®. His descriptive and exciting film scores are so popular that his soundtrack recordings have sold millions of copies. His film music is often played in orchestral concerts.

Besides writing for motion pictures, John Williams has composed many concert works, including two symphonies and several concertos. He wrote the theme music for the NBC News programs, as well as the official music for the 1984 Summer Olympics. From 1980 to 1993 he was the conductor of the Boston Pops Orchestra, one of the most famous and popular orchestras in the world.

*A scene from the film Star Wars*

# EXTENSION

## MORE MUSIC TEACHING IDEAS

Draw the grid at right on the chalkboard. Have the students:
1. Create their own rhythm patterns from the grid. Connect any four adjacent squares to form a pattern. Pat quarter notes, clap eighth notes, and snap triplets with alternating hands. (You may wish to use Copying Master 3-1 at this time.)
2. Develop memory skills. As you erase one or more of the squares, the students should try to remember the note values of the square that has been erased and perform this rhythm.

Key: D minor     Starting Pitch: D     Scale Tones: *la, ti, do re mi fa si la ti*

## SINGING A SYNCOPATED SONG

"Joshua Fought the Battle of Jericho" tells the biblical story of how     CD2:14, CD7:26
the Israelites, under Joshua, captured the town of Jericho.

**Piano Accompaniment on page PA 22**

### Joshua Fought the Battle of Jericho

With gradually increasing intensity throughout            African American spiritual (arr. M.J.)

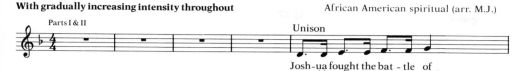

85

# LESSON 5

**Focus: Syncopation**

## Objectives
To experience syncopation
To read, play, and compare syncopated and unsyncopated patterns

## Materials
Recordings: "Joshua Fought the Battle of Jericho" (sung version)
"Joshua Fought the Battle of Jericho" (performance mix)
"I Saw the Light"
"Don't Let the Wind"
"Las Flores"

**1** SETTING THE STAGE
Remind students that they have already learned one spiritual, "Oh, Sinner Man" (page 44), and that "Joshua" is another.

**2** TEACHING THE LESSON
**1. Introduce "Joshua."** Have the students:
• Echo the following body percussion. (You may wish to notate it on the chalkboard or on an overhead transparency.)

• Play the body percussion pattern while listening to the recording.
• Find the syncopated pattern ♪♩♪ and identify the accompanying word. (*Jericho*)
• Discover how many times the pattern appears. (twelve times in melody)
• Play this pattern in rhythm. Say it, clap it, sing it, and sing and clap it together.

# LESSON 5

- Play the body percussion again to enhance awareness of the strong steady beat.
- Form two groups to sing the spiritual in two parts. (Changing voices should sing Part II.)
- Follow their parts in the score while listening to the recording.
- Follow the score and sing the song with recording.
- Review and rehearse selected phrases or sections as necessary.
- Sing the song and accompany themselves with body percussion.

E X T E N S I O N

## VOCAL DEVELOPMENT

Have students emphasize consonant articulation to give the spiritual rhythmic precision and to match the style of the accompaniment.

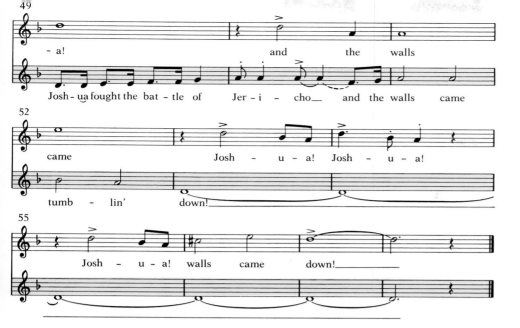

- a!                    and         the         walls

Josh - ua fought the bat – tle of   Jer – i – cho__ and the walls   came

52

came            Josh – u – a!  Josh – u – a!

tumb – lin'    down!__

55

Josh – u – a!  walls   came   down!__

This painting, by the American artist James Tissot, is his idea of how the battle of Jericho might have happened.

87

# LESSON 5

**2. Introduce alternate versions of the *Joshua* rhythm.** Have the students:
• Step the steady half-note beat as they say the refrain using rhythm A, B, or C, with rhythm A or B in the second line.
• Sing the refrain, using each of the rhythms with body percussion accompaniment.
• Sing the refrain again to identify the versions in which they can sense the beat most easily. (B and C) Discuss why. (The even half and quarter notes fit well with the body percussion.) Repeat B and C to emphasize this "matching" quality.
• Play A, B, and C again to determine which version is the most rhythmically interesting. (A) Discuss why. (The uneven rhythm has a catchy or uneven quality, known as syncopation.)
• Sing the refrain with body percussion accompaniment, using rhythm A, then rhythm B. Emphasize the differences between the uneven and even rhythms.
• Sing the entire song.
**3. Introduce information on spirituals.** Have the students:
• Discuss the background information on spirituals (see also pages 46 and 47).

Spirituals, like other folk songs, generally were not written down. They exist today because they were passed down from generation to generation of singers. Changes were introduced over time so that we now have many different versions of "Joshua."

Notice how the word *Jericho* can be sung with many different rhythms.

• Step the steady half-note beat, and clap and say each pattern.
• Sing the refrain of "Joshua" with each of the rhythms below.

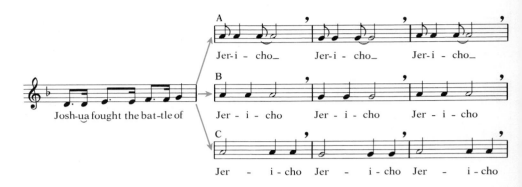

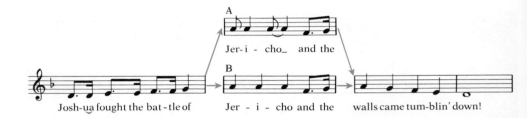

In which version can you sense the steady beat most easily?   version B or C

Which version has the most rhythmic interest?   version A

• Sing "Joshua." Bring out the catchy quality of the syncopated patterns.

88

---

# E X T E N S I O N

## COOPERATIVE LEARNING
After the students have performed the syncopated rhythm patterns in "Joshua Fought the Battle of Jericho," have them work in cooperative groups of four to identify songs in Unit 2 that contain syncopation ("I Saw the Light" and "Don't Let the Wind," both page 53, and "Las Flores," page 56). After they have identified a song that contains syncopation, each student in the group should alter the rhythm in one measure of the song to create syncopation or to eliminate syncopation. After practicing the new patterns, each cooperative group will perform the transformed rhythm pattern for the class.

## MORE MUSIC TEACHING IDEAS
Have the students make a list by title and performer/group of current popular songs that use syncopation.

A scene from *Mama I Want to Sing*

## The Spiritual — An American Style

Both "Oh, Sinner Man" and "Joshua Fought the Battle of Jericho" are spirituals. Spirituals were not well known outside the South until after the Civil War. In 1871 the Jubilee Singers, an African American choir from Fisk University in Nashville, Tennessee, traveled throughout the United States. This choir introduced the beauty of spirituals to the rest of the world while it raised money for the university. The Jubilee Singers became so famous that they were invited to tour Europe, where they also were a great success. Since then, spirituals have been performed and recorded by many groups and by individual artists such as Leontyne Price and Paul Robeson. The spiritual is now one of the best-known and best-loved forms of American music.

89

# LESSON 5

You may wish to use the following items as a basis for extended discussion.
1. The increased interest in spirituals resulted from a cross-country tour by the Jubilee Singers in 1871. These live performances demonstrated the beauty of spirituals to those outside the South who had never heard this style of music. How does new music reach a large audience today? (radio, recordings, television, films)
2. What events created the atmosphere for the success of the Jubilee Singers? (The Emancipation Proclamation of 1863 and the end of the Civil War in 1865 gave African Americans more opportunity and mobility. Development of the railroads helped people travel more easily, especially with the invention of the Pullman sleeper in 1865. The Atlantic Cable, laid down in 1865, made communication with Europe instantaneous; news no longer took weeks to get to its destination.)

### Reinforcing the Lesson

Have the students analyze and perform songs in Unit 2 that are syncopated. ("I Saw the Light" and "Don't Let the Wind," both page 53; "Las Flores," page 56)

**3 APPRAISAL**

The students should be able to:
1. Identify visually measures in "Joshua Fought the Battle of Jericho" with syncopated rhythm patterns.
2. Step, clap, say, and sing the syncopated rhythm patterns in "Joshua Fought the Battle of Jericho" while listening to the tapping of the steady half-note beat.
3. Perform accurately the syncopated patterns in "Joshua Fought the Battle of Jericho" while singing in two parts.

# REVIEW AND EVALUATION

## JUST CHECKING

### Objective
To review and test the skills and concepts taught in Unit 3

### Materials
Recordings: Just Checking Unit 3
            Unit 3 Evaluation (questions 3–5)
            *For Extra Credit* recordings (optional)
Bells, recorder, or keyboard
Copying Master 3-2 (optional)
Evaluation Unit 3 Copying Master

## TEACHING THE LESSON

**Review the skills and concepts taught in Unit 3.** Have the students:
• Look at pages 90–91, following the recorded review, and perform the activities and answer the questions.
• Review answers.
(You may wish to use Copying Master 3-2 at this time.)

## JUST CHECKING

See how much you remember.

1. As you listen to "The Star-Spangled Banner," clap the dotted eighth-note rhythm  and snap the even eighth-note rhythm .

2. To review triplets, listen to an excerpt from "Star Wars" and perform the following by clapping the quarter notes, snapping the triplets, and pat-sliding the half notes.

3. As you listen to the refrain of "Joshua," pat the steady half-note beat. Clap when you hear the syncopated pattern to the word Jer-i - cho.

4. Sing the refrain of "Joshua" with each of the rhythms below. In which version can you sense the steady beat most easily? Version B
Which version is syncopated? Version A

A
Jer-i - cho___  Jer-i - cho___  Jer-i - cho___

Josh-ua fought the bat-tle of

B
Jer - i - cho  Jer - i - cho  Jer - i - cho

C
Jer - i - cho  Jer - i - cho  Jer - i - cho

5. Listen to these excerpts from "Trav'ler." Which contains more dotted notes? a

a.
So close your eyes and dream with me

b.
and waits for us to slow our step to pause— and to ex - plore

6. Perform the following on bells, recorder, or keyboard to show your understanding of dotted rhythms.

7. The rhythm pattern ♩. ♩ can also be written:    a

   a. ♩♩♩    b. ♩. ♪    c. ♩♩♩

8. The song "Trav'ler" has two important rhythms: ♩. ♩ and ♩. ♪ Which one is an augmentation of the other? Why?

   ♩. ♩ is twice the duration of ♩. ♪

9. Perform the following on bells, recorder, or keyboard to show your understanding of the difference between the dotted eighth-note rhythm and the equal eighth-note rhythm.

91

## GIVING THE EVALUATION

Evaluation Unit 3 Copying Master can be found in the *Teacher's Copying Masters* book along with full directions for giving the evaluation and checking the answers.

## FOR EXTRA CREDIT

You may want the students to answer one of the following questions. Tell them to include at least five vocabulary terms in their answers.

1. Identify and describe musical characteristics of folk-rock music. (include comments on text, vocal register, vocal harmony, beat, and instrumentation, as well as additional comments students feel are relevant)

2. "Joshua Fought the Battle of Jericho" is a spiritual. Describe the musical characteristics of the spiritual. (include comments on text, rhythm, tempo, and form, as well as additional comments students feel are relevant)

(You may wish to play recordings to refresh students' memories.)

| ELEMENTS OF MUSIC | UNIT 4 OBJECTIVES | Lesson 1 Focus: Five-Tone Scale | Lesson 2 Focus: Major Diatonic Scale |
|---|---|---|---|
| Dynamics | Identify dynamics | Listen to and identify dynamic changes | |
| Tone Color | **Listen to and identify vocal and instrumental tone color** | Listen to and identify vocal and orchestral tone color | Sustain pitch in the upper register |
| Tempo | **Perform in slow and fast tempo** | | Experience contrasting tempi in two compositions |
| Duration/ Rhythm | **Identify an ostinato** | | |
| Pitch | Identify stepwise motion **Identify major scale** Perform a five-tone scale **Perform minor pentaton, music in minor mode Identify melodic contour** Identify sharp symbol **Perform using C-E'** | Hear, see, and perform stepwise motion Perform a melody with an octave range Identify and move to melodic contour Identify and play a five-tone scale Play melody on keyboard or bells | Identify and perform major scale Sing a melody with a wide range Read and perform melodic patterns based on the major scale Identify melodic contour Identify and perform the C major scale Improvise "answers" to melodies on keyboard or bells |
| Texture | **Identify homophonic, polyphonic, and monophonic textures** Listen to thin and thick textures **Define ostinato** | Listen to and identify monophonic and homophonic texture | Listen to, read, and perform in imitative and nonimitative polyphonic texture |
| Form | Identify and perform AABA form, round, AB form, phrases **Identify and define phrases** | Identify and perform phrase structure Identify similar and different phrases | |
| Style | Listen to music of the baroque, classical, and romantic periods Perform an American folk song Listen to music of the classical period | Listen to, perform, and discuss music of the classical/ romantic period | Listen to and perform music of the baroque period |
| Reading | | Read ♪ , ♫ , ♩ , ♩. , ♩ in 4/4 Identify dynamics *f* , *p* | Read ♩ , ♩. ♪ , ♩. in 3/4 Read 𝅝 in 4/4 Read notation G-g' |

## PURPOSE Unit 4: Melody

In this unit students will listen to and identify melodic contour and phrase structure. They will become aware of phrase structure by identifying phrases that are similar and different. Students will listen to and identify orchestral tone color, texture, dynamics, tonality (major, minor, minor pentaton), and mood in music. They will perform melodic patterns based on the major and minor scales.

## SUGGESTED TIME FRAME

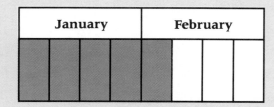

| January | February |
|---|---|

## FOCUS

- Five-tone scale
- Major diatonic scale
- Minor pentaton
- Minor scale

| Lesson 3<br>Focus: Minor Pentaton | Lesson 4<br>Focus: Minor Scale |
|---|---|
| Identify soft dynamics | Identify contrasting dynamics |
| Perform accompaniment on Orff instruments | Listen to and identify orchestral tone color |
| Identify tempo of song | |
| Perform repeated rhythmic patterns<br>Identify and play ostinati | Perform body percussion |
| Listen to and perform music based on a minor pentaton<br>Perform a melody with an octave range | Identify and perform melodic direction<br>Identify repeated phrase<br>Listen to, identify, and perform melodies in minor and major modes<br>Perform melodic accompaniments<br>Identify sharp symbol<br>Perform music with a sharp<br><br>Identify major and minor in songs |
| Perform a melody with a harmonic accompaniment<br>Identify and define ostinato<br>Play an accompaniment on Orff instruments | Listen to homophonic texture<br>Listen to contrast of thin and thick texture |
| Identify and perform phrase structure | Identify and perform melody in AB form<br>Identify similar and different phrases<br>Identify and perform phrase structure |
| Identify the mood of a song<br>Perform an American folk song | Listen to music of the romantic period |
| Read ♫ , ♩ , 𝄽 , ♩. ♪, ♩ , ◼ , o , − , ‖: :‖ in 4/4 | Read ♫ , ♩ , ♩. ♪<br>Read E major and E natural minor scales, sharp (♯) |

# TECHNOLOGY

## MUSIC WITH *MIDI*

MIDI technology allows students to manipulate musical elements and make musical decisions.

- Lesson 2, page 100: Create Using **Imitation**
- Lesson 3, page 102 *"Nine Hundred Miles"*
- Lesson 4, page 108: Create a **Rondo:** *"The Boatman's Dance"*

## VIDEO RESOURCES

Use video resources to reinforce, extend, and enrich learning in this unit.

# LESSON 1

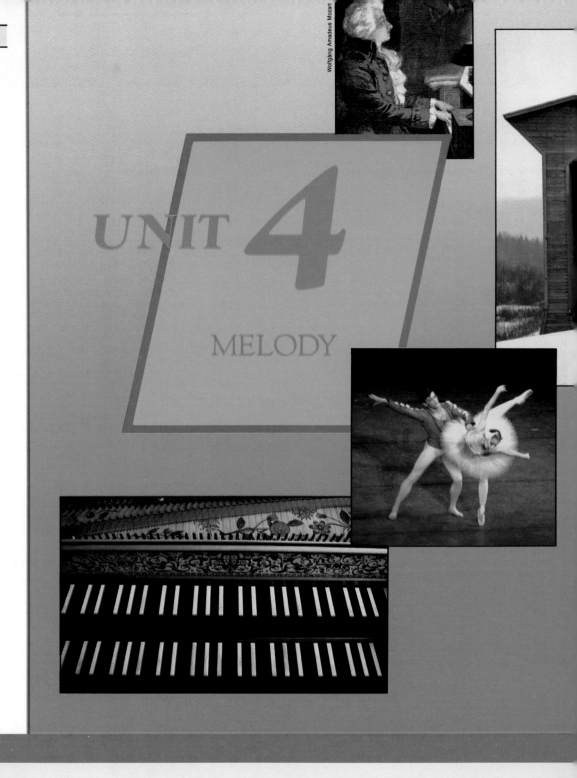

UNIT **4**

MELODY

Wolfgang Amadeus Mozart

George, 3rd Earl Cowper, with the Family of Charles Gore, Johann Joseph Zoffany, R.A., YALE CENTER FOR BRITISH ART, New Haven, CT

93

# LESSON 1

**Focus: Five-Tone Scale**

## Objectives
To identify and perform a five-tone scale
To identify and move to melodic contour
To identify phrases that are similar and different
To listen to and identify instrumental tone color, texture, and dynamics

## Materials
Recordings: "Oh, Sinner Man"
            "Ode to Joy"
            Beethoven, Symphony No.9, fourth movement
            (excerpt, with call numbers)
Bells, keyboard instruments
Copying Master 4-1: Listening Map (optional)

## Vocabulary
Melodic contour, half step, whole step

**1  SETTING THE STAGE**

Review "Oh, Sinner Man" and phrases on pages 44–45.

# LESSON 1

## 2 TEACHING THE LESSON

**1. Introduce melodic contour.** Have the students:

• Listen to "Ode to Joy" and follow the melodic contour with their hands.

• Listen again to "Ode to Joy" and identify the number of phrases. (six) Similar: 1, 2, 4, and 6. Different: 3 and 5 are identical but are different from 1, 2, 4, and 6.

• Choose a partner and create a mirror image showing each phrase. (Introduce this activity by having the class copy you in a mirror image.)

CD2:28 "Ode to Joy" is the main theme of the fourth movement of Symphony No. 9 by Ludwig van Beethoven (lood' vig vän bā' tō-ven).

• Listen to "Ode to Joy." Move your hand to show the upward and downward movement, or shape, of the melody. The shape of the melody is called the **melodic contour.**

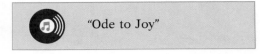

"Ode to Joy"

### "Ode to Joy," from Symphony No. 9, Fourth Movement

Ludwig van Beethoven

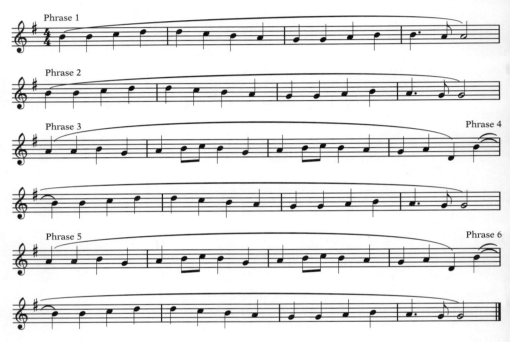

• Listen again to identify the phrases. Which phrases sound similar? Which ones sound different?  1,2,4 and 6; 3 and 5

• Create a mirror image with a partner. Move your hand in an arc to show each phrase.

94

# E X T E N S I O N

## SPECIAL LEARNERS

If your class includes physically handicapped students, preplan an activity for these students to do while the class is creating a mirror image of the phrase structure. Some alternatives might be mirror images that use movements these children can do (hand or arm movements), or having a group of students, including the handicapped student, lead the class in this activity and indicate the beginning of each phrase with one specific movement (a soft clap, for example).

"Ode to Joy" uses a five-tone scale.

The distance between two pitches that are right next to each other on the keyboard is called a **half step.**

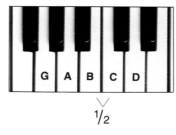

Identify the half step in this scale.    B–C

The distance between two pitches that have one key (*either* black or white) between them is called a **whole step.**

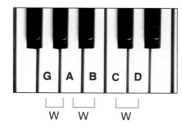

Identify two whole steps in this scale.    any two of G–A, A–B, C–D

## MORE MUSIC TEACHING IDEAS

Have the students play the third phrase of "Ode to Joy" on keyboard or bells, then play the entire song.

# LESSON 1

**2. Introduce the five-tone scale.** Have the students:
• Review the tone ladder activity from Unit 1 (pages 35–37).
• Sing the first two phrases of "Ode to Joy" on numbers, using arm levels.
• Focus on the diagrams showing the melodic contour of the first two phrases of "Ode to Joy."
• Play the first two phrases on keyboard instruments or bells.
(If only one keyboard instrument is available, have students perform individually. You may wish to have the students practice on the keyboard chart on the inside back cover.)

# LESSON 1

**3. Introduce the excerpt from Beethoven's Symphony No. 9, fourth movement.** Have the students:
• Identify the pictures used to designate orchestral tone color, texture, and dynamics.
• Listen to the recording. When numbers 1 through 4 are called, write on a sheet of paper which of the four instrument families they hear, the texture, and the dynamic level. (1. strings, monophonic, *p*; 2. strings, homophonic, *p* ; 3. strings, homophonic, *p* to *f*; 4. strings/woodwinds/brass/percussion, homophonic, *f*) Listen and read the description when numbers 5, 6, and 7 are called. (You may wish to use Copying Master 4-1: Listening Map at this time.)
• Analyze and discuss the answers.

---

**CD2:29** Listen to the way Beethoven uses the five-tone scale in the "Ode to Joy."

• When you hear the number 1 called, identify the:

strings, monophonic, soft

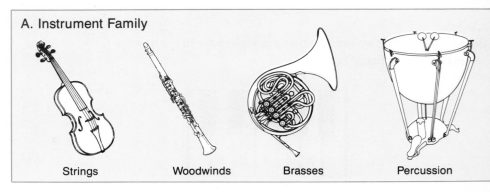

**A. Instrument Family**

Strings    Woodwinds    Brasses    Percussion

**B. Texture**

monophonic              homophonic

**C. Dynamics**

*p*                                    *f*

*piano*—soft                    *forte*—loud

• Identify the instrument families, texture, and dynamics when you hear the numbers 2 through 4 called.
• Read the descriptions below when you hear the numbers 5 to 7 called.
  5. Theme begins in woodwinds, then goes into transition with baritone.
  6. Theme sung by baritone, continues in chorus (*forte*).
  7. Theme sung by soprano, alto, tenor, and baritone soloists, concluded by chorus (*forte*).

2: strings, homophon
soft (bassoon counter
melody); 3: strings,
homophonic, soft to l
4: entire orchestra,
homophonic, loud

 Symphony No. 9, Fourth Movement (excerpt), by Ludwig van Beethoven

96

# LUDWIG VAN BEETHOVEN

Detail from Beethoven Composing the "Missa Solemnis," Josef Stieler

Ludwig van Beethoven (1770–1827), one of the world's greatest composers, was born in Bonn, Germany. He showed immense musical talent as a young child. From the age of thirteen on, he worked as a musician and also began to compose. In 1792 he moved to Vienna, Austria, the musical center of Europe. Everyone who heard his music predicted a great future for him.

Just when Beethoven was gaining recognition as one of Europe's leading composers, he began to lose his hearing. He had always been a proud, independent, and sociable man, and this discovery depressed him deeply. But Beethoven's loss of hearing did not interfere with his ability to compose. He found comfort in music and continued to work. He wrote some of his most powerful music – including the Ninth Symphony – after he became completely deaf.

In the last movement of the Ninth Symphony, Beethoven set to music the "Ode to Joy" by the German poet Friedrich Schiller (frēd' riKH shil' er). This poem is about the hope that all people might live in peace as brothers and sisters. To put this ideal in musical form, Beethoven used solo singers and chorus in a symphony for the first time.

Beethoven lived at the time of the American and French revolutions. His music expresses his own deepest emotions and love of freedom and personal dignity. The Ninth Symphony was performed at an historic concert in Germany in 1989. In that year, the Berlin Wall was taken apart. For nearly 30 years the wall had divided the city of Berlin into East and West zones. The destruction of the wall was a symbol of liberty and unity for the German people and the world.

97

# LESSON 1

### Reinforcing the Lesson
Discuss the information on Beethoven and Symphony No. 9.

## 3 APPRAISAL
The students should be able to:
1. Perform the first two phrases of "Ode to Joy" on keyboard or bells without syllables or numbers and identify the scale as a five-tone scale.
2. Identify the melodic contour of "Ode to Joy" by using appropriate arm levels while listening to the melody.
3. Identify identical and different phrases of "Ode to Joy."
4. Verbally identify the correct tone color, texture, and dynamics in the beginning of Beethoven's Symphony No. 9, fourth movement.

# LESSON 2

**Focus: Major Diatonic Scale**

**Objectives**
To read and perform melodic patterns based on the major scale
To identify and move to melodic contour

**Materials**
Recordings: "Weekend Relief"
           Pachelbel Canon
           "Nine Hundred Miles"
Bells, keyboard, or other C instruments

**Vocabulary**
C major scale, octave

## 1 SETTING THE STAGE
Review duple- and triple-meter patterns on page 16.

## 2 TEACHING THE LESSON

**1. Introduce melodic contour and meter in "Weekend Relief."** Have the students:
• Listen to "Weekend Relief" and decide if the song is in duple or triple meter. (triple meter)
• Show the melodic contour with their hands.
• Sing the song with the recording. (Changing voices can sing section B.)
• Sing section A as a round with the recording. (You may wish to have the students sing section B at the same time as section A.)

# THE MAJOR SCALE

Key: C major    Starting Pitch: C    Scale Tones: *do re mi fa so la ti do' re' mi' fa'*

CD2:30 ● Sing "Weekend Relief" in sequence and then sing section A as a round. Move your arm to show the melodic contour as you sing.

## Weekend Relief

Words by M. J.
Music by Henry Purcell (arr. V. L.)

98

# E X T E N S I O N

## THE COMPOSER

**Henry Purcell** (pər' səl) (1659?–1695)—one of the greatest English composers. As a boy, Purcell was in the choir at the Chapel Royal, where he received most of his musical training. Later Purcell served as assistant keeper of the king's instruments, keeper of the king's wind instruments, and organist at both Westminster Abbey and the Chapel Royal. Purcell is best known for writing the first great English opera, *Dido and Aeneas,* based on Virgil's *Aeneid.* He also wrote songs, church music, choral music, and chamber music, as well as incidental music for stage works.

Ⓑ

"Take this test." "Read this book." "Spell this word." "Watch this hook."

"Draw this line." Oh, my head's spin – ning a – round!

"Take this test." "Read this book." "Spell this word." "Watch this hook."

"Draw this line." Oh, my head's spin – ning a – round!

"Take this test." "Read this book." "Spell this word." "Watch this hook."

"Draw this line." Oh, my head's spin – ning a – round!

• Look at these circled notes in Section A of "Weekend Relief."
These eight pitches make up the **C major scale.**

Each day on Mon – day and Tues – day and Wednes – day and

Thurs – day and Fri – day I spend here at school!

• Play the C major scale on bells or keyboard.

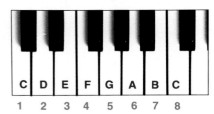

| C | D | E | F | G | A | B | C |
|---|---|---|---|---|---|---|---|
| 1 | 2 | 3 | 4 | 5 | 6 | 7 | 8 |

The musical distance from C to C is called an **octave.** Count the white keys from one C to the next one above or below it.

99

# LESSON 2

**2. Identify the major scale in "Weekend Relief."** Have the students:
• Review the tone ladder activity from Unit 1 (pages 35–37).
• Play the C major scale in triple meter, both ascending and descending, on bells or keyboard instruments.
• Determine which parts of "Weekend Relief" are based on the descending scale (parts 1 and 3 of section A).
• Play the descending C major scale with parts 1 and 3 of section A while singing the song.

**VOCAL DEVELOPMENT**

Have the students sing "Weekend Relief," substituting *vee* for the words, to aid in sustaining the pitch in the upper part of the register.

**SPECIAL LEARNERS**

Students with reading deficits may have difficulty following the words and notation in "Weekend Relief." These students will benefit from preparation of an overhead transparency of this song. Use the transparency to point out the beginning of each line that students are to sing.

# LESSON 2

**3. Introduce the melodies from the Pachelbel Canon.** Have the students:
• Form three groups.
• Read and practice each of the three melodies to prepare for performing with the recording of the Pachelbel Canon. They can sing the melodies on numbers or syllables while using arm levels.
• Play the melodies with the recording on bells, keyboard, or other C instruments.
You may wish to use the following as a basis for extended discussion.
Pachelbel's characteristic style is often referred to as *cantabile* (very singable and lyrical). Name some other songs in this text or currently popular songs in cantabile style. ("Trav'ler"; for popular songs, answers will vary)

**THE COMPOSER**
**Johann Pachelbel** (1653–1706)—was a famous German organist and composer. He taught Johann Christoph Bach, who taught *his* nephew Johann Sebastian. One of Pachelbel's sons emigrated to the American colonies to continue his family's musical profession. Johann Pachelbel was one of the earliest composers to use tonality to express the meaning of the words he set to music; he usually used major keys for joyful moods and minor keys for sorrowful ones, a practice that later became standard. This Canon was written for three violins and keyboard, but it has been arranged since for many different instruments.

# The Pachelbel Canon

CD2:31 The composer Johann Pachelbel (yoʼ hän päкнʼ əl-bel) (1653–1706) uses pitches from the major scale in this canon. The melodies are based on scales that follow one after another.

• Listen to the harmony that results when the melodies are played together.

 Canon, by Johann Pachelbel

• Read and play each of the three melodies used by Pachelbel in the Canon.
• Play the melodies in order with the recording in three groups.

Johann Pachelbel lived from 1653 to 1706. The art and architecture of this time were extremely elaborate, as in this palace room in Turin, Italy.

100

## Melodies from the Pachelbel Canon

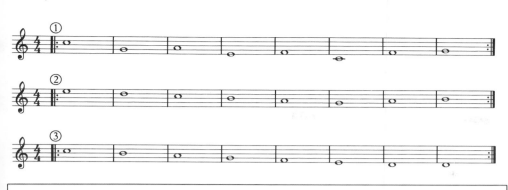

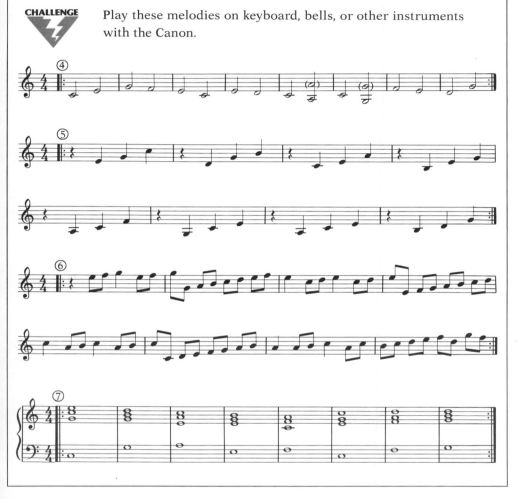

**CHALLENGE** Play these melodies on keyboard, bells, or other instruments with the Canon.

# LESSON 2

## Reinforcing the Lesson

Have the students listen to "Nine Hundred Miles," pages 102–103, for phrase structure.

**4. Introduce the Challenge!** Have the students play instrumental parts 4, 5, 6, and/or 7 with the recording. (Encourage students who already can read music to play parts 4 and 5, and students who can play keyboard to play part 6. You may wish to have students play one note each in the chords in part 7.)

## 3 APPRAISAL

The students should be able to:

1. Listen with eyes closed to several melodic patterns based on the C major scale and identify melodic contour by using appropriate arm levels.

2. Play the ascending and descending C major scale on bells or keyboard.

3. Read and play from notation several melodic patterns based on the C major scale to accompany the Pachelbel Canon.

4. Sing "Weekend Relief" in sequence and as a round with melodic and rhythmic accuracy.

## MORE MUSIC TEACHING IDEAS

Have the students improvise "answers" to phrases you improvise on bells or keyboard instruments.

# LESSON 3

**Focus: Minor Pentaton**

**Objectives**
To experience the minor pentaton
To identify and perform phrase structure
To identify the mood of a song

**Materials**
Recordings: "Nine Hundred Miles"
             "Nine Hundred Miles" (performance mix)
             "Nine Hundred Miles" (Orff accompaniment)
Orff instruments, bells, or keyboard
Copying Master 4-2 (optional)

**Vocabulary**
Ostinato

## 1 SETTING THE STAGE

Discuss the background information on "Nine Hundred Miles."

## 2 TEACHING THE LESSON

**1. Introduce the mood and phrase structure of "Nine Hundred Miles."**
Have the students:
• Listen to the first verse and decide on the general mood of the text. (sad, homesick)
• Discuss the musical descriptions that reinforce the mood of the music and text. (slow tempo, soft dynamic level, and dark vocal tone color)
You may wish to use the following item as a basis for extended discussion.
The role of railroads in the United States has changed considerably since the nineteenth century. Discuss the changes and the reasons for them. (Development of automobile, airplane, container ships, and so on has made it cheaper to ship goods and people by other means.)

# A SONG OF THE RAILROADS

CD2:32, CD7:27  Key: D minor  Starting Pitch: D  Scale Tones: *mi, so, la, ti, do re mi so la*

The building of the railroads and their importance to American life have been recorded in our folk songs. The words of these songs often describe such activities as "working on the railroad," going home, leaving home, and sending or receiving letters.

• Listen to the first verse of "Nine Hundred Miles." Which of these words describe the mood of the song?
slow, soft, dark

| slow | soft | light |
|------|------|-------|
| fast | loud | dark |

 "Nine Hundred Miles"

## Nine Hundred Miles

Traditional (arr. J. K.

1. Well, I'm walk-in' down this track, I've got tears in my eyes, Tryin' to read a
2. Well, this train that I ride on, it's one hundred coach-es long. You can hear the
3. If my love she bids me stay, I will never go a - way. Near her I will

*Refrain*

let - ter from my home.
whis - tle sound for miles._____ And if this train runs me right, I'll be
al - ways want to be._____

home to-mor-row night, 'Cause I'm nine hun-dred miles from my home._____

• Sing the song.
• Move your hands in an arc from left to right on each phrase. How many phrases do you hear in the song? four

# EXTENSION

## SIGNING FOR "NINE HUNDRED MILES"

On the first phrase, "walk" with your hands on the beat to "walkin'/down/track." The meaning of the words is signed in "runs me," which means "takes me the right direction," so we sign "direction right." Show the mood of the song with body language and especially facial expression.

Walkin'      With the palms down, move the hands forward and back, imitating feet walking.

**Tears (In My Eyes)**    Outline tears falling from the eyes.

**Read**    Hold the left hand out with the palm facing the body. The right hand imitates the eyes moving down a page and moves down the palm of the left hand.

**Letter**    The thumb of the right hand "A" touches the mouth, then moves into the open, palm-up left hand.

**From**    The left index finger points toward the right hand "X." The right hand pulls away from the left index finger toward the body and down.

**Home**    The closed right hand touches the lips, then opens to a flat palm on cheek—a place to eat and sleep.

- Play the following rhythm patterns as an accompaniment to "Nine Hundred Miles."

CD2:33

A repeated rhythm or melodic pattern is called an **ostinato** (äs-tin-ä′ tō).

### Accompaniment to "Nine Hundred Miles"

- Follow the score and sing the song with the recording. (Changing voices can sing the lower part.)
- Move their hands in an arc from left to right as they sing each phrase.
- Identify the number of phrases in the song. (four)

**2. Introduce the accompaniment to "Nine Hundred Miles."** Have the students:
- Pat or clap the rhythms of assigned parts as they sing the song.
- Play the rhythms on instruments as they sing the song. (Each student on the "cluster" part should play any two notes.)
- Take turns playing different parts.
- Discuss *ostinato* as a term for a repeated rhythmic or melodic pattern. (You may wish to use Copying Master 4-2 at this time.)

### Reinforcing the Lesson

Have half the students sing the song while the rest play the ostinati.

**3 APPRAISAL**

The students should be able to:
1. Sing the four-phrase structure of "Nine Hundred Miles" and identify the structure by moving their hands in an arc for each phrase.
2. Listen to "Nine Hundred Miles" and write a description of the mood of the text and music based on its musical characteristics, including specific references to tempo, dynamics, and vocal tone color.
3. Perform, from the score, at least two different ostinati based on the minor pentaton as an accompaniment to "Nine Hundred Miles."

| | |
|---|---|
| Train  | Rub the right hand "H" on the back of the left hand "H." Origin: movement on the tracks. |
| Runs Me (Direction)  | The index finger of the right hand "D" touches the forehead, then touches the tip of the left hand "D." |
| Right  | The right hand moves down to the left hand base of the thumb. Index fingers are extended, fingers closed. |
| Tomorrow  | The "A" position hand touches the cheek, then moves forward and down in an arc. |
| Night  | The left hand, palm down, represents the horizon. The right hand represents the sun and moves down and over the left hand for the sun setting. |
| Nine | Palm facing out, the thumb and index finger touch while the other fingers are straight up. |
| Hundred | The letter "C." |
| Miles | The right "A" moves forward in a series of arcs. |

# LESSON 4

**Focus: Minor Scale**

## Objectives
To compare the E minor and E major scales
To identify melodic contour of phrases
To identify phrases that are similar and different
To identify instrumental tone color and dynamics

## Materials
Recordings: "The Birch Tree" (sung in Russian)
Tchaikovsky, Symphony No. 4, fourth movement (excerpt, with call numbers)
Rondo "alla Turca"
"While My Guitar Gently Weeps"
Bells, keyboard, or other C instruments
Tennis balls (see *More Music Teaching Ideas*)
Copying Master 4-3: Listening Map (optional)

## Vocabulary
Minor scale, sharp

### **1** SETTING THE STAGE
Review melodic contour on page 94.

### **2** TEACHING THE LESSON
**1. Introduce melodic contour and phrase structure.** Have the students:
• Listen to "The Birch Tree" and follow the melodic contour with their hands.
• Listen again and identify the number of phrases (four) and which phrases are alike. (1 and 2; 3 and 4) Identify the form as AABB.
• Play the song on bells or keyboard or sing it in English or Russian.

# MINOR AND MAJOR

Key: E minor    Starting Pitch: B    Scale Tones: *la, ti, do re mi*

Peter Ilyich Tchaikovsky (il' yich chī-käv' skē) used the Russian folk song "The Birch Tree" in the fourth movement of his Symphony No. 4.

• Listen to "The Birch Tree" and follow the melodic contour of the music. How many phrases do you hear? Which phrases sound alike? four; phrases 1 and 2, 3 and 4

 "The Birch Tree"

• Sing "The Birch Tree" or play the melody on bells or keyboard.

**The Birch Tree**

Russian folk song

Vo  po - le  be - rë - zyn' - ka  sto - ia - la.

Vo  po - le  be - rë - zyn' - ka  sto - ia - la.

Liu,  liu,  liu - li  sto - ia - la,

Liu,  liu,  liu - li  sto - ia - la,

104

# EXTENSION

## COOPERATIVE LEARNING
Have the students work in cooperative groups of four to improvise and perform ostinati, using two to five pitches from the minor pentaton, to accompany "The Birch Tree." (You may wish to notate the minor pentaton on the board.) Within each group, students should form pairs to create ostinati using any of the word rhythms from the song. Then have the pairs share their ostinati with the other group members. Two of the students should sing the song and two should perform the ostinato, then switch parts. You may wish to have one pair from each group present its ostinato to the class while the other group members (or all the students) sing the song.

## PRONUNCIATION
1. Vo pole berëzyn'ka stoiala.
vo pol-yə' ber-yo' zin-kə stä-yä' lä
In the meadow stood a little birch tree

2. Vo pole kudriavaia stoiala
vo pol-yə' kōō-dryä' vä-yä stä-yä' lä
In the meadow stood a leafy birch tree

Liu, liu, liuli, stoiala.
lyōō lyōō lyōō' lē stä-yä' lä
Loo, loo, loo loo loo loo loo.

"The Birch Tree" uses five pitches from the **E minor scale.**

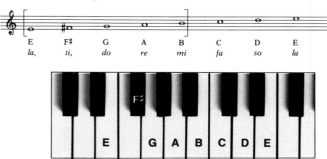

F♯ (**F-sharp**) is the black key to the right of F. A sharp *raises* a pitch one half step.

- Study the melody of "The Birch Tree." It is based on a minor scale.

The melody of "The Birch Tree" can be changed to major. This is the E major scale.

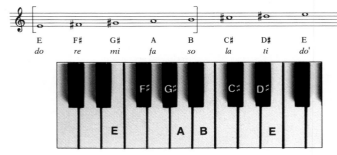

Here is the melody of "The Birch Tree" in major.
Which of the five pitches is changed to create the difference between minor and major? G is changed to G-sharp

105

**2. Introduce minor and major.** Have the students:
- Identify the first five pitches of the E minor scale used in "The Birch Tree." (E F-sharp G A B)
- Discuss the sharp symbol and its function.
- Practice playing the five pitches on keyboard instruments or bells.
- Play "The Birch Tree" on bells or keyboard.
- Listen to "The Birch Tree" played in major modality. (You or a student can play it for the class.)
- Play "The Birch Tree" in minor and major on keyboard instruments or bells.
- Identify which of the first five pitches of the scale is changed to create the difference between major and minor.

# LESSON 4

**3. Introduce instrumental tone color and dynamics in the excerpt from Tchaikovsky's Symphony No. 4.** Have the students:

• Listen to the excerpt from Tchaikovsky's Symphony No. 4 with call numbers. When numbers 1-4 are called, write on a sheet of paper which family of orchestral instruments plays ''The Birch Tree'' theme and the dynamic level they hear. (You may wish to use Copying Master 4-3: Listening Map at this time.)

1. woodwinds (oboe and bassoon) *p*
2. woodwinds (entire woodwind section) *p*
3. brass (French horns) *f*
4. brass (trombones) *f*

• Discuss how Tchaikovsky used tone color and dynamics to create variety in this composition. (He states the theme in contrasting tone colors and dynamic levels. The theme is also presented in contrasting registers from high to low.)

CD2:36● Listen to the way Tchaikovsky uses "The Birch Tree" in the fourth movement of his Symphony No. 4. When each number is called, identify the instruments that play this theme and the dynamics you hear.

*See Teaching the Lesson.*

 Symphony No. 4, Fourth Movement (excerpt), by Peter Ilyich Tchaikovsky

How does Tchaikovsky use tone color and dynamics to create variety?

Theme is stated in contrasting tone colors and dynamics, and high and low registers.

The beauty of nature inspired *The Birches*, by the American artist Neil Welliver.

106

---

# E X T E N S I O N

## SPECIAL LEARNERS

If a class includes mainstreamed students who have difficulty with writing (memory, spelling, motor movement), prepare both an overhead transparency and individual student copies of Copying Master 4-3: Listening Map. When students are directed to listen to the excerpt from Tchaikovsky's Symphony No. 4, give students some time to respond and then circle the correct answers on the overhead. This will enable exceptional learners to receive the necessary immediate feedback on their response.

## PETER ILYICH TCHAIKOVSKY

Peter Ilyich Tchaikovsky

Peter Ilyich Tchaikovsky (1840–1893) was a world-famous Russian composer. He studied at the St. Petersburg (now Leningrad) Conservatory and was, in fact, the first Russian composer to have systematic musical training in Russia. He was teaching music at the Moscow Conservatory when the wealthy widow Nadezhda von Meck (nä-dezh′ dä vän mek) asked him to write some music for her. She admired his music and agreed to guarantee him an income so that he could concentrate on composing. They wrote letters to each other for many years, although they never met.

Tchaikovsky became famous as a composer of ballets, including *Swan Lake*, *The Nutcracker*, and *The Sleeping Beauty*. He also wrote chamber music, operas, songs, and six symphonies. Tchaikovsky was a master at writing for the orchestra and combined instrumental tone colors for unusual effects. He was proud of his national heritage and often used Russian folk tunes, such as "The Birch Tree," as themes in his music.

Tchaikovsky traveled a great deal, and he went to New York City to conduct at Carnegie Hall when it opened in 1891.

A scene from *The Sleeping Beauty*, in a production by the American Ballet Theater

**4. Introduce background information on Tchaikovsky.** Have the students discuss the information on Tchaikovsky. You may wish to use the following items as a basis for extended discussion.

1. It is not uncommon for a famous composer to have a benefactor. The wealthy widow Nadezhda von Meck guaranteed Tchaikovsky an annual income so that he would not have to worry about money and could direct all of his creative energies to composing. Discuss the pros and cons of this type of arrangement. What ground rules should be determined in advance? (The amount of income should be decided; perhaps the composer should have to submit a certain number of works each year.)

2. Composers sometimes use folk melodies as themes in larger compositions. Why do they use folk tunes instead of melodies they wrote themselves? (nationalistic pride; also, listeners will identify with the music) Name other composers besides Tchaikovsky who used famous folk melodies in their music. (Copland, *Appalachian Spring*; Gould, *American Salute*; Ives, *Variations on "America"*)

## CURRICULUM CONNECTION: SOCIAL STUDIES

**Travel**—When Tchaikovsky visited New York in 1891, travel was quite hard. He went overland from St. Petersburg to Batum on the Black Sea (one thousand miles); sailed through the Bosphorus, the Aegean Sea, around the tip of Greece, through the Adriatic Sea to Trieste, Italy (fifteen hundred miles); took a train to Le Havre on the French coast (another several hundred miles). The voyage from Le Havre to New York was three thousand miles; Tchaikovsky would have seen the new Statue of Liberty in New York Harbor when he arrived. Students may wish to compare his trip with travel today.

# LESSON 4

**5. Introduce minor and major tonalities.** Have the students:
• Listen to a portion (the first 45 seconds) of Rondo "alla Turca" and determine if it begins in major or minor. (minor)
• Perform the body percussion to the minor and major sections of the composition. The order is: m, M, m, M, m—M, m, M, m, M, m, M—m, M, m, M—M.
• Listen to the opening portion of "While My Guitar Gently Weeps" to determine if the song begins in major or minor. (minor) As they listen to the entire song, perform the body percussion to the major and minor sections. The order is: m (intro), m, M, m, m, M, m (coda).

## Major and Minor?

CD2:37–38
Mozart's Rondo "alla Turca" has melodies in major and minor.

• Listen to the opening theme. Decide if the music begins in major or minor. Pat the steady beat as you listen when the music is in minor. Snap your fingers on the steady beat when the music is in major.

 Rondo "alla Turca" (toor' ka) by Wolfgang Amadeus Mozart (volf' gäng ä-mä-dā' oos mōt' särt)

In "While My Guitar Gently Weeps," you will hear changes from minor to major.

• Listen to the opening section and decide if the music begins in minor or major. As you listen, pat the strong beat when you hear minor and snap your fingers when you hear major.

"While My Guitar Gently Weeps," by George Harrison

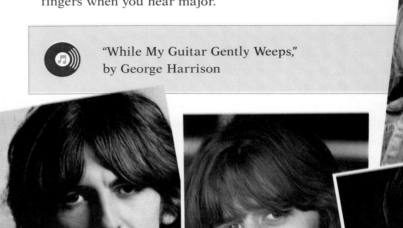

The Beatles:

John Lennon

George Harrison

Ringo Starr

Paul McCartney

108

## THE COMPOSER
**Wolfgang Amadeus Mozart** (1756–1791)—was born in Salzburg, Austria. His great talent was evident very early; his father took him and his older sister Nannerl on tours all over Europe. Mozart's father, an excellent musician, gave Wolfgang solid musical training. He also studied with Johann Christian Bach. In 1781 Mozart settled in Vienna. He wrote operas, symphonies, chamber music, piano music, sacred music, and many other works, all unsurpassed in melodic beauty and expressiveness. The Rondo "alla Turca" (in the Turkish style) is the last movement of his Piano Sonata in A major, K. 331.

You can play this melodic accompaniment to "While My Guitar Gently Weeps" on recorder or bells.

## Melodic Accompaniment to "While My Guitar Gently Weeps"

109

**6. Introduce the melodic accompaniment to "While My Guitar Gently Weeps."** Have the students:
• Practice the rhythms.
• Read and play the melodic accompaniment.

## 3 APPRAISAL

The students should be able to:
1. Listen to the first five pitches of several parallel major and minor scales and signal with eyes closed that the third pitch is higher in major and lower in minor.
2. Signal major and minor sections in Rondo "alla Turca" and "While My Guitar Gently Weeps."
3. Identify the melodic contour of "The Birch Tree" by using appropriate arm levels and, with eyes closed, signal the numbers of the phrases that are alike (1 and 2; 3 and 4).
4. Verbally identify orchestral tone color and dynamics in an excerpt from the fourth movement of Tchaikovsky's Symphony No. 4.

## MORE MUSIC TEACHING IDEAS

Have the students:
1. Choose eight to ten currently popular songs and bring recordings to class. Listen and decide which songs are based on the major scale or the minor scale, or both.
2. Form a circle for the Circle Ball Game. Listen to Rondo "alla Turca" or "While My Guitar Gently Weeps." Pass a tennis ball to the right on the strong beat when the music is in minor; pass the tennis ball to the left when the music is in major.

## THE COMPOSER

**George Harrison**—lead guitarist of the Beatles, was born in Liverpool, England, in 1943. Like his fellow Beatles, he is a self-taught musician. Although John Lennon and Paul McCartney wrote most Beatles songs, Harrison influenced their sound. He studied the Indian sitar with Ravi Shankar and played it in his songs. Probably his most famous song for the Beatles is "Something" (1969). After the group broke up in 1970, he pursued his own career. He produced the benefit concerts for Bangladesh in 1971, paving the way for the Live Aid and Farm Aid concerts of the 1980s.

# REVIEW AND EVALUATION

## JUST CHECKING

### Objective
To review and test the skills and concepts taught in Unit 4

### Materials
Recordings: Just Checking Unit 4
            Unit 4 Evaluation (questions 3–12)
            *For Extra Credit* recordings (optional)
Bells or keyboard instruments
Copying Master 4-4 (optional)
Evaluation Unit 4 Copying Master

## TEACHING THE LESSON

**Review the skills and concepts taught in Unit 4.** Have the students:
• Follow the recorded review with pages 110 and 111; perform the activities, and answer the questions.
• Review their answers.
(You may wish to use Copying Master 4-4 at this time.)

## JUST CHECKING

See how much you remember.

1. Listen to the first two phrases of "Ode to Joy." Move your hand up and down to show the contour, or shape, of the melody.

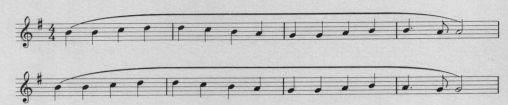

2. Listen to the first section of "Weekend Relief" and show the direction of the melody with your hand.

3. "Weekend Relief" is based on the:    a
     a. major scale     b. minor scale

4. Show the phrase structure of "The Birch Tree" by moving your hands in an arc from left to right. How many phrases does the song have? four

5. "The Birch Tree" is based on the:   b
     a. major scale              b. minor scale

6. Listen to these two different melodies. In which example are the pitches adjacent to each other (in stepwise motion)? Which example has skips between the pitches of the melody? first; second

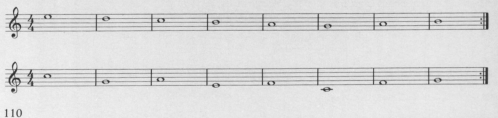

110

7. Listen to these four selections and decide if they are based on a major or minor scale. major; minor; minor; major

8. Play the following melodies on bells or keyboard.

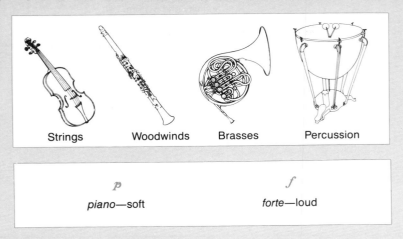

Which melody is based on a major scale? A minor scale? Change the minor example to make it major. (You will need to change only one note.) 1; 2; add C-sharp

9. Listen and identify the instrument families and dynamics you hear in this excerpt from the fourth movement of Symphony No. 4 by Tchaikovsky. brasses, strings, woodwinds; *forte*

| Strings | Woodwinds | Brasses | Percussion |

*p*            *f*

*piano*—soft       *forte*—loud

111

# REVIEW AND EVALUATION

## GIVING THE EVALUATION

Evaluation Unit 4 Copying Master can be found in the *Teacher's Copying Masters* book along with full directions for giving the evaluation and checking the answers.

## FOR EXTRA CREDIT

You may want to have the students answer one of the following questions.

1. Describe at least three ways in which Beethoven creates musical variety in the many repetitions of the "Ode to Joy" theme in the fourth movement of Symphony No. 9. (varies instrumental tone color, adds soloists, chorus, changes texture and dynamics)

2. List at least five musical characteristics that contribute to the expressive quality of "Nine Hundred Miles." (slow tempo, soft dynamic level, dark tone quality, legato, long phrases)

# UNIT 5 • OVERVIEW

| ELEMENTS OF MUSIC | UNIT 5 OBJECTIVES | Lesson 1<br>Focus: Dorian Mode | Lesson 2<br>Focus: Mixolydian Mode |
|---|---|---|---|
| Dynamics | **Listen to and identify changing dynamics** | Perform accents | Perform a composition with changing dynamics<br>Perform a *crescendo*<br>Identify dynamics |
| Tone Color | **Perform instrumental accompaniments**<br>Listen to early blues ensemble, synthesizer, folk instruments | Perform ostinati on Orff instruments<br>Sing with more resonance | Hear French horn<br>Perform an accompaniment on Orff instruments |
| Tempo | Distinguish and perform slow and fast tempi | | Perform a song in a fast tempo |
| Duration/ Rhythm | Perform syncopated rhythm pattern<br>**Perform rhythmic ostinato**<br>**Identify and perform legato and staccato articulation** | Perform body percussion<br>Perform ostinato accompaniment<br>Listen to and perform syncopation and rhythmic pattern<br>Discuss and perform *legato/staccato* | Perform body percussion ostinato<br>Listen to, identify, and clap accented notes<br>Perform instrumental accompaniment |
| Pitch | Create melodic patterns<br>**Identify and perform Dorian and Mixolydian modes**<br>**Identify blues scale, major, minor, atonal, tonal music**<br>Follow melodic sequence and melodic contour | Listen to, identify, and perform composition in Dorian mode<br>Create ostinati for Orff instruments<br>Create an accompaniment in Dorian mode | Listen to, identify, and perform Mixolydian mode<br>Identify repeated melodic patterns<br>Identify and perform flat<br>Identify melodic contour<br>Create melodies in Mixolydian mode |
| Texture | **Listen to, identify, and perform I, IV, V chords and roots**<br>**Identify and perform homophonic texture**<br>Perform thin and thick textures | Sing in two parts | |
| Form | Perform music in AB form<br>**Perform twelve-bar blues** | Perform a nonimitative polyphonic form | |
| Style | Listen to and perform Spanish folk music, blues, American folk song<br>Accompany film music | | Perform a traditional Spanish folk song<br>Listen to 20th-century English music |
| Reading | | Read ♫, ♩, 𝅗𝅥, 𝅝, 𝄆 𝄇 in $\frac{4}{4}$<br>Read articulation marks | Read ♫, ♩, 𝅗𝅥, 𝅗𝅥., 𝄼, *p*, *f*, *ff*, tie, accent, B-flat, $\frac{3}{4}$<br>C major and Mixolydian modes |

## PURPOSE Unit 5: Harmony

This unit focuses on harmony. The students will identify and perform melodic patterns and songs in the Dorian and Mixolydian modes. The students will identify and perform the I, IV, V chords in a musical selection. The unit will also introduce the blues scale. The students will perform a song in the blues style with the twelve-bar blues harmonic progression. Unit 5 also introduces and compares tonality to atonality.

## SUGGESTED TIME FRAME

| February | | | | March | | | |
|---|---|---|---|---|---|---|---|
| | | | | | | | |

## FOCUS

- Dorian and Mixolydian modes
- Recognition of I, IV, V chords
- Blues scale
- Tonality/atonality

| **Lesson 3**<br>Focus: Recognition of I, IV, and V Chords | **Lesson 4**<br>Focus: The Blues Scale | **Lesson 5**<br>Focus: Tonality and Atonality |
|---|---|---|
| | | |
| Listen to and identify change of tone color<br>Hear American folk instruments | Hear contrasting tone color (vocal and instrumental)<br>Listen to and define blues<br>Listen to and identify instruments | Perform harmonic accompaniment on bells<br>Hear synthesizer |
| | | Perform slow tempo |
| | Experience syncopation | Perform body movements showing the harmonic organization of a composition<br>Listen to, identify, and perform rhythmic patterns |
| Identify key tone or home tone<br>Identify the roots of chords | Listen to, identify, and perform blues scale<br>Read and perform twelve-bar blues harmonic progression<br>Analyze difference between blues and major scale<br>Perform chord roots from song<br><br>Improvise a blues melody<br>Perform a melody with the twelve-bar blues | Compare tonality with atonality<br>Perform, identify, and discuss tonal center<br>Identify and perform harmonic changes<br>Listen to an atonal composition<br>Identify atonal music |
| Experience and perform homophonic texture<br>Listen to, identify, and perform I, IV, V chords in harmonic accompaniment<br>Identify and perform chord changes on bells or keyboard<br><br>Perform songs with I, IV, and V | Perform homophonic texture<br>Perform I, IV, V chords | Perform song with I, iii, IV, V chords |
| | Perform twelve-bar blues progression | Listen to an extended two-part form |
| Identify and discuss folk music and instruments<br>Discuss 19th-century American folk culture | Listen to, perform, and discuss blues | Listen to and discuss film music |
| Read chord symbols I, IV, V (tonic, subdominant, dominant), and roots<br>Follow listening map; Read in the key of G major | Read blues scale, major scale,<br>chord symbols I, IV, V, natural ♮, flat ♭ | Read ♩ , ♩. , ♩· , o , ‖: :‖ in 4/4 ;<br>*Dal Segno al Coda*, chord symbols I, iii, IV, V |

# TECHNOLOGY

## MUSIC WITH *MIDI*

MIDI technology allows students to manipulate musical elements and make musical decisions.

- Lesson 1, page 114: Perform/Improvise in **Dorian**
- Lesson 2, page 116: Perform/Improvise in **Mixolydian**
- Lesson 3, page 120: Create a **Rondo:** *"The Boatman's Dance"; "Tom Dooley"*
- Lesson 4, page 126: Perform/Improvise with the **Twelve-Bar Blues**

## VIDEO RESOURCES

Use video resources to reinforce, extend, and enrich learning in this unit.

UNIT **5**

HARMONY

# LESSON 1

**Focus: Dorian Mode**

## Objectives
To identify and sing melodic patterns in the Dorian mode
To create an ostinato accompaniment using three pitches of the Dorian mode
To identify and perform legato and staccato

## Materials
Recordings: "Sing Hosanna" (part 1)
"Sing Hosanna" (part 2)
"Sing Hosanna" (parts 1 and 2)
"Sing Hosanna" (performance mix)
"Sing Hosanna" (Orff accompaniment)
Orff instruments, bells, or keyboards

## Vocabulary
Legato, staccato, Dorian mode

### 1 SETTING THE STAGE
Tell the students that they will be learning about a new kind of scale.

Wassily Kandinsky, HERMITAGE, Leningrad

July Hay, Thomas Hart Benton, THE METROPOLITAN MUSEUM OF ART, NY, Acc. No. 43.159.1

113

## THE ARTISTS
**Wassily Kandinsky** (vä-si′ lē kan-din′ skē) (1866–1944)—was a Russian painter who also lived in Germany. He thought of painting as a form of personal expression and did not think he had to show recognizable things or people. His work showed the influence of Russian folk art and Fauvism, a style full of vibrant color and bold distortions. Some of Kandinsky's paintings, such as the one shown here, are richly colored and use free forms and spontaneous lines.

**Thomas Hart Benton** (1889–1975)—was an American painter, printmaker, illustrator, teacher, and author. Known for his dramatic murals, he painted the farmers and mountain people of the Midwest and South.

# LESSON 1

## 2 TEACHING THE LESSON

**1. Introduce Part 1 of "Sing Hosanna."**
Have the students:
• Perform the body ostinato as they listen to Part 1 of "Sing Hosanna."
• Perform the body ostinato as they sing Part 1.
• Identify Part 1 of song as sounding more like minor than major.

**2. Introduce legato and staccato articulations in "Sing Hosanna."** Have the students:
• Listen to Part 2 of "Sing Hosanna." (You may wish to have students move their hands in an arc on each phrase.)
• Sing Part 2 of "Sing Hosanna," focusing on the questions. (Part 2 sounds smooth and connected; Part 1 sounds detached and crisp.)
• Discuss and define *legato* and *staccato*.
• Perform Parts 1 and 2 of "Sing Hosanna," emphasizing legato and staccato qualities. (Changing voices may sing Part 2.)

# DORIAN MODE

Key: Dorian mode on D     Starting Pitch: D     Scale Tones: *so, la, ti, do re mi fi so la*

## A New Kind of Sound

• Listen to "Sing Hosanna" and clap this ostinato.

• Clap the ostinato as you sing Part 1 of "Sing Hosanna."

### Sing Hosanna

Part 1     Piano Accompaniment on page PA 28     M. J.

Sing Ho-san-na come sing with joy!_ Sing Ho-san-na in the high-est!_

Sing Ho-san-na come sing with joy!_ Sing Ho-san-na in the high-est!_

Now is the time to sing. Lift up your voice Lift up your voice now in song!

• Decide if the music sounds more like major or minor.  minor

Part 2  *mf*

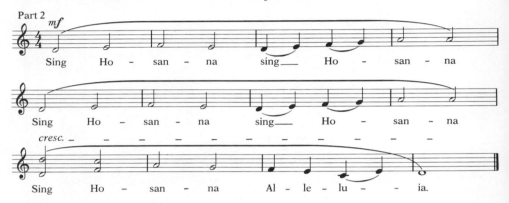

Sing Ho – san – na sing_ Ho – san – na

Sing Ho – san – na sing_ Ho – san – na

*cresc.*

Sing Ho – san – na Al – le – lu – – ia.

• Sing Part 2 of "Sing Hosanna" and compare it with Part 1.
Which part sounds smooth and connected? Part 2
Which part sounds detached and crisp? Part 1
When music sounds smooth, it is said to be performed **legato**
(le-gä′ tō). Music that sounds detached and crisp is said to be performed **staccato** (stä-kä′ tō). Notes to be played or sung staccato are written this way:

• Sing Parts 1 and 2 separately, then together. Emphasize the staccato and legato qualities.

114

## E X T E N S I O N

### VOCAL DEVELOPMENT
Have the students:
• Drop the jaw on the word *Hosanna.* (This technique will produce a more resonant tone quality.)
• Sing Part 1 of "Sing Hosanna," substituting the syllable *hing* for each word of the text to achieve a separated or *marcato* singing style.

# Dorian Mode

The melodies of "Sing Hosanna" are based on a scale using all the white keys of the keyboard from D to D. This scale is called the **Dorian mode** (dô′ rē-ən).

CD2:66

The following ostinati use pitches from the Dorian mode.
- Play these ostinati as an accompaniment to "Sing Hosanna."

### Accompaniment to "Sing Hosanna"

Arr. J.K.

**CHALLENGE** Create your own ostinati by using any three pitches from the Dorian mode. Use word rhythms from Part 1 of "Sing Hosanna."

115

**3. Introduce the Dorian mode.** Have the students:
- Discuss Dorian mode.
- Play the Dorian mode on bells or keyboard.

**4. Introduce the ostinato accompaniment for "Sing Hosanna."** Have the students:
- Practice each rhythm by pat-slide-slide-sliding the whole notes, pat-sliding the half notes, patting the quarter notes, and clapping the eighth notes.
- Transfer the rhythm patterns to barred instruments.

### Reinforcing the Lesson

Create ostinati for "Sing Hosanna." Have the students:
- Select any three pitches from the Dorian mode.
- Perform the three selected pitches with rhythm patterns found in Part 1 of the song.

### 3 APPRAISAL

The students should be able to:
1. Sing "Sing Hosanna" with melodic and rhythmic accuracy and verbally identify the mode as Dorian.
2. Perform a notated ostinato accompaniment to "Sing Hosanna" with melodic and rhythmic accuracy.
3. Create and perform an ostinato accompaniment on barred or keyboard instruments, using selected pitches from the Dorian mode.
4. Verbally define *legato* and *staccato* and vocally perform legato and staccato articulation in "Sing Hosanna."

### MORE MUSIC TEACHING IDEAS

Have the students improvise an accompaniment by using two to five pitches from the Dorian mode to add to Part 2 of "Sing Hosanna." Use any of the word rhythms found in Part 2.

# LESSON 2

**Focus: Mixolydian Mode**

**Objectives**
To sing and identify a song in Mixolydian mode
To compare the Mixolydian mode with the C major scale

**Materials**
Recordings: "Pampanitos Verdes"
"Pampanitos Verdes" (performance mix)
Prologue from *Serenade*
"Weekend Relief"

Bells or keyboard
Copying Masters 5-1 and 5-2 (optional)

**Vocabulary**
Fortissimo, Mixolydian mode, flat

## 1 SETTING THE STAGE

Tell the students they will be learning a song in Spanish.

## 2 TEACHING THE LESSON

**1. Introduce "Pampanitos Verdes."**
Have the students:
• Perform the body ostinato in a circular motion as they listen to "Pampanitos Verdes."
• Listen again and identify the repeated melodic patterns. (mm. 1–2, 4–5, 10–11, 16–17; 7–8, 13–14)
• Sing "Pampanitos Verdes" in Spanish.
• Discuss the translation.
• Discuss the information on *fortissimo*.

# MIXOLYDIAN MODE
Key: Mixolydian mode on C    Starting Pitch: G    Scale Tones: *do re mi fa so la ta do'*

## A Song from Spain

"Pampanitos Verdes" (päm-pä-nē'tōs ver'dās) is a humorous Spanish festival song about people sharing gifts.

• Perform this body ostinato in a circular motion as you listen to "Pampanitos Verdes."

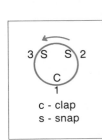

c - clap
s - snap

• Listen again to "Pampanitos Verdes" and find the repeated melodic patterns.   mm. 1–2, 4–5, 10–11, 16–17; 7–8, 13–14
• Sing the song in Spanish.

### Pampanitos Verdes

Piano Accompaniment on page PA 30

Traditional Spanish Carol
Arr. M.G.

Ya     vie-ne la     vie-ja,___        Con  el  a–gui - nal - do.___

Le     pa–re–ce     mu–cho,___        Le    vie–ne qui - tan-do.___

Le     pa–re–ce     mu–cho,___        Le    vie–ne qui - tan -do. Pam-pa–ni–tos

ver-des, Yho-jas de  li -món,  ¡La vir -gen Ma - ri - a, Ma-dre del Se - ñor!

The symbol *ff* stands for **fortissimo** (fōr-ti' sē-mō), "very loud."

# EXTENSION

## SPECIAL LEARNERS

If your class includes mainstreamed students who read below grade level, prepare an overhead transparency of the Spanish text for "Pampanitos Verdes." Separation of text and notation will allow these students to concentrate on the unfamiliar language. The inclusion of the transparency in the lesson will enable you to direct students visually to the correct phrase of the song as they are listening and singing.

## PRONUNCIATION

Ya viene    la vieja
yä vye' ne  lä vye' hä
Here comes the old woman

Con el aguinaldo,
cōn el a-gē-näl' dō
With the bonus.

Le parece     mucho,
le pä-re' se   mōō' chō
It seems like a lot to her [i.e., too much to give away],

Le viene    quitando.
le vye' ne   kē-tän' dō
She keeps it for herself

Pampanitos      verdes,
päm-pä-nē' tōs ver' des
Little green vine leaves,

Y hojas de limón,
ē ō' häs de lē-mōn'
And lemon leaves,

¡La virgen María,
lä vēr' hen mä-rē' ä
Virgin Mary,

Madre del Señor!
mä' dre del sen-yôr'
Mother of the Lord!

*Alt:*
Cantaremos alegres
kän-tä-re' mos ä-leg' res
We happily sing

esta canción.
es' tä kän-syōn'
this song.

- Clap only where the accent (>) appears as you listen to the song.
- Sing the song and clap the accents.
- Follow the dynamic markings by making:

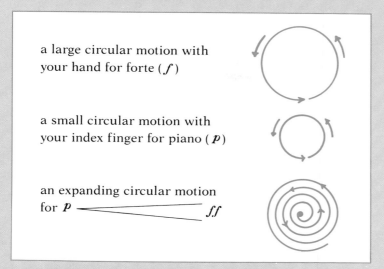

a large circular motion with your hand for forte ($f$)

a small circular motion with your index finger for piano ($p$)

an expanding circular motion for $p$ —————— $f\!f$

"Pampanitos Verdes" is based on a scale that is called the **Mixolydian mode**. To play the B♭ (B-flat) in this mode, find the black key *below* (to the left of) B. A flat *lowers* a pitch one half step.

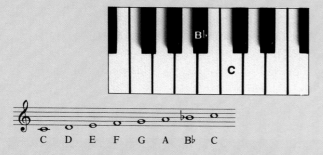

C  D  E  F  G  A  B♭  C

When you performed Pachelbel's Canon you used the C major scale.
page 101

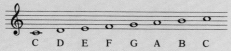

C  D  E  F  G  A  B  C

- Compare the Mixolydian mode with the C major scale. one pitch is different
- Play both the C major scale and the Mixolydian mode on keyboard or bells to help you identify the changed pitch. (B-flat)

117

# LESSON 2

**2. Analyze the accents and dynamic organization of "Pampanitos Verdes."**
Have the students:
- Clap the accents as they sing the song.
- Indicate the dynamics through movements shown. (You may wish to use Copying Master 5-1 at this time. If your class is more advanced, you may wish to use Copying Master 5-2, which has more advanced Orff parts.)

**3. Introduce the Mixolydian mode.**
Have the students:
- Listen and decide whether the Mixolydian mode sounds more like a major or a minor scale. (major) ("Pampanitos Verdes" is in Mixolydian mode on C. You may choose to identify Mixolydian mode as all of the white keys from G to G.)
- Discuss the information on the flat symbol.
- Compare the Mixolydian mode with the C major scale and identify which pitch is changed.
- Perform the Mixolydian mode and the C major scale on bells or keyboard to assist in identifying changed pitch.

## CURRICULUM CONNECTION: SOCIAL STUDIES

In Spain, the people celebrate Christmas by singing and dancing in the streets after midnight mass. Small Nativity scenes are displayed in homes and churches. According to legend, on the evening of January 5th the wise men of the Christmas story will arrive with gifts. Children put their shoes on a window or balcony, hoping that they will be filled with gifts.

# LESSON 2

**4. Introduce the use of the Mixolydian mode by Benjamin Britten in the Prologue to his** *Serenade.* **Have the students:**

• Listen to the Prologue from the *Serenade.*
• Use their hands to indicate the melodic contour of the Prologue.
• Identify the measures that contain the lowered seventh pitch of the Mixolydian mode. (mm. 7, 9)

## Another Mixolydian Melody

CD3:1 • Listen to the way Benjamin Britten uses the Mixolydian mode in the Prologue (introduction) of his *Serenade.*

 Prologue from *Serenade* by Benjamin Britten

• Follow the melodic contour of the theme with your hand as you listen.

### Serenade
#### Prologue

Benjamin Britten

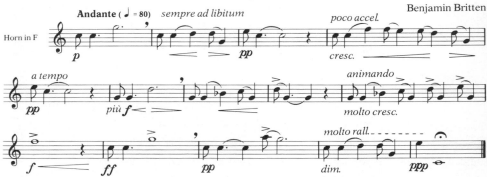

© Copyright 1944 by Hawkes & Son (London) Ltd.; Renewed 1981. Reprinted by permission of Boosey & Hawkes, Inc.

• Look back at the way the Mixolydian mode is notated. page 117
• Find the changed pitch of the Mixolydian mode. (B-flat)
• Find the same changed pitch in the score above. This pitch can also be called a *lowered* 7th in the Mixolydian mode.

Musicians rehearsing at the Aldeburgh Festival, a yearly music festival founded by Benjamin Britten

# LESSON 2

• Discuss information on Benjamin Britten.

### Reinforcing the Lesson
Review "Weekend Relief," pages 98–99, and compare the C major scale to the Mixolydian mode.

## 3 APPRAISAL
The students should be able to:
1. Identify the differences between the Mixolydian mode and the major scale, namely, that the seventh pitch in Mixolydian is lower than it is in a major scale that begins on the same pitch.
2. Sing "Pampanitos Verdes" with rhythmic and melodic accuracy and identify the mode as Mixolydian.

## BENJAMIN BRITTEN

Benjamin Britten (1913–1976), English composer, began writing music as a child and had completed many works before he was fourteen. Later in life he wrote a great deal of music for young people, including *The Young Person's Guide to the Orchestra*. This work introduces the orchestral instruments through variations on a theme by Henry Purcell. Some of Britten's other works for children are *Let's Make an Opera* and *Noye's Fludde* ("Noah's Flood"), which includes parts for a children's orchestra and chorus. for Purcell, see p. 98

Britten was a master of vocal music of all kinds, including operas, works for chorus, and songs. Probably his most famous choral work is *A Ceremony of Carols*, a setting of medieval Christmas carols with harp accompaniment.

The *Serenade* for tenor voice, French horn, and strings was composed in 1943. It opens with a beautiful horn solo.

119

## MORE MUSIC TEACHING IDEAS
Have the students create and perform melodies in Mixolydian mode.

# LESSON 3

**Focus: Recognition of I, IV, and V Chords**

**Objective**
To identify and perform the I, IV, and V chords and their roots

**Materials**
Recordings: "The Boatman's Dance"
"The Boatman's Dance"
(performed by Allegra)
"Still Reflections"
"Studio 21"
"Kum Ba Yah" (optional)
"Tom Dooley" (optional)
"When the Saints Go Marching In" (optional)
Bells or keyboard

**Vocabulary**
Dulcimer, spoons, jaw harp, tonic, key tone, dominant, subdominant, root

## 1 SETTING THE STAGE

Have the students discuss the information on "The Boatman's Dance."

## 2 TEACHING THE LESSON

**1. Introduce "The Boatman's Dance."**
Have the students sing the refrain to "The Boatman's Dance."

---

## AN AMERICAN WORK SONG

During the nineteenth century, America's rivers and canals were major highways of freight and passenger traffic. The busy waterways inspired many songs and poems. "The Boatman's Dance" is a happy song about the joys of working on a boat "floating down the river, the Ohio."

• Sing the refrain to "The Boatman's Dance."

**The Boatman's Dance**

120

---

# E X T E N S I O N

## Folk Instruments

When you listen to "The Boatman's Dance," you will hear these folk instruments.

The **dulcimer** is one of the oldest known instruments. It is mentioned in the Bible and is found all over the world. Strings are stretched across the body of the instrument, which serves as a sound board. The strings may be plucked or struck with hammers. The Appalachian dulcimer was adapted from similar European instruments. It is still popular in some areas of the country.

Musicians not only improvise music, but sometimes improvise instruments as well. Any objects that make a sound when struck can be used as percussion instruments—gourds, wooden blocks, bones, even **spoons.** Playing the spoons has become a folk tradition for accompanying singing and dancing. The player holds two spoons with the thumb and first two fingers so that the bowls of the spoons are back to back. The spoons are then shaken or struck.

The **jaw harp** is a very ancient instrument. It probably originated in Southeast Asia, but now is found widely throughout the world. It was brought to Europe during the Middle Ages and later found its way to America. The instrument consists of a small curved wood or metal frame that is held between the teeth. The elastic metal strip is stretched across the frame and plucked with the fingers. The vibrations are amplified by the mouth, and melodies can be produced.

Dulcimer

Spoons

Jaw harp

**2. Introduce the information on folk instruments.** Have the students discuss the information on folk instruments.

### COOPERATIVE LEARNING

Have the students form cooperative groups of four. Assign the roles of reader and recorder in each group. The reader should read pupil page 121 out loud for the group. After the material has been read, each group member should write down three questions about the information to share with the group. The group should then choose at least four of the best questions (being sure to include one from each group member). The recorder should write down all the questions. You may want to have one group quiz another group or the entire class.

# LESSON 3

**3. Introduce the map of "The Boatman's Dance."** Have the students:
- Listen to "The Boatman's Dance."
- Identify each change of tone color and section by placing their index fingers on the pictures that represent a change of tone color or section on the river map.
- Identify how many times they heard the refrain sung. (four times)

As you listen to the folk group Allegra perform "The Boatman's Dance," travel down the river with your index finger to follow the musical events.

 "The Boatman's Dance"

How many times did you hear the refrain? four times

122

E X T E N S I O N

## LISTENING

You may wish to use the Listening Map overhead transparency to help guide the students through the listening selection.

# A Closer Look at Chords

Remember that a chord consists of three or more pitches sounding together. The harmonic accompaniment to "The Boatman's Dance" on page 124 has three chords. They are built on the first (I), fourth (IV), and fifth (V) pitches of the scale.

The I chord is called the **tonic** chord. It is built on the most important tone of the scale, called the **key tone** or home tone. It tends to sound stable.

The tonic chord in "The Boatman's Dance" is the G major chord.
The V chord is called the **dominant** chord. It is built on the fifth pitch of the scale.

Name the dominant chord.  D major
The IV chord is called the **subdominant**.
A melody that ends with the dominant or subdominant chord tends to sound unfinished.

Listen to "Still Reflections."
With which chord does "Still Reflections" end?  I chord
With which chord does "Studio 21" end?  I chord

Show the chord changes by resting your palms on your desk when you hear the I chord. Turn your palms up when you hear the V chord.

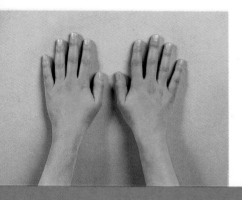
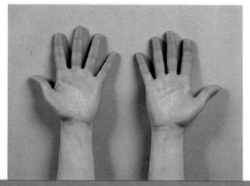

---

# LESSON 3

**4. Introduce the I, IV, and V chords.** Have the students:
• Discuss the definition of a chord.
• Label the three primary chords.
• Listen to "Still Reflections" and show that they can identify tonic and dominant chord changes as indicated. (If students are having difficulty with the small-scale motions in the text, have them move their hands down on the I chord and raise them over their heads on the V chord.)

# LESSON 3

- Listen to "Studio 21" and show that they can identify the tonic, subdominant, and dominant chord changes as indicated. (If students are having difficulty with the small-scale motions in the text, have them stretch out their arms at shoulder level on the IV chord.)
- Listen to "The Boatman's Dance" and show that they can identify the tonic, subdominant, and dominant chord changes during the refrain. (The chord changes begin with the subdominant.)
- Identify and label the root of each chord by pitch name and play the root of each chord of the refrain of "The Boatman's Dance" on bells or keyboard.
- Form three groups. Each group will play one chord on bells or keyboard with the song.
- Identify and label the root of each chord by pitch name and play the root of each chord of "Studio 21" on bells or keyboard.
- Form three groups. Each group will play one chord on bells or keyboard with the recording.

## 3 APPRAISAL

The students should be able to:
1. Listen to the I, IV, and V chords in various orders in several keys and, with eyes closed, identify them using assigned body movements or signals for each chord.
2. Perform from written notation the roots of the I, IV, and V chords in a least two keys (e.g., G and E-flat) on barred instruments or keyboard.
3. Perform from written notation the I, IV, and V chords in root position in at least two different keys (e.g., G and E-flat) on a barred instrument (played as broken chords) or keyboard instrument.

In "Studio 21" you will hear the IV (subdominant) chord, as well as the I and V chords. Put your thumbs up when you hear the IV chord.

- Use all three hand movements to show the I, IV, and V chords as you listen to "Studio 21."

- Listen again to "The Boatman's Dance." Use the three hand movements to show the I, IV, and V chord changes during lines 1 and 3 of the refrain.

The lowest pitch of each of these chords is called the **root**.

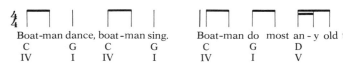

- Find the root tones of the chords above.  I=G, IV=C, V=D

- Play the root of each chord on bells or keyboard as you listen to "The Boatman's Dance."

$\frac{4}{4}$

Boat-man dance, boat-man sing.　Boat-man do most an - y old thing.
C　　G　C　　G　　　C　　G　most D　G
IV　　I　IV　　I　　　IV　　I　　V　I

- Play the root of each of these chords on keyboard or bells as you listen to "Studio 21."

I = E♭, IV = A♭, V = B♭

- Play the chords as you listen to "Studio 21" again.

124

**SPECIAL LEARNERS**

Some mainstreamed students may need a visual cue when asked to identify chord changes. The visual cue may be your doing the suggested movement, or a large set of Roman numerals, or three shapes or colors that can be pointed to on an overhead projector or chalkboard.

# LESSON 3

## Accompaniment to "Studio 21"

J.K.

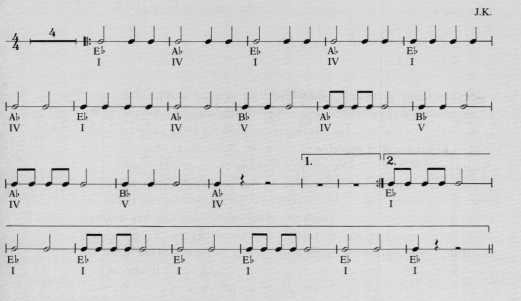

Flatboats carried goods and people during the westward movement in the United States.

*The Jolly Flatboatmen,* George Caleb Bingham

125

## MORE MUSIC TEACHING IDEAS

Have the students perform other selections that use the I, IV, and V chords:
"Kum Ba Yah" (I, IV, and V)
"Tom Dooley" (I and V)
"When the Saints Go Marching In" (I, IV, and V)

## THE ARTIST

**George Caleb Bingham** (kā' leb bing' hem) (1811–1879)—was an American painter who portrayed common people in realistic scenes of everyday life. He carefully painted typical hunters, frontiersmen, and settlers living along the Mississippi and Missouri rivers. In addition, he was active in Missouri state politics.

# LESSON 4

## Focus: The Blues Scale

### Objectives
To identify the characteristics of the blues scale
To perform a song in blues style
To perform a twelve-bar blues harmonic progression

### Materials
Recordings: "Lost Your Head Blues"
"The Walkin' Blues"
"The Twelve-Bar Blues"
Bells or keyboard instruments

### Vocabulary
Blues scale, natural, twelve-bar blues

## 1 SETTING THE STAGE
Tell the students that they will be studying a familiar musical form—the blues.

## 2 TEACHING THE LESSON

**1. Introduce the blues and its historical background.** Have the students:
• Discuss the background information on the blues.

Like ragtime, the blues was a type of music that was created by African Americans. The blues grew mainly from work songs and spirituals. Most blues songs are about loneliness or sadness or lost love, but sometimes the words express a defiant or humorous reaction to trouble.

Unlike many spirituals, which are sung at a fast tempo, the blues generally is sung at a slow tempo. Blues songs began as vocal solos without accompaniment. Instruments were later added.

The blues became popular in the early 1900s. W. C. Handy and Ferdinand ("Jelly Roll") Morton were among the first composers of blues songs. Huddie Ledbetter, also known as "Leadbelly," traveled around the South singing blues songs he heard. During the 1920s phonograph records made the blues more widely known. About this time, Bessie Smith (circa 1894–1937) was known as the "Empress of the Blues." She composed many blues songs, including "Lost Your Head Blues," and she made many recordings with other musicians.

The blues has continued to be popular and was a major influence in the development of rock music.

Blues singer Mamie Smith and the Jazz Hounds

Bessie Smith, 1924

126

# EXTENSION

## THE COMPOSER

**Bessie (Elizabeth) Smith** (1894?–1937)—"Empress of the Blues," was born into extreme poverty, in Chattanooga, Tennessee. In 1912, she joined Fat Chappelle's Rabbit Foot Minstrels, featuring Gertrude "Ma" Rainey. With Rainey as her coach, she developed a style of singing that rapidly brought her fame. In 1923, she made her first recording—"Downhearted Blues" and "Gulf Coast Blues." By 1924, Bessie Smith was one of the highest-paid African American entertainers in the country. She frequently worked with such jazz greats as Louis Armstrong, Fletcher Henderson, and Benny Goodman. Her powerful voice, her natural expressive qualities, and improvisatory abilities combined to make her the greatest blues singer of her time.

• Listen to Bessie Smith sing "Lost Your Head Blues." Identify the instruments you hear in the performance. piano and trumpet

 "Lost Your Head Blues," by Bessie Smith

Many blues songs, such as "Lost Your Head Blues," have a basic form of three phrases, each four measures long. The first two phrases have the same words. The third phrase often rhymes with the first two. There may be a musical conversation between the singer and a solo instrument. The singer will sing a phrase and the instrument will answer. The harmony of the blues is based on a set pattern of chords.

"Lost Your Head Blues" and other blues songs are based on the blues scale. This scale—along with the vocal style, tone color, form, and harmony—give the blues its special quality. The distinctive sound of the blues comes from pitches that have been "bent." These pitches are called blue notes. The blue notes are part of the **blues scale**. These altered pitches are notated with accidentals.

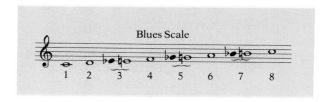

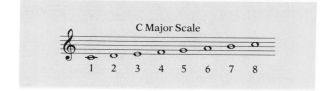

• Compare the blues scale to the C major scale by playing both scales on bells or keyboard.

To play E♭, G♭, and B♭, (E-flat, G-flat, and B-flat) find the black keys to the left of (below) E, G, and B. The symbol ♮ is called a **natural**. It tells you to return to E, G, or B. How are the major scale and the blues scale different? Blues scale has lowered third, fifth, seventh

127

## LESSON 4

• Listen to "Lost Your Head Blues" and identify the instruments heard.
• Read information about the form and harmony of the blues.
**2. Introduce the blues scale.** Have the students:
• Compare the blues scale with the C major scale by playing both scales on bells or keyboard.
• Read information on how to play E-flat, G-flat, and B-flat, and the definition of the natural symbol.
• Identify which pitches are changed in the blues scale.

### COOPERATIVE LEARNING

Place the following pitches from the blues scale on the board.

Have the students work in cooperative groups of four to improvise a blues melody, using the pitches notated on the board. Have each group form two pairs, one to improvise a blues melody and one to play the twelve-bar blues on keyboard or Auto-harp. The part improvising the blues melody should be the predominant part. Both groups should listen to each other's work and discuss the results. You may wish to have the groups switch roles and parts.

# LESSON 4

**3. Introduce "The Walkin' Blues."**
Have the students:
• Listen to "The Walkin' Blues" and learn to sing the song.

## Singing the Blues

CD3:5 "The Walkin' Blues" also is based on the blues scale.

• Learn to sing "The Walkin' Blues."

### The Walkin' Blues

Piano Accompaniment on page PA 32

Words and Music by
Bob Summers

Words and Music by Bob Summers
Copyright © 1982 by Jenson Publications
International Copyright Secured. All Rights Reserved.

128

---

# E X T E N S I O N

## COOPERATIVE LEARNING

Have the students work in cooperative groups of three to find examples within Unit 5 that have melodies which move by steps, skips, or repeated pitches. Within each group, assign a specific category to each student. The student should find an example within the unit to validate the specific category. Each member of the group will then present an example, providing documentation as to how it fits the assigned category. The validated examples for the entire group should be listed on a sheet of paper, which is signed by all of the group members.

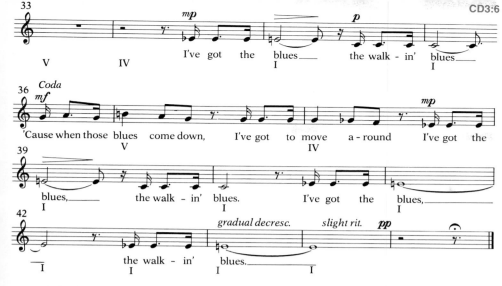

*mp* ... *p*

V      IV         I've got the blues___ the walk - in' blues___
                     I                       I

36 *Coda*    *mf*                                           *mp*

'Cause when those blues come down,   I've got to move a - round   I've got the
               V                        IV

39

blues,___      the walk - in' blues.       I've got the blues,___
I                     I                       I

42                *gradual decresc.*     *slight rit.*    *pp*

I        the walk - in'    blues.___
      I             I           I          I

- Find the lowered third (E♭) and seventh (B♭) pitches of the blues scale in the score of "The Walkin' Blues." mm. 2, 4, 8, 10, 18, 22, 34, 38, 40, 42

Which pitch frequently follows the E♭ ? E-natural

## The Twelve-Bar Blues

You can accompany "The Walkin' Blues" with a chord pattern called the **twelve-bar blues.** (*Bar* is another term for measure.)

### Twelve-Bar Blues Pattern

I   I   I   I   IV   IV   I   I   V   IV   I   I

- Use the same hand motions as you did in "The Boatman's Dance" as you listen to this pattern. pp. 123–124
- Play the root of each chord on keyboard or bells as you sing "The Walkin' Blues." I=C, IV=F, V=G
- Learn to play the chords in the twelve-bar blues. Play this chord pattern as you sing "The Walkin' Blues."

129

# LESSON 4

- Find the lowered third and seventh pitches in the melody line of "The Walkin' Blues." (mm. 2, 4, 8, 10, 18, 22, 34, 38, 40, 42)
- Identify the pitch that frequently follows E-flat. (E-natural)
- Sing "The Walkin' Blues." (Changing voices can sing Blues Repetition 1 or 2 with the entire song.)
**4. Introduce the twelve-bar blues chord pattern.** Have the students:
- Define this chord pattern as the twelve-bar blues.
- Use the hand motions from "The Boatman's Dance" (pp. 123–124) as they listen to "The Twelve-Bar Blues." (If students are having difficulty with the small-scale motions, use the larger ones.)
- Perform the root of each chord as they sing "The Walkin' Blues."
- Learn to play the twelve-bar blues on bells or keyboard with the recording. (Play the pattern twice after the four-measure introduction.)

### Reinforcing the Lesson
Have the students perform the twelve-bar blues as they sing "The Walkin' Blues."

**3 APPRAISAL**

The students should be able to:
1. Define the characteristics of the blues scale as the lowered third, fifth, and seventh pitches added to a major scale.
2. Sing "The Walkin' Blues" with dynamic changes and melodic and rhythmic accuracy.
3. Perform, from notation with chord symbols, a twelve-bar blues pattern consisting of I, IV, and V chords in root position as an accompaniment to "The Walkin' Blues."

**MORE MUSIC TEACHING IDEAS**
Have the students:
1. Improvise a blues melody on C, E-flat, F, G, and B-flat of the blues scale.
2. Perform an improvised melody accompanied by the twelve-bar blues.

**SPECIAL LEARNERS**
A transparency of the twelve-bar blues progression on pupil page 129 should be used to assist mainstreamed learners in playing the roots or entire chords of the progression. Point out each chord change as it fits into the song "The Walkin' Blues."

# LESSON 5

**Focus: Tonality and Atonality**

## Objectives
To identify and perform harmonic relationships with emphasis on tonal center
To identify and perform chord changes
To compare tonality with atonality

## Materials
Recordings: "The Boatman's Dance"
Theme from *Chariots of Fire*
(with call numbers)
*Le marteau sans maître*
Bells or keyboard instruments

## Vocabulary
Tonal center, tonal music, atonal music

### 1 SETTING THE STAGE
Review "The Boatman's Dance" page 120.

### 2 TEACHING THE LESSON
**1. Introduce the rhythm patterns found in the theme from *Chariots of Fire*.** Have the students:
• Clap each rhythm pattern as indicated.
• Perform both rhythm patterns with the recording.

---

# COMBINING HARMONY AND RHYTHM

CD3:7  • Listen to the theme from *Chariots of Fire*.

    Theme from *Chariots of Fire*, by Vangelis (van-je' lis)

The theme from the Academy Award-winning film *Chariots of Fire* is based on two rhythm patterns:

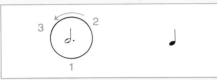

• Clap each rhythm pattern. Show the ♩. by moving your hands in a circular motion. Clap on 1 and think 2 and 3.

• Show duration of the half note in the second pattern by lifting your hand on the half note after you clap it.

clap clap clap (up)  clap clap clap (up)

• Clap rhythm pattern 1 or 2 when you hear numbers 1 or 2 called in the music.

The scenes on these two pages are from the film *Chariots of Fire*.

---

## E X T E N S I O N

### THE COMPOSER

**Vangelis**—is one of the most successful composers today even though he cannot read or write music. He was born in southern Greece in 1943 and started to play the piano by ear when he was four. In the early 1960s, he performed in two successful European rock bands, Aphrodite's Child and Formynx. He moved to Paris in 1968 and started to compose electronic scores for television documentaries and films. The soundtrack to *Chariots of Fire*, written in 1981, was ranked as 1982's best all-instrumental album. Since *Chariots of Fire*, Vangelis has written the scores to films such as *Missing*, *Blade Runner*, and *The Bounty*.

• Identify rhythm patterns 1 and 2 in the harmonic accompaniment.

• Find rhythm patterns 1 and 2 in the harmonic accompaniment.

1. mm. 5, 6, 7, 8, 9, 10, 11, 45, 46, 47;
2. mm. 13–14, 17–18

**Harmonic Accompaniment to**
**Theme from** *Chariots of Fire*

131

# LESSON 5

**2. Introduce the tonic chord.** Have the students:
• Discuss the information on repetition of the tonic chord and its function as the tonal center.
• Show the I chord through movement as indicated with the recording.
• Play the C major chord on bells or keyboard each time it appears in the score.

## Harmonic Base

The chord you heard most often in the theme from *Chariots of Fire* is the I (tonic) chord, or C chord.

Repetition of the I (tonic) chord provides a strong *tonal center*. The **tonal center** serves as the central point for all chords and pitches.

• Listen again to the theme from *Chariots of Fire*. When you hear the I chord, place your palms on your desk.

• Listen again to the theme from *Chariots of Fire*. This time, play the I chord in the harmonic accompaniment to the theme from *Chariots of Fire* on bells or keyboard. The circle ( o ) above the C chord will help you identify when to play the tonic chord (see page 131).

132

## Hearing Chord Changes

The V, IV, and i i i chords in the harmonic accompaniment move away from the tonal center. "Away" chords are marked with an *X*.

- Show that you hear the chord changes and the "away-tonic" chord changes. Turn your palms up when you hear the V chord. Put your thumbs up on other "away" chords. When you hear the tonic chord (I), put your palms on your desk.

These computer images represent the I chord as the tonal center (opposite), and the movement of chords away from the tonal center (above).

133

**3. Introduce the nontonic chords (IV and iii chords).** Have the students:
- Show the nontonic chords through movement as indicated with the recording.
- Form groups and play the accompaniment with the recording, one group playing each chord.

**4. Introduce tonality.** Have the students:
• Discuss the information and the fine art, focal point, and tonal center.
• Identify and label *tonality*.

## Tonality and Atonality

When music has a strong tonal center or pitch focus it is called **tonal music.** It is said to have *tonality*.

Like music, visual art also can have a focal point.

Skyscrapers (#3 panel of the series: "New York Interpreted"), Joseph Stella, THE NEWARK MUSEUM

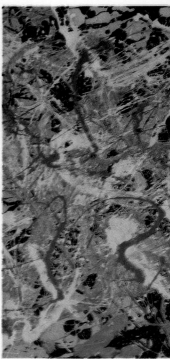

In Joseph Stella's painting *Skyscrapers*, all the lines converge to a central focal point.

134

# E X T E N S I O N

## THE ARTIST

**Joseph Stella** (1880–1946)—was an Italian-born American painter who created paintings of city subjects by combining small areas of color into large swirling patterns. He was fascinated by the noise and motion of New York City's industrialization. His painting *Skyscrapers* shows his interest in modern steel construction, electric lights, and the monumental size of the city.

Music without a strong tonal center or pitch focus is called **atonal music** and is described as having *atonality*. In atonal music, all pitches are equally important. This music does not project a feeling of tonic or pitch focus.

- Listen to *Le marteau sans maître* ("The Hammer without a Master"). It has no strong tonal center.

*Le marteau sans maître* (lə mär-tō′ säN mä′ trə), by Pierre Boulez (pē-är′ bōō-lez′)

Jackson Pollock's *Number 27* has no one central focal point. It is a kind of visual representation of the act of painting.

*Number 27, Jackson Pollock, WHITNEY MUSEUM OF AMERICAN ART, NY*

# LESSON 5

**5. Introduce atonality.** Have the students:
- Discuss the information and the fine art, the absence of a tonal center, and visual focus.
- Listen to *Le marteau sans maître* by Pierre Boulez to hear the absence of a strong tonal center or pitch focus.

## Reinforcing the Lesson

Have the students identify and define *atonality*. (It is important for students to realize that atonal music is not *deficient* because it has no tonal center. Certain twentieth-century composers have chosen to emphasize other aspects of music, such as rhythmic drive, range of dynamics, or sheer vocal or instrumental tone color. You may wish to point out that the energy in the Pollock work is actually its subject.)

## 3 APPRAISAL

The students should be able to:
1. Listen to the I, iii, IV, and V chords in root position and, with eyes closed, signal each time the tonic chord is played.
2. Listen to the theme from *Chariots of Fire* and, with eyes closed, identify the harmonic relationships with palms up for the dominant chords and thumbs up on other "away" chords.
3. Perform on keyboard or barred instruments various patterns of the I, iii, IV, and V chords from a written score with chord symbols. (Each student should play all notes of the chords simultaneously or as a broken chord.)
4. Verbally identify tonal music as having a strong tonal center or pitch focus and atonal music as not having a tonal center or pitch focus.

135

## THE ARTIST

**Jackson Pollock** (pol′lok) (1912–1956)—was an American artist who started a new way of painting. Instead of drawing or planning a painting in the traditional way, he dripped, poured, and splashed paint from all sides onto huge canvases lying on the floor. Since he threw different kinds of paint into motion in all speeds and directions, his paintings, such as *Number 27*, are webs of color that show paint moving and interacting with great freedom.

## THE COMPOSER

**Pierre Boulez**—one of the outstanding musical forces of the twentieth century, was born in Montbrison, France, in 1925. He first studied mathematics and science, then switched to music. In the mid-1950s, Boulez began to promote serial and other experimental forms of music. Later, as the conductor and music director of the New York Philharmonic, he featured works by Schoenberg, Berg, Webern, Varèse, and other modernists. *Le marteau sans maître* ("The Hammer without a Master"), a cantata for alto and six solo instruments, was written in 1955. It is based on poems by René Char, one of the leading poets of the French Resistance.

# REVIEW AND EVALUATION

## JUST CHECKING

### Objective
To review and test the skills and concepts taught in Unit 5

### Materials
Recordings: Just Checking Unit 5 (questions 1–5 and 7)
　　　Theme from *Chariots of Fire*
　　　Unit 5 Evaluation (questions 3–7)
　　　*For Extra Credit* recordings (optional)
Bells or keyboard
Copying Master 5-3 (optional)
Evaluation Unit 5 Copying Master

## TEACHING THE LESSON

**Review the skills and concepts taught in Unit 5.** Have the students:
• Perform the activities and answer the questions on pages 136–137. (For this review, examples for questions 1, 2, 3, 4, 5, and 7 are included in the "Just Checking Unit 5" recording. Have the students answer these questions first. Then have them answer the other questions in the review, using the recordings in the unit where necessary.)
• Review their answers.
(You may wish to use Copying Master 5-3 at this time.)

## JUST CHECKING

See how much you remember.

1. Listen to the following three melodies and identify which melody is based on a mode, a blues scale, or a major scale.
   major; mode; blues

2. Listen to "Still Reflections." Show the chord changes by putting your palms down on your desk when you hear the I chord. Turn your palms up when you hear the V chord.

3. Listen to the following four examples and decide if the music feels detached and crisp (*staccato*) or smooth and connected (*legato*). legato; staccato; legato; legato

4. Listen to the following four examples and decide if the music is tonal or atonal. tonal; atonal; tonal; tonal

5. Show the dynamic contrasts in "Pampanitos Verdes" by making a large circular motion with your hand for forte (*f*) and a small circular motion with your index finger for piano (*p*). Show the crescendo *p*━━*f* by using an expanding circular motion.

a large circular motion with your hand for forte (*f*)

a small circular motion with your index finger for piano (*p*)

an expanding circular motion for *p*━━*ff*

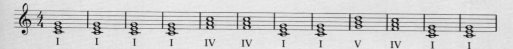

6. Play the twelve-bar blues pattern by playing the roots of the I, IV, and V chords on bells or keyboard.

7. Use three movements to show the I, IV, and V chords as you listen to "Twelve-Bar Blues." Show the chord changes by putting your palms on your desk when you hear the I chord. Turn your palms up when you hear the IV chord. Put your thumbs up when you hear the V chord.

8. Play the C chord or I (tonic) on bells or keyboard to show the strong tonal center in the theme from *Chariots of Fire.*

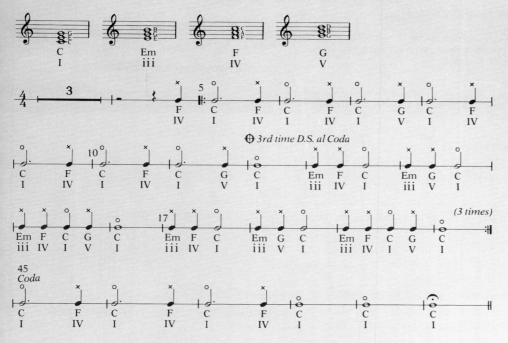

137

## GIVING THE EVALUATION

Evaluation Unit 5 Copying Master can be found in the *Teacher's Copying Masters* book along with full directions for giving the evaluation and checking the answers.

## FOR EXTRA CREDIT

You may want to have the students answer one of the following questions.

1. Identify and describe at least five elements of the blues. (Began among black Americans, from work songs and spirituals, usually express loneliness or sadness, slow tempo, melody based on blues scale, accompanied by twelve-bar blues harmony)

2. Describe music that is tonal and music that is atonal. (In tonal music, one pitch—the tonic—is the most important. In atonal music, all pitches or chords are equally important and do not project a feeling of home base or pitch focus. Both tonal and atonal music have "away" chords. All chords in atonal music are "away" chords. Repeating the tonic chord provides a strong tonal center for tonal music. The most common "away" chords in tonal music are the subdominant and the dominant chords.)

(You may wish to play recordings to refresh students' memories.)

| ELEMENTS OF MUSIC | UNIT 6 OBJECTIVES | Lesson 1<br>Focus: Form—Repetition | Lesson 2<br>Focus: Form—Adding New Ideas to Repetition |
|---|---|---|---|
| Dynamics | **Identify dynamic changes** | | Identify the dynamic scheme of a composition |
| Tone Color | Hear string bass, orchestra, tone color variations<br>**Perform accompaniments on classroom instruments**<br>Perform spoken music | Play guitar, keyboard, Autoharp, or bells | Listen to tone color used for variety |
| Tempo | **Identify *accelerando*, tempo changes** | | Identify, hear, and move to *accelerando*<br>Identify tempo changes |
| Duration/ Rhythm | **Identify repeated patterns**<br>Identify syncopation<br>Hear meter changes, augmentation | Identify, read, and perform repeated rhythm patterns<br><br>Identify visual repetition | Identify and perform melodic rhythm |
| Pitch | **Perform melodic ostinato using G Em C D chords or roots**<br>Identify upper and lower registers | Perform harmonic progression by playing chords or roots<br><br>Play chord pattern with songs | Perform melodic ostinato<br><br>Play motives |
| Texture | Listen to, identify, and perform homophonic and polyphonic textures<br>**Perform homophonic and polyphonic textures** | Listen to and perform ostinati in homophonic texture<br>Perform harmonic ostinato on instruments<br>Play I, vi, IV, V chords | Identify thin and thick textures in orchestral arrangement<br><br>Create a layered sound composition |
| Form | **Identify theme and variations**<br>**Identify subject and episode** | Perform repeated harmonic and rhythmic patterns on instruments | Identify theme repetition |
| Style | Listen to American popular music, romantic style, minimalist style, baroque style in 20th-century orchestration, American nationalistic music, jazz | Perform guitar chords with American popular music | Listen to late romantic orchestral music, minimalist style |
| Reading | | Read chord pattern I, vi, IV, V (G, Em, C, D) | Read ♩♫ in ⁴⁄₄<br>Read ⟨, ⟩, *f*, *p*, grace note, tie |

## PURPOSE Unit 6: Repetition: The Basis of Form

In this unit the students will gain an understanding of how repetition functions as a unifying element of form in music and visual art. The two types of repetition in music that are exemplified are harmonic and rhythmic repetition. The students will identify repetition with imitation in the fugue as well as performing a spoken fugue. The unit discusses how variety and interest can be added to jazz and other styles through variations in tone colors, dynamics, and melody.

## SUGGESTED TIME FRAME

| March | | | | April | | | |
|---|---|---|---|---|---|---|---|
| | | ▓ | ▓ | ▓ | ▓ | | |

## FOCUS

- Repetition
- Adding new ideas to repetition
- Repetition with imitation
- Repetition with variation

| **Lesson 3**<br>Focus: Form—Repetition with Imitation | **Lesson 4**<br>Focus: Repetition with Variation |
|---|---|
| Perform using dynamics | Identify forte, piano, and ◁══ ══▷<br>Hear dynamic variations |
| Listen for solo and combinations of orchestral instruments<br>Listen to and perform a spoken fugue | Identify changes in instrumental tone color<br>Hear "slap bass" accompaniment<br><br>Vary tone color through use of solo and group singing |
|  | Identify tempo changes |
| Listen to and perform from spoken-music score | Listen to and identify syncopation<br>Experience compound meter, augmentation, meter changes<br><br>Vary a song with augmentation and diminution |
| Listen to a composition in minor mode<br>Identify pitch level changes of the subject | Listen to and identify upper and lower registers<br>Perform and discuss a song in minor mode with a range of A-a<br>Hear melodic ostinato |
| Listen to and perform polyphonic compositions<br>Perform fugue<br><br>Create a spoken-fugue subject | Perform a unison song |
| Identify subject and episode in a fugue | Listen to and identify theme and variation<br><br>Create variations on a song |
| Listen to baroque music in 20th-century orchestral transcription | Listen to 20th-century American jazz and nationalistic music |
| Read ♫♫ , ♫♩ , ♫♫ , ♪, ⁊ , ♫ , ♫ , ♩, 𝄽 , 𝄼<br>*p* , *f* , *mp* , *ff* , ══▷ , > <br>Follow listening map | Follow listening chart and map |

# TECHNOLOGY

## MUSIC WITH *MIDI*

MIDI technology allows students to manipulate musical elements and make musical decisions.
- Lesson 2, page 145: Analyze **Expressive Elements**: *"In the Hall of the Mountain King"* by E. Grieg
- Lesson 3, page 148: Analyze a **Fugue**: *"Little Fugue in G Minor"* by J. S. Bach; Create Using **Imitation**

## VIDEO RESOURCES

Use video resources to reinforce, extend, and enrich learning in this unit.

# LESSON 1

## UNIT 6

### REPETITION: THE BASIS OF FORM

Zon en Maan, M.C. Escher, CORDON ART, Baarn, Holland

# E X T E N S I O N

## THE ARTISTS

**Alexander Calder** (kol'dər) (1898–1976)— was an American sculptor best known for his *mobiles*. These are made of metal forms hanging from thin wires. The forms move around when pushed by air currents, so they constantly change their arrangement and the appearance of the whole sculpture.

**M.C. (Maurits Cornelis) Escher** (1889– 1971)—was a Dutch graphic artist. He often drew interlocking figures such as the birds in *Zon en Maan*. Escher's prints frequently present viewers with optical illusions that at first glance look like normal three-dimensional scenes, but upon closer study they also look normal from another perspective. The viewer knows that the two or even several perspectives cannot exist at the same time, but they are interwoven so skillfully that the illusion succeeds.

CD3:28

Everything has form. **Form,** or shape, helps us know what an object is. It allows us to call an object by name. Sometimes many small forms are combined to create a much larger form.

These pictures contain repetition. **Repetition** results when a form, line, or color appears more than once. Which of these pictures contain the most repetition of form, line, or color? Answers may vary.

Like many works of visual art, many kinds of music contain repetition. The form of a musical composition may result from repeated rhythms, harmonies, and melodies.

139

CD3, CD4

# LESSON 1

**Focus: Form—Repetition**

**Objectives**
To identify repetition in art and music
To identify and play repeated rhythms
To play a repeated harmonic accompaniment
To become familiar with repetition as a unifying element

**Materials**
Recordings: "Rhythmic Repetition Montage"
"Harmonic Repetition Montage"
*American Quodlibet* (optional)

Bells, keyboard, guitar, or Autoharp

**Vocabulary**
Repetition, four-chord set

**1 SETTING THE STAGE**
Have the students listen to "Rhythmic Repetition Montage" as they enter the room.

**2 TEACHING THE LESSON**
**1. Introduce form and repetition.**
Have the students:
• Discuss the information on form and repetition.
• Decide which of the pictures on pages 138–139 contain the most repetition.

# LESSON 1

**2. Identify the rhythm patterns in "Rhythmic Repetition Montage."**
Have the students:
• Practice and perform the rhythm patterns as indicated.
• Match the recorded compositions in "Rhythmic Repetition Montage" with the rhythm patterns.
• Read and perform each example with recording.

# REPETITION BUILDS FORM

• Perform each of the following rhythms. Pat the quarter notes, clap the eighth notes, and tap the sixteenth notes on the top of your hand. Perform the half notes ( ♩ ) with a pat-slide motion. Make a silent, palms-up motion on the rests ( 𝄽 ).

• Listen to "Rhythmic Repetition Montage." Match each rhythm with a part of the montage. 4, 2, 1, 3

"Rhythmic Repetition Montage"

140

---

# E X T E N S I O N

## SPECIAL LEARNERS
Many mainstreamed students may have difficulty with the sequence of motor tasks described in the pupil edition for these rhythmic patterns. If there are mainstreamed students in the class, have the class pat the longer notes, clap the shorter notes, pat-slide on the half notes, and use a silent, palms-up motion on the rests. This will enable the students to succeed in experiencing the rhythmic variety contained in the Montage.

## MORE MUSIC TEACHING IDEAS
Have the students identify patterns of repetition within the classroom environment (ceiling tiles, windows, and so on).

# Repetition: Harmony

Some music contains repetition in repeated chord patterns. One of the most often used patterns is the **four-chord set.**

- Learn to play the four-chord set on bells, keyboard, or guitar. The chords shown here are G major, E minor, C major, and D major. The Xs over some strings mean that those strings should not be played.

Four-Chord Set

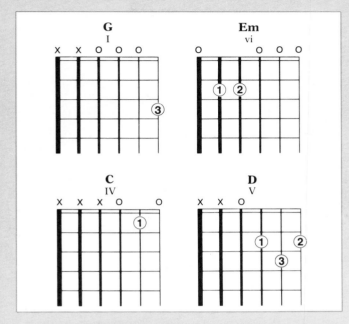

- Play the following rhythms. Change chords as shown. Strum *down* on each chord.

141

**3. Introduce harmonic repetition and the four-chord set.** Have the students:
- Play the root of each chord in the four-chord set.
- Play the chord in the four-chord set on bells, keyboard, guitar, or Autoharp. (If the Autoharp is used, retune the E major 7 chord to E minor.)
- Practice changing chords in each measure as indicated.

# LESSON 1

- Perform the ''Harmonic Repetition Montage'' with the recording. (There is a four-beat introduction.)

(If students are having difficulty changing from $\frac{4}{4}$ to $\frac{2}{4}$ and back, have them clap the first beat of each measure of both $\frac{4}{4}$ and $\frac{2}{4}$, and pat their laps on the remaining beats.)

CD3:29 Each song in the "Harmonic Repetition Montage" uses the four-chord set.

- Listen to "Harmonic Repetition Montage" and play this harmonic accompaniment on guitar, keyboard, or bells.

"Harmonic Repetition Montage"

Elton John

A scene from the film *Grease*

Gene Chandler, composer of "Duke of Earl"

"Duke of Earl"

142

---

## EXTENSION

### SPECIAL LEARNERS

If a class includes mainstreamed students who have visual disabilities or difficulty with visual-motor coordination tasks, prepare an overhead transparency of pupil pages 142 and 143. Point to the beginning of each measure on the transparency so the students will be able to follow the harmonic progression.

"Crocodile Rock"

"Blue Moon"

"Duke of Earl"

The repeated rhythms and harmonies give unity to "Harmonic Repetition Montage."

143

# LESSON 1

### Reinforcing the Lesson
Have the students summarize how repetition of rhythm and harmony give unity to a musical composition.

## 3 APPRAISAL
The students should be able to:
1. Verbally define repetition in music and the visual arts as a basic technique for providing unity in a composition.
2. Listen to several phrases that contain examples of either repetition (rhythmic or harmonic) or no repetition and, upon a second hearing with eyes closed, signal during the playing of the repetitions.
3. Examine a selection of visual art reprints and verbally identify the reprints that demonstrate the most obvious use of repetition to unify the composition.
4. Perform accurately from notation the repeated rhythm patterns in "Rhythmic Repetition Montage."
5. Perform accurately from notation the four-chord set as a harmonic accompaniment to "Harmonic Repetition Montage" on bells, keyboard, or guitar.

## MORE MUSIC TEACHING IDEAS
Have the students use the four-chord set to accompany other songs. The following is an accompaniment to "Swing Low, Sweet Chariot," which is part of *American Quodlibet* on page 197.

# LESSON 2

**Focus: Form—Adding New Ideas to Repetition**

**Objectives**
To identify changes of tempo and dynamics

**Materials**
Recordings: "Do You Hear the People Sing?"
"In the Hall of the Mountain King"
*In C*

**Vocabulary**
Accelerando

## 1 SETTING THE STATE

Review "Do You Hear the People Sing?" page 13. Determine what is changed in the repetition of the A sections. (Voices, instruments, and dynamics are changed. The first A section is sung by a soloist, the other two A sections have voices added to form a chorus. The first A section is played on a keyboard, the other two A sections are played by an orchestra. The first A section is *mp*, the other two A sections are *ff* and *fff*.)

## 2 TEACHING THE LESSON

**1. Introduce repetition with additions.** Have the students identify repetition and repetition with additions in the picture.

# REPETITION PLUS

We see many kinds of repetition around us. Sometimes when a shape is repeated, something new is added for variety. What is repeated here? What has been added?

The Russian artist Kazimir Malevich used repeated shapes in his painting *Morning in the Village After a Snowstorm.*

144

# Repetition: Melody

"In the Hall of the Mountain King," by Edvard Grieg, has repetition of a melody. As in the picture on page 144, Grieg adds something new to each repetition.

- Perform the steady half-note beat ( 𝅗𝅥 ) with a pat-slide motion as you listen.

 "In the Hall of the Mountain King" from *Peer Gynt* (pēr gint) Suite No. 1 by Edvard Grieg (ed′ värd grēg)

- What happens to the tempo of the steady half-note beat? gradual increase in speed

This change in tempo is called **accelerando** (ä-chel-er-än′ dō).

- Clap the rhythm of the melody as you listen again.

Edvard Grieg (1843–1907) wrote many compositions inspired by the folk tales of his native Norway. "In the Hall of the Mountain King" was part of the music for a play about the Norwegian folk hero Peer Gynt. Peer was a young man who roamed throughout the world, pursuing adventure and power. He sometimes was dishonest and tricked other people. In the Mountain King's underground palace, Peer was chased by goblins. Grieg adds something new to the melody by changing the tempo, dynamics, and instruments to represent Peer Gynt's increasing terror as he runs faster and faster to escape.

 **CHALLENGE** Form two groups. One group will clap the steady half-note beat while the second group claps the rhythm of the melody.

145

**2. Introduce repetition with addition in "In the Hall of the Mountain King."** Have the students:
- Perform the steady half-note beat as they listen to the recording.
- Describe the change in tempo. (gradual increase in the speed of the steady beat)
- Define and label *accelerando*. (You may want to compare *accelerando* to the word *accelerator* as it refers to the gas pedal of a car.)
- Perform the rhythm of the melody as indicated.
- Perform the Challenge! activity. Have the class divide into two groups and perform the rhythm of the melody against the steady beat with the recording.

**3. Introduce the composer Edvard Grieg.** Have the students:
- Discuss the information on Edvard Grieg. You may wish to use some of the following items as a basis for extended discussion.

1. Discuss the meaning of the word *inspired*. Is this a necessary ingredient for all creative efforts? (answers will vary) Name some examples of inspired music and the source of the inspiration. (example: "The Star Spangled Banner"; the sight of the American flag over Fort McHenry at dawn showed Francis Scott Key that the fort had not been captured)

2. Relate the musical term *accelerando* to other areas. (automobiles and heartbeats accelerate) Does acceleration always result from an extreme emotion such as fear or excitement? Why? (answers will vary)

# LESSON 2

**4. Introduce the dynamics in "In the Hall of the Mountain King."** Have the students listen again and determine which diagram represents the dynamics of the work. (3, crescendo)

**5. Summarize how Grieg creates unity and variety in "In the Hall of the Mountain King" through repetition and repetition with additions.** Have the students:
• Answer the questions.
• Examine the diagram that represents accelerando and crescendo.

• Listen again. Which diagram represents the changing dynamics and use of instruments in this selection? 3, crescendo

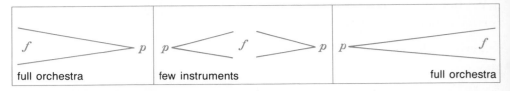

| | | |
|---|---|---|
| _f_ ———————▷ _p_ | _p_ ◁——— _f_ ———▷ _p_ | _p_ ◁——————— _f_ |
| full orchestra | few instruments | full orchestra |

Grieg gives his composition unity by repeating one melody and one rhythm pattern throughout. He gives it variety through tempo, dynamics, and tone color.

1. How does he use tempo to add tension and excitement? by specifying an accelerando of the steady half-note beat

2. How does he change the dynamics? by starting at piano and using a crescendo until the dynamic level reaches forte at the end

3. How does he vary the tone color? by gradually adding instruments until the entire orchestra is playing

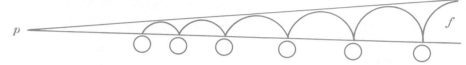

Repetition with the addition of something new gives "In the Hall of the Mountain King" its form.

Repetition of circular shapes with the addition of squares and rectangles gives form to this computer image.

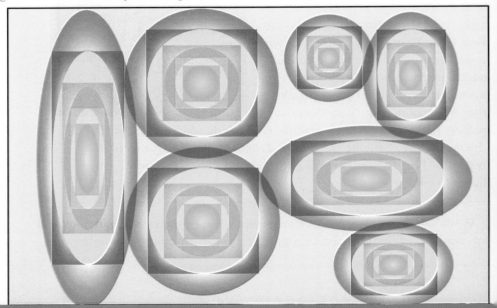

### COOPERATIVE LEARNING

Have the students work in cooperative groups of four. Each member of the group will create a four-measure ostinato using pitched or unpitched instruments. (Encourage students to use the pentatonic scale or Dorian mode.) The group members then perform their patterns in succession. As each pattern is added, the texture will thicken and dynamics will increase, forming a long crescendo. Assign one student the role of conductor to bring in the individual ostinato patterns and indicate the crescendo. The patterns should be notated by an appointed recorder in a simple line score to be read and performed by the entire class.

- Listen to *In C*, a twentieth-century example of repetition with addition. CD3:31

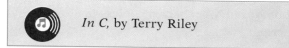

*In C,* by Terry Riley

- Play this melody on bells or keyboard as you listen to *In C.*

American composer Terry Riley repeats the pitch C on the piano throughout the work. Each of the other eleven performers adds something new to the repetition of C by gradually adding fifty-three melodies! Here are the first seven of them.

Notice that Terry Riley does not use meter signatures or bar lines.

How does the composer use dynamics and tone color to create variety? Answers will vary.

147

**6. Introduce repetition in minimalism.** Have the students:
- Listen to *In C* and play the melodic accompaniment.
- Discuss how the composer adds variety to the music. (variations in tone colors, dynamics, short melodies)

### Reinforcing the Lesson

Have the students compare the different ways Grieg and Riley use repetition with addition.

### 3 APPRAISAL

The students should be able to listen to several examples in which the melody remains the same and then is repeated with either tempo or dynamic changes and, with eyes closed, signal tempo or dynamic change for each example.

---

### MORE MUSIC TEACHING IDEAS

Create a layered sound composition. Have the students:
1. Form groups of three or four. Each group will create a four-measure ostinato using percussion or pitched instruments. (Encourage students to use a pentatonic scale or Dorian mode.)
2. Perform their patterns in succession continuing throughout the composition.
3. As each pattern is added, the texture will thicken and dynamics will increase, forming a long crescendo. (Encourage students to notate their patterns.)
If equipment is available, you may wish to tape-record or videotape these compositions for replay and evaluation.

### MORE MUSIC TEACHING IDEAS

Have the students learn to play the seven motives from *In C* on bells or keyboard. They can create a composition based on a random model as follows:
1. Number each of seven sticks to correspond to each of the seven motives from *In C.*
2. Drop the sticks and read from left to right to determine the order of the motives of the composition.
3. Perform the motives in the order determined by the random ordering of the sticks.

### THE COMPOSER

**Terry Riley**—avant-garde American composer, was born in California in 1935. He studied composition at the University of California at Berkeley. Later, he studied the rich traditions of Indian music and culture. Riley is a leading innovator of minimal music. His compositions explore the contrast between complexity and simplicity. Riley's output includes ballets, symphonic music, and chamber music. *In C* for orchestra, one of the earliest minimal compositions, was first performed in 1965. Its simple, repeated rhythm patterns create a complex musical effect when combined.

# LESSON 3

**Focus: Form—Repetition with Imitation**

## Objectives
To identify repetition with imitation in the fugue
To identify and label the main parts of a fugue
To perform a spoken fugue for three voices

## Materials
Recordings: "Bottletop Song" (optional)
"Geographical Fugue" (optional)
"Go Now in Peace" (optional)
"Weekend Relief" (optional)
*Spoken Fugue for Three Voices*
"Little Fugue in G Minor"

## Vocabulary
Subject, imitation, episode

## 1 SETTING THE STAGE

You may wish to have the students review the word rhythms on page 17 of the teacher's edition and the Challenge! on page 52. You also may wish to review some or all of the following: "Bottletop Song," p. 18; "Geographical Fugue," p. 24; "Go Now in Peace," p. 34; and "Weekend Relief," pp. 98–99.  CD1:11–12, 16, 23; CD2:30

## 2 TEACHING THE LESSON

**1. Introduce** *Spoken Fugue for Three Voices*. Have the students:
• Read through part I of *Spoken Fugue for Three Voices*.
• Form three sections.
• Perform the *Spoken Fugue for Three Voices*.

---

# REPETITION WITH IMITATION

CD3:32  You will hear the main theme, or **subject,** of the fugue imitated two times by different voices. **Imitation** results when a part copies what has already been stated in another part.

 *Spoken Fugue for Three Voices*

• Perform the *Spoken Fugue for Three Voices*.

### Spoken Fugue for Three Voices
M. J.

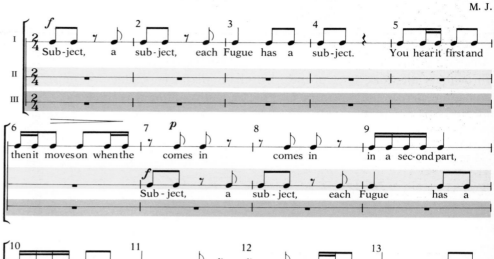

148

---

# EXTENSION

### EXTRA HELP

If your class has difficulty performing all three parts of the *Spoken Fugue*, use only parts I and II.

149

# LESSON 3

**2. Introduce Bach's "Little Fugue in G Minor."** Have the students:
• Discuss the information on J. S. Bach and the "Little Fugue in G Minor."
You may wish to use some of the following items as a basis for extended discussion.
1. Discuss the concept of fame. Name some famous contemporary musicians. (answers will vary) How does fame affect a person's life? (answers will vary) Was Bach able to enjoy the rewards of his fame? (yes and no—he was famous but only among his fellow musicians and a few wealthy patrons)
2. Define the musical use of the word *voice*. (an individual vocal or instrumental line of a work) How does this relate to the standard interpretation of "voice"? (answers will vary) Discuss other meanings such as the "voice" of the people, and so on.
• Listen to the subject. (You may wish to play it or use the first statement of the subject on the recording.)
• Listen to the first four statements of the subject and show the length of the subject by moving the right hand in a circular motion. Show each of the three imitations by alternating hands and changing direction.
• Identify the instruments playing the first four entrances of the subject. (oboe, English horn, bassoon, bassoon)

Detail from *Johann Sebastian Bach*, Elias Hausmann, STADTGESCHICHTLICHES MUSEUM, Leipzig

CD3:33  Johann Sebastian Bach (1685–1750) was one of the greatest musicians of all time. He came from a German family of professional musicians. He wrote music for organ and other keyboard instruments, as well as works for orchestra, small groups, and chorus. Bach was famous for his ability to make up music on the spot (improvise) as he played. Bach worked very hard, composing and playing music for royal courts and church services. In addition, he directed the choir, gave music lessons, and composed new music for all Sundays and special religious services of the year.

Bach based each movement of his music on a single mood or emotion such as joy or sadness. He would keep the mood, as well as the tempo and rhythm, consistent throughout the movement. Whether he used simple or complex melodies, he almost always composed in polyphonic style.

Bach wrote the "Little Fugue in G Minor" early in his career. It was originally composed for the organ and later arranged for orchestra.

• Listen to the "Little Fugue in G Minor." The subject is repeated on different pitches. Identify the instruments you hear stating the first four entrances of the subject.  oboe, English horn, bassoon, bassoon

Subject

 "Little Fugue in G Minor" by Johann Sebastian Bach

150

---

# E X T E N S I O N

## SPECIAL LEARNERS

Preplan for any class that includes students with visual learning disabilities by making a transparency of page 151 in the pupil edition. These students will be more successful coordinating the auditory activity with the visual task if each number is pointed to on a transparency.

## Identify the Subject

These are the repetitions or imitations of the subject of the "Little Fugue in G Minor."

Many manuscripts of Bach's music have been preserved. The one shown here is of a work for keyboard.

- Listen to the "Little Fugue in G Minor" again. Show the pitch level (register) of each entrance of the subject by pointing your hand up or down.

151

- Show the length of the subject by moving their hands in a large circular motion as they listen to the recording.
- Using the diagram as a model, indicate the pitch level of each entrance of the subject as directed.

# LESSON 3

**3. Introduce *episode* and its symbol in preparation for listening to the "Little Fugue in G Minor."** Have the students:
• Discuss the information on how to follow the listening map.
• Listen to the recording and follow the map to identify the number of episodes (five) and statements of the subject (nine). (Call number 6 is a false entrance followed by a full statement of the subject.)

## Reinforcing the Lesson

Have the students summarize by labeling diagram 2 as polyphonic texture. (You may wish to refer to the discussion of musical texture on page 19.)

## 3 APPRAISAL

The students should be able to:
1. Identify, by raising their hands with eyes closed, each of the four first entrances of the subject in the "Little Fugue in G Minor."
2. Verbally identify two parts of a fugue as subject and episode, and define subject as the main theme that is imitated and episode as contrasting sections to the subject.
3. Perform, with rhythmic accuracy, the three different voice parts in *Spoken Fugue for Three Voices*.

• Follow the map of the "Little Fugue in G Minor." You will hear the subject imitated by different instruments and in different registers. The symbol ⌒⌒ represents each statement of the subject. The *contrasting* sections are called **episodes.** They are shown by the symbol ✖.

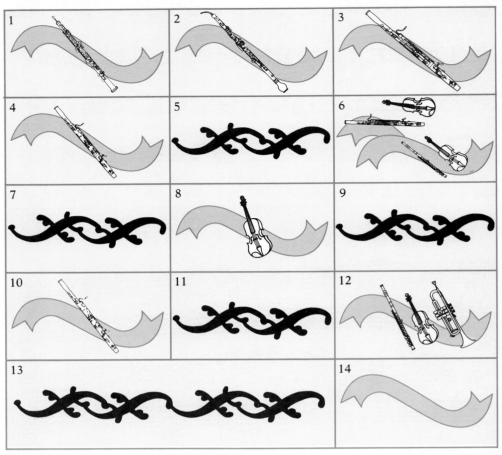

• How many statements of the subject and episodes do you hear?   9 statements of subje[ct]
Remember that texture in music refers to the way in which sounds are combined. Which of the following diagrams best shows the texture of "The Little Fugue in G Minor"?   2    5 episodes

1. ∼∼∼∼∼

2. ∼∼∼∼
  ∼∼∼∼
  ∼∼∼∼
  ∼∼∼∼

3. ∼∼∼∼∼
  ▪ ▪ ▪ ▪

152

---

## LISTENING

You may wish to use the Listening Map overhead transparency to help guide the students through the listening selection.

## MORE MUSIC TEACHING IDEAS

Have the students create a spoken fugue subject by choosing a topic such as sports, foods, or popular musicians and focusing on vocabulary associated with that topic. For example, if sports were selected, a possible fugue subject might be:

golf___ ten - nis   bas-ket-ball and hock - ey

# REPETITION WITH VARIATION

- What is the original idea in each picture? Demuth: numeral 5; Vasarely: square shapes
- What has been changed in each picture to provide visual interest and contrast? Demuth: 5s are different sizes; Vasarely: forms are varied in shape and color

**Variation** results when an idea is changed or altered.

*I Saw the Figure 5 in Gold*, by Charles Demuth

*I Saw the Figure 5 in Gold, Charles Henry Demuth, THE METROPOLITAN MUSEUM OF ART, NY*

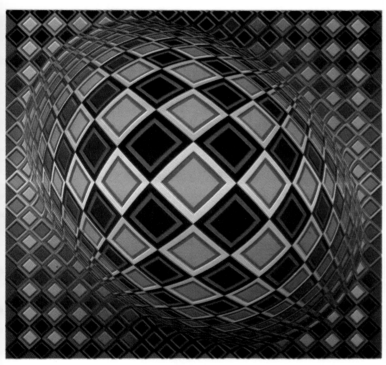

*Teke*, by Victor Vasarely

153

# LESSON 4

**Focus: Repetition with Variation**

### Objectives

To identify repetition with variation in visual art and music

To analyze how a theme is changed to create musical variety

### Materials

Recordings: "Joshua Fought the Battle of Jericho"

Variations on "Joshua Fought the Battle of Jericho"

"When Johnny Comes Marching Home"

"When Johnny Comes Marching Home" (performance mix)

*American Salute*

### Vocabulary

Variation, jazz, theme and variations

## 1 SETTING THE STAGE

Have the students identify the original or main idea in each work of art and how each is varied.

# EXTENSION

### THE ARTISTS

**Charles Demuth** (də-mōōth′) (1883–1935) —was an American painter and illustrator and a pioneer of modern art in this country. He often painted pieces of signs, buildings, street lights, and letters. *I Saw a Figure 5 in Gold* is based on a poem about a fire engine. The golden numerals on the red background are the colors of a fire engine, and the repetition of the numeral is used to suggest the sudden loud approach of the truck.

**Victor Vasarely** (vä-sä-rel′ē) (1908–1997) —was born in Hungary and worked in France. He was interested in optical patterns that seem to move, and experimented with geometrical shapes and bright color combinations that give the illusion of three dimensionality or movement. He believed this kind of art is an expression of the geometry found in nature and is thus appealing to all viewers.

# LESSON 4

## 2 TEACHING THE LESSON

**1. Introduce jazz as a style of music that contains variation.** Have the students:
• Discuss the information given.
• Review "Joshua Fought the Battle of Jericho" on pages 85-87.

## Jazz—Repetition and Variation

Jazz is a uniquely American style of music that is based on variation. It had its roots in earlier American music, including ragtime and the blues. Since its beginnings in the African American community of New Orleans around the turn of the century, jazz has continuously evolved into many different styles. Dixieland, swing, Big Band, bebop, free form, and jazz-rock are only some of the popular jazz styles.

The consistent elements of the different styles of jazz are improvisation and variation, a steady, prominent meter, and syncopated rhythms. Instruments have varied from the trumpet, clarinet, banjo, piano, and drums of early jazz to synthesizers.

Milt Hinton has played string bass for jazz recordings, as well as pop and television music, for over fifty years, sharing his music with many people. Known as a "musician's musician," he is highly regarded in the jazz field.

Left, Milt Hinton in about 1953, when he was featured with the Louis Armstrong All-Stars. Above, Milt Hinton in a recent performance

## EXTENSION

- Listen to Milt Hinton perform and talk about his variations on the song "Joshua Fought the Battle of Jericho."  CD3:34

 Variations on "Joshua Fought the Battle of Jericho" by Milt Hinton

| | |
|---|---|
| 1. Milt talks about "Joshua..." | Milt sings and plays "Joshua" |
| 2. "Going into battle..." | Introduction: _p_ dynamic level; wide leaps becoming smaller; weak beat |
| 3. "Here he [Joshua] comes..." | Theme: "Joshua" in low register; slow tempo |
| 4. "Here is a little boy telling the story...an' a girl says..." | Theme: "Joshua" in high register |
| 5. "Then...choir..." | Bridge: based on harmony and rhythms of "Joshua"; register changes; syncopation |
| "Oh, here comes the soldiers..." | Rhythm becomes stronger |
| 6. "Here they come... Here comes Joshua..." | Variation 1: "Joshua" theme with syncopation; variation on melody; "slap bass" accompaniment |
| 7. "He's gonna work on the walls now..." | Variation 2: Repeated leaps growing wider (opposite of Introduction) creates increasing tension; variation based on harmony |
| 8. "There goes the wall..." | Melody descends (representing the walls "tumbling down") and ritardando |
| 9. "Walls come tumbling..." | Coda: soft chords |

155

# LESSON 4

**2. Introduce Milt Hinton's variations on "Joshua Fought the Battle of Jericho."** Have the students:
• Follow the listening chart as he discusses his music.
• Discuss how the song was varied.

## MORE MUSIC TEACHING IDEAS

Choose a song and explore ways of creating variations on it. Have the students:
1. Sing in unison.
2. Sing the song in a minor mode.
3. Divide note values in half (diminution).
4. Double note values (augmentation).
5. Sing the song as a round.
6. Alternate between class singing a phrase and a solo voice or instruments performing subsequent phrases.

# LESSON 4

**3. Introduce "When Johnny Comes Marching Home."** Have the students:
• Discuss information on "When Johnny Comes Marching Home."
• Sing the song. (Changing voices can sing the entire song.)

**4. Introduce theme and variations in *American Salute*.** Have the students:
• Discuss the use of "When Johnny Comes Marching Home" as the thematic material for *American Salute*.

You may wish to use some of the following items as a basis for extended discussion.

1. What skills does an orchestral arranger need in order to do the job effectively? (knowledge of ranges and tone colors of instruments; sensitivity to the music and feeling for appropriate arrangement) With which elements of music would an arranger work? (melody, harmony, rhythm) Why is it possible to be an arranger without being a composer? (arranger does not compose)

2. Why is music able to convey national pride to the listener so effectively? (associations of patriotic themes or ideas with music) Consider the role of music in propaganda. Cite specific examples. (television commercials, school songs, and so on)

## A Civil War Song

CD3:35; CD7:30

Scale Tones: *mi, so, la, ti, do re mi*

Starting Pitch: D

Key: D minor

Singing can cheer you up and can make hard work seem easier. "When Johnny Comes Marching Home" was written to help cheer the soldiers fighting in the Civil War. In 1863 Patrick Gilmore, a bandmaster in the United States Army, composed the words. He set them to the Irish folk song "Johnny I Hardly Knew Ye."

• Sing this song about soldiers returning home from the war.

### When Johnny Comes Marching Home

Piano Accompaniment on page PA 29

Words by Patrick Gilmore
Irish folk melody

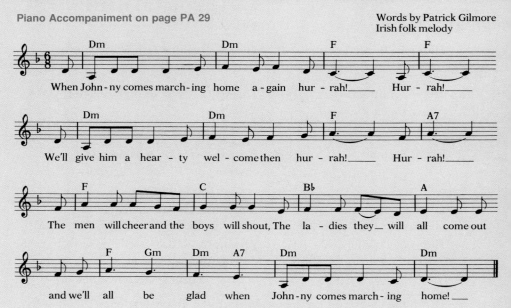

When John-ny comes march-ing home a-gain hur – rah!____ Hur – rah!____

We'll give him a hear-ty wel-come then hur-rah!____ Hur-rah!____

The men will cheer and the boys will shout, The la – dies they __ will all come out

and we'll all be glad when John-ny comes march-ing home!____

"When Johnny Comes Marching Home" has been used in many different ways. William McKinley used it as a theme song in his presidential campaign in the late 1890s. The song became popular again during the Spanish-American War (1898) and World War I (1914–18).

Large-scale compositions have been based on this catchy melody. American composer Morton Gould combines American popular styles and folk melodies with a traditional form. In his *American Salute,* he took "When Johnny Comes Marching Home" as his theme and "dressed it up" by composing variations on the melody.

156

During the Civil War, many soldiers on both sides posed for souvenir portraits. Above, an unknown Union soldier. Right, Private Walter M. Parker, 1st Florida Cavalry, C.S.A.

157

# LESSON 4

• Follow the map of *American Salute* and identify how the composer varies the theme to create musical interest and variety.
1–4: changes in instrumental tone color
5: adds notes to the melody and changes in tone color
6: use of syncopation
7: adds ostinato pattern and places the melody in long note values
8–9: varies the instrumental tone color
10: changes in tempo and dynamics

CD3:36 • Follow the map of *American Salute*. Listen to the theme and identify how each variation changes the melody, rhythm, texture, dynamics, tone color, and tempo.

 *American Salute* by Morton Gould

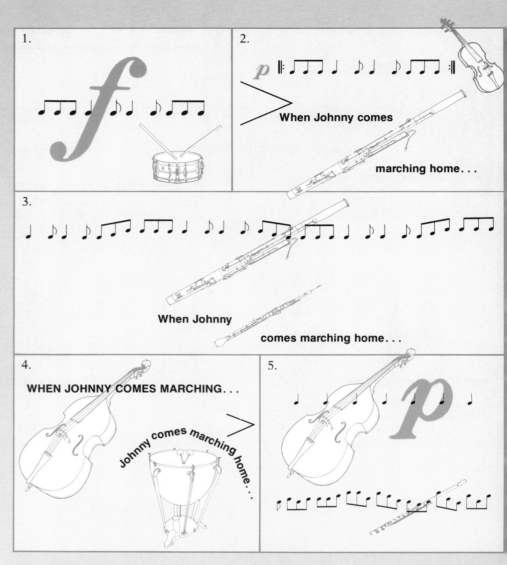

158

# EXTENSION

## THE COMPOSER

**Morton Gould** (1913–1996)—American composer and conductor, was born in New York City. He was an accomplished musician at an early age. His creative output was enormous and ranges from symphonic works to scores for Broadway, Hollywood, and television. Gould brought together unusual combinations of folk and traditional orchestral instruments. He also combined American popular styles and folk melodies with traditional formas and techniques, as in *American Salute*. Gould was committed to providing high-quality music for student groups. In 1986, Morton Gould was elected president of ASCAP, the American Society of Composers, Authors, and Publishers, the oldest performing rights organization in the world.

## LISTENING

You may wish to use the Listening Map overhead transparency to help guide the students through the listening selection.

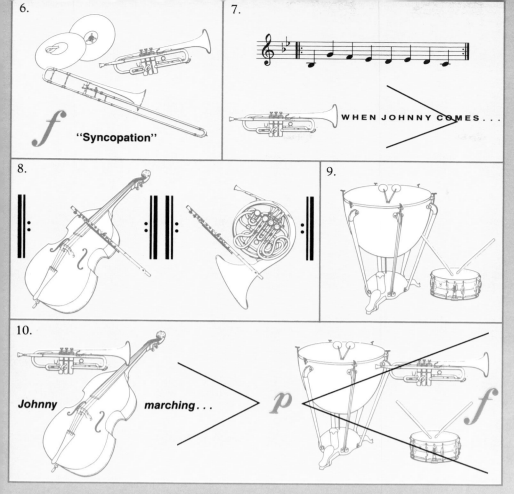

**6.** *f* "Syncopation"

**7.** WHEN JOHNNY COMES...

**8.**

**9.**

**10.** Johnny marching... *p* *f*

Repetition of the theme, "When Johnny Comes Marching Home,"
gives unity to *American Salute*. Different rhythms, melodies,
textures, dynamics, tone colors, and tempo give it variety. The form
of *American Salute* is **theme and variations.**

 **CHALLENGE** Choose your favorite television or movie theme. Create your own
variations on the theme by changing any of the following: tempo,
rhythm, texture, dynamics, or tone color.
If the theme is too long, choose a short phrase that everyone will
recognize.

159

# LESSON 4

## Reinforcing the Lesson
Have the students:
• Summarize how unity and variety are
built into the variations on "Joshua" and
*American Salute*.
• Identify and label theme and variation
form.
• Respond to the Challenge!

### 3 APPRAISAL
The students should be able to:
1. Examine several appropriate visual art
examples that clearly present a single idea
with variations and verbally identify the
idea and one dimension that has been
changed (color, shape, size, etc.).
2. Identify techniques used to vary the
song "Joshua Fought the Battle of Jericho"
by Milt Hinton and the theme in *American
Salute*.
3. Listen to brief excerpts from familiar
songs with variations created by changing
tempo registers, rhythmic styles, or pitches
and identify the technique used for the
variation.

# REVIEW AND EVALUATION

## JUST CHECKING

### Objective
To review and test the skills and concepts taught in Unit 6

### Materials
Recordings: Just Checking Unit 6 (questions 1, 4–6, and 9)
*In C*
*Spoken Fugue for Three Voices*
Unit 6 Evaluation (questions 3–7)
*For Extra Credit* recordings (optional)
Bells, keyboard, or guitar
Copying Master 6-1 (optional)
Evaluation Unit 6 Copying Master

## TEACHING THE LESSON

**Review the skills and concepts taught in Unit 6.** Have the students:
• Perform the activities and answer the questions on pages 160–161. (For this review, examples for questions 1, 4, 5, 6, and 9 are included in the "Just Checking Unit 6" recording. Have the students answer these questions first. Then have them answer the other questions in the review, using the recordings in the unit where necessary.)
• Review their answers.
(You may wish to use Copying Master 6-1 at this time.)

---

## JUST CHECKING

See how much you remember.

1. Perform this rhythm pattern by patting the quarter notes and clapping the eighth notes.

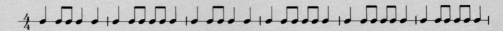

2. Perform the following chord pattern on bells, keyboard, or guitar.

3. To review melodic repetition, play one of these melodies on bells or keyboard as you listen to *In C*.

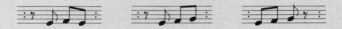

4. Listen to an excerpt from "In the Hall of the Mountain King." Pat the steady beat to experience the *accelerando*. "In the Hall of the Mountain King" is an example of: a

    a. repetition with additions
    b. no repetition
    c. jazz

160

5. Listen to an excerpt from the "Little Fugue in G Minor" and raise your hand each time you hear the subject. The "Little Fugue in G Minor" is an example of: b
    a. ABA form
    b. repetition with imitation
    c. repeated chord progression

6. Listen to excerpts by Milt Hinton performing variations on "Joshua Fought the Battle of Jericho" to identify changes in tempo, register, and rhythmic style, one at a time. Show changes in tempo by rolling your hands; register by pointing higher or lower; rhythmic style by snapping your fingers.

7. Review the *Spoken Fugue for Three Voices*. Identify three vocabulary words found in *Spoken Fugue for Three Voices*. subject, episode, polyphony

8. Which of the following diagrams best shows the texture of the *Spoken Fugue for Three Voices*? 2

9. As you listen to an excerpt from *American Salute*, name three ways the composer, Morton Gould, creates variations on the theme "When Johnny Comes Marching Home." changes the rhythm, dynamics, and tone color

161

## GIVING THE EVALUATION
Evaluation Unit 6 Copying Master can be found in the *Teacher's Copying Masters* book along with full directions for giving the evaluation and checking the answers.

## FOR EXTRA CREDIT
You may want to have the students answer the following questions.
1. Identify and describe five means by which composers create variety in repetitions of a theme. (changes in dynamics, texture, tempo, instrumentation, melodic patterns, rhythm patterns, register)
2. Give two reasons why Milt Hinton's performance of "Joshua Fought the Battle of Jericho" is an example of musical variation. (repeats one theme, changes are added through tone color, tempo changes, dynamics)
(You may wish to play recordings to refresh students' memories.)

| ELEMENTS OF MUSIC | UNIT 7 OBJECTIVES | Lesson 1 Focus: Form–Contrast | Lesson 2 Focus: Form–Repetition After One Contrast |
|---|---|---|---|
| Dynamics | **Listen to and identify repetition and contrast in dynamics** | | Perform repeated and contrasting dynamic levels |
| Tone Color | Perform on pitched and unpitched instruments<br>Listen to Renaissance ensemble | Hear Renaissance instruments and American folk instruments | Hear small orchestra |
| Tempo | Listen to tempo contrasts | | Listen to tempo changes |
| Duration/ Rhythm | **Perform *legato* and *staccato* articulation** | | Perform *legato* and *staccato* articulation |
| Pitch | Review Dorian mode<br>Perform vocal improvisations<br>**Perform melodic accompaniment using C-D¹** | Perform Dorian or pentatonic melody | Sing a song with a range of B♭-e♭¹ |
| Texture | Listen to and perform homophonic and polyphonic textures | | Perform a song with contrasts of polyphonic and homophonic textures |
| Form | **Listen to and identify sections of equal and unequal length<br>Identify contrasting sections and repetitions<br>Review ternary form<br>Identify rondo and suite** | Discuss contrast in music<br>Sing and perform movements to a song in binary form<br>Identify and perform contrasts between sections<br>Listen to and identify a composition in AB form<br>Identify and perform sections of unequal length<br><br>Improvise AB composition | Perform phrases and sections of equal and unequal length<br>Identify and perform contrasts and repetition at the sectional level<br>Listen to and identify ternary form |
| Style | Listen to Renaissance, American and English folk music, orchestral music | Listen to and discuss music of the Renaissance<br>Perform an American folk song | Listen to and discuss 20th-century Russian orchestral music |
| Reading | | Read ♩,𝄽,♩,♩., ¾,𝄆𝄇,tie | Read *ritardando, a tempo* |

## PURPOSE Unit 7: Form: Repetition And Contrast

In this unit the students will identify repetition and contrast in music and visual art. They will perform music that contains contrast and identify contrasts of articulation, dynamics, and form. The students will experience music in AB form, ABA or AABA form (ternary), and rondo form. As part of the unit the students will have the opportunity to create an improvised rondo.

## SUGGESTED TIME FRAME

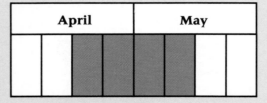

| April | | | | May | | | |
|---|---|---|---|---|---|---|---|

## FOCUS

• Contrast
• Repetition after one contrast (ternary form)
• Repetition with more than one contrast (rondo form)
• Repetition and contrast

| **Lesson 3**<br>Focus: Form–Repetition with More than One Contrast | **Lesson 4**<br>Focus: Repetition and Contrast |
|---|---|
| | Listen to and identify dynamic contrasts |
| Perform a melodic accompaniment on recorder and bells | |
| | |
| Move to steady beat<br>Perform a rhythmic dance<br>Experience syncopation<br>Listen to and move to duple meter | Identify *staccato* and *legato* articulation |
| Perform a melodic accompaniment<br>Sing a melody in Dorian mode<br>Perform notated and improvised sections on classroom instruments<br>Identify repeating and contrasting sections of a melody<br>Sing a song with the range of B-c' | |
| | Listen to a composition in homophonic texture |
| Listen to and identify rondo form<br>Perform a rondo by singing and improvising over ostinato<br><br>Create a composition in rondo form<br>Create visual diagrams in AB, ternary, and rondo form | Identify suite<br>Listen to and identify AABCCBAA form<br>Identify and perform repetition and contrast<br><br>Identify repetition and contrast in popular songs |
| Perform an Israeli folk song and dance in rondo form | Listen to and discuss 20th-century English orchestral music |
| Read ♫ , ♩ , 𝄽 , 𝅗𝅥 , 𝅗𝅥. , ²⁄₂ , ⁴⁄₄ , double note score, dance directions and notation, recorder and bell notes C D E F G A B C D | Follow listening chart |

# TECHNOLOGY

## MUSIC WITH *MIDI*

MIDI technology allows students to manipulate musical elements and make musical decisions.

- Lesson 1, page 166: *"Cripple Creek"*
- Lesson 3, page 172: *"Hine Ma Tov"*
- Lesson 3, pages 172, 175: Create a **Rondo:** *"The Boatman's Dance"*

## VIDEO RESOURCES

Use video resources to reinforce, extend, and enrich learning in this unit.

# LESSON 1

## UNIT 7

### FORM: REPETITION AND CONTRAST

**THE ARTIST**

**Victor Vasarely**
See page 153.

Repetition and contrast occur everywhere, in art and in the world around us.
To **contrast** means to be different from or unlike.

*La Galope, Paul Gavarni, THE METROPOLITAN MUSEUM OF ART, NY*

*Detail from Dance of Augsburg Patricians (attributed to Vogtherr)*

163

# LESSON 1

Focus: Form—Contrast

**Objectives**
To identify contrast in musical and visual examples
To identify, perform, and move to music containing contrast

**Materials**
Recordings: Courante
 "Cripple Creek"
Bells or keyboard instruments

**Vocabulary**
Contrast

## 1 SETTING THE STAGE

Have the students identify contrast in the pictures on pages 162–163 (contrasts of shapes, sizes, and colors).

# LESSON 1

## 2 TEACHING THE LESSON

**1. Introduce contrast in music.** Have the students:
• Discuss the use of contrast in music.
• Listen to the courante to identify the musical characteristics that are changed to create contrast between the A and B sections. (The B section is longer and has a contrasting melody; bells are added.)
• Play the melodic descant on bells or keyboard with recording.

CD3:48 You can hear contrast in music when tone color, tempo, dynamics, melody, rhythm, or form change.

• Listen to this dance from the Renaissance (1450–1600). What changes provide contrast? The B section is longer and has a contrasting melody; bells are added.

Courante (koo-ränt′) from *Terpsichore* (turp-si′ kō-rē) by Michael Praetorius (prā-tō′ rē-us)

• Listen to the dance again. Play the melodic accompaniment on bells or keyboard to sense the contrast between the two sections.

*A section*—first melody; A section repeats

*B section*—contrasting melody; bells are added; longer than A;
B section repeats

164

# EXTENSION

## SPECIAL LEARNERS

If you have any mainstreamed students with visual learning disabilities, use an overhead transparency of pupil page 164, color-coding each section. Divide the class into two groups, assigning a section to each. Each group will pick up from the previous one as each new section begins. Point to each line on the transparency as each group plays its part. This will enable mainstreamed students to follow the melodic accompaniment with more ease.

# MICHAEL PRAETORIUS

Michael Praetorius (1571–1621) was a German composer and author. He served as official composer in various German cities and courts of the nobility. Praetorius and several other composers compiled *Terpsichore*, a collection of music for dancing, in 1612. Following the custom of the time, Praetorius did not call for specific instruments in the music. People simply played the dances on whatever instruments were available to them.

Besides composing, Praetorius wrote many books about music. His writings, illustrated with drawings, are a major source of information about the music and musical instruments of his time.

During the Renaissance, dances were very formal occasions, as this painting shows.

Ball at the Court of Henry III, anonymous, LOUVRE, Paris

165

# LESSON 1

• Discuss the information on Michael Praetorius.
**2. Reinforce contrast through singing.** Have the students:
• Sing "Cripple Creek" on page 42.
• Discuss the information on the verse-refrain structure of "Cripple Creek" and label it as AB form.
• Review the form of the courante as AB.

## Reinforcing the Lesson

Have the students:
• Follow the directions and decide if the movement for "Cripple Creek" matches the form of the song. (yes)
• Learn the dance.
You may wish to use the following suggestions.
1. Regardless of the group's level of skill, begin by using the directions given in the pupil edition (Version 1). All three versions are based on these basic steps.

# LESSON 1

2. Have the students identify the difference between the movement patterns of the A section and the B section. In the A sections (verses) the movement is six steps *forward* (counterclockwise) or *backward* (clockwise) around the circle, each pattern ending with three steps in place. In the B sections (refrains) the movement is *toward* and *away from the center of the circle* (four steps toward center and two steps away from the center, followed by three steps in place).

3. When all can perform the basic steps easily, teach the more advanced versions and combine them as parts of the dance according to the skill of your class. For example, you might do the basic version during the first two verses and refrains and then do the intermediate or advanced versions for the rest of the song.

Version 2, for intermediate dancers

Formation: Double circle of partners, all facing counterclockwise (holding hands is optional).

Movement for each verse: Same steps as in Version 1 except that partners walk beside each other, forward and backward.

Movement for the refrain: Face partners and do-si-do (walk around partner passing right shoulder to right, back to back, left shoulder to left) and stamp three times in place, facing partner.

(Think: Walk, 2, 3, 4, back, 2, stamp, stamp, stamp)

Repeat this pattern, starting the do-si-do with the *left* shoulder.

Interludes and coda: Use the Version 1 clapping pattern or change to:

clap
stamp

L   R   L       R   L   R

## Contrast in a Folk Song

• Sing "Cripple Creek." page 42
• What is the form of "Cripple Creek"? AB form

How does it compare to the form of the courante? the same; both are in AB form

The steps and patterns used in folk dances often correspond to the form of the music.

• Follow these directions and decide if the movements for "Cripple Creek" match the form of the song. yes
Form a circle, all facing counterclockwise, hands at sides.

### Introduction

Bend and straighten your knees in time with the music.

### Movement for Each Verse

Take one step forward on each steady beat ( ♩ ), except on the seventh beat, when you take two small steps in place.

(Think: forward 2,    3,    4,    5,    6,    7 and 8)

Keep facing forward as you repeat the pattern walking backward (moving clockwise):

(Think: back    2,    3,    4,    5,    6,    7 and 8)

---

# EXTENSION

## SPECIAL LEARNERS

In any class that has mainstreamed students who are unable to participate in the dance for "Cripple Creek," divide the class into two groups. Have one group perform the steps to "Cripple Creek" while the other plays different unpitched instruments during each section. The group playing the instruments should be a mixture of regular and mainstreamed students.

## Movement for the Refrain

Face the center of the circle and take four steps forward.

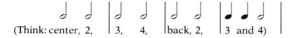

(Think: center, 2, 3, 4)

Keep facing center of circle and walk backward stepping this pattern:

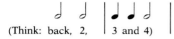

(Think: back, 2, 3 and 4)

Repeat both parts of the pattern.

(Think: center, 2, 3, 4, back, 2, 3 and 4)

## Movement for Each Interlude and Coda

clap
stamp

Folk festivals with music and dancing are popular all over the United States.

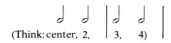

# LESSON 1

Alternate feet as shown, or stamp same foot throughout, keeping weight on the other foot.

Version 3, for experienced dancers
Formation: Double circle, partners facing each other and holding both hands. (Those in the inner circle face outward.)
Movement for each verse: Inner circle begins with left foot, outer circle with right foot, so that all are moving counterclockwise. Take six sliding steps followed by three steps in place.
(Think: Slide and 2 and 3 and 4 and 5 and 6 and stamp, stamp, stamp)
Repeat the pattern, moving clockwise.
Movement for the refrain: Partners do a right-shoulder do-si-do as in Version 2, ending with three steps in place.
(Think: Walk, 2, 3, 4, back, 2, 3 and 4)
Partners do a left-shoulder do-si-do, and the inner circle moves diagonally left (counterclockwise) to next partner. Dance the next verse and the refrain with the new partner.
Interludes and coda: Use combinations of previous clapping patterns or create new ones. Experiment with a burst of movement and sound on the last note.

## 3 APPRAISAL

The students should be able to:
1. Observe visual symbols or designs as well as examples of musical patterns and verbally identify the similar and contrasting patterns.
2. Listen to the Courante from *Terpsichore* and with eyes closed, signal the beginning of the contrasting section.
3. Identify the contrasting sections in "Cripple Creek" by performing the movements accurately, and verbally identifying similar and contrasting movements.
4. Verbally identify two contrasting sections in a composition as binary form.

## MORE MUSIC TEACHING IDEAS

Have the students:
1. Read "The Termite" by Ogden Nash on page 21 and determine the form of the rhyme scheme. (*aabb*)
2. Improvise a composition in AB form on Orff instruments.
• Perform a sixteen-beat-long melody and accompaniment in Dorian mode or on a pentatonic scale for the A section.
• Improvise a sixteen-beat-long contrasting B section in Dorian mode or on a pentatonic scale.
• Describe the contrast between the A and B sections.

# LESSON 2

**Focus Form—Repetition After One Contrast**

**Objective**
To identify repetition after one contrast in musical and visual examples

**Materials**
Recordings: "Galop" (excerpt), from Suite No. 2 for Small Orchestra, by Stravinsky
"Our World"
"Our World" (performance mix)

## 1 SETTING THE STAGE
Review ternary form, page 31.

## 2 TEACHING THE LESSON

**1. Introduce repetition in music.** Have the students:
• Discuss the information on repetition and contrast.
• Listen to the recording of "Galop" to identify repetition and contrasts of sections and list the answers on a separate sheet of paper.
• Identify the form of "Galop."

---

## LISTENING FOR REPETITION AND CONTRAST

CD4:1 Composer Igor Stravinsky (ē' gôr strä-vin' skē) organized "Galop" into repeated and contrasting sections.

• Listen to "Galop." When a number is called, decide whether you hear repetition or contrast.

 "Galop" (excerpt), from Suite No. 2 for Small Orchestra, by Igor Stravinsky

1. **Section A** (full orchestra, loud, accented and fast)

2. **Repetition of Section A**     or     **Contrasting Section B** ?     contrast

3. **Repetition of Section A**     or     **Repetition of Section B**     or     **Contrasting Section C** ? repetition of section A

• Listen again. How is the B section different from A? smooth and connected
• Which of the following represents the form of "Galop"? ABA

  AAA     AAB     ABA     ABB     ABC

168

---

# EXTENSION

## SPECIAL LEARNERS
If a class includes mainstreamed students who have difficulty in remembering and writing answers simultaneously, prepare an overhead transparency of pupil page 168 to use with this lesson so the students will not have to listen to "Galop" *and* concentrate on writing the answers.

## LISTENING
You may wish to use the Listening Map overhead transparency to help guide the students through the listening selection.

# IGOR STRAVINSKY

Igor Stravinsky (1882–1971) was one of the most influential composers of modern music. He was born and grew up in Russia, then lived in France and later in the United States. He never went to music school, but he studied orchestration with Nicolai Rimsky-Korsakov.

Stravinsky first became famous when he composed three ballets in Paris between 1909 and 1913. The first two—*The Firebird* and *Petrushka* (pe-trōōsh' kä)—were easy to listen to and quickly became popular. The third ballet, *The Rite of Spring*, was so unconventional that the audience rioted at the first performance.

Stravinsky's many works include ballets, symphonies, and music for chorus. Like Rimsky-Korsakov, he was a master of orchestration and used tone colors for startling effects.

Stravinsky composed the Suite No. 2 for Small Orchestra in 1922. It consists of several of Stravinsky's short piano pieces. Stravinsky himself arranged them for orchestral instruments.

This is a visual representation of the form of "Galop."

● What form do you see? ABA or ternary form

169

● Discuss the information on Igor Stravinsky.

You may wish to use some of the following items as a basis for extended discussion. Discuss the use of the word *influential*. Name other people in the twentieth century who were influential in political or social affairs. (Martin Luther King, Jr., social justice; Eleanor Roosevelt, social reform; Mahatma Gandhi, social and political justice, nationalism, independence of India; Winston Churchill, political leadership)

**2. Introduce repetition and contrast in visual art.** Have the students identify that the picture is based on ABA form.

# LESSON 2

**3. Introduce a song using repetition and contrast.** Have the students:

• Listen to "Our World" and identify the order of the repeated and contrasting sections of the song. (A, mm. 2–10; A, mm. 11–17; B, mm. 18–27; A, mm. 28–38)

• Listen again and identify other musical characteristics that provide contrast between the A and B sections. (The A section is in major and is moderately loud, mezzoforte; B is in minor and performed at a softer dynamic level.)

• Sing the song, emphasizing musical contrast.

## Three-Part Form

Key: E♭ major and G minor     Starting Pitch: B♭

• Listen to the repeated and contrasting sections. You will hear the A section repeat *before* you hear the B section.

• Sing the song. Be sure to emphasize the contrasting sections.

Piano Accompaniment on page PA 36

Scale Tones:
E♭ major: *so, la, ta, ti, do re ma mi fa so la ta ti do'*
G minor: *mi si la ti do'*

### Our World

Words by Jane Foster Knox
Music by Lana Walter

170

Words by Jane Foster Knox

# EXTENSION

## SPECIAL LEARNERS

Students who are poor readers or who have visual disabilities may have difficulty following the notation when the song changes from single to double staff format. Prepare a transparency of pages 170–171 of the Pupil Edition and point to the staff that has the melody. This procedure will enable different learners to follow the order of the song sections.

## SIGNING FOR "OUR WORLD"

In sign language the meaning of the phrase is signed. For example, to "make it so" means to make it happen or succeed; therefore the sign is "succeed." The signing begins with measure 29.

Think

The index finger points to the brain.

Race (People)

Using "P" palms-down hands, circle alternately in front of the body.

Find

With palm down, index finger and thumb close, as in picking up something.

World

Circle the right "W" forward, down, up, and around the left "W," as in the world revolving.

Fair/Lovely

The "O" hand starts at the chin, opens while circling the face, coming back to rest again at the chin.

The last A section differs a little from the first ones. Remember that when music contains a repetition after one contrast, it is in ternary form. It can be labeled ABA.

# LESSON 2

### Reinforcing the Lesson

Have the students identify and label a repetition after one contrast as *ternary form*.

## 3 APPRAISAL

The students should be able to:

1. Verbally identify repetitions and contrasts in visual art as well as accurately signal repeating sections and contrasting sections in Stravinsky's "Galop," and "Our World."

2. Verbally identify repetition after one contrast as ternary form.

---

**Loving**  With closed fists, cross hands over the heart.

**Caring**  Place open palms over the heart.

**Make It So (Succeed)**  Index fingers move up, making two loops, as in moving up the ladder toward success.

**Sharing** Move the upright open palm of the right hand back and forth across the open, palm-up left hand.

**Know** Fingers touch forehead.

### VOCAL DEVELOPMENT

Practice the A sections of the song on the syllable *hing* to achieve a marcato style. Practice the B section on a sustained *oo* vowel to provide a contrasting legato style of singing.

### COOPERATIVE LEARNING

Have the students work in cooperative groups to find examples within the textbook of songs or listening examples of AB and ternary form. Within each group, assign one student to identify AB or ternary selections. After the individual members of the group have found specific examples, they should present them to the group with a validation as to why they fit the assigned categories. The examples should then be listed by category on a sheet of paper to be signed by all of the group members to validate the answers.

# LESSON 3

**Focus Form—Repetition with More than One Contrast**

## Objectives
To identify repetition after more than one contrast in music as rondo form
To move to a composition in rondo form
To create an improvised rondo

## Materials
Recordings: "Hine Ma Tov"
"Hine Ma Tov" (performance mix)
"Sing Hosanna"
Bells, recorders, or keyboard instruments

## Vocabulary
Rondo

### 1 SETTING THE STAGE

Have the students listen to "Hine Ma Tov" and identify the repeated and contrasting sections. (You may wish to focus on the text repetitions.)
A section mm. 1–8, 17–24, and 33–40, highlighted in green
B section mm. 9–16, highlighted in orange
C section mm. 25–31, highlighted in yellow

### 2 TEACHING THE LESSON

**1. Learn "Hine Ma Tov."** Have the students:
• Learn the A section of the song and sing with the recording.
• Learn the entire song.

---

## REPETITION WITH MORE THAN ONE CONTRAST

• Listen to "Hine Ma Tov," an Israeli song about peace and harmony.

 "Hine Ma Tov" (hē´nā mä tov)

### Hine Ma Tov

Words from Psalm 133 verse 1
Music by Moshe Jacobson

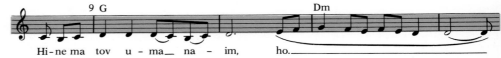

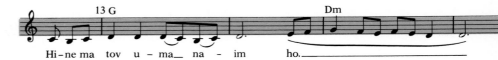

172

# EXTENSION

## PRONUNCIATION

Hine    ma tov uma    naim,
hē-nay´ mä töv o͞o´ mä nä-ēm´

Shevet achim    gam yachad.
shev´ et ä-кнēm´ gäm yä´ кнäd

---

Hi - ne ma tov u - ma na - im, she - vet a - chim gam ya - chad.

Hi - ne ma tov u - ma na - im, she - vet a - chim gam ya - chad.

© by Moshe Jacobson, Israel.

The form of "Hine Ma Tov" can be outlined as:

A    B    A    C    A

This form is called **rondo** form.

• Play this melodic accompaniment to "Hine Ma Tov" on recorder and bells.

• Identify and label repetition with more than one contrast as rondo form.

**2. Introduce the melodic accompaniment to "Hine Ma Tov."** Have the students:

• Identify the A, B, and C sections of the melodic accompaniment to "Hine Ma Tov." (The A section is highlighted in green, the B section in orange, and the C section in yellow.)

• Identify how the B and C sections are different from each other and from the A section. (The B section is to be played on bells, the C section is to be played on bells and recorder, and the A section is to be played on recorder.)

• Review G, A, B, C, and D on recorder or bells.

• Play the melodic descant with recording.

• Form two groups, with one group singing the song while the other plays the melodic accompaniment.

**3. Introduce repetition and contrast in the dance to "Hine Ma Tov."** Have the students:
• Prepare the basic movements.
• Do the dance with the song.

## Song and Dance

The traditional folk dance to "Hine Ma Tov" has repeated and contrasting steps. How does the form of the dance relate to the form of the song? patterns are arranged in rondo form

### "Hine Ma Tov" Dance

• Do the steps in place as you read the directions below.

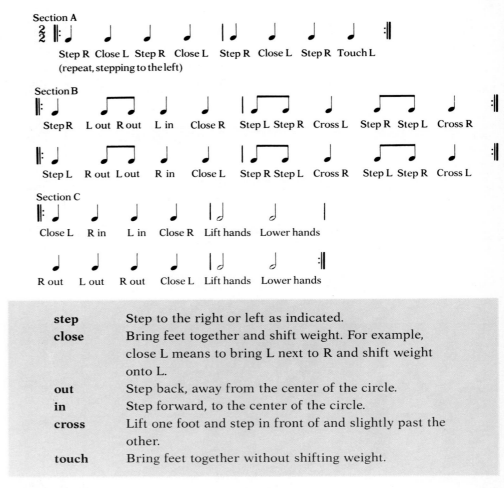

| step | Step to the right or left as indicated. |
|---|---|
| close | Bring feet together and shift weight. For example, close L means to bring L next to R and shift weight onto L. |
| out | Step back, away from the center of the circle. |
| in | Step forward, to the center of the circle. |
| cross | Lift one foot and step in front of and slightly past the other. |
| touch | Bring feet together without shifting weight. |

• Perform the dance in a single circle, hands joined at shoulder height with arms bent and elbows down (in "W" position).

174

E X T E N S I O N

### SPECIAL LEARNERS

If there are any mainstreamed students who are unable to participate in the movement exercises, divide the class into two groups. Have one group perform the steps to the "Hine Ma Tov" dance while the other performs the melodic accompaniment on bells or keyboard. The group playing the melodic accompaniment should be a mixture of regular and mainstreamed students. Prepare an overhead transparency of pupil page 173 to point to each section as it begins.

# Improvise with Rondo Form

You can create a rondo with part 1 of "Sing Hosanna." Choose one of the ostinati on page 115.

Key: Dorian mode on D    Starting Pitch: D    Scale Tones: *la, do re mi fi so la*

## Sing Hosanna

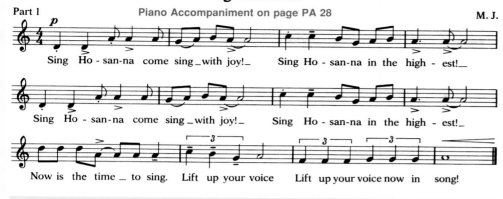

Part 1          Piano Accompaniment on page PA 28          M. J.

Sing Ho - san-na come sing _ with joy! _    Sing Ho - san-na in the high - est! _

Sing Ho - san-na come sing _ with joy! _    Sing Ho - san-na in the high - est! _

Now is the time _ to sing.  Lift up your voice    Lift up your voice now in    song!

**A**  Sing part 1 with the ostinato.

**B**  Improvise a bell or keyboard part using these pitches over the ostinato.

D  F  G  A  C  D

**A**  Sing part 1 again over the ostinato.

**C**  Improvise new melodies, using rhythms of the words over the ostinato.

**A**  Sing part 1 again over the ostinato.

This computer image represents rondo form.

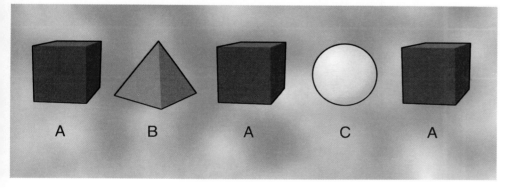

A    B    A    C    A

# LESSON 3

## Reinforcing the Lesson

Have the students:
• Review "Sing Hosanna," with ostinati (pp. 114–115).
• Practice improvising a melody on bells using the pitches D F G A C D.
• Practice a vocal improvisation using the rhythm of the words of "Sing Hosanna."
• Perform their improvised rondo.

## 3 APPRAISAL

The students should be able to:
1. Verbally identify "Hine Ma Tov" as being in rondo form since it has repeating sections after more than one contrasting section.
2. Accurately perform the movements for the folk dance to "Hine Ma Tov."
3. Create a composition in rondo form by singing or playing a familiar melody for the first and repeating sections and improvising at least two contrasting sections using voice and/or classroom instruments.

## MORE MUSIC TEACHING IDEAS

Have the students improvise a composition in rondo form using Orff instruments:
1. Perform a sixteen-beat-long melody and accompaniment in Dorian mode or on a pentatonic scale for the A section.
2. Improvise a sixteen-beat-long contrasting B section in Dorian mode or on a pentatonic scale.
3. Repeat the A section.
4. Improvise a sixteen-beat-long contrasting C section in Dorian mode or on a pentatonic scale.
5. Repeat the A section.
6. Compare and contrast the A, B, and C sections.

## CURRICULUM CONNECTION: ART

**Illustrating Form**—Have the students design visual diagrams to represent AB, ternary, and rondo forms, using triangles for A, circles for B, and squares for C.

## LESSON 4

**Focus: Repetition and Contrast**

**Objective**
To identify and perform repetition and contrast in music

**Materials**
Recording: March from *Folk Song Suite* by Vaughan Williams
Tennis balls
Copying Master 7-1: Listening Map (optional)

**Vocabulary**
Suite

### 1 SETTING THE STAGE
Have the students discuss the information on the suite.

### 2 TEACHING THE LESSON

**1. Introduce the March from the Folk Song Suite.** Have the students:
• Listen to the recording of the March. Identify repetition and contrasts of sections and list their answers on a separate sheet of paper. (You may wish to use Copying Master 7-1: Listening Map at this time.)
• Listen again to identify the contrasts of legato, staccato, and dynamics.
1 Section A  staccato  *p*
2 Section A  staccato  *f*
3 Section B  legato  *p*
4 Section C  staccato  *ff*
5 Section C  staccato  *ff*
6 Section B  legato  *p*
7 Section A  staccato  *p*
8 Section A  staccato  *f*

**2. Introduce tennis ball activity for experience of repetition and contrast.**
Have the students:
• Prepare to perform the tennis ball activ-

---

## CONTRAST IN FORM

**CD4:5** A **suite** is a large-scale musical work consisting of several individual smaller forms linked together. Each of these forms is based on repetition and contrast. In the art on page 162, the image you see is a result of many shapes repeated and contrasted.

• Listen to the March from *Folk Song Suite* by Ralph Vaughan Williams. Listen for repeated and contrasting sections.

 March from *Folk Song Suite* by Ralph Vaughan Williams

• Listen to the March again. Identify the form by the use of staccato and legato and changes in dynamics.  *See Teaching the Lesson.*

Ralph Vaughan Williams uses legato, staccato, and changes in dynamics to provide contrast for the A, B, and C sections of the March.

| 1. | A | bounce | catch | bounce | catch |
|----|---|--------|-------|--------|-------|
| 2. | A | bounce | catch | bounce | catch |
| 3. | B | roll | two | three | catch |
| 4. | C | bounce | catch | toss | catch |
| 5. | C | bounce | catch | toss | catch |
| 6. | B | roll | two | three | catch |
| 7. | A | bounce | catch | bounce | catch |
| 8. | A | bounce | catch | bounce | catch |

• Listen to the March again. Move a tennis ball to the steady beat as indicated.

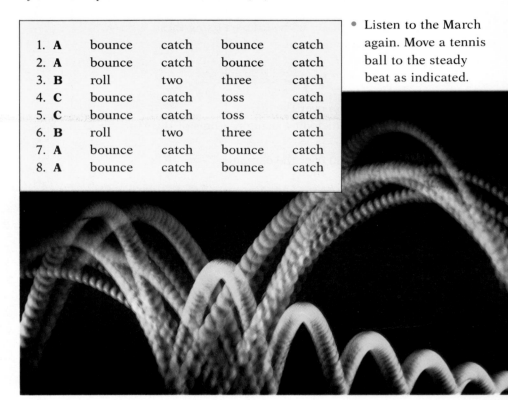

---

# EXTENSION

**MORE MUSIC TEACHING IDEAS**
Have the students select and bring recordings of popular songs that have repetition and contrast.

## RALPH VAUGHAN WILLIAMS

Ralph Vaughan Williams (1872–1958), a great English composer, was born in Gloucestershire, England. His interest in music was sparked by his grandmother, who encouraged him to study piano and violin. He later went on to study composition and organ at Trinity College, Cambridge.

Vaughan Williams had great pride in his homeland. He loved his country's folk music—"the lilt of the chorus in a music hall . . . the children dancing to a barrel organ . . . the cries of street peddlers." Throughout his life, he was an active collector of English folk songs. His own music was greatly influenced by the many songs he collected and wrote down. The *Folk Song Suite* uses some of his favorites. The "March" from this suite contrasts dynamics and textures by using different combinations of instruments.

Besides composing, Vaughan Williams was involved in many other aspects of musical life. He wanted to make all English people aware of their rich musical heritage. He taught, wrote about music, conducted at choral festivals, and always encouraged young musicians.

177

# LESSON 4

ities by practicing the patterns for the A, B, and C sections.
• Perform tennis ball movement activities with recording.

**3. Introduce the composer Ralph Vaughan Williams.** Have the students discuss the information on Ralph Vaughan Williams.

You may wish to use some of the following items as a basis for extended discussion:

Ralph Vaughan Williams was a very successful and popular composer. Why do you think he was so well liked by his fellow citizens? (enthusiasm for native folk music, skill at communicating, helpfulness to young musicians) Name some American composers who also had a special message for their own people.

(Morton Gould, *American Salute*, pp. 156–159; Aaron Copland, *Appalachian Spring*, based on American folk music; Bruce Springsteen, "Born in the U.S.A.," "My Home Town")

## Reinforcing the Lesson

Have the students summarize Vaughan Williams' use of articulation and dynamics to provide contrast in the A, B, and C sections of March.

### 3 APPRAISAL

The students should be able to:

1. Listen to Vaughan Williams' March from the *Folk Song Suite* and with eyes closed, using different signals for A, B, and C sections, identify repeating and contrasting sections.

2. Listen to Vaughan Williams' March from the *Folk Song Suite* and, using a prepared form that lists all the repeating and contrasting sections in order (A A B C C B A A), write the most correct dynamic symbol ($p$, $f$, or $ff$) and articulation word (staccato or legato) for each section.

## COOPERATIVE LEARNING

After identifying the A A B C C B A A form of "March" from the *Folk Song Suite*, have the students work in cooperative groups to draw a listening map of the piece. The musical characteristics to be highlighted on the map are the musical constructs developed in the lesson: form, articulation, and dynamics. Encourage any other generalized descriptions that would help a listener follow the maps. When the maps are completed, collect them and redistribute each to another group. Each group should try to follow the new map. Provide an opportunity for students to render constructive suggestions.

## SPECIAL LEARNERS

If there are any students in the class with auditory learning disabilities, prepare an overhead transparency of Copying Master 7-1: Listening Map as well as individual student copies. As the listening selection is played, pause at the end of each section to allow the students to fill out the chart. Then fill in the correct responses on the transparency. This will help mainstreamed students to coordinate the auditory activity with the visual task.

# REVIEW AND EVALUATION

## JUST CHECKING

**Objective**
To review and test the skills and concepts taught in Unit 7

**Materials**
Recordings: "Cripple Creek"
"Shifting Meters"
"Hine Ma Tov"
Courante
Unit 7 Evaluation
(question 3)
*For Extra Credit* recordings
(optional)
Drumsticks, recorder, bells, or keyboard
Copying Master 7-2 (optional)
Evaluation Unit 7 Copying Master

## TEACHING THE LESSON

**Review the skills and concepts taught in Unit 7.** Have the students:
• Perform the activities and answer the questions on pages 178–179 using the recordings from the unit.
• Review their answers.
(You may wish to use Copying Master 7-2 at this time.)

---

## JUST CHECKING

See how much you remember.

1. Listen to "Cripple Creek." Pat the steady beat during the verse (or A section) and snap during the refrain (or B section).

2. Listen to "Shifting Meters." Show the form by conducting in duple meter during the A section.
Conduct in triple meter during the B section.

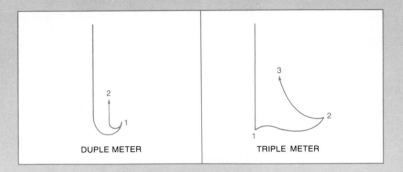

DUPLE METER          TRIPLE METER

3. Listen to "Hine Ma Tov." Show the A sections by performing the following pattern:

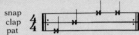

4. Choose one of the works of art on pages 162–163 and describe ways in which the artist achieved contrast.   Answers may vary.

5. Which of these diagrams represents ternary form? Which represents rondo form?   ABA; ABACA

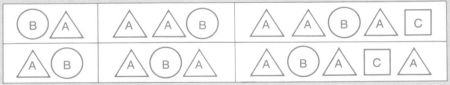

178

6. Perform the following examples. Use them to create your own ternary and rondo forms.

A — recorder, bells, or keyboard
B — sticks (tap together) / sticks (tap on desk tops)
C — snap / clap / pat

R L R L

7. Play this melodic accompaniment on bells or keyboard to show the contrast between the two sections.

8. Review "Our World" and describe how contrast is achieved.
The B section is in minor. The B section is more legato than the A section.

179

## GIVING THE EVALUATION

Evaluation Unit 7 Copying Master can be found in the *Teacher's Copying Masters* book along with full directions for giving the evaluation and checking the answers.

## FOR EXTRA CREDIT

You may want to have students answer the following question.
Describe how dance movements may be used as a means of showing musical form. (Contrasting dance movements for contrasting sections of music will reflect the form. Ideally they should also reflect the musical character of the selection.)
(You may wish to play recordings to refresh the students' memories.)

| ELEMENTS OF MUSIC | UNIT 8 OBJECTIVES | Lesson 1 CORE Focus: Composers Make Decisions | Lesson 2 Focus: Composers Make Decisions About Tone Color |
|---|---|---|---|
| Dynamics | Identify dynamic changes | Hear dynamic changes | |
| Tone Color | **Identify marching band, orchestra, families of instruments, blend and contrast** **Identify decisions about tone color and tone colors in scores** Create a composition with various tone colors | Identify orchestral tone color Identify decisions made by composers concerning tone color Identify various tone colors Identify brass, strings, woodwinds, and percussion Play using two tone colors | Identify band and orchestra tone colors Discuss tone colors available in the late 19th century Identify and discuss appropriate tone colors for given compositions Identify form through tone color changes Compare performances using different tone colors |
| Tempo | **Perform rhythms in steady tempo** | Perform rhythms in steady tempo | |
| Duration/ Rhythm | Listen to and perform beat and beat subdivisions | Read and perform a rhythm accompaniment with beat subdivisions | Follow a steady beat listening map |
| Pitch | Perform G A B C D on recorder, bells, or keyboard Sing four partner songs | | |
| Texture | Identify thin and thick textures Perform in polyphonic texture | | Listen to thin and thick textures |
| Form | **Identify march form** Improvise rondo form Perform four-part quodlibet | | Identify the form of a march (AABBC bridge C bridge C) |
| Style | Listen to and perform to American march, baroque music, film music | Listen to and perform with film music | Discuss John Philip Sousa and the development of the march style |
| Reading | | Read ♪ , ♪. ♪ , ♩ , 𝄽 , ▬ , ▬ , ‖: :‖ in 𝟰/𝟰 | Follow listening map |

## PURPOSE Unit 8: Tone Color

This unit focuses on the decisions composers make in writing music. The students will experience how blending and contrasting tone colors are used in music and how changes in tone color enhance musical interest. The students will listen to identify tone color and create a composition that displays the effects of tone color.

## SUGGESTED TIME FRAME

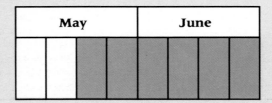

| May | | | June | | | |
|---|---|---|---|---|---|---|
| | | | | | | |

## FOCUS

- Decisions about tone color
- Choosing colors to provide contrast
- Blending tone colors

| **Lesson 3**<br>Focus: Composers Choose Tone Colors to Provide Contrast | **Lesson 4**<br>Focus: Blending Tone Colors |
|---|---|
| Identify dynamic change and contrast<br>Create a portion of a composition with dynamic contrasts | |
| Listen to and identify instrumental and vocal tone colors<br>Identify tone color found in musical scores<br>Create a portion of a composition using various tone colors of classroom instruments | Listen to and identify tone colors that blend<br>Listen to and differentiate between blending and contrasting tone colors<br>Listen to and identify tone color families<br><br>**Identify examples of blending tone colors** |
| Perform a rhythm accompaniment on sticks<br>Create a portion of a composition using contrasting rhythms | Perform a quodlibet with a steady beat<br>Perform a quodlibet with rhythmic accuracy |
| Perform a melodic accompaniment on recorder, bells, or keyboard<br>Create, notate, and perform a composition using pitched and unpitched instruments | Perform four partner songs with melodic accuracy |
| Listen to and identify thin and thick textures in musical scores | Perform nonimitative polyphonic texture |
| Determine the form of a composition<br>Create and notate a composition for classroom instruments with contrasting tone colors | Experience repetition and contrast<br>Perform a quodlibet of four songs |
| Determine texture and tone color used in rock and baroque music | |
| Read ♩♩ , ♩. , *p* , *f* , < , > , *f* > *p*<br>Follow listening chart<br>Read musical score | |

# TECHNOLOGY

## MUSIC WITH *MIDI*

MIDI technology allows students to manipulate musical elements and make musical decisions.

• Lesson 3, page 194 Create a **Rondo**: *"The Boatman's Dance"*

## VIDEO RESOURCES

Use video resources to reinforce, extend, and enrich learning in this unit.

# LESSON 1

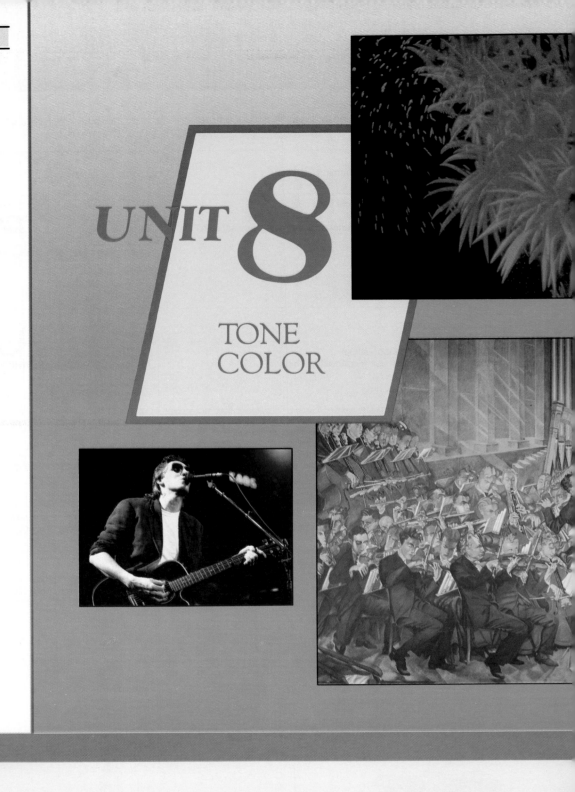

UNIT 8

TONE COLOR

Emerson String Quartet

Symphony, Maximilian Mopp, NEW YORK GRAPHIC SOCIETY, LTD.

As you listen to "Tone Color Montage 1,"
match the tone color you hear
with the correct picture.

 "Tone Color Montage 1"

181

# LESSON 1

**Focus: Composers Make Decisions**

**Objectives**
To identify decisions made by composers
about tone color
To perform a rhythm accompaniment with
drumsticks

**Materials**
Recordings: "Tone Color Montage 1"
Theme from *Raiders of the Lost
Ark*
"Procession of the Nobles"
Drumsticks or substitutes

## 1 SETTING THE STAGE

Have the students listen to "Tone Color
Montage 1" and match each tone color they
hear with the correct picture on pages 180
and 181.

# LESSON 1

**2 TEACHING THE LESSON**

**1. Introduce the fact that composers make decisions.** Have the students:
• Identify music of composers shown.
John Williams, Theme from *Star Wars*
Morton Gould, *American Salute*
Bessie Smith, ''Lost Your Head Blues''
Elton John (and Bernie Taupin), ''Crocodile Rock''
• Discuss the decisions composers make.

Morton Gould

Bessie Smith

Elton John

John Williams

In writing music, composers make musical decisions.

"How fast should this composition be performed?"
"Should this be louder?"
"What instruments would sound best?"

182

- Use the matched grip to perform this rhythmic accompaniment to the theme from *Raiders of the Lost Ark*, by John Williams.
for matched grip, see p. 3

**Theme from *Raiders of the Lost Ark***
**Rhythm Accompaniment**

♩ = on desk
✗ = strike stick in air

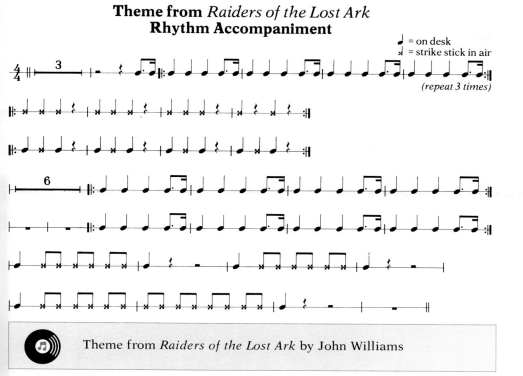

(repeat 3 times)

♪ Theme from *Raiders of the Lost Ark* by John Williams

Harrison Ford as Indiana Jones in a scene from *Raiders of the Lost Ark*

# LESSON 1

**2. Introduce the rhythmic accompaniment to the theme from *Raiders of the Lost Ark*.** Have the students:

• Listen to the theme from *Raiders of the Lost Ark* and identify the tone colors they hear. (orchestra, mostly brass; line 1: *mp* brass; line 2: low brass *mp*; line 3: brass and strings *f* line 4: brass and strings; line 5: brass, strings, woodwinds; line 6: full orchestra with percussion; line 7: brass and percussion)

• Play the rhythmic accompaniment to the theme from *Raiders of the Lost Ark*, focusing on the contrasts of tone color of the two different sticking techniques. The normal note heads represent striking the drumstick on a desk and the X-shaped note heads represent striking the sticks together in the air. (You may wish to have students choose different unpitched percussion instruments when they perform the rhythmic accompaniment.)

• Discuss possible reasons for the different tone colors in the theme as well as the different sticking tone colors in the accompaniment. (give variety, blend, contrast, interest, show thematic changes, mood, or setting)

## Reinforcing the Lesson

Have the students review "Procession of the Nobles" (page 30) and identify the musical decisions about tone color Rimsky-Korsakov made in composing this work.

### 3 APPRAISAL

The students should be able to:
1. Verbally identify at least three musical decisions composers make that affect tone color and provide one example from a familiar composition.
2. With drumsticks, perform a simple rhythm accompaniment with rhythmic accuracy.

## SPECIAL LEARNERS

If the class has mainstreamed students who have visual disabilities or difficulty tracking abstract symbols, divide the class into six groups, assigning a line to each. The sixth group will have the last two lines. Each group will pick up from the previous one. Prepare an overhead transparency of pupil page 183, color-coding each line, to point to each line as it begins.

# LESSON 2

**Focus: Composers Make Decisions About Tone Color**

### Objectives
To identify and discuss the appropriate tone color to be used for a march
To discuss tone colors available in the late nineteenth century
To listen to a march performed with various tone colors

### Materials
Recordings: *The Stars and Stripes Forever* (band version)
*The Stars and Stripes Forever* Montage
''Little Fugue in G Minor'' (orchestral version)
''Little Fugue in G Minor'' (organ version; excerpt)
Copying Master 8-1 (optional)

## 1 SETTING THE STAGE
Discuss the information on marches and bands.

## 2 TEACHING THE LESSON

**1. Introduce the listening map for *The Stars and Stripes Forever*.** Have the students:
• Listen to *The Stars and Stripes Forever* as they follow the Parade Route Guide. (Each square is equal to one measure or two beats.)

CD4:13 **Follow the Parade Route**

You have heard and seen marches being performed at parades, sports events, and at concerts. The strong steady beat of the march makes it easy to move to the music. Wind and percussion instruments are usually used in a marching band. They have a powerful and unique tone color. One of the most famous marches is *The Stars and Stripes Forever* by John Philip Sousa.

• "March" along with this composition by following the Parade Route Guide below. Move to the next square every two beats.

 *The Stars and Stripes Forever,* by John Philip Sousa (soo'sä), band version

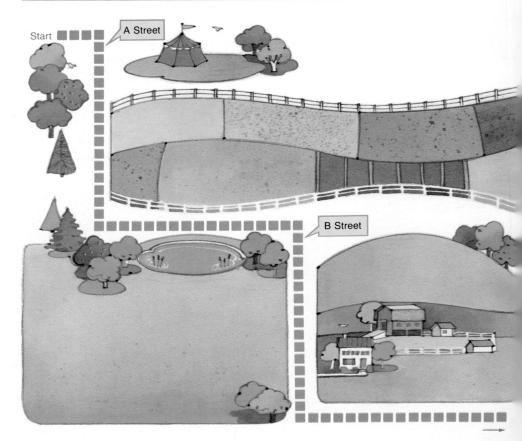

184

# EXTENSION

### LISTENING
You may wish to use the Listening Map overhead transparency to help guide the students through the listening selection.

Examine the Parade Route Guide.

How many different sections can you find?

Are any of the sections the same? None of the sections are the same

What is the overall form of this march? AA, BB, C, Bridge, C, Bridge, C

How do Sousa's changes in tone color help identify the form?
He uses contrasts of tone color to emphasize the different sections.

• Identify the form of *The Stars and Stripes Forever* by focusing on the questions in the text.

The march has four sections:
   A Street
   B Street
   C Street (three times)
   Bridge (twice)

The overall form of the march is AA, BB, C, Bridge, C, Bridge, C. Sousa uses contrasts of tone color to emphasize the different sections of the march. Point out the piccolo part in the last section. (You may wish to use Copying Master 8-1 at this time.)

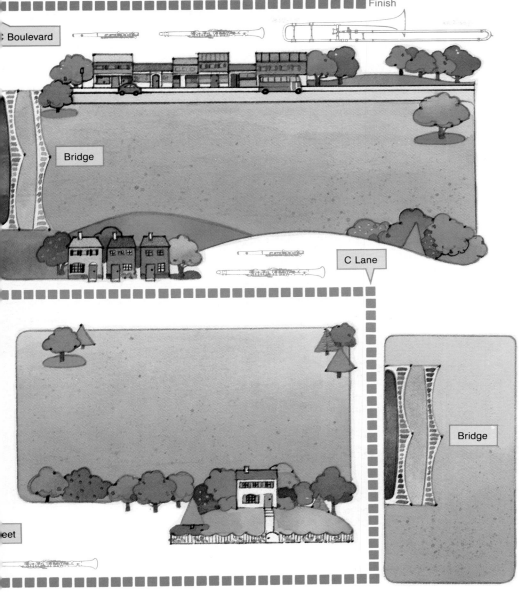

Finish

Boulevard

Bridge

C Lane

Bridge

eet

185

**2. Introduce decisions about tone color selection.** Have the students:
• Discuss the tone color resources which were available to John Philip Sousa in the late 1800s and identify the instruments shown.
• Follow the listening guide as they listen to *The Stars and Stripes Forever* performed on different instruments.
• Discuss Sousa's choice of the band as the most appropriate tone color for *The Stars and Stripes Forever*. (*The Stars and Stripes Forever* is a march. The marching band is the most appropriate tone color because the marching band instruments are portable, loud, and produce a variety of tone colors. The organ and piano are not normally outdoor instruments and are stationary. The accordion does not usually play marches and the sound is not loud enough for a parade. An orchestra is stationary.)

**3. Introduce John Philip Sousa.** Have the students discuss the information on John Philip Sousa.

You may wish to use some of the following items as a basis for extended discussion.

1. Discuss some of the reasons why Washington, D.C., is a world center. (It is the center of our government, many famous people from all over the world visit the city, Kennedy Center, Cherry Blossom Festival, the Washington Redskins football team.)

2. How might Sousa's life have been different if he had run away from home at the age of thirteen and joined a circus band? (Answers will vary, but direct students to different possibilities for choice.)

3. Discuss the effect of environment on the development of a person's values. Relate this to Sousa's career choice. (Answers will vary.)

CD4:14 **Composers Make Decisions About Tone Color**

When John Philip Sousa composed *The Stars and Stripes Forever* he decided to use the tone color of a marching band.

• Listen to these sections of *The Stars and Stripes Forever* for different tone colors.

 *The Stars and Stripes Forever* Montage

Why do you think Sousa chose the tone color of the marching band?

186

# JOHN PHILIP SOUSA

John Philip Sousa (1854–1932), known as the "March King," was born in Washington, D.C. During the Civil War Sousa's father was a member of the Marine Corps Band. John Philip watched him perform in concerts and parades that helped to raise the spirits of the people. By the time John Philip was a teenager, he could play several band instruments, as well as the violin.

When John Philip was thirteen, he decided to run away and join a circus band. His father found out and encouraged the boy to enlist in the Marine Corps Band instead. His experience in the Marine Corps Band gave Sousa excellent musical background. At twenty-six, he became the conductor of the Marine Band. Sousa required high musical standards of the members of the Marine Band. He also was concerned with improving the quality of band instruments. One of his suggestions led to the invention of the sousaphone, a special kind of tuba that the player can carry while marching.

In 1890, Sousa left the Marine Band and founded his own band. He and his band toured the world and were acclaimed everywhere.

187

# LESSON 2

### Reinforcing the Lesson

Have the students review the orchestral version of the "Little Fugue in G Minor" (page 150), then listen to the organ version. Compare these performances in terms of their use of tone color: In which version is the subject easier to hear? (answers will vary) What might have influenced the arranger in selecting the instruments to perform the subject? (answers will vary)

## 3 APPRAISAL

The students should be able to:
1. Verbally identify at least three reasons why the tone color of a band may be appropriate for a march.
2. Listen to several versions of a march (i.e., *The Stars and Stripes Forever*) performed by different instruments or ensembles and verbally identify the tone color changes and suggest at least two additional ways that tone color could be changed using instruments available in the late nineteenth century.

## COOPERATIVE LEARNING

After the students have read about John Philip Sousa, have them form three groups for brief discussions on the three extended discussion items in the lesson, then report back to the class. Divide the class into groups by having the students counting off by threes. Identify the three meeting areas of the room. Group 1 should discuss why Washington, D.C., is considered a world center. Group 2 should discuss how Sousa's life might have been different if he had run away at the age of thirteen to join a circus band. Group 3 should discuss the effect of environment on the development of a person's values, relating this to Sousa's career choice. Each group should choose a spokesperson to give a brief report on the group's discussion and conclusions.

# LESSON 3

## Contrast in Visual Art

When you look at a work of art, you focus on many different things about it. Sometimes a painting shows something that is easy to recognize.

*Early Sunday Morning, Edward Hopper, WHITNEY MUSEUM OF AMERICAN ART, NY*

**Focus: Composers Choose Tone Colors to Provide Contrast**

### Objectives

To identify families of tone colors from pictures

To identify individual instrumental and vocal tone colors from pictures and by sound

To identify and name the tone colors in a musical score

To create and notate a musical composition illustrating contrast

### Materials

Recordings: "Tone Color Montage 2" (with call numbers)
    *Contrast I*
    *Contrast II*, A section

Drumsticks, bells, recorder or keyboard

Tape recorder (if available)

### Vocabulary

Score

## 1 SETTING THE STAGE

Have the students:

• Discuss the Hopper painting, focusing on its pictorial qualities.

• Examine the other painting and determine how lines, shapes, and colors build contrast. (Shapes are different and are contrasting in color.)

When you first look at the work of art shown below, your attention may be drawn to the contrasts. What are some of the contrasts you see?

Shapes are different and are contrasting in color.

*The Frozen Sounds, No. 1, Adolph Gottlieb, WHITNEY MUSEUM OF AMERICAN ART, NY*

# EXTENSION

## CURRICULUM CONNECTION: FINE ARTS

Have the students look at the two paintings on this page and decide which one shows repetition. (the top painting) Ask them to identify the shapes that are repeated. (the windows, the line of the roof) Have them look at the other painting and identify the shapes. (circle, half circle, rectangle)

Give each student an envelope that contains a combination of various-sized triangles, squares, rectangles, and circles cut from construction paper. Have the students arrange the shapes into easily recognizable patterns, such as all triangles, triangle/square/triangle, and so on. Have the students choose a classroom instrument for each of the four shapes—triangle, square, rectangle, circle.

Have them create a composition based on their arrangement of the shapes.

Then have them arrange the shapes into a random design. Have them create another composition based on this new design.

## THE ARTISTS

**Edward Hopper** (1882–1967)—was an American painter who painted realistic scenes of everyday life. He portrayed subjects such as bridges, railroads, street scenes, and lighthouses. He is known for painting still, peaceful scenes that seem to have fresh air and clear light.

**Adolph Gottlieb** (ā′dolf got′lēb) (1903–1974)—was an American painter. Some of his paintings, such as *The Frozen Sounds, No. 1,* are similar to landscapes, with a horizon and simple shapes suspended in the sky above it. Contrasting colors and shapes are balanced and not much movement or emotion is expressed.

# Identifying Tone Color Contrasts

The following chart shows some of the instrumental tone colors
that composers use.

• Identify each tone color you hear and match it with a picture. c, b, d, c, c

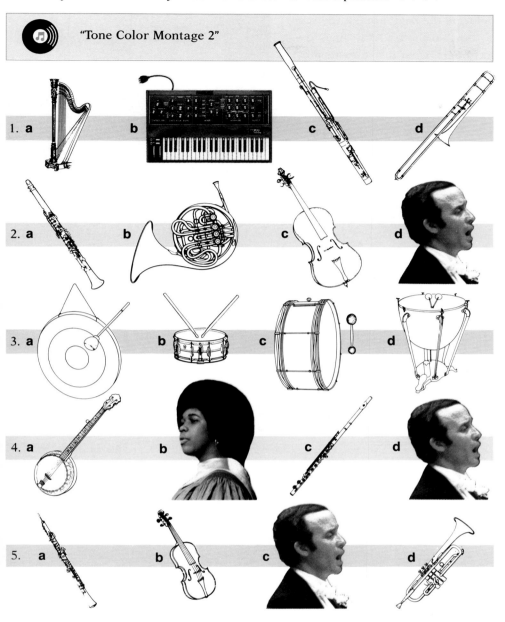

"Tone Color Montage 2"

1. a   b   c   d

2. a   b   c   d

3. a   b   c   d

4. a   b   c   d

5. a   b   c   d

189

**1. Review the basic tone colors available to composers.** Have the students:
• Identify the tone color families by name. (strings, woodwinds, brass, percussion, voices)
• Listen to "Tone Color Montage 2" and match the picture with the tone color they hear as each number is called.

# LESSON 3

**2. Introduce musical scores.** Have the students:
• Discuss the information on musical scores.
• Examine the musical scores and identify the tone colors used. (The instruments and voices in the Bach are: trumpet; flute; oboes; violins; viola; soprano, alto, tenor, bass voices; organ.)

## Focusing on Contrasts

A musical **score** is the notation of a composition, showing all the parts to be played or sung.

Below is the beginning of the score of "Born in the U.S.A." Besides the vocal part, what instruments are called for in this score?

piano/keyboard, guitar

Bruce Springsteen

### Born in the U.S.A.

Words and music by
Bruce Springsteen

Moderate Rock ( ♩ = 120)

1. Born down in a dead man's town, the first kick I took was when I

The score shown below is part of a composition by Johann Sebastian Bach. Many of the instruments Bach used are similar to those used today. The instruments he chose are indicated on the left side of the score.

• Which instruments and voices did he decide to use? shown on score
• Find a section of the score where all the instruments and voices are performing. mm. 1–5
• Find a contrasting section of the score in which the fewest instruments and voices are performing. mm. 6–7

### Cantata No. 78, Jesu der du meine Seele

J.S. Bach

• Find a portion of the score where all tone colors are used. (mm. 1–5)
• Find the portion of the score where the fewest tone colors are used. (mm. 6–7)

# LESSON 3

**3. Introduce *Contrast I*.** Have the students:
• Listen to decide in which measures only a few instruments are playing and when all the instruments are playing. (few: mm. 13–20, 23–24, 27–28; all: mm. 1–12, 21–22, 25–26, 29–31)
• Identify the measures in which brass and percussion tone colors are featured. (mm. 5–12, 21–22, 25–26)
• Identify the measures in which woodwind tone colors are featured. (mm. 13–20, 23–24, 27–28)
• Discuss how the changes in tone color enhance musical contrast. (answers will vary)

CD4:17 *Contrast I* emphasizes contrasting tone colors.

• Listen closely to the contrasts in the music. When do you hear mostly brass and percussion? When do you hear mostly woodwinds? The A sections have mostly brass and percussion, the B section mostly woodwinds.

 *Contrast I*

On White II, Wassily Kandinsky, MUSÉE NATIONAL D'ART MODERNE, Paris

Notice the contrasting shapes and forms in this painting.

192

**THE ARTIST**

**Wassily Kandinsky**
See page 113.

- Play the rhythmic accompaniment on sticks.
- Play the melodic accompaniment on recorder, bells, or keyboard.
- Decide where you want to play either or both accompaniments to emphasize contrast.

**Contrast I**

Theldon Myers

193

- Play the rhythm accompaniment to *Contrast I* on sticks with the recording.
- Play the melodic accompaniment to *Contrast I* on recorder, bells, or keyboard with the recording.
- Form two groups and play both accompaniments to *Contrast I* with the recording.
- Make suggestions as to the measures where the accompaniments should play alone, combine, or rest so that contrast can be emphasized. (answers will vary, but guide student responses so that the form of the work is outlined)
- Play the accompaniments with the recording, using students' suggestions.

**SPECIAL LEARNERS**

Mainstreamed students with poor reading and/or visual skills will benefit from the use of an overhead transparency of pupil page 193. The use of a transparency will enable the student to be visually cued to the correct line of the *Contrast I* accompaniment.

**Creating Contrasts**

# LESSON 3

**4. Introduce** *Contrast II.* Have the students:
• Listen to the A section of *Contrast II.*
• Examine the score to *Contrast II* on page 195 and answer the questions. (tone colors of sticks and drums, the rhythm pattern ♫ ♩ ♩ ♫, and the following dynamic plan: *f* ⟶ *p*)
• Read the information in preparation for creating and notating two contrasting sections as indicated.

● Listen to the A section of *Contrast II.*

 *Contrast II*, A section

What are the tone colors, rhythms, and dynamics of this section? See box A on p. 195.

You will compose sections B and C and create a rondo.

● Select classroom instruments to contrast with the tone colors of the A section. Decide on the length of sections B and C.

This chart gives you some suggestions.

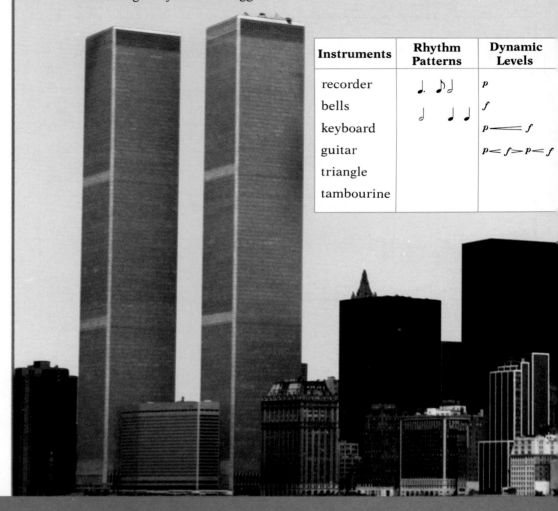

| Instruments | Rhythm Patterns | Dynamic Levels |
|---|---|---|
| recorder | ♩. ♪♩ | *p* |
| bells | ♩ ♩ ♩ | *f* |
| keyboard | | *p* ⟨ *f* |
| guitar | | *p* ⟨ *f* ⟩ *p* ⟨ *f* |
| triangle | | |
| tambourine | | |

- Make your decisions and write them down.
- Practice and play your composition.
- Copy and complete this chart.

## Contrast II

|  | A | B | A | C | A |
|---|---|---|---|---|---|
| This section is: | 15 seconds | ? | 15 seconds | ? | 15 seconds |
| The tone color is: | sticks, drums | ? | sticks, drums | ? | sticks, drums |
| The rhythm pattern is: | ♫ ♩ ♩ ♫ | ? | ♫ ♩ ♩ ♫ | ? | ♫ ♩ ♩ ♫ |
| With the dynamics: | *f* ══ *p* | ? | *f* ══ *p* | ? | *f* ══ *p* |

Contrast is all around us. The skyline of New York City contains buildings of contrasting shapes, sizes, and styles.

# LESSON 3

- Practice and play their composition.
- Record the compositions and evaluate them to determine if contrast is achieved.

### Reinforcing the Lesson

Have the students identify how the use of contrasting tone colors helps to create musical interest in other musical compositions. (answers will vary)

### 3 APPRAISAL

The students should be able to:

1. Look at pictures of families of instrumental tone colors while listening to excerpts of compositions written for keyboard, voice, string, brass, woodwind and percussion families and identify the instrumental family.

2. Listen to several performances of a single composition or song for solo voice or instrument in which tone color is changed and verbally identify the change.

3. Look at a score for instruments and voices and verbally identify the tone colors used in the composition.

4. When a repeating musical phrase is given, create and notate two different musical phrases or sections that contrast with the given musical phrase and demonstrate decisions regarding length, tone color, rhythm, and dynamics.

# LESSON 4

**Focus: Blending Tone Colors**

**Objectives**
To identify examples of tone colors that blend
To identify families of tone colors from recorded examples

**Materials**
Recordings: *American Quodlibet*
"Tone Color Montage 3"
"Saints Montage"

**Vocabulary**
Orchestration, quodlibet, blend

## 1 SETTING THE STAGE

Discuss the information on orchestration.

## 2 TEACHING THE LESSON

**1. Introduce *American Quodlibet*.** Have the students:
• Discuss the information on orchestration and the quodlibet.
• Learn each song in the quodlibet.
• Sing *American Quodlibet*, emphasizing the combination of voices within each section.

## BLENDING TONE COLORS

CD4:19 Remember that *orchestration* is the selection of instrumental tone colors for a composition. Sometimes when composers **orchestrate**, or arrange, a composition, they use tone colors from the same family of instruments. *American Quodlibet* has been arranged for voices. A **quodlibet** consists of several songs or melodies that can be performed together.

• Form four groups. Each group should sing its song alone.
• Combine all four songs.

*Recording Session* is by the American artist Romare Bearden.

196

# EXTENSION

## SPECIAL LEARNERS

If there are mainstreamed students who have aural learning disabilities or are weak singers, divide the class into two groups, making sure that the stronger singers are equally divided. The mainstreamed students also may need a visual starting cue since all the songs do not begin on the downbeat.

## THE ARTIST

**Romare (Howard) Bearden** (1914–1988)— was an American artist who lived across from the Apollo Theatre in Harlem and was inspired by the great jazz musicians who played there. In the *Recording Session*, he blended images about jazz, strong black lines, and distinctly colored shapes into a collage that looks like a stained glass window.

**American Quodlibet**  Scale Tones: See below.

When the Saints Go Marching In – *do re mi fa so*

arr. V.L.

F

Oh when the   saints _____ go  march - in'   in, _____ Oh when the

C7                                          F

saints  go  march - in'   in, _____ Oh Lord  I   want    to   be    in  that

Bb                          F          C7          F

num - ber _____   when  the   saints   go   march - in'   in.

F Nobody Knows the Trouble I've Seen – *so, la, do re mi fa so*

No - bod - y   knows   the   trou - ble   I've   seen,

C7                    F

No - bod - y   knows   my   sor - row.   No - bod - y   knows   the

Bb                    F          C7          F

trou - ble  I've   seen.   Glo - ry   hal - le - lu - jah!

F Good Night, Ladies – *so, do re mi fa*

C7

Good   night,   la - dies,   Good   night,   la - dies,

F              Bb                    F          C7          F

Good   night,   la - dies, _____ we're   go - ing   to  leave   you   now.

F Swing Low, Sweet Chariot – *so, la, do re mi so la*

Swing   low,   sweet   char - i - ot,

C7                              F

com - in'  for   to   car - ry   me   home;   Swing _____ low,   sweet

Bb                          F          C7          F

char - i - ot, _____ com - in'  for   to   car - ry   me   home. _____

When you sang *American Quodlibet,* you combined the tone colors
of the individual voices in your group. At the same time the tone
colors of all groups combined to create a whole.

197

# LESSON 4

- Discuss the information on *American Quodlibet.*

**2. Introduce blending color in visual art.** Have the students identify the individual colors used by both artists, and discuss how they blend to make a whole.

# Blending Color in Visual Art

- Identify the individual colors in each painting.

  Monet: blue-purple, pale yellow, gold; Frankenthaler: rose, tan, lavender, blue, green

*Rouen Cathedral in Full Sunlight,* by Claude Monet

198

# EXTENSION

### THE ARTIST

**Claude Monet** (klôd mō-nā′) (1840–1926) —was a French painter and the founder of the painting style called Impressionism. He used short brush strokes and patches of color to quickly capture his personal impressions of a scene. He often painted the same field or building over and over to show how the changing light of day affected the way it looked. One building he painted several times was Rouen Cathedral.

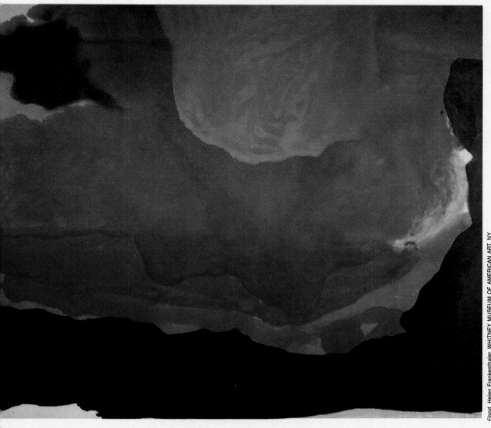

*Flood*, by Helen Frankenthaler

he colors in these paintings have a strong, unified quality. Even
hough you can identify individual colors, they seem to blend with
ach other. The total tone color of the paintings results from the
ombinations of the individual colors.

199

## THE ARTIST

**Helen Frankenthaler** (frank-ən-thä′lər)
(b. 1928)—is an American painter who
experiments with color. Inspired by Jackson
Pollock's drip-painting (see page 135), she
developed the soak-stain technique, in
which she pours layers of thinned paint to
soak into raw canvas. The color pools run
into one another, sometimes overlapping or
leaving some canvas bare. The color and texture thus become the most important elements of her paintings.

# LESSON 4

**3. Introduce blending of orchestral instruments.** Have the students:
• Discuss the information on blend.
• Sing *American Quodlibet* and decide which section of the class has the best blend.
• Listen to "Tone Color Montage 3" and identify the family of tone color and match it with the correct picture.

## Blending Instruments

CD4:20 The instruments in a tone color family sound similar because their tone is produced in a similar way. When instrumental or vocal tone colors are so similar that they merge, their sound is called a **blend**.

• Listen to each section of your class sing its song from *American Quodlibet*.
• Which section has the best blend?  answers will vary
"Tone Color Montage 3" contains examples of instruments blending.
• Identify each family of instruments and match the tone color you hear with the correct picture.  steel band: brass band: children's chorus

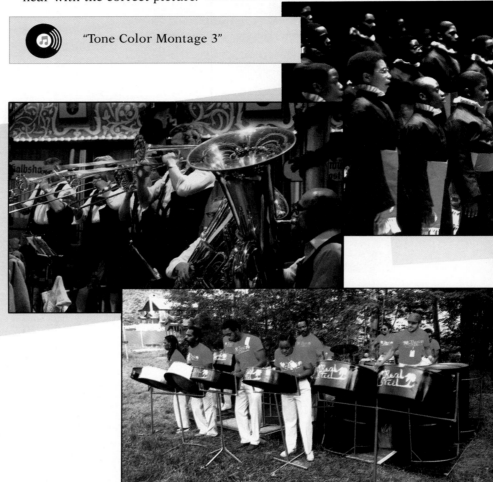

"Tone Color Montage 3"

200

**CURRICULUM CONNECTION: SCIENCE**

Set up a mini-acoustics laboratory to explore the basic properties of a sine wave. Stretch a Slinky on the floor, with one person at each end. Experiment with making small and large waves with the Slinky. The "largeness" or "smallness" of the wave is called its *amplitude*. Have the students repeat the experiment of making small and large waves and listen to the dynamic level of the tone that is produced. (The larger the amplitude, the louder the tone. The smaller the amplitude, the softer the tone.)

The number of waves per second is called the *frequency*. Experiment with making a few waves as well as many waves with the Slinky to determine how the number of waves affects the pitch. (The greater the frequency,

the higher the pitch. The smaller the frequency, the lower the pitch.)

# Listening for Blend and Contrast

Just as contrasting visual colors can be combined, different instrumental tone colors can be blended together.

 "Saints Montage"

As you listen to "Saints Montage" decide which sections you think have blending or contrasting tone colors. Answers may vary.

201

**4. Identifying blending and contrasting tone colors in "Saints Montage."** Have the students discuss blending and contrasting tone colors.

### Reinforcing the Lesson

Listen to "Saints Montage" and identify which sections have tone colors that blend together and which sections have tone colors that contrast.

### 3 APPRAISAL

The students should be able to:
1. Verbally identify tone color families from recorded examples.
2. Listen to several examples of recorded compositions that demonstrate blended and contrasting tone colors and, with eyes closed, signal the contrasting tone color sections.

## MORE MUSIC TEACHING IDEAS
Have the students find other recorded examples of blending tone colors.

# REVIEW AND EVALUATION

## JUST CHECKING

**Objective**
To review and test the skills and concepts taught in Unit 8

**Materials**
Recordings: Just Checking Unit 8 (questions 1–3, 6, and 7)
*Contrast I*
*American Quodlibet*
Unit 8 Evaluation (question 3)
*For Extra Credit* recordings (optional)
Drumsticks, recorder, bells, or keyboard
Copying Master 8-2 (optional)
Evaluation Unit 8 Copying Master

## TEACHING THE LESSON

**Review the skills and concepts taught in Unit 8.** Have the students:
• Perform the activities and answer the questions on pages 202–203. (For this review, examples for questions 1, 2, 3, 6, and 7 are included in the "Just Checking Unit 8" recording. Have the students answer these questions first. Then have them answer the other questions in the review, using the recordings in the unit where necessary.)
• Review their answers.
(You may wish to use Copying Master 8-2 at this time.)

---

## JUST CHECKING

See how much you remember.

1. Listen to the steady beat and perform these patterns on the drumsticks. Provide tone color contrast by playing the ♩ lines on your desk top and tapping sticks together when you see ♩.

*(repeat 3 times)*

2. Play this melody on recorder, bells, or keyboard with two different accompaniments. Decide which accompaniment you think blends best with each instrument.

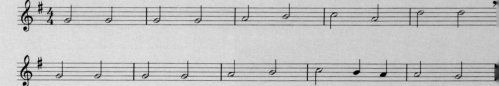

3. Listen to two excerpts from *The Stars and Stripes Forever.* Discuss how the composer achieved contrast through his choice of:  1: brass, woodwinds, and percussion, loud; 2: mostly woodwinds, softer
   instrument families (tone color)
   dynamics

4. Listen to *Contrast I* and determine how the composer used instrumental tone colors to achieve blend and contrast. The A sections have mostly brass and percussion, the B section mostly woodwinds.

5. Sing *American Quodlibet* to review the blending of voices.

202

Listen to the following examples on the recording and decide if you hear blending or contrasting tone colors. answers will vary

As you listen to these musical examples, identify the families of instruments you hear. c) brass, b) strings, d) woodwinds

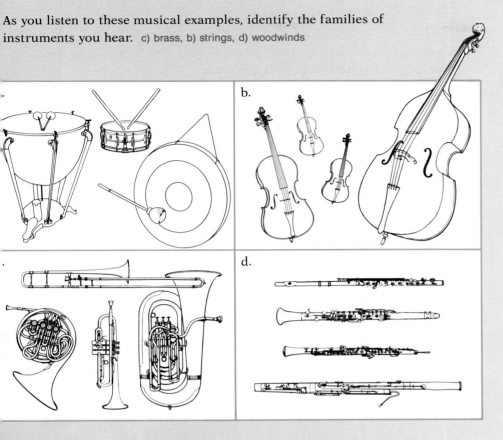

Examine the instruments found in your music classroom. Which combination of instruments would create contrasting tone colors? Which combinations would create blending tone colors? answers will vary

Make a list of all the instruments in your classroom. Which of these instruments would you use if you were writing music to be performed at your school's pep rally? Which would you use if you were writing a composition to be played at assembly? Why? answers will vary

203

# REVIEW AND EVALUATION

## GIVING THE EVALUATION

Evaluation Unit 8 Copying Master can be found in the *Teacher's Copying Masters* book along with full directions for giving the evaluation and checking the answers.

## FOR EXTRA CREDIT

You may want to have students answer one of the following questions.
1. Identify three contrasting tone colors in *The Stars and Stripes Forever* and describe why they contrast. (Piccolo, trumpet, and snare drum. The three different tone colors are used to emphasize the form of the march.)
2. Identify three decisions composers make about tone color. Why do they use different tone colors? (Decisions about tone color deal with blend, contrast, and the setting where music will be performed. They use different tone colors to create musical interest.) (You may wish to play recordings to refresh students' memories.)

# YEAR-END REVIEW

**Objective**
To review and test the skills and concepts taught through Grade 7

**Materials**
Recording: Year-End Review
Drumsticks, recorder, bells, or keyboard

## TEACHING THE LESSON

**Review the skills and concepts taught in Grade 7.** Have the students:
• Follow the recorded review with pages 204–205, perform the activities, and answer the questions.
• Review their answers.

## YEAR-END REVIEW

CD4:37–47

1. Listen and decide if the musical texture of each of these examples is monophonic, polyphonic, or homophonic.
   a. "Bottletop Song" (version 1)  monophonic
   b. "Bottletop Song" (version 2)  polyphonic
   c. "Do You Hear the People Sing?"  homophonic

2. Listen and identify the instrument families you hear in this excerpt from "Procession of the Nobles."  brass, percussion

3. Perform these rhythms from the rhythmic accompaniment for *The Entertainer*.

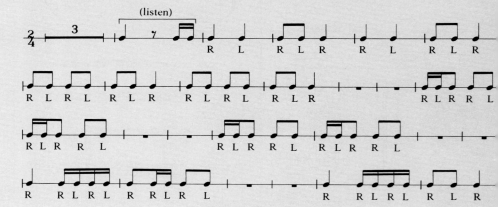

4. To review triplets, listen to an excerpt from "Star Wars" and perform the following by clapping the quarter notes, snapping the triplets, and pat-sliding the half notes.

204

5. Play the following melodies on bells or keyboard.

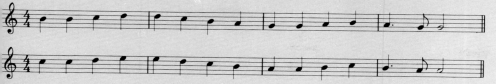

Which melody is based on a major scale? A minor scale?
Change the minor example to make it major. (You will need to
change only one note.) 1; 2; add C-sharp

6. Play the twelve-bar blues pattern by playing the roots of the I,
IV, and V chords on bells or keyboard.

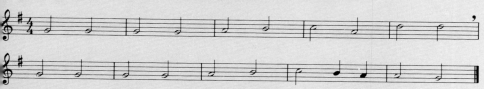

I    I    I    I    IV   IV   I    I    V    IV   I    I

7. Listen to an excerpt from the "Little Fugue in G Minor" and
raise your hand each time you hear the subject. The "Little
Fugue in G Minor" is an example of: b

a. ABA form    b. repetition with imitation    c. repeated chord progression

8. Which of these diagrams represents
ternary form? Which represents rondo form?
ABA; ABACA

9. Play this melody on recorder, bells, or
keyboard with two different accompaniments. Decide which
accompaniment you think blends best with each instrument.

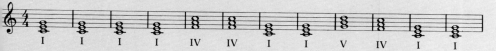

10. Listen to excerpts from the A and B sections of *The Stars and Stripes Forever*.
Discuss how the composer achieved contrast through his choice of:

| instrument families (tone color) | dynamics |

A: brass, woodwinds, and percussion, loud; B: mostly woodwinds, softer

205

# KEYBOARD AND GUITAR

207

# KEYBOARD AND GUITAR

# KEYBOARD

**Focus: Learning to Play Keyboard Instruments**

**Objective**
To develop performance skills at the keyboard

**Materials**
Recordings: Chopin, Etude in E minor
"Crocodile Rock"
"A Horse with No Name"
Keyboard(s)

**Vocabulary**
Keyboard, black keys, white keys, treble clef, bass clef

## TEACHING THE LESSON

**1. Introduce playing the keyboard.**
Have the students:
• Listen to and compare the two recordings.

# KEYBOARD INSTRUMENTS

These listening examples are both played on keyboards. How do they sound alike? How are they different?

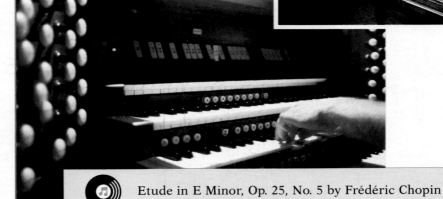

 Etude in E Minor, Op. 25, No. 5 by Frédéric Chopin

 "Crocodile Rock," by Elton John and Bernie Taupin

208

# The Keyboard

- If you have a portable keyboard, place it on your lap or on a desk.
- If you have a piano available, sit comfortably so that the middle of the keyboard is in front of you.

The keyboard is made up of sets of white and black keys.

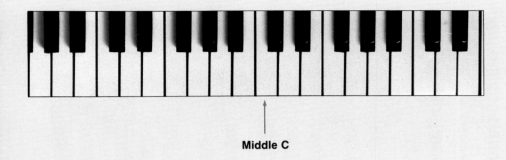

**Middle C**

- Start on middle C with your *right* hand and play all the white keys to the right to hear each pitch.
  Do the pitches become higher or lower? higher
- Start on middle C with your *left* hand and play all the white keys to the left to hear each pitch.
  Do the pitches become higher or lower? lower

- Find each set of *two* black keys up and down the keyboard. A full piano keyboard has seven sets of two black keys. How many sets of two black keys does your keyboard have? Answers will vary.
- Find each set of *three* black keys up and down the keyboard.
- Now experiment by playing both black and white keys.

209

# KEYBOARD

- Start on middle C with the right hand and play all the white keys to the right.
- Identify whether the pitches become higher or lower. (higher)
- Start on middle C with the left hand and play all the white keys to the left.
- Identify whether the pitches become higher or lower. (lower)
- Locate each set of two black keys up and down the keyboard.
- Identify how many sets of two black keys their keyboard has.
- Locate each set of three black keys up and down the keyboard.
- Identify how many sets of three black keys their keyboard has.

# KEYBOARD

- Examine the picture of both hands on keyboard playing C, D, E, F, and G with fingers 1, 2, 3, 4, and 5.
- Identify and play all the Ds up and down the keyboard.
- Identify and play all the Cs and Es up and down the keyboard.
- Clap or pat the rhythm to "Lightly Row" before reading it with finger numbers.
- Play the song.

## Playing a Keyboard Instrument

You can play this simple tune.

- Keep your arm straight but relaxed. The fingers of both hands are numbered from 1 to 5, with both thumbs being 1.
- Place the pads of your right thumb and fingers on the keys. Your thumb should be on middle C. The picture below shows the names and locations of the notes.

- Clap or pat the rhythms of this song before you play it.

**Lightly Row**

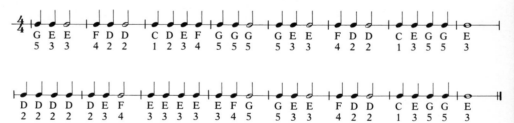

| G | E | E | F | D | D | C | D | E | F | G | G | G | G | E | E | F | D | D | C | E | G | G | E |
| 5 | 3 | 3 | 4 | 2 | 2 | 1 | 2 | 3 | 4 | 5 | 5 | 5 | 5 | 3 | 3 | 4 | 2 | 2 | 1 | 3 | 5 | 5 | 3 |

| D | D | D | D | D | E | F | E | E | E | E | E | F | G | G | E | E | F | D | D | C | E | G | G | E |
| 2 | 2 | 2 | 2 | 2 | 3 | 4 | 3 | 3 | 3 | 3 | 3 | 4 | 5 | 5 | 3 | 3 | 4 | 2 | 2 | 1 | 3 | 5 | 5 | 3 |

210

# Keyboard Music

Pitches can be shown on the staff. The treble clef (𝄞) shows the location of the higher-sounding pitches. The bass clef (𝄢) shows the location of the lower-sounding pitches.

    The treble and bass clefs are combined on the grand staff, shown below. The right hand generally plays notes in the treble clef. The left hand generally plays notes in the bass clef. To play the songs in this section you will need to find these notes on the keyboard. The notes shown here are played on the white keys.

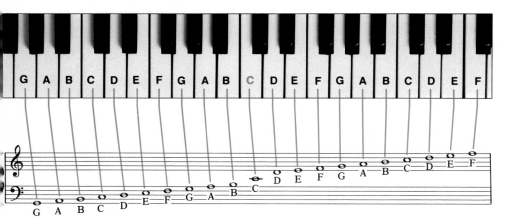

Bruce Hornsby

211

**2. Introduce reading staff notation at the keyboard.** Have the students:
• Discuss the information on reading the treble and bass clefs.
• Practice reading and playing pitches in the treble clef as indicated.
• Practice reading and playing pitches in the bass clef as indicated.

# KEYBOARD

**3. Introduce the left and right hands together.** Have the students:
• Locate the five-finger position in both hands.
• Pat or clap the rhythm of each part.
• Practice the right- and left-hand parts to "Lightly Row" separately before putting hands together.

## Putting It All Together

Now you are ready to put the right and left hands together. To play this song, your right thumb should be on middle C. The fifth finger of your left hand should be on the next C *below* middle C.

- Pat or clap the rhythm of each part before you play it.
- Practice the right- and left-hand parts separately. Then practice both parts together.
- Check your place on the keyboard diagram on page 211.

Howard Jones with keyboard

## Lightly Row

212

# A Rock Keyboard Accompaniment

Now you can play an accompaniment to the song "A Horse with No Name," by the group America.

- Place the third finger of your right hand on the B *above* middle C.
- Place the third finger of your left hand on the E *below* middle C. F-sharp is the black key between F and G.
- Pat or clap the rhythm of each part before you play it.
- Practice the right- and left-hand parts separately. Then practice both parts together.

## A Horse with No Name

- Keep the third finger of your right hand on the B above middle C.

The left hand part contains two chords.

| For the first chord: | For the second chord: |
|---|---|
| • Place your fifth finger on the E below middle C. | • Place your fifth finger on the D below middle C. |
| • Place your third finger on G. | • Place your third finger on F-sharp. |
| • Place your thumb on B. | • Place your thumb on A. |

The eyeglasses ( 👓 ) here and in other songs tell you to watch out for changes in the music.

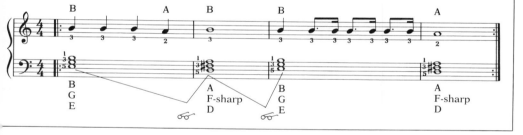

213

---

**4. Prepare students to perform a harmonic accompaniment on keyboard to "A Horse with No Name."** Have the students:
- Practice, then perform, the right- and left-hand parts as an accompaniment to "A Horse with No Name."
- Practice the Challenge! (Observe E minor and D major chord changes in the left hand.)
- Perform the E minor and D major chord changes with the right and left hand together as a harmonic accompaniment to "A Horse with No Name" with the recording.
- Form two groups. One group will play the guitar accompaniment on page 219 while the other group plays the keyboard accompaniments. Perform with the recording.

## APPRAISAL

The students should be able to:
1. Identify sets of two and three black keys on the keyboard.
2. Read, identify, and locate C, D, E, F, and G on the keyboard.
3. Locate the five-finger position using fingers 1, 2, 3, 4, and 5.
4. Read and identify melodies in treble and bass clefs.
5. Read and perform a harmonic accompaniment to "A Horse with No Name."

KEYBOARD AND GUITAR **213**

# GUITAR

• Listen to the following compositions for guitar. How do they sound alike? How do they sound different? Answers may vary.

**Focus: Learning to Play the Guitar**

### Objective
To develop performance skills on the guitar

### Materials
Recordings: *Guajira* (excerpt)
"Paint It Sad"
"A Horse with No Name"
"Tom Dooley"
"Kum Ba Yah"

Guitars
Copying Master A-1 (optional)

### Vocabulary
Fret, neck, sound hole, saddle, bridge, body, string, fingerboard, tuning peg, nut, downward strum, upward strum, open string, fret position, chord diagram, tablature

## TEACHING THE LESSON

**1. Introduce playing the guitar.** Have the students:
• Listen to and compare the two recordings.

*Guajira*, by Leo Brouwer

"Paint It Sad," by L. Raub and B. Chase

A seventeenth-century Italian guitar

A modern acoustic guitar

An electric guitar

214

# KNOW YOUR GUITAR

Learn the parts of the guitar from this picture. The surrounding pictures show other instruments. What do they have in common with the guitar?

All are stringed instruments.

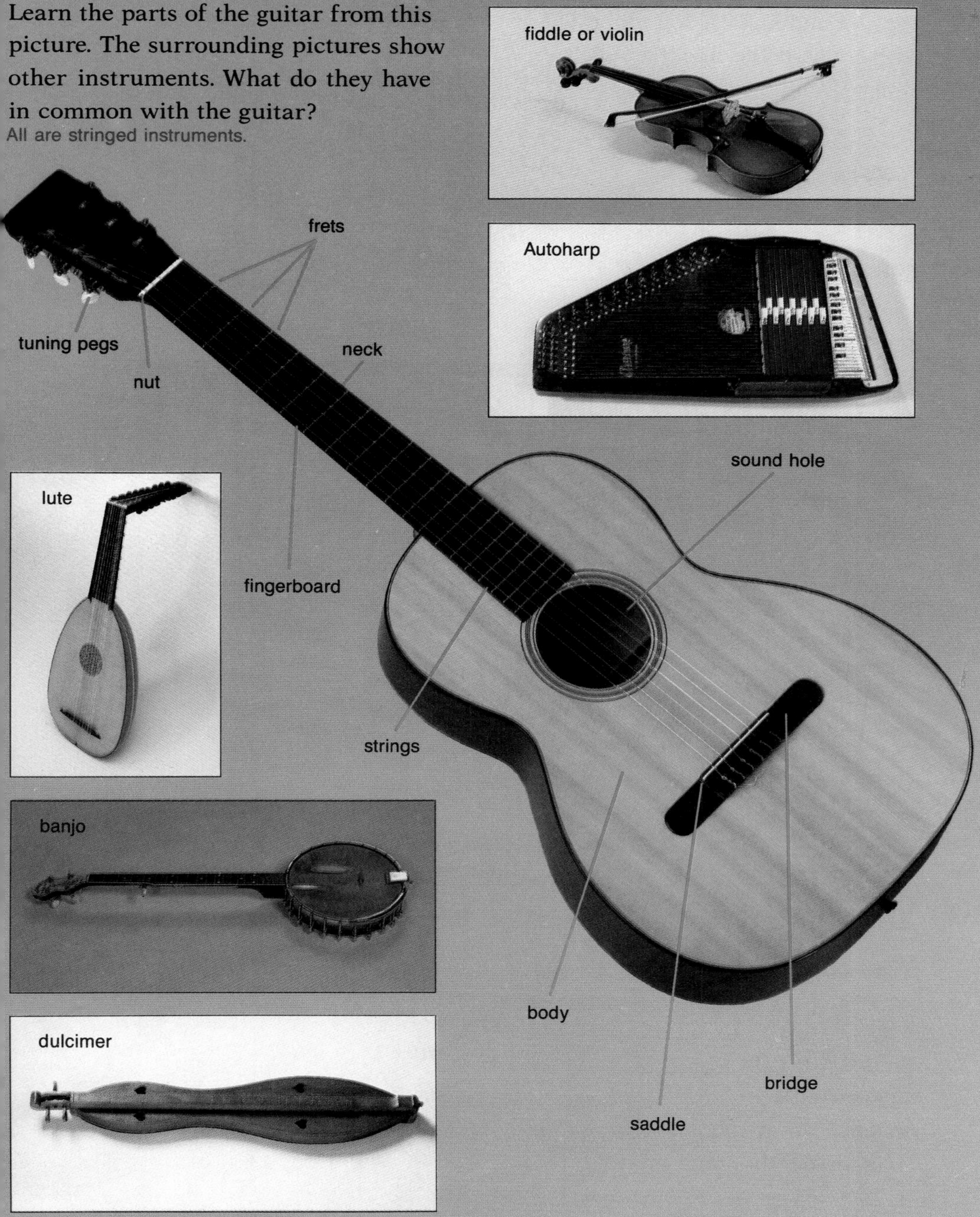
fiddle or violin
Autoharp
frets
tuning pegs
nut
neck
lute
fingerboard
sound hole
strings
banjo
dulcimer
body
saddle
bridge

215

# GUITAR

- Discuss the information on the parts of the guitar.
- Identify and label the parts of the guitar.

# GUITAR

• Discuss the strings and tuning of the guitar. (If some students know how to tune the guitar, have them help those who do not.)

## Strings

The first string on a guitar is the thinnest and highest sounding. The sixth string is the thickest and lowest sounding.

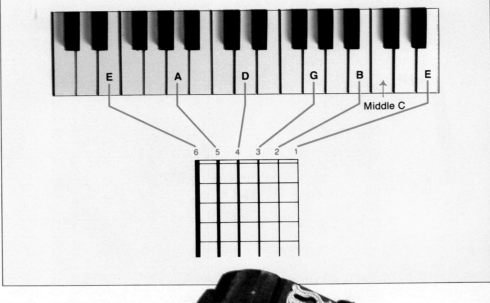

Middle C

## Tuning

The tuning most often used on guitar is pictured on a keyboard and the guitar. Find E A D G B E on the keyboard. Use the tuning pegs on your guitar to make each guitar string make the same sound as the correct key.

216

## Holding Your Guitar

You support the guitar with your hands and body. To do this, rest the guitar on your thigh and hold it against your chest with your right arm. You may want to tilt the guitar slightly at first so that you can see the fingerboard.

### Left-Hand Position

- Place the pad of your left thumb in the center of the back of the guitar neck.
- Keep the palm of your hand off the neck.
- Curve your fingers over the strings. The fingers are numbered from index (1) to little finger (4). The thumb, labelled T in the photograph, is not given a number.

### Right-Hand Position

- Hold your right hand over the strings near the sound hole. Your wrist should be slightly bent and your fingers curved.

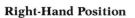

217

**2. Introduce holding the guitar.** Have the students:
- Discuss the information on the left-hand position.
- Discuss the information on the right-hand position.

# GUITAR

**3. Introduce strumming technique.**
Have the students:
• Discuss the information on upward and downward strums.
• Practice the upward and downward strums.
• Perform the rhythm patterns, using a downward and upward strum.

## Strumming Your Guitar

When you strum the guitar with your right hand, you can use either a downward or upward strumming motion.

• Curve your fingers and brush downward across the strings with your fingernails for a downward strum.

• Pull your fingers upward across the strings for an upward strum.

When you strum with your right hand and your left-hand fingers are *not* on the guitar strings, you are strumming on what are called *open strings*.

• Play the following rhythm patterns, using the downward ( ⊓ ) and upward ( ∨ ) strums. The notes indicate the rhythm to use. The numbers below the notes will help you count the beats. Always strum *down* on the first beat of a measure unless the music is marked otherwise.

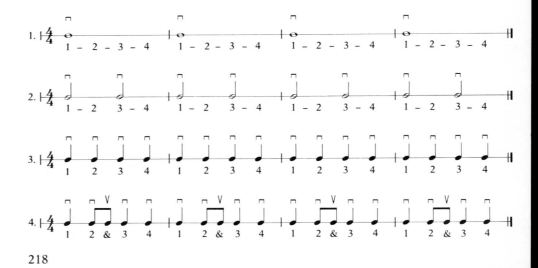

218

# Playing Chords

To play chords, you strum over the sound hole with your right hand and place your left fingers in the correct *fret positions*. Fret positions are string spaces between frets (the metal bars across the neck) where fingers are placed.

A chord diagram or frame shows where the fingers of your left hand should be placed on the fingerboard to fret, or form, a chord. The number in the circle tells you what finger to use. The circle shows you where your finger belongs. An *O* for *open* means that *no* finger is on the string. That string is open or unfretted.

**4. Introduce playing chords on the guitar.** Have the students:
• Discuss information on playing chords and fret positions.
• Note the picture of the guitar fingerboard.
• Examine the diagrams to form the E minor and D 6/9 chords.
• Practice playing the E minor and D 6/9 chords.

**5. Prepare students to perform a harmonic accompaniment on guitar to "A Horse with No Name."** Have the students:
• Review procedures for playing the guitar. (You can play these chords on the Auto-harp by retuning the E major chord to E minor and using the D major chord.)
• Practice playing the rhythms using the E minor and D 6/9 chords.
• Choose one line to play as a harmonic accompaniment to "A Horse with No Name."
• Form two groups. Group 1 will play the guitar accompaniment while Group 2 plays the keyboard accompaniment on page 213.

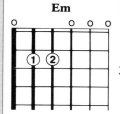

**Em**

1. 1st finger on 5th string, 2nd fret position

2. 2nd finger on 4th string, 2nd fret position

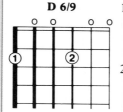

**D 6/9**

1. 1st finger on 6th string, 2nd fret position

2. 2nd finger on 3rd string, 2nd fret position

Lines 1 to 4 are harmonic accompaniments to "A Horse with No Name." They use the same chords but different rhythms.

• Practice by playing the rhythms. Choose one line to play as an accompaniment to "A Horse with No Name."

## A Horse with No Name — Harmonic Accompaniment

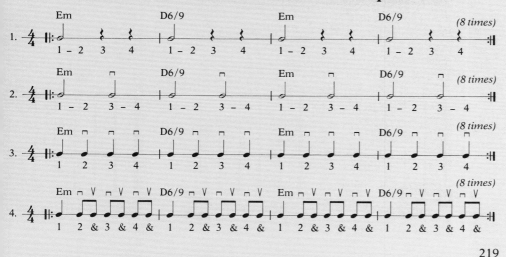

219

# GUITAR

**6. Introduce the bass part to "Tom Dooley."** Have the students:
- Sing the folk ballad "Tom Dooley."
- Discuss the information on guitar tablature.
- Perform the bass part to the song.

(You may wish to use Copying Master A-1 at this time to perform a bass accompaniment to "A Horse with No Name.")

CD4:52 ● Sing this folk ballad.

## Tom Dooley

Traditional

Hang down your head, Tom Doo - ley, Hang down your head and cry,

Hang down your head, Tom Doo - ley, Poor boy, you're bound to die.

So far you have used your right hand to strum and your left hand to play chords on the guitar. You can use your right thumb to play a bass part to "Tom Dooley." This bass part is plucked on the open fourth (D) and fifth (A) strings.

You can write this bass part in a notation called *tablature*. Tablature is a horizontal picture of the six guitar strings divided into measures. An O written on the strings indicates that the string is played open (no fretting). This entire part is played on two open strings. The rhythm is shown above the strings. The rhythm for this part is in whole notes.

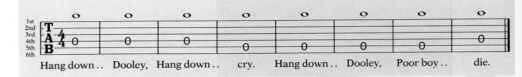

Hang down.. Dooley, Hang down.. cry. Hang down.. Dooley, Poor boy.. die.

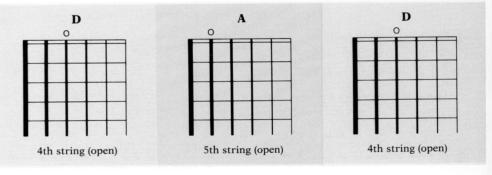

| D | A | D |
|---|---|---|
| 4th string (open) | 5th string (open) | 4th string (open) |

220

## Playing a Melody

You can play melodies with your right thumb. Here is a portion of tablature connected to a chord frame. It has both open and fretted strings. Your left hand frets some strings.

CD4:53

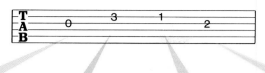

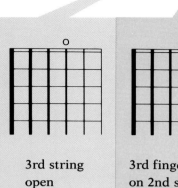

3rd string
open

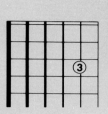

3rd finger
on 2nd string,
3rd fret position

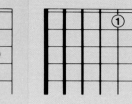

1st finger
on 2nd string,
1st fret position

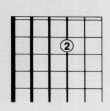

2nd finger on
3rd string,
2nd fret position

• Play the melody to the folk song "Kum Ba Yah" from this tablature. Notice that a string can be played open or fretted in the same song.

### Kum Ba Yah

Traditional

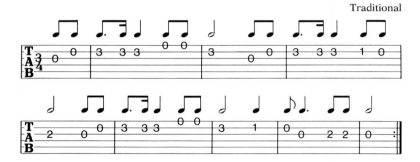

221

# GUITAR

**7. Introduce playing a melody on the guitar.** Have the students:
• Discuss the information on playing a melody.
• Perform the melody to the folk song "Kum Ba Yah."

## APPRAISAL

The students should be able to:
1. Identify and label the parts of the guitar.
2. Demonstrate the proper playing position for the guitar.
3. Read and play downward and upward guitar strum patterns.
4. Play the E minor and D 6/9 chords on the guitar.
5. Perform a bass part to a song on the guitar.
6. Perform a melody on the guitar.

# LESSON 1

 You will be listening to these examples of American popular music during this section:

"The River of Dreams," by Billy Joel

"In Your Eyes," by Peter Gabriel

"Can't Stop Lovin' You," by Edward and Alex Van Halen, Sammy Hagar, and Michael Anthony

"Dreams," by Stevie Nicks

"More Than a Woman," by Barry, Robin, and Maurice Gibb

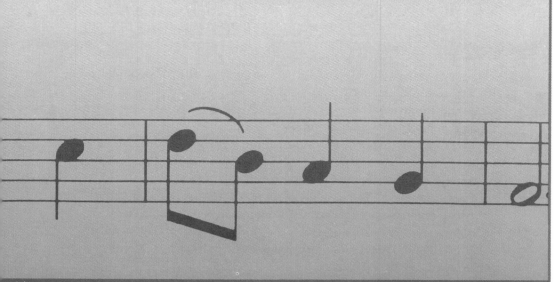

"California Sound"

"Blowin' in the Wind," by Bob Dylan

"Fifties Montage"

"Rock Around the Clock," by Max B. Friedman and Jimmy DeKnight

"Foggy Mountain Breakdown," by Lester Flatt and Earl Scruggs

"St. Louis Blues," by W. C. Handy

CD4, CD5

# LESSON 1

**Focus: Style—History of American Popular Music**

**Objective**
To identify styles of popular music of the 1980s and 1990s

**Materials**
Recordings: "The River of Dreams"
"In Your Eyes"
"Can't Stop Lovin' You"

**Vocabulary**
Innovation, rock, rhythm and blues, rap, alternative rock

# AMERICAN POPULAR MUSIC: 1950 TO THE PRESENT

# LESSON 1

## TEACHING THE LESSON

**1. Introduce American popular music.** Have the students:
• Read and discuss the first two paragraphs on the pupil page.
• Discuss the reasons why parents have sometimes objected to popular music. (harsh and strident sound combined with more aggressive performance behaviors by the performing artists, lyrics considered rebellious or inappropriate)
• Discuss how the emergence of the guitar as a popular musical instrument contributed to the popularity of American popular music. (It helped to make the music more accessible and participation more affordable. The simple chord structure of many songs offered an opportunity to "play along" with the popular music heroes.)
• Discuss how the use of the synthesizer and other electronic keyboards have changed American popular music since the 1980s. (They can produce special sound effects and new tone colors, eliminate the use of many musicians, and need less equipment than a full band. Some music is more technically oriented, requiring knowledge of electronic equipment and computers as well as the keyboard.)
**2. Introduce Billy Joel.** Have the students:
• Read the last two paragraphs on the page.
• Listen to "The River of Dreams." (You may wish to have the students play along using the accompaniments on pages 274–275.)
• Discuss other music by Billy Joel or other popular musicians who combine popular music styles. (For example, jazz was combined with pop when Sting teemed up with the jazz saxophone player Branford Marsalis. Mannheim Steamroller combined classical with rock. Blood, Sweat, and Tears combined rock and jazz. Simon and Garfunkel combined folk and rock.)

The music of the United States focuses strongly on the freedom and the expression of the individual. The American styles of jazz and blues allow individuals to express themselves creatively by improvising melodies and rhythms within musical forms. Another means of creative expression is **innovation**. When using innovation artists take established styles and musical forms and use their personal visions to create something new.

American music has had many great innovators. As a result, American popular music has gone through many changes. New styles have been created along the way. Popular music today includes rap, rock, rhythm and blues, alternative music, folk rock, and many other styles.

Musicians such as Billy Joel, Paul Simon, and Stevie Wonder have combined different musical styles to create innovative music. Billy Joel uses a gospel influence in his song "The River of Dreams." Listen to the call and response between the lead vocalist and the choir. This element is typical of gospel music. You will find a guitar accompaniment and a keyboard accompaniment to this song on pages 274–275.

Jazz artists such as saxophonist Branford Marsalis have teamed up with rock stars like Sting to create new blends of music. Many examples of mixing styles can be found in rap music, where "samples" of older songs are mixed with new raps and new beats.

Billy Joel

## BIOGRAPHY

**Paul Simon** (1941– )—is considered one of the leading songwriters of rock and folk music. He first rose to prominence in the late 1950s with Art Garfunkel as his writing partner. Simon & Garfunkel's music blended folk and rock styles, and with such songs as "The Sounds of Silence," "I Am a Rock," and "Bridge Over Troubled Water," they became one of the most successful duos in rock history. Simon has recorded many solo projects as well, most notably the albums *Still Crazy After All These Years* and *Graceland,* which featured African musicians, including Youssou N'Dour and Ladysmith Black Mambazo.

Peter Gabriel

**3. Introduce musicians who borrow musical ideas from other countries.** Have the students:
• Read page 225.
• Listen to "In Your Eyes" for the combination of African and British styles.
• Discuss other musicians they know who use styles from other countries. (For example, the Beatles combined styles from England and India. Richie Valens combined Mexican folk music with American rock and roll. The Gypsy Kings combined flamenco with American pop music.)
• Discuss what they think will happen to music styles in the future as communication and interaction with other musicians around the world becomes faster and easier.

## Music in a Changing World

Just as musicians in the United States have borrowed ideas from each other, they have also borrowed musical ideas from other cultures. In recent years people have become increasingly aware that they share this planet with neighbors from all over the world. This awareness can be heard in music—when popular music of the United States is combined with music from other countries. Artists such as Paul Simon (singer), The Chieftains (Irish folk musicians), Pat Metheny (jazz guitarist), and Mickey Hart (drummer for the Grateful Dead), have worked with musicians from many nations to create new and innovative music.

Similarly, British singer Peter Gabriel has made popular recordings with musicians from all over the world. He has worked with the Russian folk singers of the Dimitri Pokrovsky Ensemble, the Middle Eastern percussionist Hozzam Ramzy, and violinist Shankar from southern India. He has also recorded with musicians from Africa such as singers Youssou N'dour and Papa Wemba and percussionist Manu Katche. Listen to the variety of voices in Peter Gabriel's song "In Your Eyes."

Hear how this arrangement combines African lyrics and vocal styles with the English lyrics sung by Gabriel himself.

Paul Simon

225

### BIOGRAPHY

**Peter Gabriel** was born in 1950 in England. The flamboyant frontman of the group Genesis from 1968 to 1975, he was known for masks and weird costumes. He left the group for a solo career. Gabriel works with experimental, rock, pop, and world music. He fuses various elements such as complex African rhythms and African tone colors with the latest music technology. Gabriel and WOMAD (World of Music Arts and Dance) have brought together musicians from all over the world to England for massive outdoor festivals of global pop music. Gabriel has produced several world-wide hits.

# LESSON 1

**4. Introduce rock.** Have the students:

• Read the first two paragraphs and listen to "Can't Stop Lovin' You." (You may wish to have the students play the accompaniments on pages 279–281.)

• List various rock styles they know, adding the names of the various groups or musicians who use those styles. (for example, heavy metal, rock and roll, folk rock, jazz rock, rockabilly, progressive rock, hard rock, blues rock, country rock, bubble-gum rock)

• Name some rock groups or musicians who are important to them and explain why. (For example, the performers play or sing better, the lyricists write more meaningful lyrics, the music is more energetic, the composers create more interesting melodies, the tone colors are more appealing.)

## Rock

Rock and roll has undergone many changes since it was first played in the 1950s. Because of its many variations, such as alternative rock, heavy metal, and pop rock, it appeals to a wide variety of people. Rock songs often reflect the attitudes and issues of the times.

Van Halen's music has the intense energy of classic rock and roll. This energy is certainly apparent in lead guitarist Eddie Van Halen's playing. Listen for the wide variety of different guitar sounds in Van Halen's "Can't Stop Lovin' You." Eddie Van Halen, like Jimi Hendrix in the 1960s, has been an important rock-guitar innovator. You will find guitar and keyboard playalongs to this song on pages 279–281.

Eddie Van Halen

Bon Jovi

Queen Latifah

---

E X T E N S I O N

## BACKGROUND

**Van Halen** is a heavy-rock band that has been popular since the late 1970s. The Van Halen brothers, Eddie and Alex, grew up in Holland. Eddie Van Halen is a guitarist who uses innovative techniques and wild guitar sounds. He also plays keyboards. Alex Van Halen plays drums and Michael Anthony plays bass in the group. David Lee Roth was replaced by Sammy Hagar in 1986 as a singer in the group. The group played a lot of local gigs (playing engagements) before they made their first album.

## MORE MUSIC TEACHING IDEAS

Have each student chart the length of time a song remains popular, either through such things as Top-40 charts or through personal preferences. Students could trace a hit song for a period of weeks or months to see how long it remains in one spot on the charts. Students might also list their favorite song each week for a period of weeks or months. Compare and evaluate the results of the various charts.

## BACKGROUND

### Electric Guitar

An electric guitar has pickups that translate string vibrations into electrical impulses. An amplifier modifies (strengthens) these impulses, and loudspeakers turn the electrical impulses back into sound. Most electric guitars are set up like a regular guitar.

Pickups are mounted under the strings. Knobs on the body adjust tone and volume. Additional controls are often added for special effects. Other special-effects devices are operated with foot pedals. The wah-wah, fuzz, fuzz-wah, phaser, and fuzzphaser pedals are some of the devices used.

There are two kinds of electric guitar: electro-acoustic and solid-body. Electro-acoustic guitars began in the 1930s. The

## Rhythm and Blues

Rhythm and blues combines the expressive soul of blues with the strong rhythms of rock and roll. Rhythm and blues, or R&B, often features virtuosic singing and complex harmonies. Boyz II Men, a popular R&B group of the 1990s, creates a rich texture by blending the group's four voices. They have also introduced elements of rap into some of their arrangements. Contemporary R&B songs often have a very new sound because they use the latest techniques in music recording.

Boyz II Men

## Rap

Rap, or hip-hop, is an American innovation that started in the late 1970s. Rap, like jazz, was created primarily by African Americans and uses improvisation. Clever and elaborate rhyme schemes bring out the rhythms of the words in unexpected ways. When spoken or "rapped" to a powerful drum beat, the rhythms of the words are made even stronger.

Rapping is often done to instrumental records that feature strong beats, similar to the Jamaican tradition of "toasting." "Sampling" is another rap technique involving the use of previously recorded music from another source. A rap, as well as other instrumental and vocal parts, is added to the older song, creating an exciting blend of styles. Rappers like Puff Daddy, Will Smith, and the outspoken Queen Latifah have used the driving intensity of this style to express important social issues of the times.

# LESSON 1

**5. Introduce rhythm and blues.** Have the students:
- Read the first paragraph.
- List and discuss other rhythm and blues musicians and songs they may know. (For example, Louis Jordan, Muddy Waters, the Drifters, the Coasters, B.B. King, Ray Charles, Aretha Franklin, Natalie Cole. You may wish to point out that some musicians work in several styles.)

**6. Introduce rap.** Have the students:
- Read the second and third paragraphs.
- List and discuss other rap musicians and songs they may know. (For example, Sugarhill Gang, L.L. Cool J., Grandmaster Flash. You may wish to call attention to the use of rap in such things as commercials.)
- Create a rap on an issue that is important, for example, ecology. Find a rhyme scheme. Accompany the rap with a strong rhythm using available percussion, body percussion, or found sounds.

solid-body guitar started in the late 1940s. A solid-body guitar can sustain tone much longer than other kinds of guitars and can use greater amplification.

**CAREER**
**Electric Guitarist**

An electric guitarist is often a member of a band. The guitarist learns how to play the instrument through lessons and/or by observing and listening to other guitarists. A skilled guitarist puts in many hours of practice to develop playing skills before rehearsing and performing with other musicians. The electric guitarist needs to keep up with the latest developments in equipment. The electric guitarist may have a variety of instruments, amps, and special effects to be used for different styles. The electric guitarist may also double as a singer, songwriter, bassist, keyboardist, or in other areas.

**MORE MUSIC TEACHING IDEAS**

Have the students investigate the use of movement and dance styles, such as break dancing and mime, with rap. Give possible reasons why these movement styles are used.

# LESSON 1

**7. Introduce alternative rock.** Have the students:
• Read page 228.
• Name other alternative rock groups they may know. (for example, R.E.M., Sonic Youth)
• Compare various recordings of alternative rock and the more slick "produced"-sounding rock recordings for such things as tone color, mixes, quality of lyrics and melodies, emotional quality or mood, and dynamic level.

Alanis Morissette in concert

R.E.M. in concert

## Alternative Rock

For many people in the early 1990s, mainstream rock and roll lacked the freshness it had back in the 1950s. Many of the new rock-and-roll recordings sounded too "produced." They seemed to be made by a giant record company instead of by individual artists. Young people began to look for an "alternative" kind of music with a new sound and a more personal message.

Groups from Seattle, like Nirvana and Pearl Jam, helped to define this new music. With lyrics that are emotional and honest, their songs deal directly with problems and anxieties that young people face. The rough, distorted guitars give the music the "grunge" sound that is sometimes associated with this style.

228

# EXTENSION

## BACKGROUND
### Sound Systems

A musical program attended by large numbers of people usually requires amplification. **Sound systems** are made up of various devices used to control the sound. The devices are usually connected with cords, though some equipment is cordless.

A **microphone** (mike) changes sound into electric energy. The energy travels to a loudspeaker or other instrument that changes it back into sound. Mikes are designed and specialized for the type of work they do. A mike is usually placed on a stand or attached in some way to the person or instrument that is being amplified. A pickup acts as a microphone and attaches to or is built into an instrument.

A **mixer** balances and controls the sound. Additional equipment, such as cassette or compact disc players, can be connected to the system. A preamplifier and an **amplifier** (amp) make the sound louder.

A **loudspeaker** (speaker) is an electric device that reproduces sound. Some speakers are specialized to reproduce only pitches in a certain range. These usually produce a better quality sound than single speakers. A tweeter reproduces high-pitched sounds, a squawker reproduces sounds in the middle range of pitch, and a woofer reproduces low-pitched sounds. Speakers come in all sizes.

**Monitors** are speakers placed near the performers to help them hear and check the sound.

## MORE MUSIC TEACHING IDEAS

1. If you have access to sound system equipment in the classroom or auditorium, show students how the equipment is connected. Prepare or have students prepare diagrams of how to connect the various pieces. You may wish to have the students work in small groups to hook up the sound system. Stress safe and careful handling of equipment.
2. Discuss the use of the proper equipment for the sound needs. For example:
—Use equipment with the right amount of power for the size of the area. If it is too powerful, the sound may be distorted and too loud. If it is too weak, the sound will not be heard well.
—Use equipment that best enhances the sound.

## Music with a Social Message

Popular music is an influential medium because it is listened to and, through music videos, seen by so many people. Many rock stars who are in the spotlight realize the power of this medium. They use their music and fame to help make a difference. In the 1980s and 1990s, popular musicians bonded together on important issues. Live Aid, the giant rock festival of 1985, was an example. Live Aid was put together by Bob Geldolf of the Boomtown Rats to help people who were suffering from famine in Africa. Over 40 groups, many of whom reunited for this one occasion, were part of this enormous musical event.

Similar projects to help people suffering from famine were the "We Are the World" song and Band Aid. Farm Aid was an event that raised money to help farmers in the American Middle West. Many songs provide messages of concern for humanity and the ecology of our planet.

Human Rights Concert, Wembley

**8. Introduce music with a social message.** Have the students:
• Read page 229.
• Name musicians and groups who have participated in events such as Live Aid. (for example, The Who, Paul McCartney, Tina Turner, Queen, Sting, Elton John)
• List songs that they know that have a message of concern for humanity. (for example, "Our World," "Let There Be Peace on Earth," "[Life Is a] Celebration," "Lean on Me," "Harmony")
• Discuss any local events or benefits that have been held to help others.
• Discuss some of the problems that need to be solved in putting on a large concert such as Live Aid. (for example, space for the audience, amplification, advertising, contacting the many performers, keeping all the equipment organized)
• Discuss where they have seen sound systems and the equipment involved. (Call attention to the diversity of systems, ranging from home systems, small and large concert halls, outdoor systems, recording studios. See *Background*.)

## APPRAISAL

The students should be able to identify the musical characteristics of rock, rhythm and blues, rap, and alternative rock.

—Place monitors and loudspeakers where they are most effective.
—Make sure cords are organized and out of the way so people don't trip. This precaution may involve taping cords down.
—Find the right mixer settings for the room and for the sounds being amplified. (Live or dead rooms need to be treated in different ways.)
—Use the right kind of connecting jacks.
—Do a sound check to make sure everything is adjusted correctly and you don't get feedback.
**3.** Discuss the qualities of equipment available, from beginner's equipment to that of professional musicians. If possible, have students aurally compare pieces of equipment of various qualities.

# LESSON 2

**Focus: Style—History of American Popular Music**

### Objective
To identify characteristics of a synthesizer
To identify contemporary women musicians
To identify styles of popular music of the 1970s

### Materials
Recordings:  "The River of Dreams"
"A Horse with No Name"
"Dreams"
"More Than a Woman"

### Vocabulary
Pop, folk rock, funk, disco

## TEACHING THE LESSON

**1. Introduce the sound of the synthesizer.** Have the students:
• Listen to "The River of Dreams" focusing on the sound of the synthesizer. (This sound can be heard in the introduction and between the refrains. The keyboards used on the recording are synthesizer, piano, and Hammond organ. You may wish to teach the guitar and keyboard accompaniments to the song, pages 274–275 at this time.)
• Respond to the following:
1. A synthesizer is essentially a specialized computer which interprets musical inputs in order to produce musical sounds. Discuss what kinds of components might be in a synthesizer. (tone generator, amplifier, keyboard, sequencer, sampler, computer, and so on) Find pictures of synthesizers or other electronic keyboards to bring to class.

## Women Contributors to Popular Music

Women performers have played a major role in the development of rock and roll and other popular music styles. Early contributors include Brenda Lee and Connie Francis, top performers in the 1950s, and all-women groups of the 1960s, such as the Supremes.

During the 1970s singer-songwriters such as Joni Mitchell and Carole King became well known. Joni Mitchell influenced many musicians with her innovative songs and vocal style. Carole King's album *Tapestry* was one of the biggest-selling recordings of the 1970s. Artists such as Aretha Franklin, Tina Turner, and Barbra Streisand have turned out hit after hit for over three decades.

Barbra Streisand

Whitney Houston

Mariah Carey

230

# EXTENSION

### ELECTRIC KEYBOARDS

The **electronic organ** was originally developed to imitate the pipe organ. The electronic organ was much less expensive. Other electronic organs developed that did not imitate the pipe organ.

An **electric piano** is an electronic keyboard instrument designed to imitate the piano. Electrical impulses generated by vibrations are modified by an amplifier and converted back into sound by loudspeakers.

A **synthesizer** manufactures (or synthesizes) sounds electronically from the different components of sound waves. It can create any sound whose characteristics can be precisely identified in acoustical terms.

A synthesizer may or may not be a keyboard instrument.

A **sampler** is a device that plays back digital recordings of actual sounds. Its sounds are more realistic than a synthesizer because the sounds are actual samples of the real instrument. A sampler may or may not be a keyboard instrument.

### SYNTHESIZER HISTORY

The first synthesizers were used as early as 1929. They were used in the studio with tape recorders to create recorded electronic compositions. It wasn't until the 1970s that synthesizers became common. MIDI synthesizers came into use in 1983. They range in quality from relatively inexpensive beginner instruments to the sophisticated instruments used by professional musicians.

atalie Cole

Pat Benatar

Laurie Anderson

anet Jackson

Women have increasingly been recognized as composers and producers as well as performers. Performance artists such as Laurie Anderson and Kate Bush combine visual arts, dance, vocal and instrumental performance, poetry, and the latest in technological effects to create innovative art forms. Pat Benatar broke ground as one of the first successful solo women in hard rock. Madonna, Bonnie Raitt, and Whitney Houston are performers who made a big impact in the 1980s and 1990s. Vocalists of the 1990s such as Lauryn Hill, Alanis Morissette, and Janet Jackson provide inspiration in the field of popular music to women of the future.

231

2. How might the skills needed to play a synthesizer contrast with the skills needed to play other popular instruments? (Besides keyboard skills, a synthesizer player needs to know how to program the synthesizer and hook up the various parts of the equipment. The player needs to think of tone color and special effects more since there are many choices. The player needs to stay current on the latest synthesizer technology and upgrade equipment when newer sounds and effects are desired.)

3. Some synthesizers are not dependent on the limitations and ranges of specific musical instruments or human performing skills. Discuss how this advantage might affect tone quality, interval ranges, sustaining times, and so on. (They can imitate many instruments, play intervals outside of major and minor scales, and have almost unlimited sustaining time with no fade.)

2. **Introduce women in popular music.** Have the students:

• Read pages 230–231 and discuss the information on women in popular music.
• Respond to the following:

1. List important, contemporary women from the following professional fields: medicine (Dr. Helen Taussig), sports (Katarina Witt, Bonnie Blair, Nancy Lopez, Billy Jean King), law (Sandra Day O'Connor).

2. List other women musicians of the past or present. (for example: composers—Amy Beach, Teresa Carreño, Ruth Crawford-Seeger, Thea Musgrave; performers—Dolly Parton, Alicia de Larrocha, Midori, Ella Fitzgerald, Aretha Franklin, Kiri Te Kanawa; groups—Sweet Adelines, Sweet Honey in the Rock, Andrews Sisters)

## MORE MUSIC TEACHING IDEAS

1. Demonstrate (or have students demonstrate) functions, effects, and tone colors of electric keyboards that are available.

2. Play or have a student play a song accompaniment on electric keyboard and change the tone colors. Discuss which sounds worked best and why.

3. Discuss the two types of electronic instruments below and list other examples:
—where natural sounds are produced in traditional ways such as blowing, scraping, beating, and then amplified electronically, as in the electric guitar.
—where electronically-generated sounds are produced and then amplified electronically, as in the Hammond organ or synthesizer.

# LESSON 2

**3. Introduce styles of the 1970s.** Have the students:
• Read the first paragraph on page 232 and discuss the information on pop music of the 1970s.
• Listen to the recording of "Dreams." (You may wish to teach the guitar and keyboard accompaniments to the song, pages 277–278, at this time.)
• Read the second paragraph on page 232 and discuss the information on folk rock in the 1970s.
• Listen to "A Horse with No Name" used in Unit 3, Lesson 3, pages 76–81. (You may wish to teach the guitar accompaniments to the song, page 219, and the keyboard accompaniments, page 213, at this time.)
• Read paragraphs 3 and 4 and discuss the information on funk and disco.
• Listen to "More Than a Woman," written by the Bee Gees (Barry, Robin, and Maurice Gibb) for the movie *Saturday Night Fever*.

## Styles of the Seventies

Singer-songwriter David Bowie and groups such as the Eagles and the Carpenters wrote many popular songs which captured the musical styles of the 1970s. These songs were often very melodic and featured smooth sounds. The smooth sounds resulted from innovative musical arrangements and recording techniques far more advanced than those of the 1960s. The song "Dreams," from the group Fleetwood Mac, exhibits the smooth melodies of 1970s pop music. Guitar and keyboard accompaniments as well as the lyrics to "Dreams" appear on pages 276–278.

In the 1960s folk music became very popular. By the 1970s it had merged with rock music to create the style of folk rock. Folk rock emphasized meaningful lyrics and smooth vocal harmonies. Musicians such as James Taylor, Harry Chapin, Neil Young, and the group Crosby, Stills and Nash wrote many popular songs in the folk-rock style. Crosby, Stills and Nash, in particular, were well known for their complex harmonies. Another folk-rock group, America, produced a hit record in 1972 with their song "A Horse with No Name." You will find guitar accompaniments to this song on page 219 and two keyboard accompaniments on page 213.

Fleetwood Mac. Stevie Nicks, the composer of "Dreams," is on the right

232

# EXTENSION

## BIOGRAPHY

**Stephanie (Stevie) Nicks** was born in 1948 and raised in California. She was the vocalist of Fritz before becoming part of the pop-rock group Fleetwood Mac, where she remained from 1975–1993. She has made several gold- and platinum-selling albums both with and without Fleetwood Mac.

The **Bee Gees** are a trio of brothers from England—Barry (1947–), and twins Robin and Maurice (1949–). They first performed together in 1955. The Bee Gees recorded top-selling albums in the 1970s and 1980s. They composed the soundtracks for *Saturday Night Fever* and *Staying Alive*. In addition to singing as a group, each of them has had solo careers.

Karen and Richard Carpenter

James Taylor

An important musical development of the 1970s was a style called funk music. This music had its roots in soul music of the 1960s. Funk featured complex and vibrant rhythms. A prominent instrument in funk was the electric bass guitar. It made the music "funky" with its intricate and syncopated bass lines. Kool and the Gang, Parliament, and Earth, Wind and Fire are examples of 1970s funk bands.

During the 1970s another style of music emerged called disco. Like rock, disco had a beat. This beat was so strong and steady that it was perfect for dancing. By 1975 people were listening and dancing to disco music by Donna Summer, Diana Ross, and others. Not only were young people caught up in the disco craze, but so were their parents and grandparents. Disco even had its own movie, *Saturday Night Fever*, starring John Travolta. The soundtrack—with songs by the Bee Gees and other groups—became one of the best-selling albums of all time.

John Travolta in *Saturday Night Fever*

233

• Respond to the following:
1. Mainstream pop and disco music were popular at the same time. Explain how this occurrence was possible. (Music was fulfilling the needs of a diverse population and several age groups.)
2. List adjectives to describe pop and disco. (pop: smooth, melodic; disco: driving, rhythmic)

## APPRAISAL

The students should be able to:
1. Identify characteristics of a synthesizer.
2. Identify at least three women musicians.
3. Identify the musical characteristics of pop, folk rock, funk, and disco.

# LESSON 3

**3. Introduce the folk style.** Have the students:
• Discuss the folk style of the 1960s.
• List topics that would be relevant to sing about if folk music were prevalent in the 1980s. (answers will vary)

## Popular Music in the 1960s

It was during the 1960s that popular music "grew up." The music was rebellious, sometimes experimental, sometimes traditional, but always exciting.

## Hard Rock

During the late 1960s, rock expressed a new musical freedom. Along with the music came what was termed the "hippie" movement. Young men and women let their hair grow very long and wore outlandish clothes in a rebellion against more conservative adult society. Songs of the late sixties were often five, eight, or ten minutes long. Jimi Hendrix and Jeff Beck played long, intricate solos on electric guitar accompanied by a hard, driving beat.

Jimi Hendrix in performance

Above and below, the Woodstock Music and Art Fair, August 1969

The real home of this music was not the radio. It was at places like Woodstock—big, open-air festivals with dozens of rock bands playing in front of hundreds of thousands of people over the course of two or three days.

234

Left, the Beach Boys in the early 1960s. Below, the Beach Boys in performance at the Washington Mall, July 4, 1984

# LESSON 3

**2. Introduce the "California sound."** Have the students:
• Discuss the "California sound."
• Listen to "California Sound," containing songs made popular by the Beach Boys.
• Respond to the following questions:
1. How did the Beach Boys influence the younger generation? (They promoted what teenagers liked—surfing, cars, beach life.)
2. What has contributed to the Beach Boys' continued success for over thirty-five years? (The subject matter is clean and has lasting appeal, their style has not changed greatly, they appeal to a wide age group and continue to appeal to younger crowds.)

## The California Sound

During the early 1960s, the Beach Boys—three brothers, their cousin, and their best friend—used five-part vocal harmony and lively guitar melodies to create a sound known as "surf rock." Their songs were about the joys of surfing, cars, and being teenagers. During the mid-1960s they reeled off many hits such as "Surfin' Safari," "Surfin' U.S.A.," and "Surfer Girl."

As the Beach Boys grew older their sound matured, with Brian Wilson writing complex vocal harmony parts for the group and using sophisticated recording studio techniques. Their 1966 hit "Good Vibrations" is one of their best-known songs in this later style. It influenced other groups to update their music and recording quality. The Beach Boys have performed popular music for over thirty-five years.

235

# LESSON 3

**3. Introduce the folk style.** Have the students:

• Discuss the folk style of the 1960s.
• List topics that would be relevant to sing about if folk music were prevalent today. (Answers will vary.)

Peter, Paul and Mary

The New Christy Minstrels

The Kingston Trio

## The Folk Style

During the 1960s folk music had an important influence on popular music. Groups such as the Weavers; Peter, Paul and Mary; the Kingston Trio; and the New Christy Minstrels adapted traditional American folk music to the vocal styles of the time. Folk music became popular all over the nation.

One of the most important changes in popular music during the 1960s was an emphasis on the lyrics of the songs. The words became as important as the music. One person responsible for this change was the folk singer Bob Dylan.

236

# LESSON 3

• Listen to "Blowin' in the Wind." (You may wish to teach the guitar and keyboard accompaniments to the play-along version of the song, pages 265–266, at this time.)

Bob Dylan

Joan Baez

   Before Dylan, popular songs were frequently about love. Dylan wrote songs that expressed his feelings and opinions. Playing acoustic guitar and harmonica, Dylan sang about social topics, politics, and his experiences traveling across America.

   When Bob Dylan began playing concerts in 1961, Joan Baez was already world famous for her recordings of folk music. She recorded many of Dylan's songs herself and helped bring him to fame. They were two of the best-known folk singers of the 1960s.

   One of Dylan's most enduring songs is "Blowin' in the Wind." You will find a guitar accompaniment, a keyboard accompaniment, and the lyrics to this song on pages 264–266.

237

## MORE MUSIC TEACHING IDEAS

Some styles of music, such as musical theater and opera, require excellent diction from the performers. Popular music artists, however, are often not as crisp or clear. This is because personal style and expressive intent can override consideration to diction. Ask students if they can recall being mistaken about a song lyric. How did "their" version of the lyric differ from the actual lyric? The class may want to compile a list of "misheard lyrics."

# LESSON 3

**4. Introduce African American contributions to popular music.** Have the students:
- Discuss the information on Motown.
- Listen to "Motown Montage."

## Motown

The groups that made the "Motown Sound" famous during the 1960s came from Detroit (the "Motortown"), Michigan. Many of them recorded for Motown Records. The Motown style was spirited, danceable music sung by African American groups such as the Supremes, the Temptations, and the Four Tops.

Motown Records' slogan was "The Sound of Young America," and that is exactly what the Motown sound was. It combined the soul of American rhythm and blues music and gospel music with pop influences. The songs were well written and arranged, using many of the best studio musicians and the best recording techniques of the time. Motown Records searched for talent within the African American community. They encouraged young musicians to become polished performers and to write their own songs.

One of the best known of the early Motown groups was a female vocal trio, the Supremes. Led by Diana Ross, the Supremes had hit after hit during the 1960s. Their success continued until 1969, when Diana Ross left the group for a solo career.

- Listen to "Motown Montage."

The Supremes. Diana Ross is at the center.

🎵 "Motown Montage"

The Temptations

238

The Four Tops

Another leading Motown artist was Stevie Wonder, who had his first record, "Fingertips Part 2," in 1963 at the age of thirteen. Although he was blind from birth, "Little" Stevie (as he was called then) could play drums, bongos, harmonica, piano, and organ, as well as sing. He went on to have many hits during the 1960s. Stevie Wonder remains a successful song writer and performer today.

Ray Charles

James Brown

Aretha Franklin, "Lady Soul"

## Soul

Besides the Motown performers, other African American musicians were popular during the 1960s. They performed "soul music," which drew from the gospel and blues heritage of African Americans. Soul music was emotional and expressive like gospel music. Its popularity reflected the growing pride among America's African American community. That pride is evident in songs like James Brown's 1968 hit "Say It Loud—I'm Black and I'm Proud." Other soul singers such as Wilson Pickett, Otis Redding, and Aretha Franklin enjoyed success with songs that featured strong rhythms and vibrant horn sections. Many soul artists from the 1960s are still popular, for example, Aretha Franklin, Tina Turner, Lionel Richie, and Ray Charles. They have influenced a new generation of soul musicians such as Erykah Badu, Brian McKnight, and Lauryn Hill.

Stevie Wonder

• Discuss the information on soul music.
• Respond to the following:
1. Discuss the Motown style. (spirited, makes you want to dance, music which synthesized many types of music)
2. Discuss some of the contributions that older soul artists have made to the new generation of soul artists. (Ideas have been influenced by earlier artists and new versions of old songs have been created, for example, "Lean on Me," "Earth Angel," "Stand by Me.")

### APPRAISAL

The students should be able to define the musical characteristics of hard rock, the folk style, the California sound, and Motown.

# LESSON 4

**Focus: Style—History of American Popular Music**

**Objective**
To identify styles of popular music of the 1950s

**Materials**
Recordings: ''Fifties Montage''
          ''Rock Around the Clock''

**Vocabulary**
Rhythm and blues

## TEACHING THE LESSON

**1. Introduce popular music of the 1950s.** Have the students:

• Discuss the information on popular music in the 1950s.

• Listen to ''Fifties Montage,'' containing songs popular in the 1950s.

• Respond to the following:

1. List other rock-and-roll groups of the 1950s. (Bill Haley and the Comets, Fats Domino, Little Richard, Jerry Lee Lewis) Describe how they contributed to the development of rock-and-roll music. (They were the pioneers of the style, set the standard for others to follow.)

2. Discuss the characteristics of early rock-and-roll music. (steady beat, simple chord progressions, simple rhythms, songs of love and romance, danceable)

Buddy Holly and the Crickets

## Popular Music in the 1950s

The big rock festivals of the late 1960s were a far cry from the simple rock and roll of the 1950s. When rock and roll began in the mid-fifties, there were no high-tech recording studios and no synthesizers. Popular songs were often about the boy or girl next door or had titles like "Splish, Splash, I Was Taking a Bath."

The origins of rock and roll were here in the United States. This musical style grew out of American gospel, blues, and country and western music. The greatest influence on rock and roll was African American rhythm and blues. Rhythm and blues developed when musicians combined the melancholy melodies and harmonies of the blues with the emotion of gospel music, and added a dance beat. Rhythm and blues also featured the electric guitar and tenor saxophone. White pop groups such as the Crew Cuts rerecorded African American rhythm and blues songs and introduced white teenagers to rhythm and blues. The Crew Cuts' 1954 hit "Sh-Boom" usually is considered to be the first real rock-and-roll recording. "Sh-Boom" was originally recorded by an African American group, the Chords.

240

Ritchie Valens

Bill Haley and the Comets

CD5:9

• Listen to the recording of "Rock Around the Clock." (You may wish to teach the guitar and keyboard accompaniments to the song, pages 268–269, at this time.)

However, it wasn't until Bill Haley and the Comets recorded "Rock Around the Clock" in 1954 that rock and roll took off. More teenagers knew "Rock Around the Clock" than any previous rock-and-roll record because they heard it in the 1955 movie *Blackboard Jungle*, a film about high school students. The popularity of "Rock Around the Clock" made Bill Haley and the Comets the first big success of rock and roll. You will find guitar accompaniments, a keyboard accompaniment, and the lyrics to "Rock Around the Clock" on pages 267–269.

Two other early rock-and-roll artists of this period were Buddy Holly and Ritchie Valens. Buddy Holly was one of the first rock-and-roll performers to be involved in all aspects of his music. He composed and arranged his songs, besides producing the recordings. Ritchie Valens had several big hits in his six-month career, including "La Bamba." His life story was the subject of a recent film, also called *La Bamba*. Tragically, both Holly and Valens died in the same plane crash in 1959.

241

## MORE MUSIC TEACHING IDEAS

Have students investigate changes in dance styles over the last six decades. Ask them to interview older relatives and friends to find out what dances were popular in their teenage years. Ask students to note especially the changes in popularity that partner dancing has undergone. Do they know any partner dances? With what recent dance crazes are they familiar?

# LESSON 4

**2. Introduce Chuck Berry.** Have the students:
• Discuss the information on Chuck Berry.
• Respond to the following question: How did the stage behavior of pop performers change as rock and roll developed? (Movements became more stylized—jumps, "moon walks," spins, group synchronized choreography, and so on.)

Chuck Berry doing the duckwalk, about 1965. He still continues to record and tour.

## Chuck Berry, Rock-and-Roll Innovator

Bill Haley's songs were typical of early rock and roll. They had simple melodies; a strong, steady beat; and understated electric guitars.

Chuck Berry took 1950s rock and roll one giant step further. He brought the lead guitar to the forefront of the band. His songs "Maybellene," "School Days," and "Sweet Little Sixteen" were about everyday life. Teens recognized themselves in the words of his songs.

Chuck Berry also was the first great showman of rock and roll, moving across the stage with his guitar slung low while doing a step called the "duck walk." His song "Johnny B. Goode" was about a backwoods country boy who makes it big in rock and roll—a dream of many young musicians.

242

# Elvis: The King

One young musician who dreamed of making it big in rock and roll was a truck driver from Tupelo, Mississippi, named Elvis Presley. Elvis eventually became the biggest star in rock-and-roll history. Even though he died in 1977, Elvis is still referred to as the "King of Rock and Roll."

Elvis brought a raw energy to early rock-and-roll music. He caused near-riots among swooning teenage girls when he sang in concerts. By 1956, Elvis was the biggest star of popular music. He is still idolized by millions of fans. Hundreds of Elvis Presley imitators— even in Broadway musicals—still imitate his way of dressing and his singing style in front of enthusiastic crowds.

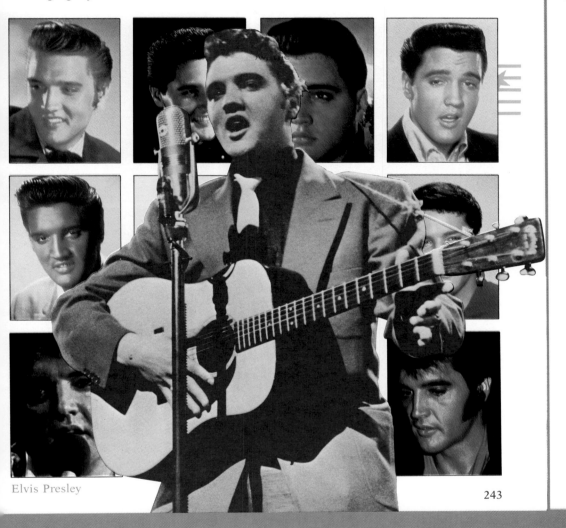

Elvis Presley

243

## LESSON 4

**3. Introduce Elvis Presley.** Have the students:
• Discuss the information on Elvis Presley.
• Respond to the following question: Why is Elvis Presley called the "King of Rock and Roll"? (He brought rock and roll to everyone's attention by his energetic performances, "boy next door" image, and exciting music.)

# LESSON 4

**4. Introduce other rock and roll artists of the 1950s.** Have the students discuss the information on other rock and roll artists of the 1950s.

## APPRAISAL

The students should be able to define the characteristics of popular music of the 1950s.

## Other Rock and Rollers of the 1950s

While Elvis Presley and Chuck Berry sang and played guitar, Jerry Lee Lewis and Little Richard sang and pounded out their music on the piano. Jerry Lee Lewis would push his piano stool away from the piano, sometimes playing with his feet. Little Richard was famous for jumping on top of the piano and dancing wildly. Both performers brought energy and emotion to the rock and roll of the 1950s.

Other 1950s stars, such as the Everly Brothers, played more sedate music. Brothers Don and Phil Everly were from a family of country and western musicians. They brought the smooth vocals, pleasant harmonies, and acoustic guitars of country music to rock and roll. Their big hits from the 1950s include "Bye Bye Love" and "Wake Up, Little Susie."

Little Richard

Jerry Lee Lewis

244

Johnny Horton also drew on the country music tradition for his rock music. In 1959 his "Battle of New Orleans" was a number-one hit. Horton's song featured a military-style beat on the snare drum, while the lyrics describe a battle fought during the War of 1812.

American rock-and-roll music of the 1950s influenced young people around the world. The Beatles, an English group, got their start playing American rock and roll. The Beatles went on to become the world's best-known rock group.

Left, Johnny Horton
Below, the Everly Brothers

## LESSON 5

**Focus: Style—History of American Popular Music**

**Objective**
To identify styles of popular folk music

**Materials**
Recording: "Country Music Montage"
"Foggy Mountain Breakdown"

**Vocabulary**
Country and western, bluegrass

## TEACHING THE LESSON

**1. Introduce country and western music.** Have the students:
• Discuss the information on country and western music.

## Country and Western Music

Before the rock and roll of the 1950s, several other types of music were popular throughout America. Among these were country and western music and bluegrass music. Although both of these styles trace their origin to rural American folk music, they are quite different.

Country and western music, or country music, had many sources—old ballads, cowboy songs, Mexican music, and Appalachian music, to name just a few. The earliest country performers sang and played this traditional music. The most common instruments were acoustic guitar, string bass, banjo, pedal-steel guitar, and fiddle. Most of the songs had four-line verses in duple meter and used three or four simple chords.

At first many people did not care for the nasal singing style and unpolished sound of this music. During the 1920s Jimmie Rodgers, recognized as the "father of country music," and the fiddler Roy Acuff began to write and record more commercial country music. Jimmie Rodgers also was influenced by the blues he heard sung by the African Americans he worked with on the railroads.

Hank Williams, Sr.

Minnie Pearl

June Carter

246

Nashville, Tennessee, became a center for the writing and recording of country music. It is also where the Grand Ole Opry was located until it moved to nearby Opryland. Starting in 1939, national radio broadcasts from the Grand Ole Opry introduced many country artists, such as the Carter family, Patsy Cline, and Loretta Lynn, to the American public.

When radio expanded during the 1940s and 1950s, country music became more popular. It also began to change. It sounded less like "hillbilly" music and more like the commercial music of the time. Singers Hank Williams and Minnie Pearl were stars during this period.

During the 1960s and 1970s, large-scale orchestrations with string and brass sections became popular. Chet Atkins, Glen Campbell, and Johnny Cash were leading stars. Country musicians flocked to Nashville.

Roy Acuff

Johnny Cash (left) and Waylon Jennings

# LESSON 5

- Listen to the "Country Music Montage."
- Respond to the following:

1. Discuss the development of country and western music from its roots to the present. (new instrumentation, large-scale orchestrations, different type of singing, more emphasis on promotion today, biggest-selling variety of music in nation)

2. How does country and western music reflect current trends in society today? Give examples. (songs of economic depression, Farm Aid, love songs, songs of travel, music packaged for mass appeal, videos, choreography)

Reba McEntire

CD5:10

Some country songs, such as Tammy Wynette's "Stand By Your Man" (1968) and John Denver's "Take Me Home, Country Roads" (1971) became big "crossover" hits. They did well on both the country and pop charts. At the same time, the "New Nashville" sound developed. It featured smooth orchestrations, background vocals, and electric guitars instead of fiddles. Charley Pride, Kenny Rogers, and Dolly Parton became popular with this new sound. Meanwhile, artists like Willie Nelson and Emmy Lou Harris went back to the simpler roots of country music.

In the early 1990s, record stores began using new technology that reported record sales more accurately. Overnight the music industry realized that country music sold nearly as many recordings as mainstream pop. This new realization made country music even more popular because the record industry now promoted country music with as much effort as it gave mainstream music. Garth Brooks was one of the first country stars to receive mainstream recognition. Country music videos, tours, and concerts of groups such as Alabama began to take on the major proportions of mainstream pop and rock. Faith Hill, Reba MacEntire, Vince Gill, Alan Jackson, and Patti Lovelace are among the country music stars of the 1990s.

- Listen to "Country Music Montage" to hear the many styles of country music.

"Country Music Montage"

Faith Hill

Garth Brooks

Vince Gill

248

Lester Flatt (left) and Earl Scruggs (right) in performance

CD5:11

## Bluegrass

Bluegrass music, or "string band music" as it is sometimes called, uses acoustic stringed instruments such as five-string banjo, fiddle, mandolin, guitar, and bass. Bluegrass singing features a high-pitched, nasal sound. This style became established in the late 1940s, and bluegrass music remained relatively unchanged since.

One of the first musicians to make bluegrass more popular was Bill Monroe. His group, called the Bluegrass Boys, enjoyed success during the mid-1940s, with Earl Scruggs playing banjo and Lester Flatt playing guitar. In 1948, Flatt and Scruggs left the Bluegrass Boys to form the Foggy Mountain Boys. Their most popular song was the rousing "Foggy Mountain Breakdown." You will find a guitar accompaniment and a keyboard accompaniment to this song on pages 262–263.

Bill Monroe

# LESSON 5

**2. Introduce bluegrass.** Have the students:
• Discuss the information on bluegrass.
• Listen to the recording of "Foggy Mountain Breakdown." (You may wish to teach the guitar and keyboard accompaniments to the song, pages 262–263, at this time.)
• Respond to the following:
The bluegrass style has not really changed since its beginning in the late 1940s. Discuss possible reasons why this style of music, unlike other styles (rock, jazz, country and western) has remained the same. (Bluegrass calls for specific instruments and specific styles of singing and playing; its popularity is enduring.)

## APPRAISAL

The students should be able to trace the development and define the musical characteristics of country and western music and bluegrass.

249

# LESSON 6

**Focus: Style—History of American Popular Music**

**Objective**
To identify styles of popular music of the 1940s, 1930s, and 1920s

**Materials**
Recordings: ''When the Saints Go Marching In'' (performed by Louis Armstrong)
''When the Saints Go Marching In'' (scat version)
''Forties Montage''
''Harlem Speaks''

**Vocabulary**
Dixieland, scat singing, Swing, Big Band

## TEACHING THE LESSON

**1. Introduce early jazz styles.** Have the students discuss the information on early jazz styles.

## Early Jazz Styles

New Orleans, Louisiana, is often called the birthplace of American jazz. The early jazz style called Dixieland developed there during the early 1900s. Dixieland bands consisted of five to eight musicians who played piano, bass, drums, banjo, clarinet, trombone, and trumpet (or the trumpetlike cornet).

Three of the most important musicians in jazz history hailed from New Orleans: pianist Ferdinand "Jelly Roll" Morton, cornetist Joseph "King" Oliver, and one of the greatest jazz artists, Louis Armstrong.

Born in New Orleans, King Oliver rose to fame in Chicago during the 1920s when he hired cornetist Louis Armstrong to play in his group, the Creole Jazz Band. Armstrong stayed with the Creole Jazz Band until about 1924.

King Oliver's Creole Jazz Band. Left to right, Johnny Dodds, Baby Dodds, Honoré Dutrey, Louis Armstrong, Joe Oliver, Lil Hardin Armstrong, Bill Johnson

250

Louis Armstrong set new directions for jazz by improvising unusual solos and performing them in an expressive style. He also is said to be the inventor of a vocal style known as "scat singing." Instead of singing words, Armstrong uttered sounds like "de-de-de" and "lat-dat-da-da" to imitate various instruments. Later Ella Fitzgerald and Al Jarreau used this style with great success.

Louis Armstrong made jazz popular not only because of his tremendous musical abilities but also because of his showmanship and captivating personality. He traveled and performed all over the world until his death in 1971.

• Listen to Armstrong's performance of "When the Saints Go Marching In." You will find guitar and keyboard accompaniments on pages 272–273.

 "When the Saints Go Marching In," performed by Louis Armstrong

• Now listen to a performance of the song using scat singing.

Louis Armstrong

251

# LESSON 6

**2. Introduce Louis Armstrong.** Have the students:
• Discuss the information on Louis Armstrong.
• Listen to Armstrong's performance of "When the Saints Go Marching In." (You may wish to teach the guitar and keyboard accompaniments to the song, pages 272–273, at this time.)
• Listen to the scat version of the song.
• Respond to the following:
1. Try some "scat singing." What are some of the problems encountered in trying to scat sing? (use of the voice as an instrument, which vowels to use and when to use them) How does scat singing enhance the music? (provides unique tone color)
2. In what way did Louis Armstrong help improve the political climate between the United States and the Soviet Union? (He became a Goodwill Ambassador between the two countries.) What was his famous nickname? (Satchmo—short for "satchel mouth," because of his big, warm smile) What common link did he provide to the two countries? (music)

# LESSON 6

**3. Introduce the hit parade and the Big Bands.** Have the students:
• Discuss the information on the hit parade.
• Identify the artists shown.

Glenn Miller (first in line) and his orchestra

*The Wizard of Oz*

Paul Whiteman (conducting) and his orchestra

## The Hit Parade and the Big Bands

From 1935 through the 1940s, many people listened to the top songs of the era on a radio program called "Your Hit Parade." Frank Sinatra, Judy Garland, and the Andrews Sisters all rose to fame during this period.

Some of the most popular songs on "Your Hit Parade" were performed by Big Bands. The catchy rhythm of this era was called "Swing." Through the 1930s and 1940s, people danced to Big Band Music.

252

Frank Sinatra

The Andrews Sisters

Benny Goodman
(playing clarinet) and his orchestra

**4. Introduce the Big Band Era.** Have the students:
• Discuss the information on the Big Bands.
• Listen to "Forties Montage."
• Respond to the following:
1. What did the dancers do while the instrumentalists improvised solos during a dance selection? (stopped to listen, then resumed dancing)
2. What other name applied to the music of the late thirties through the forties? (swing) What were some characteristics of this style? (syncopation, large band, dancing to music)
3. Contrast Big Band dancing to rock and roll dancing. (closer, smoother, more structured dance steps) Name two dances of this time. (jitterbug, foxtrot)

The Big Band was literally big, consisting of thirteen to eighteen musicians who played trumpets, trombones, saxophones, piano, guitar, drums, and bass, as well as vocalists. The leader usually served as the band's soloist. The Glenn Miller Orchestra and bands led by Duke Ellington, Tommy Dorsey, Jimmy Dorsey, Benny Goodman, Count Basie, Harry James, and Stan Kenton played before packed houses in dance halls and ballrooms across America.

 "Forties Montage"

253

# LESSON 6

**5. Prepare to listen to "Harlem Speaks."** Have the students:
• Discuss the information on Duke Ellington.
• Listen to "Harlem Speaks."
• Respond to the following:
1. Discuss the impact of improvisation in jazz music. (requires experimentation, development of musical ideas, expression of soloist, most important element of style)
2. Identify the different instruments featured in the improvisations of "Harlem Speaks."

## APPRAISAL

The students should be able to trace the development and define the musical characteristics of Dixieland, the Big Bands, and other jazz styles.

Pianist and band leader Duke Ellington contributed to the fusion of Big Band music with instrumental jazz during the 1930s. Members of Ellington's orchestra, such as John Hodges on saxophone or Charles "Cootie" Williams on trumpet, improvised solo parts "on the spot." This kind of improvisation has always been one of the basic features of jazz.

• Follow the improvisations in "Harlem Speaks," recorded by the Ellington orchestra in 1933.

 **"Harlem Speaks"**

1. *Introduction*

2. *Verse 1*  trumpet solo (Freddie Jenkins)

3. *Verse 2*  alto saxophone (Johnny Hodges)

4. *Verse 3*  trumpet with mute ("Cootie" Williams)

5. *Verse 4*  trombone with mute ("Tricky Sam" Nanton)

6. *Verse 5*  saxophone chorus

7. *Verse 6*  full band with trombone and clarinet featured

Duke Ellington (center) and his orchestra. Freddie Jenkins is seated at far right; Johnny Hodges is seated behind the guitarist; "Cootie" Williams is seated in the front row at right; "Tricky Sam" Nanton is seated in the front row at left.

Scott Joplin

Eubie Blake (at the piano)
and Noble Sissle

James P. Johnson

# LESSON 7

**Focus: Style—History of American Popular Music**

**Objectives**
To identify styles of popular music from 1900 to 1920

**Materials**
Recordings: *The Entertainer* (complete piano version)
"St. Louis Blues"
"Lost Your Head Blues"

**Vocabulary**
Blues

## TEACHING THE LESSON

**1. Introduce ragtime.** Have the students:
• Discuss the information on ragtime. (You may wish to have the students listen again to the piano version of *The Entertainer* used in Unit 2, Lesson 3.)
• Respond to the following question: What made Scott Joplin the "King of Ragtime"? (developed style of ragtime, brought originality and expressiveness to ragtime)

## Ragtime

Ragtime, another style of American popular music, began in the African American communities of midwestern cities such as St. Louis and Sedalia, Missouri, at the turn of the century.

Ragtime is exciting to hear and difficult to play because the melody has complex, syncopated (off-the-beat) rhythms against a simple, steady beat in the accompaniment. Many later jazz musicians borrowed characteristics of ragtime. The strong syncopated rhythms, simple repeated chord patterns, and lively spirit of this music quickly made it popular.

Scott Joplin (1868–1917) was called the "King of Ragtime." His *Maple Leaf Rag* became very popular when it was first published as sheet music in 1899. Joplin is best remembered today for his rag *The Entertainer*, which was heard in the 1973 movie *The Sting*. The entire soundtrack to *The Sting* consists of music by Joplin.

As the ragtime craze swept across the country, many composers were attracted to this spirited music. Among them were James Scott, James P. Johnson, Euday L. Bowman, May Aufderheide, and Eubie Blake. They and others published hundreds of ragtime piano pieces, songs, and dances.

255

# LESSON 7

**2. Introduce the blues.** Have the students:
- Discuss the information on the blues.
- Listen to the recording of "St. Louis Blues." (You may wish to teach the guitar and keyboard accompaniments to the song, pages 270–271, at this time.)

## THE BLUES

The roots of jazz lie in the blues. The blues grew out of the spirituals and work songs of the post-Civil War period. The tempo of blues songs is slow, and the subject matter is almost always unhappy, reflecting everyday troubles—mainly unhappy love.

W. C. Handy and Ferdinand "Jelly Roll" Morton were among the first composers of blues songs early in the twentieth century. Handy was probably the first to make the blues available to the general public with publication of "Memphis Blues" in 1912 and "St. Louis Blues" in 1914. You will find a guitar accompaniment and a keyboard accompaniment to "St. Louis Blues" on pages 270–271.

Billie Holiday

Huddie Ledbetter
("Leadbelly")

Ferdinand "Jelly Roll" Morton

Although W. C. Handy's and Jelly Roll Morton's songs helped make the blues popular, it was Bessie Smith who really brought this music to the American people. With her powerful voice and her ability to communicate the emotions expressed in her songs, Bessie Smith affected audiences wherever she performed.

Billie Holiday was another popular woman singer. Although she did not sing many "classic" blues songs, she gave a blues inflection to the music she sang, mainly pop tunes.

Huddie Ledbetter (known as "Leadbelly") was one of the most important African American singer-guitarists of all time. He wandered through the South, learning and composing blues songs.

Bessie Smith

W. C. Handy

257

## LESSON 7

- Identify two important female singers of the blues. (Bessie Smith, Billie Holiday)
- Respond to the following:
1. Why did people call this kind of music the *blues*? (slow tempo, unhappy subject matter)
2. What were the songwriters usually "blue" about? (unhappy love, troubles of life)
3. What is the special element in vocal quality which determines greatness? (ability to communicate emotion)
4. Discuss some differences between blues and ragtime. (Blues has a sadder quality and tends to emphasize the lyrics. Ragtime has a lively spirit and is more rhythmic and syncopated.)
- Turn to page 127 and listen to "Lost Your Head Blues."
- Identify the problems expressed through the text.

**3. Introduce music of the turn of the century.** Have the students:
• Discuss the information on the turn of the century.

Lillian Russell, a popular singer

Pianos or organs could be found in many homes at the turn of the century.

A ticket to a concert by Jenny Lind, another famous singer

## The Turn of the Century

Different groups brought a variety of popular music to many areas of the country before 1900. As America expanded and developed, musicians traveled in minstrel shows, barbershop quartets, bands, and vocal groups, and as solo performers. They presented music through formal and informal concerts. A great deal of this music grew from specific events or places. "Erie Canal" and "When Johnny

258

Barbershop quartets first became popular around the turn of the century.

An early phonograph. A needle traced tiny grooves on a wax cylinder to reproduce recorded sounds.

• Respond to the following:
1. List some reasons for the diverse musical tastes of the American people. ("melting pot" population, large country, many geographical locations, varied occupations of people)
2. List two composers who contributed to our musical culture at the turn of the century. (John Philip Sousa, Scott Joplin)

## APPRAISAL

The students should be able to trace the development and define the musical characteristics of the blues and ragtime.

Comes Marching Home" are just two examples. Stephen Foster wrote about other aspects of American life in songs such as "Beautiful Dreamer" and "Oh! Susannah." The band leader and composer John Philip Sousa wrote many marches, including *The Stars and Stripes Forever*. All of these types of music contributed to America's rich musical heritage.

259

# REVIEW AND EVALUATION

**Objective**
To review American Popular Music from 1900 to present

**Materials**
Recordings: Looking Back (questions 12, 13, 14, 15)
"More Than a Woman"
"Dreams"
"The River of Dreams"
"Motown Montage"
"Foggy Mountain Breakdown"
Copying Master A-2, A-3 (optional)
Evaluation American Popular Music I and II Copying Masters

## TEACHING THE LESSON

**Review the skills and concepts taught in American Popular Music.** Have the students:

• Perform the activities and answer the questions on pages 260–261. (For this review, examples for questions 12–15 are included in the "Looking Back" recording. Have the students answer these questions first. Then have them answer the other questions in the review.)

• Review their answers. (You may wish to use Copying Masters A-2 and A-3 at this time.)

## LOOKING BACK

See how much you remember.

1. Listen to a portion of "More Than a Woman" and describe the musical characteristics of disco music. strong, steady beat, not syncopated, commercially oriented

2. Listen to a portion of "Dreams" and identify the musical characteristics of mainstream-pop style. Rich vocal harmonies, layers of guitars, and the use of multiple keyboards. The melodies are tuneful and the rhythm lacks the hard, driving character of disco.

3. Name one popular-music superstar from each decade: the 1960s, the 1970s, the 1980s, and the 1990s. Give a fact about each. Answers will vary.

4. Listen to a portion of "The River of Dreams." Identify the musical characteristic that Billy Joel borrowed from another style of popular music. call and response between lead vocalist and choir borrowed from gospel music

5. The Beach Boys and their musical style, known as "surf music," have continued to enjoy popularity for over thirty-five years. Describe the special qualities of this musical style. close vocal harmony; melodic guitar parts; and words that focus on the joys of surfing, cars, and being teenagers

6. Listen to a portion of "Motown Montage" and describe the musical characteristics of this style from Detroit. driving percussion, very spirited, based on combination of rhythm and blues with gospel-style writing

7. Name some of the sources from which country and western music developed. rural American folk music, old ballads, cowboy songs, Mexican music, Appalachian music

8. Listen to "Foggy Mountain Breakdown." Identify the tempo, style, and instruments used. fast, bluegrass, banjo and guitar

9. Name three popular recording artists from the 1940s. Frank Sinatra, Judy Garland, and the Andrews Sisters

260

10. Name at least two conductors of the Big Band era. Glenn Miller, Tommy Dorsey, Benny Goodman, Count Basie, Harry James, Stan Kenton

11. Name two early composers of blues songs. W. C. Handy and "Jelly Roll" Morton

12. Listen to this singing style and describe scat singing. sounds uttered to imitate various instruments

13. Listen to examples of two styles of popular music that influenced the development of the Dixieland early jazz style. Name the two styles. blues and ragtime

14. Listen to the following examples and name each style and period in which it was popular. Choose from the following time periods. 1. big band, 1930–1950; 2. ragtime, 1890–1910

    1890–1910          1910–1930          1930–1950

15. Listen to the following examples. Name each style and the period in which it was popular. Choose from the following time periods. 1. rock and roll, 1950–1960; 2. rock 1990–2000

    1950–1960          1960–1970          1970–1980
    1980–1990          1990–2000

# REVIEW AND EVALUATION

## GIVING THE EVALUATION

Evaluation American Popular Music I and II can be found in the *Teacher's Copying Masters* along with full directions for giving the evaluation and checking the answers.

# ACCOMPANIMENTS AND LYRICS

**"Foggy Mountain Breakdown"**

## Materials
Recording: "Foggy Mountain Breakdown"
Copying Master A-4 (optional)

## TEACHING THE ACCOMPANIMENT

**1. Prepare to perform a harmonic accompaniment on guitar to "Foggy Mountain Breakdown."** Have the students:
• Review the E minor chord.
• Practice playing the G major and D major chords.

---

## Foggy Mountain Breakdown

"Foggy Mountain Breakdown" is a standard song among bluegrass bands. Bluegrass tunes are often played at a fast tempo. In a "breakdown" song, each musician takes a turn playing the melody as a solo.

You can accompany "Foggy Mountain Breakdown" with three chords, E minor, which you have already learned (see page 219), G major, and D major.

The X at the top of a string on the chord diagram indicates that the string is not to be played. Avoid strumming the fifth and sixth strings when you play the G major and D major chords. Remember that a string marked with an O should be played open.

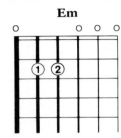

**Em**

1. 1st finger on 5th string, 2nd fret

2. 2nd finger on 4th string, 2nd fret

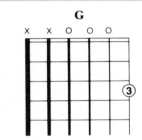

**G**

3rd finger on 1st string, 3rd fret

262

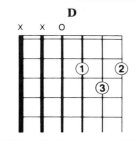

**D**

x x o

1. 1st finger on 3rd string, 2nd fret

2. 2nd finger on 1st string, 2nd fret

3. 3rd finger on 2nd string, 3rd fret

## Guitar Accompaniment to "Foggy Mountain Breakdown"

*(11 times)*

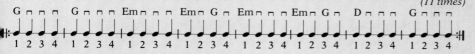

can also play a keyboard accompaniment to "Foggy Mountain Breakdown."

## Keyboard Accompaniment to "Foggy Mountain Breakdown"

nacle Overlook, Cumberland Gap National Heritage Park, Tennessee

# ACCOMPANIMENTS AND LYRICS

• Practice the guitar accompaniment to "Foggy Mountain Breakdown," changing chords as indicated.

• Play the guitar chords as a harmonic accompaniment to "Foggy Mountain Breakdown" with the recording. (You may wish to use Copying Master A-4 at this time.)

**2. Prepare to perform a harmonic accompaniment on keyboard to "Foggy Mountain Breakdown."** Have the students:

• Practice, then perform, right- and left-hand parts separately, then together.

• Perform the keyboard accompaniment to "Foggy Mountain Breakdown" with the recording.

• Form two groups. Group 1 will play the guitar accompaniment while Group 2 plays the keyboard accompaniment. (You may wish to use Copying Master A-4 at this time.)

# ACCOMPANIMENTS AND LYRICS

## "Blowin' in the Wind"

**Materials**
Recording: "Blowin' in the Wind" (play-along version)
Copying Master A-5 (optional)

## TEACHING THE ACCOMPANIMENT

**1. Prepare students to perform a harmonic accompaniment on guitar to "Blowin' in the Wind."** Have the students:
• Discuss the information on "Blowin' in the Wind."
• Sing the words to the song.

## Blowin' in the Wind

"Blowin' in the Wind," by Bob Dylan, deals with one of the most serious social issues of the early 1960s—the struggle by African Americans for civil rights. Although "Blowin' in the Wind" sounds simple when played on the guitar, the song's lyrics have a powerful message.

### Blowin' in the Wind
Words and music by Bob Dylan

How many roads must a man walk down
    before you call him a man?
How many seas must a white dove sail
    before she sleeps in the sand?
Yes, 'n' how many times must the cannonballs fly
    before they're forever banned?
The answer, my friend, is blowin' in the wind,
the answer is blowin' in the wind.

Yes, 'n' how many times must a man look up
    before he can see the sky?
Yes, 'n' how many ears must one man have
    before he can hear people cry?
Yes, 'n' how many deaths will it take till he knows
    that too many people have died?
The answer, my friend, is blowin' in the wind,
the answer is blowin' in the wind.

Yes, 'n' how many years can a mountain exist
    before it is washed to the sea?
Yes, 'n' how many years can some people exist
    before they're allowed to be free?
Yes, 'n' how many times can a man turn his head
    and pretend that he just doesn't see?
The answer, my friend, is blowin' in the wind,
the answer is blowin' in the wind.

# E X T E N S I O N

## CURRICULUM CONNECTION: SOCIAL STUDIES

Music can reflect and comment on social issues, such as war, riots, racial violence, and ecology. Have the students look at the text and listen to "Blowin' in the Wind." Ask them to determine what social issue is reflected in the words of the song. (racial injustice) Ask them how the music supports the meaning of the text. (slow tempo, soft dynamic level, vocal tone quality)

Have the students examine the text of "Our World" on page 170 and determine what social issue is reflected in the words of the song. (ecology) Ask them to decide how the music in the repeated and contrasting sections of the song helps to reflect the mood of the text. (The A section is in a major mode, has a fast tempo, and expresses a general mood of optimism. The B section is in a minor mode, is slower and legato, and expresses a general mood of anxiety.)

You can accompany "Blowin' in the Wind" on the guitar with four chords: D major, G major, A major, and E minor. You have already learned all of them except A major.

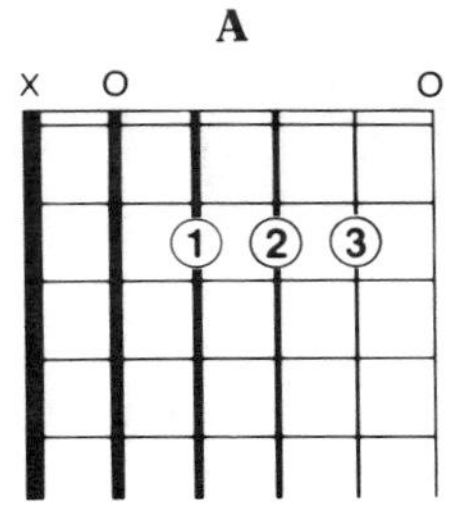

**A**

1. 1st finger on 4th string, 2nd fret
2. 2nd finger on 3rd string, 2nd fret
3. 3rd finger on 2nd string, 2nd fret

**Guitar Accompaniment
to "Blowin' in the Wind"**

$\frac{4}{4}$

*Verses 1–3*

D    G    D    D    G    D

D    G    D    D    G    A

D    G    D    D    G    D

*Refrain*

G    A    D    Em    A    D

*Coda*

G    A    D    Em    A    D

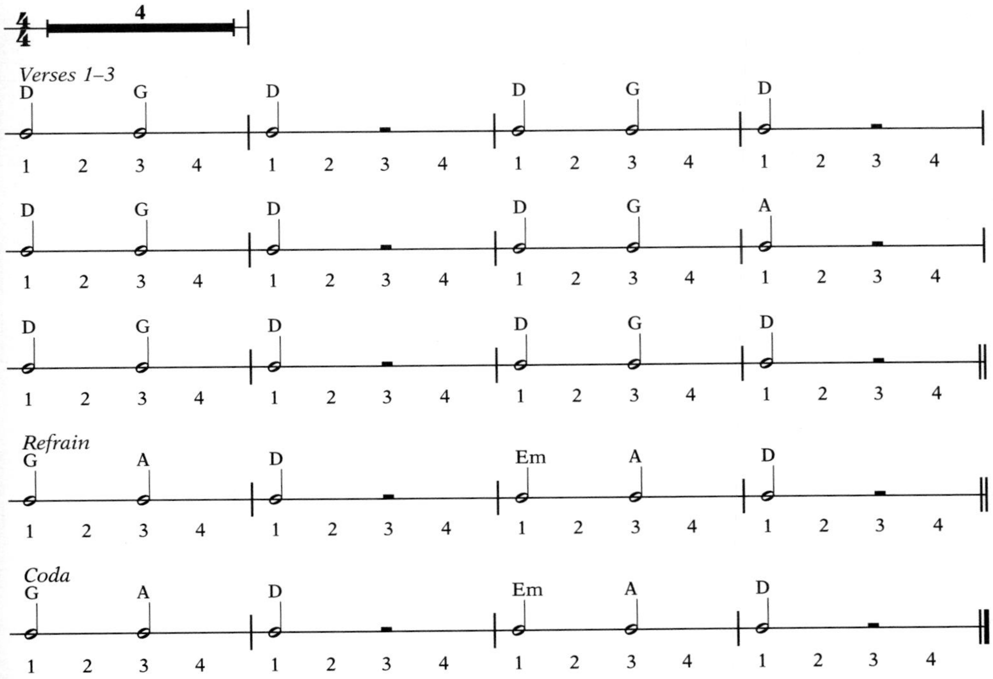

# ACCOMPANIMENTS AND LYRICS

• Review the D major, G major, and E minor chords.
• Practice playing the A major chord.
• Practice the guitar accompaniment, changing chords as indicated.
• Play the harmonic accompaniment to "Blowin' in the Wind" with the recording. (You may wish to use Copying Master A-5 at this time.)

265

# ACCOMPANIMENTS AND LYRICS

**2. Prepare students to perform a harmonic accompaniment on keyboard to "Blowin' in the Wind."** Have the students:
• Practice, then perform, right- and left-hand parts separately, then together.
• Perform the keyboard accompaniment to "Blowin' in the Wind" with the recording.
• Form two groups. Group 1 will play the guitar accompaniment while Group 2 plays the keyboard accompaniment. (You may wish to use Copying Master A-5 at this time.)

Bob Dyl[an]

You can also accompany "Blowin' in the Wind" on the keyboard.

### Keyboard Accompaniment to "Blowin' in the Wind"

# Rock Around the Clock

"Rock Around the Clock" is generally recognized as the song that helped bring worldwide popularity to rock and roll.

## Rock Around the Clock
### Words and music by Max B. Friedman and Jimmy DeKnight

Introduction

One, two, three o'clock, four o'clock, rock.
Five, six, seven o'clock, eight o'clock, rock.
Nine, ten, eleven o'clock, twelve o'clock, rock.
We're gonna rock, around, the clock tonight.

1. Well, get your glad rags on, join me hon', we're gonna have some
   fun when the clock strikes one,
   We're gonna rock around the clock tonight, we're gonna rock,
   rock, rock 'til the broad daylight,
   We're gonna rock, gonna rock around the clock tonight.

2. When the clock strikes two, three and four, and the band slows
   down we'll yell for more,
   We're gonna rock around the clock tonight, we're gonna rock,
   rock, rock 'til the broad daylight,
   We're gonna rock, gonna rock around the clock tonight.

3. Instrumental Verse

4. When the chimes ring five, six, and seven, we'll be rockin' up
   in seventh heaven,
   We're gonna rock around the clock tonight, we're gonna rock,
   rock, rock 'til the broad daylight,
   We're gonna rock, gonna rock around the clock tonight.

5. When it's eight, nine, ten, eleven too, I'll be going strong and
   so will you,
   We're gonna rock around the clock tonight, we're gonna rock,
   rock, rock 'til the broad daylight,
   We're gonna rock, gonna rock around the clock tonight.

6. Instrumental Verse

7. When the clock strikes twelve we'll cool off, then, start a-rockin'
   round the clock again,
   We're gonna rock around the clock tonight, we're gonna rock,
   rock, rock 'til the broad daylight,
   We're gonna rock, gonna rock around the clock tonight.

267

# ACCOMPANIMENTS AND LYRICS

## "Rock Around the Clock"

**Materials**
Recording: "Rock Around the Clock"
Copying Master A-6 (optional)

## TEACHING THE ACCOMPANIMENT

**1. Prepare to perform a harmonic accompaniment on guitar to "Rock Around the Clock."** Have the students:
• Discuss the information on "Rock Around the Clock."
• Sing the words to the song.

# ACCOMPANIMENTS AND LYRICS

- Review the D major and A major chords.
- Practice playing the E7 chord.
- Practice the guitar accompaniment, changing the chords as indicated.
- Play the harmonic accompaniment to "Rock Around the Clock" with the recording. (You may wish to use Copying Master A-6 at this time.)
- Read the directions on page 221 on how to play a bass part from tablature.
- Practice the bass part to "Rock Around the Clock," then play it with the recording.

You can accompany "Rock Around the Clock" on the guitar with the A major and D major chords. The song also uses the E7 chord.

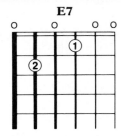

1. 2nd finger on 5th string, 2nd fret

2. 1st finger on 3rd string, 1st fret

## Guitar Accompaniments to "Rock Around the Clock"

- Learn a bass part to "Rock Around the Clock" from the tablature below.

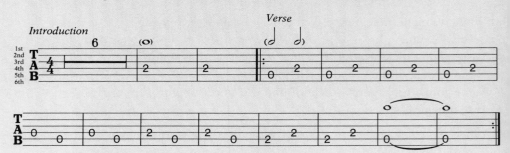

Turn to page **220** for directions on how to play a bass part from tablature.

268

The repeated chords in this keyboard accompaniment are a trademark of early rock-and-roll keyboard style.

## Keyboard Accompaniment to "Rock Around the Clock"

*Introduction*

*Verses*

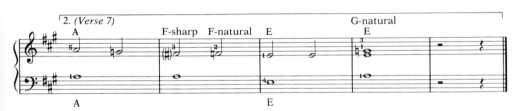

# ACCOMPANIMENTS AND LYRICS

**2. Prepare to perform a harmonic accompaniment on keyboard to "Rock Around the Clock."** Have the students:
• Practice right- and left-hand parts separately, then together.
• Practice, then perform, left- and right-hand parts together as an accompaniment to "Rock Around the Clock" with recording.
• Form two groups. Group 1 will play the guitar accompaniment while Group 2 plays the keyboard accompaniment. (You may wish to use Copying Master A-6 at this time.)

# ACCOMPANIMENTS AND LYRICS

**"St. Louis Blues"**

**Materials**
Recording: "St. Louis Blues"

## TEACHING THE ACCOMPANIMENT

**1. Prepare to perform a harmonic accompaniment on guitar to "St. Louis Blues."** Have the students:
• Discuss the information on "St. Louis Blues."
• Review the D major, G major, and A major chords.
• Practice the guitar accompaniment to "St. Louis Blues," changing chords as indicated.
• Play the guitar chords as a harmonic accompaniment to "St. Louis Blues" with the recording.
• Discuss the information on the blues shuffle and sixth chords.
• Practice the blues shuffle, changing chords as indicated.
• Play the blues shuffle as an accompaniment to "St. Louis Blues."

# St. Louis Blues

One of the earliest and most famous blues songs is "St. Louis Blues," written by W.C. Handy in 1914.

You can play a basic blues accompaniment for "St. Louis Blues" using the D, G, and A chords with this strum pattern of alternating long and short sounds.

When you can play the pattern easily, practice the entire twelve-bar blues pattern of the song. Accent the second and fourth beats slightly.

**Guitar Accompaniment to "St. Louis Blues"**

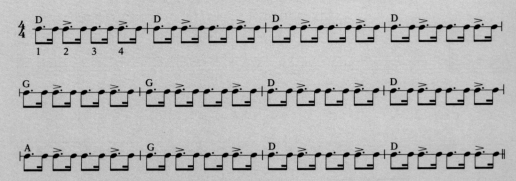

Another accompaniment pattern often used with blues is the *blues shuffle*. It is played by adding the sixth of the scale on the second and fourth beats of each measure.

• Practice these new sixth chords and add them to the basic chord pattern above.

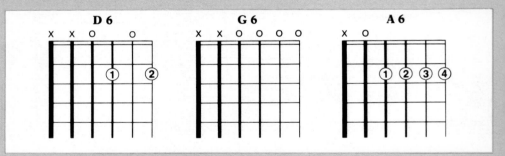

270

The blues shuffle pattern for each chord is written this way.

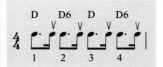 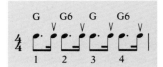 

You can also accompany "St. Louis Blues" on the keyboard.

## Keyboard Accompaniment to "St. Louis Blues"

**2. Prepare to perform a harmonic accompaniment on keyboard to "St. Louis Blues."** Have the students:
• Practice, then perform, right- and left-hand parts separately, then together.
• Perform the keyboard accompaniment to "St. Louis Blues" with the recording.
• Form two groups. Group 1 will play the guitar accompaniment while Group 2 plays the keyboard accompaniment. Perform with the recording.

# ACCOMPANIMENTS AND LYRICS

### "When the Saints Go Marching In"

**Materials**
Recording: "When the Saints Go Marching In" (performed by Louis Armstrong)
Copying Master A-7 (optional)

## TEACHING THE ACCOMPANIMENT

**1. Prepare to perform a harmonic accompaniment on guitar to "When the Saints Go Marching In."** Have the students:
• Discuss the information on "When the Saints Go Marching In."
• Review the G major chord.
• Practice playing the C major and D7 chords.
• Practice the guitar accompaniment to "When the Saints Go Marching In," changing chords as indicated.
• Play the guitar chords as a harmonic accompaniment to "When the Saints Go Marching In" with the recording. (You may wish to use Copying Master A-7 at this time.)

## When the Saints Go Marching In

"When the Saints Go Marching In" is a spiritual. According to popular belief, "When the Saints Go Marching In" was played slowly in funeral marches in New Orleans early in this century. A happy, fast-tempo version of the song also became popular with jazz bands in New Orleans.

You can accompany "When the Saints Go Marching In" on the guitar with three chords: G major, which you have already learned, C major, and D7.

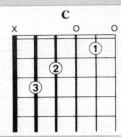

1. 1st finger on 2nd string, 1st fret
2. 2nd finger on 4th string, 2nd fret
3. 3rd finger on 5th string, 3rd fret

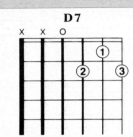

1. 1st finger on 2nd string, 1st fret
2. 2nd finger on 3rd string, 2nd fret
3. 3rd finger on 1st string, 2nd fret

### Guitar Accompaniment to "When the Saints Go Marching In"

272

Street musicians playing jazz in the French Quarter of New Orleans, Louisiana

**2. Prepare to perform a harmonic accompaniment on keyboard to "When the Saints Go Marching In."** Have the students:
• Practice, then perform, the left- and right-hand parts separately and together.
• Perform the keyboard accompaniment to "When the Saints Go Marching In" with the recording.
• Form two groups. Group 1 will play the guitar accompaniment while Group 2 plays the keyboard accompaniment. (You may wish to use Copying Master A-7 at this time.)

You can also accompany "When the Saints Go Marching In" on the keyboard.

## Keyboard Accompaniment to "When the Saints Go Marching In"

273

# ACCOMPANIMENTS AND LYRICS

## "The River of Dreams"

**Materials**
Recording: "The River of Dreams"
Copying Master A-8 (optional)

## TEACHING THE ACCOMPANIMENT

**1. Prepare to perform a harmonic accompaniment on guitar to "The River of Dreams."** Have the students:
• Discuss the information on "The River of Dreams."
• Review the G major, C major, and D major chords.
• Practice each of the three parts.
• Follow the performance routine and find where they should play.
• Listen to the recording and follow the routine without playing.
• Play the part with the recording. (You may wish to use Copying Master A-8 at this time.)

## The River of Dreams

Billy Joel's 1993 hit song "The River of Dreams" includes lead and backup singers as well as piano, synthesizer, Hammond organ, guitar, bass, and percussion.

You can accompany "The River of Dreams" on the guitar with the G, C, and D chords.

• Choose one of the three parts to play. Follow the routine below, playing your part when you get to each colored box.

### Guitar Accompaniment to "The River of Dreams"

In the middle of the night. . .

night. . .

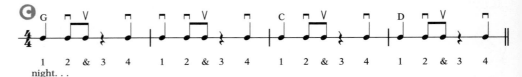

night. . .

**PERFORMANCE ROUTINE**

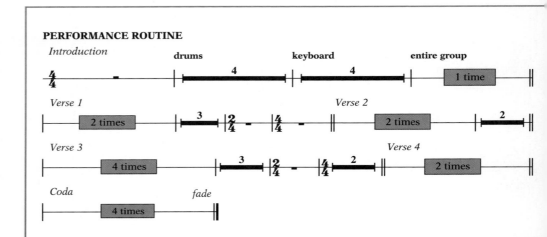

You can also accompany "The River of Dreams" on the keyboard.

- Choose one of the four parts to play. Follow the order of the song outlined on page 274.

Billy Joel

## ACCOMPANIMENTS AND LYRICS

**2. Prepare to perform a harmonic accompaniment on keyboard to "The River of Dreams."** Have the students:
- Practice each of the three parts, right- and left-hand parts separately, then together.
- Follow the performance routine and find where they should play.
- Listen to the recording and follow the routine without playing.
- Play one of the parts with the recording. (You may wish to use Copying Master A-8 at this time.)
- Form two groups. Group 1 will play the guitar accompaniment while Group 2 plays the keyboard accompaniment. (You may wish to use Copying Master A-8 at this time.)

### Keyboard Accompaniment to "The River of Dreams"

275

# ACCOMPANIMENTS AND LYRICS

### "Dreams"

**Materials**
Recording: "Dreams"
Copying Master A-9 (optional)

## TEACHING THE ACCOMPANIMENT

**1. Prepare to perform a harmonic accompaniment on guitar to "Dreams."**
Have the students:
• Discuss the information on "Dreams."
• Sing the words to "Dreams" with the song.

## Dreams

"Dreams," one of Fleetwood Mac's hits, featured the voice of Stevie Nicks, who wrote the song.

**Dreams**
Words and music by Stevie Nicks

Now here you go again
You say you want your freedom
Well who am I to keep you down
It's only right that you should
Play the way you feel it
But listen carefully to the sound
Of your loneliness
Like a heartbeat...drives you mad
In the stillness of remembering what you had
And what you lost...
And what you had...
And what you lost

Thunder only happens when it's raining
Players only love you when they're playing
Say...women...they will come and they will go
When the rain washes you clean...you'll know

Now here I go again, I see the crystal visions
I keep my visions to myself
It's only me
Who wants to wrap around your dreams and...
Have you any dreams you'd like to sell?
Dreams of loneliness...
Like a heartbeat...drives you mad
In the stillness of remembering what you had...
And what you lost
What you had...
And what you lost

Thunder only happens when it's raining
Players only love you when they're playing
Say...women...they will come and they will go
When the rain washes you clean...you'll know

276

Words and Music by Stevie Nicks

You can accompany "Dreams" on the guitar using the G major chord, which you have already learned, the A minor chord, and the F major 7 chord.

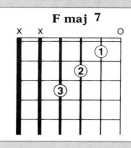

**F maj 7**

1. 1st finger on 2nd string, 1st fret

2. 2nd finger on 3rd string, 2nd fret

3. 3rd finger on 4th string, 3rd fret

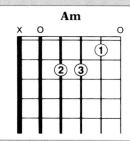

**Am**

1. 1st finger on 2nd string, 1st fret

2. 2nd finger on 4th string, 2nd fret

3. 3rd finger on 3rd string, 2nd fret

### Guitar Accompaniment to "Dreams"

- Review the G major chord.
- Practice playing the F major 7 and A minor chords.
- Practice lines 1–5, changing chords as indicated.
- Play lines 1–5 (with repeats) as a harmonic accompaniment to "Dreams" with the recording. (You may wish to use Copying Master A-9 at this time.)

277

# ACCOMPANIMENTS AND LYRICS

**2. Prepare to perform a harmonic accompaniment on keyboard to "Dreams."** Have the students:

• Practice, then perform, right- and left-hand parts separately, then together.

• Practice the chord changes in the right- and left-hand parts of the Challenge!

• Perform the two keyboard accompaniments to "Dreams" with the recording.

• Form two groups. Group 1 will play the guitar accompaniment while Group 2 plays the keyboard accompaniment. (You may wish to use Copying Master A-9 at this time.)

Stevie Nicks of Fleetwood Mac in performance

You can also accompany "Dreams" on the keyboard.

## Keyboard Accompaniment to "Dreams"

This is a more advanced keyboard accompaniment.

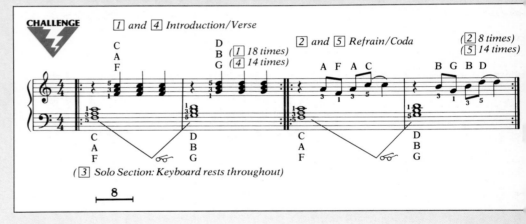

278

# Can't Stop Lovin' You

The words to this song were written by the members of the hard-rock group Van Halen. Members of the group sing and play guitar, keyboards, drums, and bass.

You can accompany "I Can't Stop Lovin' You" on the guitar with the G, Em, C, and D chords.

## Guitar Accompaniment to "Can't Stop Lovin' You"

Make up your own strum patterns to the song.

279

CD5:2

# ACCOMPANIMENTS AND LYRICS

## "Can't Stop Lovin' You"

**Materials**
Recording: "Can't Stop Lovin' You"
Copying Master A-10 (optional)

### TEACHING THE ACCOMPANIMENT

**1. Prepare to perform a harmonic accompaniment on guitar to "Can't Stop Lovin' You."** Have the students:
• Discuss the information on "Can't Stop Lovin' You."
• Review the G major, E minor, C major, and D major chords.
• Practice the two rhythms and changing chords.
• Follow the order of the score as they listen to the song.
• Play the guitar part with the recording. (If students have difficulty changing chords, assign groups of students to play the individual chords.)

## ACCOMPANIMENTS AND LYRICS

**2. Prepare to perform a harmonic accompaniment on keyboard for "Can't Stop Lovin' You."** Have the students:

• Practice right- and left-hand parts using good fingering technique. (right thumb on D, left thumb on G)

• Practice with both hands together.

• Listen to "Can't Stop Lovin' You," following the score (without playing).

• Play the keyboard part as they listen to the recording.

• Form two groups. Group 1 will play the guitar accompaniment while Group 2 plays the keyboard accompaniment. (You may wish to use Copying Master A-10 at this time.)

You can also play a keyboard accompaniment.

### Keyboard Accompaniment to "I Can't Stop Lovin' You"

1. There's a time. . .
2. You can change. . .

280

*Introduction*    *New Segment*

**lead guitar solo**

I'm so twisted and tied    And when it's over

*Refrain and Coda*

Eddie Van Halen (right)
Sammy Hagar (left)

281

# MAKING A RECORDING

**Focus: Performing on a Recording**

### Objectives
To explore the history of music recording
To identify some careers and decisions made in making a recording
To explore the career of vocalist
To record and critique a song

### Materials
Recordings: Recorded Lesson: The History of Recording
"Ac-cent-tchu-ate the Positive" sung by Aretha Franklin
Copying Master MR-1 (optional)

## MAKING A RECORDING

**1. Consider the role recorded music plays in daily life.** Have the students:
• List a typical day's activities, noting which ones involve recorded music. (for example, woke up to Top-40 hit playing on the radio, watched television show that included background music, watched MTV, listened to cassette or CD on way to school)
• Determine a class average of daily time spent listening to recorded music.
• Speculate how their musical experiences would differ if all the music they heard had to be performed live. (Choices might be limited to local musical groups or musicians on tour. Informal music-making might increase.)
• Check the weekend paper or other sources and list the live concerts available in their community.

282

# E X T E N S I O N

### COOPERATIVE LEARNING
Cooperative groups can work together throughout this unit to do the recording projects. The projects can be as simple or sophisticated as available resources allow. If no recording equipment is available, students might plan the recordings, rehearse the music, hold mock recording sessions, and record their experiences in writing.

A member of each group should write notes about the decisions and actions of the group. This task could be done on a rotating basis through the unit.

### MORE MUSIC TEACHING IDEAS
1. Have the students visit a record store and make a chart listing the categories of music available there. Compare the number of recordings in each category. Propose reasons for the numbers. Compare the names of record companies found in each category. Analyze which companies produce the most varieties and which companies are limited to one or a few styles.
2. Have the students prepare a report on the care and workings of a CD player/CD or cassette player/cassette (or record, DAT, reel-to-reel, cartridge). Include diagrams as needed.
3. Have the students discuss some of the current brands of audio equipment and compare experiences using them. Com-

pare the quality, features, and cost of the equipment.
4. Have the students discuss "sound etiquette." For example: If people are trying to hold a conversation, should music be playing? Why? When is it more appropriate to use earphones?
5. Have the students recommend ways to protect their hearing when using audio equipment. (For example, Do not turn the volume all the way up when using earphones. Do not listen to extremely loud music for long periods of time. Give their ears a rest periodically from controllable sounds. Use earplugs or move away from the speakers at concerts that are too loud.)

# MAKING A RECORDING

**2. Learn about history of the recording processes.** Have the students:
• Look at the unit opener photographs and discuss the historical evolution of the recording process.
• Listen to Recorded Lesson: The History of Recording. (You may wish to use Copying Master MR-1 at this time. This is a time line of important developments in recording sound.)

## JOURNAL/ASSESSMENT

Students might keep a journal to record their decisions and experiences with recordings, to answer questions posed in the unit, to assess the music they make, or to record their investigations into recordings, technology, and music. The journal could be used for assessment.

# MAKING A RECORDING

## THE STARS OF THE SHOW

**Discuss the importance of the performers.** Have the students:
- Read the top of pupil page 284 and discuss what they like about their favorite vocalists.
- Describe the vocal qualities of their favorite vocalists.

## ARETHA FRANKLIN

**Read about a recording artist and learn about aspects of the recording industry.** Have the students:
- Read about Aretha Franklin.
- Listen to "Ac-cent-tchu-ate the Positive" sung by Aretha Franklin.
- Name other songs sung by Aretha Franklin that they know and categorize them by style.
- Discuss qualities a performer would need in order to succeed as a recording artist.
- Play the accompaniment to "Ac-cent-tchu-ate the Positive" on unpitched percussion instruments.
- Propose ways to vary the accompaniment to enhance the song.

## The Stars of the Show
CD5:26

Whose name springs to mind at the thought of a favorite song on the radio? What makes that song appealing? The song's appeal may come from a lively rhythm, a catchy tune, or a meaningful message. However, what really sells the song is the performance of the singer. We like the singer's impressive vocal skills, distinctive vocal tone color, style of pronouncing certain words, and choices of how phrases are shaped.

### Aretha Franklin, Vocalist

ARETHA FRANKLIN'S unique vocal quality and powerful, expressive performance style have made her the "Queen of Soul." Aretha grew up in Detroit and was strongly influenced by the gospel music she heard in church. Top African American performers such as Mahalia Jackson and Clara Ward helped mold the young singer. Aretha joined her father's church choir at age 9, became their star soloist at 12, and began cutting solo recordings at 14.

When Aretha went to New York at age 17 she attracted attention as a "soul" singer. Aretha combined the expressive style of gospel singing with the exciting new developments in rhythm and blues and rock and roll. She has recorded numerous albums during her long and successful career. *Amazing Grace*, recorded with James Cleveland in 1972, became a double platinum album. Aretha has won 15 Grammy® Awards and was the first woman to be inducted into the Rock and Roll Hall of Fame.

- Listen to "Ac-cent-tchu-ate the Positive" sung by Aretha Franklin. Notice how she embellished the melody with altered or added pitches, words, and rhythms.
- Play the accompaniment to "Ac-cent-tchu-ate the Positive" on unpitched percussion instruments.

"Ac-cent-tchu-ate the Positive" sung by Aretha Franklin

284

## CAREERS

Many professionals are involved in creating a recording. Share the following information with the class. Invite the students to explore further the careers that interest them as well as the training needed for those careers.

Before a musician is able to make a recording with a record company, the **artist** (musician) often prepares a **demonstration tape** (demo) of three or four of his or her best songs. Often these songs are composed by the artist. The artist's **personal manager,** who represents the musician in business agreements, brings the demo to the attention of the Artist and Repertoire (A & R) department of a record company. If A & R people like the demo, they may sign the artist to make a recording.

The contract between the artist and the record company is usually handled with the help of a **music business attorney** who represents the artist's interests. The recording contract deals with royalties (payment to the artist for each copy sold), advances (money paid to the artist ahead of time), and artistic control of the product.

The artist must also decide which performing rights society is most beneficial to join. Performing rights are the rights paid for public performances of songs, including radio, television, concerts, and other performance places.

Additional **studio musicians** are often hired to sing or play at a recording session. They are a supplement or substitute for the artist's own group. Many of the musicians belong to the American Federation of Musicians, a union which regulates wages and working conditions.

Aretha Franklin, far left

## A Song for the Record

It's your turn to be a star!

Create

- Choose a song you'd like to record. Consider the variety of vocal combinations available. Some verses could be sung as solos, others as duets or in a group. Decide who will perform the song with you.

- Think about how you will interpret the song. Should the singers perform the song exactly as in the printed music, or are there elements of the song you'd like to change? After you've made these decisions, rehearse the song.

- Consider the results of the rehearsal. Does the song sound the way you want? Is there anything you'd like to change?

- Record your performance when you're finished rehearsing the song.

### THINK IT THROUGH

How would you improve your recording? In what ways might different technology improve the result?

285

# MAKING A RECORDING

## A SONG FOR THE RECORD

**Sing and record a song to a pre-recorded instrumental track.** Have the students:
- Identify favorite songs in the pupil book and list musical elements that contribute to their enjoyment of each piece. (for example, the mood and subject of the song, the tone colors of the singers, the arrangement)
- Choose a song to record.
- Discuss practical considerations such as:
—What are the vocal requirements?
—Who will sing each part?
—Will the song be performed exactly as notated in the book or will the performers make changes? (for example, changes in dynamics, tempo, and vocal harmonies)
—What kind of instrumental accompaniment will be used? (piano accompaniment, Performance Mix or Divided Track instrumental accompaniment on the compact discs, their own accompaniment)
- Rehearse the song. Evaluate the result and make changes as needed.
- Plan the technical aspects of the recording. Consider the number of microphones available, where they should be placed, and use of other available equipment.
- Record the performance of the song on a cassette recorder as they sing with the compact disc accompaniment or their own instrumental accompaniment. (Recording equipment such as a karaoke machine might record from CD to cassette directly to produce a cleaner sound.)
- Play back and evaluate their recorded performance, listing musical and technical elements that sound different than expected. Decide what they would change to improve the recording. Rerecord their performance if necessary.

# MAKING A RECORDING

## Focus: Songwriting and Arranging

### Objectives
To examine the creative processes of songwriting and arranging
To compare two different arrangements of a melody
To create an arrangement for a song

### Materials
Recordings: "When the Saints Go Marching In" Playalong
Recorded Lesson: Interview with Bruce Hornsby
"Cruise Control"
"Sound Vision" Playalong

## THE RECORDING STARTS WITH A SONG

**Play a melody to two different arrangements.** Have the students:
• Read page 286.
• Practice the melody of "When the Saints Go Marching In."
• Play the melody with the two recorded accompaniments. Then compare the results. Which accompaniment best enhanced the song? Why?
• Suggest other accompaniment options and discuss how these options would alter the perception of the song.

# Start with a Song

For much of the music we hear, our attention and admiration are focused on the musicians who are performing. Their photographs grace the covers of the compact discs we buy. The performer's vocal and instrumental skills are displayed to best advantage for all to enjoy.

In addition to the performers, many others work behind the scenes to contribute to that all-important final product—the recording.

Before any recordings are made, before any CDs or cassettes are sold, and before a performer becomes a star, a good song must be chosen.

• Play "When the Saints Go Marching In" on recorder, bells, or keyboard. Then play it with two different accompaniments. How do the accompaniments affect the song?

Bruce Hornsby (seated, center) with some of the musicians with whom he has collaborated

286

---

# EXTENSION

## BACKGROUND
### Music Technology
An arranger may work with musical ideas in his or her head, try them out on piano or guitar, or try them out using sophisticated music technology. An arranger may use a sequencer to experiment with ideas. A **sequencer**, similar to a tape recorder, records and plays musical information. It can be a stand-alone machine, a part of an electronic instrument, or a computer software program. A **sequence** is a musical arrangement stored (as a sequence of digital information) as a MIDI file. Sequences are usually stored on disk. A sequencer also allows you to create, manipulate, store, and edit (change) sequences.

An arranger may use a **computer** to compose, record, play, and notate music. This very versatile tool can save the arranger much time and drudgery.

### MORE MUSIC TEACHING IDEAS
1. Call attention to the copyright notice on the bottom of the first page of copyrighted music. Discuss benefits and drawbacks of copyright laws. Have the students research basic copyright rules and find out what kind of music is usually in the public domain. Have them find out how to register a copyright.

2. Have the students discuss different approaches to songwriting. Which is created first—lyrics or music? An example of a song for which the music was composed first was "Yesterday" by Paul McCartney. While working on the music he originally used the words *scrambled eggs* in the melodic phrase which eventually became *yesterday*. On the album *Graceland* Paul Simon wrote his material by improvising stream-of-consciousness lyrics over pre-recorded instrumental tracks until he achieved a finished song. David Bowie used an abstract modern-art method when he cut up all his lyrics, threw them on the floor, and sang them in the order in which he picked them up.

## When the Saints Go Marching In

African American Spiritual

# Bruce Hornsby
### Songwriter, Arranger, Vocalist, and Pianist

A native of Williamsburg, Virginia, Bruce Hornsby has used his many talents to create new and interesting music. In 1986 he was honored with the Best New Artist Grammy® award. Besides being an innovative songwriter, singer, and pianist, Bruce is also an arranger. An arranger chooses the textures, tone colors and instruments to use on a particular song. Bruce not only chooses the instruments, but also selects specific musicians to play the parts. Guitarist Pat Metheny, saxophonist Branford Marsalis, and banjo player Bela Fleck contribute interesting jazz solos to Bruce Hornsby's songs. Bruce invited The Grateful Dead's guitarist Jerry Garcia to cut solos on some of his songs such as "Cruise Control."

In addition to combining the artistry of different musicians in his arrangements, Bruce also creatively mixes different styles of music. The verses of his songs, for example, are often arranged in a pop style while the solo sections feature complex jazz rhythms and harmonies. In this way his music bridges the gaps among different musical forms. The result is something new and original that combines the best elements of each style.

- Listen as Bruce Hornsby talks about the creative process used in songwriting and arranging.

- Listen to "Cruise Control" by Bruce Hornsby. Listen to the different instruments and what they contribute to the music. Which instruments most strongly convey the rhythm or "groove" of the song? Which instruments hold long notes that create textures above the groove? These are important elements in the song's arrangement.

 "Cruise Control" by Bruce Hornsby

287

## MAKING A RECORDING

### MEET BRUCE HORNSBY

1. **Meet a songwriter/arranger and learn about the creative process.** Have the students:
- Look at the photo and find Bruce Hornsby seated in the center. (Musicians from left to right: Gregory Hines, Don Henley, Bonnie Raitt, Pat Metheny, Bruce Hornsby, Bob Weir, David Hollister, and Levi Little. They were part of a PBS "In the Spotlight" Special—Bruce Hornsby and Friends.)
- Read about Bruce Hornsby.
- Listen to Recorded Lesson: Interview with Bruce Hornsby.
- Discuss what they learned about songwriting and arranging.
2. **Listen to "Cruise Control."** Have the students:
- Listen to "Cruise Control," focusing on elements that were used to compose or arrange this song using the following questions to get started.
1. Is the melody interesting?
2. Are there repeated rhythms?
3. What kind of dynamics are used?
4. What kind of tempo is used?
5. How would you describe the texture?
6. Can you identify the form?
7. What is the style?
8. What instruments or voices were used?
9. How does the accompaniment enhance the melody?
10. If you were arranging this song, what might you have done differently?

3. Have the students discuss musicians who use diverse musical skills such as performing, composing, and arranging, and those who specialize in only one area. Stevie Wonder excels at performing, composing, and arranging. Through multitrack recording he sometimes plays all the parts himself: lead vocals, vocal harmonies, keyboards, bass parts, and drums.

Relatively inexpensive multitrack cassette-recorders make it possible for beginning musicians to not only write and sing their own songs, but to experiment by playing different instruments and creating different arrangements as well.

### BIOGRAPHY

Bruce Hornsby is a composer, arranger, and performer. As he was growing up, his parents encouraged him to listen to a broad range of pop music by performers such as Elvis Presley, Little Richard, and Pat Boone. Bruce played guitar in a band at age 12, but music was only a sideline until about age 17. His older brother John introduced Bruce to various recordings of popular music, including some that were very piano-oriented. When a grand piano was bequeathed to his mother, Bruce started playing piano by ear, picking songs off of records. His mother, seeing that he was becoming serious about the piano, made sure he took lessons. Bruce earned a degree in Jazz and Studio Music from the University of Miami. He has performed with Bonnie Raitt, Stevie Nicks, Don Henley, Willie Nelson, Phil Collins and many others, as well as toured with the Grateful Dead for a year and a half.

Bruce started composing at about age 22. He spent time developing his own style and eventually, after numerous rejections, landed his first record deal. After that other record companies became interested. Some of his albums include *The Way It Is, Harbor Lights, and Hot House.* Bruce has contributed to over 50 albums. His stylistic diversity is reflected in his three Grammy® awards and seven Grammy® nominations.

# MAKING A RECORDING

## SOUND VISION

**Create and record an arrangement of "Sound Vision."** Have the students:
• Read pupil page 288 and examine the instrumental score at the bottom of the page.
• Determine what information is shown on that score. (instrumentation, pitches, rhythms, number of parts, and so on)
• Listen to "Sound Vision" and discuss possible rhythm patterns and percussion tone colors to add to the piece. (Create patterns or use the patterns on page 289.)
• Listen again, trying out the chosen rhythm patterns.

## Arranging a Song CD6:3

Once a song is composed, it needs an arrangement. The choices an arranger makes will present the song to its best advantage. The arranger decides on the instruments and writes the rhythms and harmonies to be played in the accompaniment.

Different arrangements of the same song can change the song's overall feel or mood. For example, the arranger may decide to feature a wailing guitar solo instead of a saxophone solo. The arranger may choose to add complex percussion rhythms instead of standard rhythm patterns.

• Listen to "Sound Vision," which is partially arranged.

**Create**

• Try out a few of the following rhythm patterns with the song or create some of your own. Which ones sound most appropriate?

• Decide when to play and how many times to play each pattern. Experiment with combinations of several patterns.

• Choose instruments to play each of the chosen rhythm patterns. Decide which instrumental tone colors sound the most satisfying with the song.

• Record your arrangement of the piece.

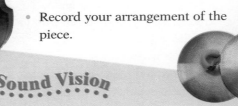

## Percussion Parts for "Sound Vision"

• Discuss which rhythm patterns seem to fit best and evaluate which elements contribute to a satisfying arrangement. (For example, do they prefer a thick texture of many overlapping rhythms or a thinner texture with one or two prominent rhythms? Should the rhythms repeat or should different ones occur? Should the rhythms be played all the time?)
• Choose percussion instruments or found sounds on which to play each of the rhythm patterns.
• Practice all parts together with "Sound Vision."
• Record the completed arrangement.
• Discuss the *Think It Through* question.

### THINK IT THROUGH

What happened to the arrangement when you added parts?

289

# MAKING A RECORDING

**Focus: Working in a Recording Studio**

## Objectives
To examine the process of recording and mixing tracks
To explore the career of recording engineer
To create a multiple-part recording by over-dubbing or by multitrack recording

## Materials
Recordings:  Recorded Lesson: Interview with Al Schmitt
Recorded Lesson: Mixing a Multitrack Recording
"Sound Vision" Playalong

## Vocabulary
Producer, recording engineer, multitrack recording, overdubbing

## IN THE STUDIO

**Learn about the professional recording and mixing process.** Have the students:
• Read about professional recording on page 290.

## MEET AL SCHMITT

**Meet a recording engineer and learn about recording and mixing music.** Have the students:
• Read about Al Schmitt, a recording engineer.
• Listen to Recorded Lesson: Interview with Al Schmitt.
• Discuss new information they learned from the interview about making a recording, mixing, or the career of recording engineer.
• List other recording engineers or producers they know. (Call attention to the information on cassette or CD jackets, which often lists these people.)

# In the Studio

Professional recordings are most often made in a multitrack recording studio. These recording studios have sophisticated electronic equipment. The equipment is controlled through a giant control panel. Most of the equipment is in a control room away from the performers. The performers work in special soundproof rooms. Two key people, the producer and the recording engineer, are needed to create a good recording.

The job of a **producer** is to capture on a recording the talent and creativity of the performers. A producer who is "producing" a single artist, such as a vocalist, might hire the additional musicians who will work best on a particular song. Producers who work with bands often help by choosing the band's best material, determining the lengths of songs, and deciding where to use vocal harmonies.

The **recording engineer** works the recording equipment in the recording studio. The engineer must check that the voices and instruments are miked in a manner to produce the best sound. Each instrument usually has its own microphone and is recorded on a separate track. As many as 24, 48, or more tracks can be used.

MEET *Al Schmitt*   RECORDING ENGINEER

290

---

# EXTENSION

## MORE MUSIC TEACHING IDEAS

1. Explore further the careers of studio musician, record producer, or recording engineer.
2. Have the students explore how CDs and/or cassettes are actually manufactured once the final mix leaves the recording studio and explain the process to the class.
3. Have the students explore how various parts of a sound system or recording studio work and explain their findings to the class. (See page 229 for information on sound systems. Various audio magazines and books are also good information sources.)

## CAREERS
### Recording Engineer

Some recording engineers acquire in college the technical knowledge to operate the recording equipment. Others start out as apprentices and work their way up to small and then large sessions. In addition to knowledge of the equipment, a recording engineer must also have music and business knowledge to run a recording studio. An engineer needs patience and tact in dealing with producers and musicians. Engineering specialties include maintenance engineers (who maintain and repair equipment) and mastering engineers (who work in mastering studios and convert tapes to disc).

## BACKGROUND
### Hi-fi and Lo-fi

As music recording technology developed, high-fidelity (hi-fi) sound became a goal. High fidelity means sound is reproduced with a high degree of faithfulness to the original sound. High-fidelity equipment was in use by 1958 and has continued to improve. The search to capture and reproduce high-quality sound led to much higher expenses in recording and more expensive play-back equipment.

The expense of making a recording using the latest equipment is beyond the budget of most young musicians. Recently, the development of "alternative music" recorded on inexpensive "home studio" equipment has led to an appreciation of

These tracks can be recorded on multitrack tape or, with the help of digital technology, directly on the computer.

When the recording session is finished, the engineer and producer work together to do the "mixdown." During the mixdown, the best tracks are picked and effects such as reverb are chosen. The volumes of the separate tracks are decided so that when they are combined, they create a balanced whole. The result of all this work is the master recording. The master recording is then sent out to be manufactured as the CDs and cassettes you buy in the store.

## MIDI

In the recording studio many kinds of electronic music equipment are used. One way that varied equipment can work together is if each component is equipped with MIDI. MIDI stands for Musical Instrument Digital Interface. It is a standard language that allows musical instruments made by different manufacturers to communicate digitally with each other and with computers. Equipment such as computers, MIDI piano keyboards, drum machines, sequencers, tone generators (sound sources), mixers, and lighting can exchange information if it is equipped with MIDI.

Al Schmitt is a six-time Grammy® winner who has worked on recordings for Steely Dan, George Benson, and Natalie Cole. When he started his career there were none of today's technical schools to teach sound engineering. Al got into the business from the ground up—by making coffee and sweeping the floor in a recording studio. He paid careful attention to the details of recording sessions and used what he learned to become the successful engineer that he is today. He feels that this kind of commitment, along with an ability to work well with others, is important to success as a recording engineer.

• Listen to Al Schmitt as he describes recording and mixing music.

291

creativity and experimentation over slick and expensively-produced "mainstream" music. This development led to the term *lo-fi*. Lo-fi can encourage young musicians, showing them that big professional studios are not necessarily better than an inexpensive "home studio" unit.

# MAKING A RECORDING

## RECORDING MULTIPLE PARTS

1. **Plan, practice, and record multiple parts.** Have the students:
• Listen to the Recorded Lesson: Mixing a Multitrack Recording to hear how the overall sound is influenced by the mixing process.
• Choose a song with multiple vocal and/or instrumental parts to record. (Choose a song they recorded previously in this unit, a new song, or "Sound Vision.")
• Discuss and plan which vocal and/or instrumental parts will be recorded and in what order. (For example, students might record themselves singing the song, then overdub several instrumental parts, one at a time.)
• Find the best placement of microphones by testing several sites.
• Record the first part.
• Play back the recording, assessing and approving (or re-recording) the performance before continuing.
• Record the second part. Play back the recorded first part on one tape recorder while playing the second part live. Use the second tape recorder to record both parts being played together.
• Continue this overdubbing process as many times as necessary to record the desired number of parts.
• Discuss the *Think It Through* question.

## Recording Multiple Parts

• Listen to how a song recorded on multiple tracks is mixed.

### Create

• Create your own arrangement of "Sound Vision" using the parts on pages 293 and 289. Then record the arrangement.

If you have a multitrack recorder or a sequencer, you can record each part on a different track. This is called **multitrack recording**.

If you have two cassette recorders, you can record each part on top of the others. This is called **overdubbing.** Overdubbing allows the same performer to perform many parts.

Follow these directions to overdub using two cassette recorders.

1. Decide in what order you will record each part.

2. Record one part at a time.

3. Record the first part on one cassette recorder. Then play the first part back as you perform the second part along with the recording.

4. Record both parts at the same time on your other cassette recorder.

5. Repeat this process for each part planned.

**Cassette Player A**          **Cassette Player B**

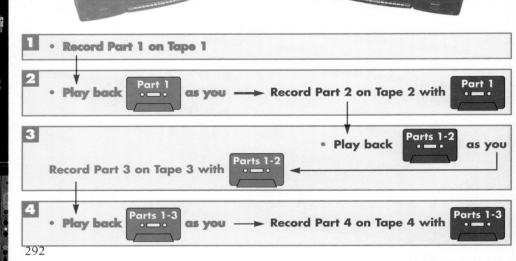

**1** • Record Part 1 on Tape 1

**2** • Play back Part 1 as you ⟶ Record Part 2 on Tape 2 with Part 1

**3** • Play back Parts 1-2 as you
Record Part 3 on Tape 3 with Parts 1-2

**4** • Play back Parts 1-3 as you ⟶ Record Part 4 on Tape 4 with Parts 1-3

292

---

## E X T E N S I O N

### MORE MUSIC TEACHING IDEAS

1. Have a student who is familiar with MIDI describe and demonstrate the parts of a MIDI workstation. A MIDI workstation often has a computer, computer software, tone generator, powered speakers, MIDI keyboard(s), and other MIDI equipment connected together.
2. Refer to the *Music with MIDI* User's Manual for more information on MIDI. If the class has MIDI equipment, you may wish to have the students do one or more of the projects in *Music with MIDI* and demonstrate MIDI features to the class.

### BACKGROUND
#### MIDI Controllers

MIDI controllers generate and transmit MIDI information. A controller permits a musician to control several MIDI instruments and sounds through one instrument. MIDI controllers include: keyboard controllers, guitar controllers, percussion controllers, and wind controllers.
• A variety of keyboards are equipped with MIDI. These can be linked together and run by a *keyboard controller*. All of the effects, including the pitch bend and pedaling, are converted to MIDI data.
• A basic *guitar controller* (as well as violin or bass controllers) is made by adding a pitch-to-MIDI converter to the instrument.
• A *percussion controller*, often called a drum

machine, is a synthesizer that produces percussion sounds.
• A *wind controller* is played by blowing. It's fingering is similar to the fingering on a soprano recorder. Through MIDI technology the instrument can make many different instrument sounds.
• *Experimental controllers* have been developed that translate hand and/or finger movements into MIDI data. Engineers and musicians continue to develop unusual ways to create MIDI information. Some of these ways may become popular, others may only be used by the few who take the time to learn to "play."

- Choose some of these parts to play with "Sound Vision." Decide when to play them, whether they should repeat, and what instruments would sound the best.

### Melodic Parts for "Sound Vision"

**2. Record multiple parts using multi-track equipment (optional).** Have the students:

• Follow the procedure as on page 292. This time, record each part on a different track using multitrack equipment.

• Play back each track, assessing and approving (or re-recording) the performance before continuing.

• Mix the completed tracks using available technology.

**THINK IT THROUGH**

Evaluate your recording. Discuss the accuracy of the parts. How might you change your method of recording to improve the sound? What part of the recording worked well? What would you do differently?

293

## MORE MUSIC TEACHING IDEAS

1. Demonstrate or have a student demonstrate how to use a keyboard controller to control one or more other keyboards or MIDI instruments.

2. Have students play a song on MIDI controllers or other MIDI instruments and then manipulate the information using other MIDI equipment. For example, play a melody on a wind controller and record it on a sequencer. Add a second track to the sequence using another controller (such as a drum machine). Add a third track, such as chords, on a keyboard or guitar controller. Play back, and evaluate the result and revise as needed.

## BACKGROUND
### Uses of MIDI

Generally, MIDI technology works best with instruments such as keyboards and drum machines. Playing these instruments is much like pushing buttons, which is the easiest way for a computer to "hear" what you are playing. However, almost any instrument can be adapted to operate in MIDI language. Bluegrass/jazz musician Bela Fleck uses MIDI with his banjo. Pat Metheny creates unusual jazz with his MIDI guitar, as does Michael Brecker with his MIDI sax. There's even a MIDI harp which allows instant retuning of the entire set of strings by just pressing a button.

# MAKING A RECORDING

**Focus: Marketing Recordings**

## Objectives
To analyze and create music advertising
To examine the career of video producer
To create a music video

## Materials
Recordings: Recorded Lesson: Interview
  with Lee Rolontz

## Vocabulary
Storyboard

## SELLING THE RECORDING

**Learn about how recordings are marketed.** Have the students:
• Read page 294.
• Discuss the articles pictured.
• Share experiences about music promotional items or advertisements they have used or seen. Which of these advertisements were most effective? Which did students enjoy the most? Why?

# Selling the Recording

You've created a wonderful recording that you want everyone to hear. How do you make sure people find out about it?

Recording companies have marketing teams for this job. The marketing teams determine who will be most likely to buy a recording, where the recording might be used, and where the recording will be sold. They choose from various ways of advertising including radio or television commercials, posters, T-shirts, bumper stickers, newspaper or magazine ads or articles, and promotional parties.

Often the publicity tries to give a specific image to the recording. Sometimes the performer may be the key to sales. Other times a particular song or style is highlighted. People are hired to write commercials, create the art work, and take the photographs.

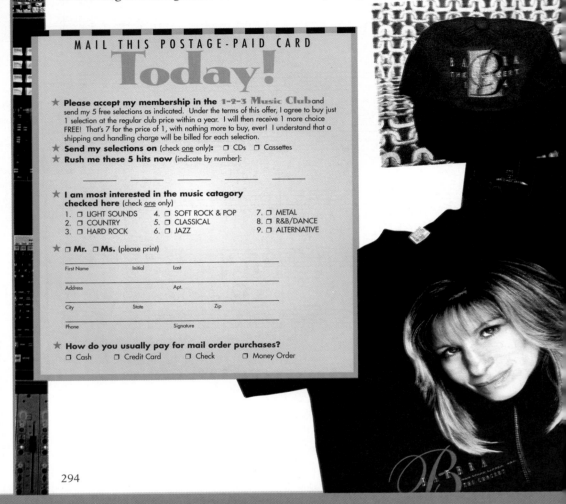

294

---

# E X T E N S I O N

## CAREERS

### Music Director/Program Director
Once a recording is made and advertising is created, many people are involved in convincing the public to purchase the recording. The music director or program director at a radio station usually makes the decisions on which recordings are aired. Some stations play only one style of music such as soul, classical, or Top 40. The Top-40 format makes a recording popular faster because there is intense exposure to the song. This kind of exposure also shortens the life span of the recording's popularity.

### Disc Jockey
A disc jockey conducts and announces a radio or television program of musical recordings. The disc jockey often adds comments between the recordings about the music or other subjects. In large markets, disc jockeys work with engineers whose job is to cue the recordings, monitor the sound, punch in the commercials, and make sure that the station signal is operating correctly. In small stations the same person may be the disc jockey, announcer, and engineer. Sometime the jobs of program director and music director are also part of a disc jockey's work. Disc jockeys may cue their own records, operate a control board, write and produce commercials, set up microphones, answer telephones, do public service announcements, as well as report weather or sports and offer bits of humor. Personality is a big factor in a disc jockey's success.

### Music Critic
A music critic reviews music and gives an opinion about its quality. He or she may review a live performance or a recording. The critic may comment on the performance and the music itself. The reviews appear in newspapers or magazines. The music critic may note an effective line of lyrics or describe some amazing part of the performance. The critic may also report that the instruments were out of tune or the words were uninspired. The critic may compare a recording with others the same group has made or with another recording of the same song.

## Advertise Your Recording

Think of the recording you made in class. Consider who you've created your recording for and how it is to be used. What message does your recording communicate? Is your recording a love song, or is it a jingle to advertise a school event?

Determine where it will be heard. Will you need to make cassette copies to sell, or will your school play it over the public address system?

Choose ways to advertise your recording. What kind of message do you want your advertising to communicate?

- Design a poster to advertise your recording.

- Design a cassette or CD jacket cover, complete with photos or artwork, song lyrics, recording artist biographies, and other important information. You may wish to use a favorite CD jacket as a model.

## ADVERTISING YOUR RECORDING

**Create advertising for a recording product.** Have the students:
- Choose one completed (or planned) recording project for an advertising campaign.
- Define their target audience. (For example, their market may be members of a school club, the entire class or school, or perhaps an specific segment of the general public.)
- Discuss practical ways to advertise to their market. (For example, create flyers and posters, or make announcements over the school public address system or during an assembly.)
- Determine how many copies might be sold and plan how the recording will be duplicated.

## CREATE

**Design a poster and packaging for a recording.** Have the students:
- Decide on a theme for a poster advertising their recording and determine what kinds of words and visual images would support that theme.
- Design and create the promotional poster.
- Display the advertisements if possible.
- Design a cassette or CD jacket cover for their recording. Include information such as song titles, composers, performers, length of songs, and so on.

295

# MAKING A RECORDING

## AND . . . ACTION!

**Explore music videos.** Have the students:
• Read the left side of page 296 and answer the *Think It Through* question.
• Give examples of music videos that are direct interpretations of the song, tell stories, use abstract visual images, use computer graphics, use claymation, and/or show musicians performing the song.
• Discuss the elements in music videos they know that were most effective in promoting the song, most interesting, most artistic, and/or most musical.
• Discuss whether or not music videos made them want to buy a recording of the song.

## MEET LEE ROLONTZ

**Explore the career of video producer.** Have the students:
• Read about Lee Rolontz, a video producer in New York.
• Listen to Recorded Lesson: Interview with Lee Rolontz, in which she discusses the process of creating music videos.
• Describe what information they found most interesting about creating music videos or being a video producer.
• Share other information they know about making music videos or video producers.

## And... Action!

A music video is often an important part of the marketing of a song or musical group. Think of a favorite music video. Once you see the images, does it change the experience of listening to the music?

### THINK IT THROUGH

Do visual images enhance music or does music enhance visual images? In what ways?

Some music videos are direct interpretations of the songs. They tell with images what the song says with words and music. Some music videos tell stories. Other videos employ more abstract visual images, using special effects such as computer graphics, lighting, and claymation. Some music videos may simply show the musicians performing the song. Since the invention of MTV, video making has become quite an art.

Directors are continually searching for new ways to express a song with images. Since music technology rapidly changes, the ways music is presented will continue to change.

296

## Meet Lee Rolontz VIDEO PRODUCER

Lee Rolontz runs a major New York video production company. As a producer, she is involved in the many different aspects that go into making a music video. Lee has produced videos for many noted musicians including Soul Asylum, Bruce Springsteen, Mariah Carey, Billy Joel, Mary Chapin Carpenter, and Bob Dylan.

• Listen as Lee Rolontz describes the process of creating music videos.

# EXTENSION

## MORE MUSIC TEACHING IDEAS
Have students find out how to take proper care of videotapes and videodiscs and report to the class.

## CRITICAL THINKING
How has the use of earphones changed the ways people listen to music?
What kind of recording format do you think will be invented in the future?
What improvements would you make to current music technology?

## BIOGRAPHY
Lee Rolontz is a video producer in New York City. Lee was involved in music since she was a teenager and always liked movies. She worked for a music magazine, music managers, and for record companies but always ended up doing things involving film. She was able to learn everything about film production through hands-on experience. She found out that she liked film better than music and continued in that direction. Many of the videos she makes can be seen on MTV, VH1, television, and home video. She has worked with Mariah Carey, Michael Bolton, Luther Vandross, Sophie B. Hawkins, Soul Asylum, and others.

## Plan a Music Video

Plan scenes for a music video. Decide on a song, then discuss the kinds of images that might illustrate different parts of the song.

Think about the mood you want to show. To create different moods for the music, you can vary the lighting and the camera angles. Performers can use particular actions and express different emotions.

### Create

• Draw pictures of each scene for your music video. These pictures, or **storyboards**, will help you plan the filming of the video.

• Plan and rehearse the video. Then set up the equipment and shoot your video. Play it back for the class and discuss the results.

**THINK IT THROUGH**

How might technology change the way music is advertised and distributed in the future?

# MAKING A RECORDING

## PLAN A MUSIC VIDEO

**1. Create a music video.** Have the students:

• Discuss songs that would be good choices for a music video, evaluating story line or theme, characters, mood, phrase structure, instrumentation, and so on.

• Choose a completed recording project or a professionally recorded song for their video and describe its characteristics.

• Discuss what images might work for each part of the song and what visual enhancements such as lighting, camera angles, or color might help illustrate the song.

• Plan scenes and draw storyboards for each part of the song. The storyboards should show the setups of shots to be filmed. Then display the storyboards in sequence as they listen to the song. Revise as needed.

**2. Film the music video.** Have the students:

• Scout locations for the scenes, design sets, gather props, assign acting roles if applicable, and stage and rehearse actors.

• Learn to run available equipment. (The school media specialist may be helpful.)

• Set up the equipment and shoot the video. (If editing the footage is not an option, then the filming of each scene must be planned and shot in sequence. Scenes must be timed and shot to conform exactly to each part of the music.)

• Edit the footage (if equipment is available). (Video editing gives more flexibility in the filming process because extraneous footage can be cut out later and scenes can be intercut.)

• Discuss the results.

• Find opportunities to show the video.

• Discuss the *Think It Through* question.

## BACKGROUND
### Audio and Audiovisual Transmission

Professional **radio** broadcasting has been around since the 1920s. Early radio broadcasts used live music because the primitive phonograph records of the time could not hold very much music. As recording technology improved, more and more recorded music was broadcast. As television developed, radio became even more exclusively a transmitter of music.

Music and technology advanced with the addition of visual images to sound. The silent **motion picture** was invented in the late 1800s. It wasn't until the 1920s that a sound track was added to film. The sound was recorded in a narrow band along the side of the film. Improvements to sound and image continue to be made in motion pictures.

Black and white **television** became widely used in the 1950s. Color TV began in 1953. Most TV programs use some kind of music. Today some TVs have stereo sound. Television music programs may be simultaneously broadcast on radio where better quality sound can be received. Some cable channels now carry only music programs.

Development of the **videotape** began in the 1940s. Videotapes became part of home entertainment in the 1970s. Prerecorded tapes can be bought or rented. Also tapes can be recorded with a home video camera or by taping off a TV.

The **videodisc** has been in use since the 1970s. It is similar to a phonograph record but carries both sound and pictures. The videodisc player is attached to a TV set and is used primarily for viewing prerecorded movies.

Improved **computer technology** in the 1990s has led to greater use of audio and visual materials on such mediums as CD-ROM and the Internet, as well as video games.

# MUSIC LIBRARY

298

## E X T E N S I O N

### POSTURE

Correct posture is the first step toward developing correct breathing for singing. Have students come forward in their chairs as though they are about to stand. They should sit tall with their shoulders relaxed and down. As soon as students know the correct posture, you can simply say "singing position" and they should automatically assume this position. If students are standing, ask them to stand firmly on both feet with feet slightly separated.

### BREATHING

As soon as correct posture is established, work on proper breathing. Breathing deeply gives the energy necessary to support the singing tone. The following three exercises should make students aware of the meaning of diaphragmatic breathing.

1. Have the students place their hands on their abdomens and feel the impulse as they make the sound *ch ch ch*, like an old-fashioned locomotive. With their hands on their abdomens they can feel the intake and release of air.

2. Have them blow out old air, inhale new air to the count of 1–3, and exhale on a hiss to the count of 1–5. Repeat, exhaling to the count of 1–7. Extend the count each time to increase breath control.

3. Ask students to breathe in and then sing on one breath the alphabet up to the letter *k* on middle line B. To increase breath control, repeat, each time adding another letter of the alphabet. Remind students that breathing more deeply produces a fuller, more supported tone.

### ACCOMPANIMENTS

The piano accompaniments and recorded accompaniments help set the style of the songs.

Divided track recordings can be used to help teach parts. The vocal parts can be isolated by adjusting the balance between the left and right speakers. A group can sing with its part to develop security or that part can be turned down or off and the group can sing with the other part.

A performance mix recording can be used to develop independent singing and as an accompaniment for a performance.

Students may wish to create their own accompaniments on appropriate instruments.

# Music Library

299

## AUDIENCE/PERFORMER

Give students the opportunity to be members of an audience as well as performers in class. As an audience, students should be encouraged to show approval at appropriate points in the performance and to offer appropriate comments after the performance by writing reviews or offering suggestions.

Give students the opportunity to show appropriate performance behavior in the classroom as well as in actual concerts. Determine where each part should stand in a "concert" situation, and review how to stand, sit, and bow in unison.

## FOLLOWING A CONDUCTOR

Remind students to watch the conductor of the group for visual directions. Demonstrate the various conducting movements used and explain what they mean: meter patterns, dynamics, articulations, tempos, attacks and cut offs. Give students the opportunity to be conductors and to refine their conducting techniques.

# MUSIC LIBRARY

**Focus: Group Singing**

## Objectives

To analyze music notation

To perform vocal music in three parts

To develop increased confidence in using the singing voice

## Materials

Recordings: "A Place in the Choir"
"A Place in the Choir"
(performance mix)

Guitar, Autoharp, percussion, synthesizer, keyboard, mallet instruments (optional)

## TEACHING THE LESSON

**1. Introduce group singing.** Have the students:

• Read and discuss the information on group singing. (Emphasize the long tradition of people singing for enjoyment.)

• Discuss opportunities for singing in their community.

• Listen to "A Place in the Choir" and identify the "singers" in the choir.

**2. Introduce Warm-ups 1 and 2.** Have the students:

• Discuss the need for warm-ups. (Singers warm up their voices much as athletes warm up their muscles before engaging in strenuous sports.)

• Perform Warm-ups 1 and 2. (See page 301 below.)

Why do people sing? Singing is a means of expressing yourself. Singing also stimulates your mind, touches your spirit, and demonstrates physical skill.

Group singing has been a popular activity for hundreds of years. A singing group such as a chorus, a choir, or a special ensemble may be highly trained or the group may be made up of amateurs who love to sing. What opportunities exist in your communty for singing? Every voice in the group is important. Each person adds to the sound of the whole. We all have a "place in the choir"!

Whenever you learn a new song, take the time to analyze and study the music notation. If you are learning a song in parts, notice how the parts are written. Follow each part all the way through so you know where to focus your eyes. "A Place in the Choir " has places where one, two, or three parts sing. The melody is in Part 1.

Identify the pitches and rhythms that you know, and find the pitches and rhythms that are not yet known. For example, the eighth note followed by a dotted quarter note in measure 9 may be new. Find any tempo, dynamic, and articulation markings. Locate symbols related to form such as repeat signs and first and second endings. Read through the lyrics and find their meaning. Try to determine the style and flavor of the song. How would you describe the mood of "A Place in the Choir"?

300

- Learn the melody to "A Place in the Choir." Add the other two parts when you are ready.

- Assign a tempo to each verse.

CD6:7, CD8:1

Key: G major, A♭ major     Ranges I: C–E♭¹, II: G₁–F, III: D♭–A♭

### A Place in the Choir

Piano Accompaniment on page PA 40

Words and music by Bill Staines
Arranged by M.J.

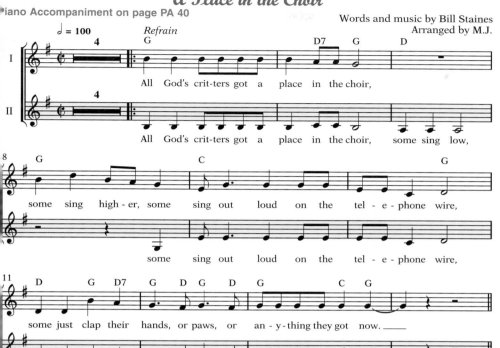

All God's crit-ters got a place in the choir,

All God's crit-ters got a place in the choir, some sing low,

some sing high-er, some sing out loud on the tel-e-phone wire,

some sing out loud on the tel-e-phone wire,

some just clap their hands, or paws, or an-y-thing they got now. ____

some just clap their hands, or paws, or an-y-thing they got now. ____

---

## MUSIC LIBRARY

**3. Introduce "A Place in the Choir."** Have the students:

- Read about how to prepare to sing a song, and examine the notation. (Be sure students can identify repeat signs, indications for Parts I-II-III, and the first and second endings.)
- Listen to the song while following the score, and describe the mood of the song. (lighthearted, joyful)
- Identify and discuss any difficulties in following the musical score. Listen again if needed.

---

## WARM-UPS

Encourage the students to use good singing posture and think about what they are doing vocally as they sing the warm-ups. Model the warm-ups for the class as needed.

1. Use Warm-up 1 to develop good diction by using the lips, teeth, and tongue to shape the sounds.
2. Use Warm-up 2 to extend the vocal range. Help students strive for a smooth, even quality of tone between low and high pitches. Encourage boys to start in the upper part of their vocal range. Have individuals or small groups sing, and make suggestions regarding the evenness of sound quality.

## WARM-UP 1

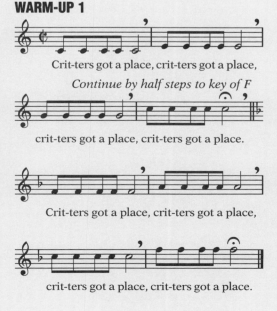

Crit-ters got a place, crit-ters got a place,

*Continue by half steps to key of F*

crit-ters got a place, crit-ters got a place.

Crit-ters got a place, crit-ters got a place,

crit-ters got a place, crit-ters got a place.

## WARM-UP 2

Hah ____

*Continue sequence to key of G*

Hah ____

Hah ____

# MUSIC LIBRARY

**4. Teach the verses of "A Place in the Choir."** Have the students:

• Listen, follow the musical score, and sing the verses softly along with the recording.

• Sing the verses in sections, small groups, individually, with and without accompaniment and/or vocal modeling. Repeat as needed.

• Practice using good diction to make the lyrics understood and to give the song a rhythmic quality. (Explain that *diction* refers to the way words are pronounced.)

**5. Teach the refrain of "A Place in the Choir."** Have the students:

• Identify the refrain of the song. (measures 5–14 and 32–41)

• Follow the score as you vocally model Part III, starting at measure 32.

• Sing Part III. (Observe if boys are singing in the lower octave. These may be changed voices and could be assigned to Part III.)

• Listen and follow the score as you model Part II.

• Sing Part II. (Boys who are singing this part comfortably at pitch level may have changing or unchanged voices and can be assigned to Parts I or II.)

• Form two groups and sing Parts II and III together, with keyboard accompaniment.

• Compare Part II with Part I. (Part II is lower in pitch and uses the same words and rhythms; rests fall in different places.)

• Read and sing Part I. (Challenge students to sing this based on what they already know of the song.)

• Follow the score as you model Part I.

302

## MORE MUSIC TEACHING IDEAS

1. Have the students play the chord roots or chords on keyboards or mallet instruments (G, C, D, D7; Ab, Db, Eb, Eb7). The chords in G major could also be played on Autoharp or guitar. Have the students improvise appropriate rhythms for the chords.

2. Have students create percussion ostinatos to add to the song. You may wish to have them notate the ostinatos and exchange patterns.

3. Have students sing various verses as solos.

4. Have students add vocal sound effects to imitate the various "critters." Sound effects might also be created from synthesizer sounds.

*Refrain*
*3 times: part III; parts III & II; parts III, II, I and claps on offbeats*

All God's crit-ters got a place in the choir, some sing high-er, some

All God's crit-ters got a place in the choir, some sing low, some

All God's crit-ters got a place __ in the choir.

sing out loud on the tel-e-phone wire, some just clap their

sing out loud on the tel-e-phone wire, some just clap their

Some sing out and some just clap their

hands, or paws, or an-y-thing they got now. __

*last time*

hands, or paws, or an-y-thing they got now. __

*last time*

hands, or paws, or an-y-thing they got now. __

**THINK IT THROUGH:** Determine which tempos were most effective.
Suggest ways of improving your performance.

303

# MUSIC LIBRARY

• Sing Part I. (Boys who are singing the higher pitches comfortably may have unchanged voices and can be assigned to Part I.)
• Sing Parts I and II together with and without accompaniment. Repeat as needed to secure pitch and rhythmic accuracy.
• Practice singing all three parts until everyone can sing each part. (Assign specific parts at the end of this exercise. Part III might be given to changed and treble voices; Part II cambiatas and treble voices; Part I unchanged treble voices. Each group may consist of both boys and girls.)
**5. Perform "A Place in the Choir."** Have the students:
• Sing the song with all three parts.
• Add the offbeat clapping at the end of the song.
• Choose a tempo for each verse. Then perform the song using those tempos.
• Discuss *Think It Through*.

## APPRAISAL

The students should be able to:
1. Analyze "A Place in the Choir" for known and new material.
2. Sing "A Place in the Choir" in three parts.
3. Sing with increased confidence.

# MUSIC LIBRARY

**Focus: Balance**

**Objectives**
To perform quarter-note triplets in a Cuban song
To develop choral balance

**Materials**
Recordings: "Guantanamera"
  Pronunciation:
  "Guantanamera"
  "Guantanamera" (perfor-
  mance mix)
Keyboard, mallet instruments, Latin per-
cussion (optional)

## TEACHING THE LESSON

**1. Introduce "Guantanamera."** Have the students:
• Read the information on the song. (Call attention to the order of the song and the meaning of *D.C. al Fine* and *Fine.*)
• Read about balance and the quarter-note triplet.
• Discuss why balance is important. (*Balance* is adjusting the volume of the parts so that all parts can be heard well and the melody is clearly heard. Balance creates unity in the choral-ensemble sound.)
• Practice clapping quarter-note triplets to a half-note beat.
• Listen to the song.
• Identify who is singing. (soloist, three-part chorus)
• Identify the languages in the song. (Spanish and English)

"Guantanamera" is a Cuban song. The Spanish verse is based on the poetry of José Martí (hō-sā mär-tē´), a Cuban patriot, author, journalist, and poet of the 1800s. Martí's poetry is sensitive and sincere. The verse of "Guantanamera" speaks of heartfelt poems he wishes to share. Martí dedicated his life to Cuba's struggle for independence from Spain.

**PREPARING** *to Sing "Guantanamera"*

When a group is singing in two or more parts, the group must work to balance the parts. This means that each part should stand out a bit more than the other parts. The melody of "Guantanmera" is in Part 1.

Notice the rhythm in measure 18. There is a quarter-note triplet on the word *morrime (die I would)*. This means that there are three quarter notes within the time of a half note.

$$\overset{\overline{\phantom{x}}3\overline{\phantom{x}}}{\downarrow\downarrow\downarrow} = \downarrow$$

• Try singing the verse as a solo. Add Parts II and III when you have learned the melody.

# EXTENSION

## MORE MUSIC TEACHING IDEAS

1. Have the students play the chord roots or chords on keyboard or mallet instruments. This can be simplified by playing only on the downbeats.
2. Have the students create rhythm ostinatos and play them using Latin percussion instruments. You may wish to have the students notate the ostinatos.
3. Explain that this song has evolved through changes made by a variety of people. Have the students choose a song and change various aspects of it. For example, have a student create new words to a verse, then pass it on to another who changes those words somewhat, then to another who changes some of the rhythms or pitches in the song, and so on. If students know another language, translate the song into that language. Discuss the results. What changes seemed to be improvements? What changes seemed to detract from the song?
4. Have the students sing this popular Cuban song from memory.

## PRONUNCIATION

Guantanamera, guajira Guantanamera.
gwän-tän-ä-meh'-rä gwä-hē'-rä gwän-tän-ä-meh'-rä

Yo soy un hombre sincero
yō sō e̅ ōōn ōm'-bre sēn-se'-rō

de donde crece la palma.
de dän'de krä'seh lä päl'mä

Y antes de morirme quiero
e̅ än'tes de mō-rēr-me kēe-rō

Echar mis versos del alma
ā-chär mēs ver'sos del äl'mä

# Guantanamera

CD6:8–9, CD8:2

Words and music by José Fernandez Dias
Music adapted by Julian Orbon and Pete Seeger
Lyrics adapted by Julian Orbon based on a poem by José Martí
Arrangement and English Words by MMH

Key: F major  Ranges I: C–D¹, II: B♭₁–B♭, III: F₁–F

Piano Accompaniment on page PA 46

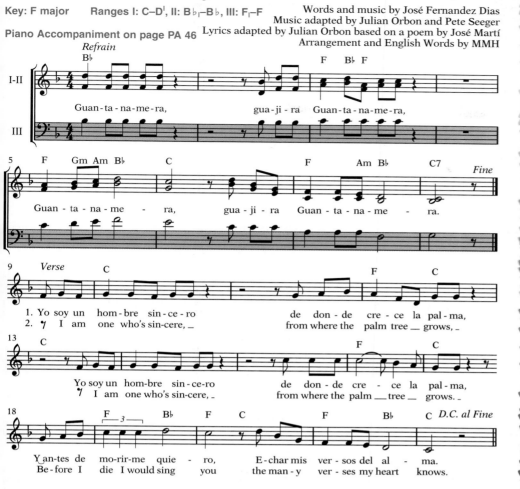

**Refrain**

Guan-ta-na-me-ra, gua-ji-ra Guan-ta-na-me-ra,

Guan-ta-na-me-ra, gua-ji-ra Guan-ta-na-me-ra. *Fine*

**Verse**

1. Yo soy un hom-bre sin-ce-ro    de don-de cre-ce la pal-ma,
2. I am one who's sin-cere, _    from where the palm tree _ grows, _

Yo soy un hom-bre sin-ce-ro    de don-de cre-ce la pal-ma,
I am one who's sin-cere, _    from where the palm _ tree _ grows. _

Y an-tes de mo-rir-me quie-ro,    E-char mis ver-sos del al-ma,
Be-fore I die I would sing you    the man-y ver-ses my heart knows.

*D.C. al Fine*

**THINK IT THROUGH:** Evaluate the balance among the vocal parts in your performance. Suggest ways to improve the balance.

305

# MUSIC LIBRARY

**2. Teach Guantanamera.** Have the students:
- Sing the melody (Part I) using a neutral syllable such as *loo*.
- Listen to "Pronunciation: 'Guantanamera'" and practice pronouncing the Spanish words. (See *Pronunciation* below.)
- Sing the melody in Spanish.
- Learn Parts II and III using a neutral syllable such as *doo* to aid in rhythmic accuracy. (Boys can be assigned to the parts best suited to their ranges. Review bass clef as needed. Girls can sing Parts I and II.)
- Sing all three parts first using a neutral syllable, then using words.
- Sing the verses as solos or as small groups.
- Form three groups, each made up of students with the appropriate range, and sing the song.
- Discuss balance between vocal parts.
- Discuss *Think It Through*.

## APPRAISAL

The students should be able to:
1. Identify and perform quarter-note triplets in "Guantanamera."
2. Balance the three parts in "Guantanamera."

# MUSIC LIBRARY

**Focus: Group and Solo Singing**

**Objectives**
To sing alone and in a two-part group
To identify ABA form

**Materials**
Recordings: "Cum-ma-la Be-stay"
"Cum-ma-la Be-stay" (performance mix)
Pitched instruments, keyboard, unpitched percussion (optional)

## TEACHING THE LESSON

1. Introduce "Cum-ma-la Be-stay." Have the students:
• Read about the song.
• Listen to the song, softly patting the half-note beat and following Part I. (Call attention to the cut-time meter signature. Explain that this means that there are two beats in a measure and the half note gets the beat.)
• Listen again and follow Part II.

Part of the fun of singing in a group is the variety of sounds you can produce. "Cum-ma-la Be-stay" uses a soloist as well as a group. After the Part I melody is learned, the lower voices can add the Part II harmony part.

This song needs some movement! Plan how you want to move. Use the lyrics and the form of the song to get you going. What parts are the same? First and last sections of the ABA form are the same, the group echoes the soloist in the A sections, various phrases are the same.

💡 **THINK IT THROUGH:** Compare your movement ideas with others. Which ideas most effectively fit with the style of the music? Why?     Key: F major     Ranges 1: C–C¹, II: A₁–D

Piano Accompaniment on page PA 48

## Cum-ma-la Be-stay
Words and Music by Donny Burke, Jerry Vance, and Terry Philips
Arranged by M. J.

---

# EXTENSION

## MORE MUSIC TEACHING IDEAS

1. Have the students play part or all of the melody on pitched instruments. You may wish to have instruments alternate during the A sections, matching the solo/all markings.

2. Have the students practice reading letter names in bass clef. Part II is limited to five pitches: G A B♭ C D. Have the students play Part II on bass instruments such as low mallet instruments or keyboard.

3. Have the students play chord roots or chords with the song. (F, B♭, C7) Encourage them to play the harmony by ear.

4. Have the students use unpitched percussion instruments to play the unpitched notes in the song.

5. Have the students play Parts I and II, chords, and percussion parts together.

6. Have the students make up new words to the song. For example, they might use new nonsense words or create a new verse for the B section. They could also choose new movements to do.

7. Have the students sing the two parts as a duet or as a small ensemble.

8. Have the students sing the song from memory.

**2. Teach "Cum-ma-la Be-stay."** Have the students:
• Speak in rhythm, then sing Part I (melody). (Use vocal modeling as needed. Boys can sing down an octave if needed.)
• Correct any diction that is not uniform or is incorrect.
• Determine the form. (ABA)
• Identify other musical characteristics of the song. (major key, steady pulse, repeated rhythms and melodies, alternates Solo and All)
• Learn Part II by echo singing. (This part can be sung by boys with changing or changed voices.)
• Practice both parts together with and without accompaniment.
• Sing the song in two parts with a soloist or small group singing the B section.
• Describe the style of singing that is appropriate for this song. (energetic, focused, fun)
**3. Create movement for "Cum-ma-la Be-stay."** Have the students:
• Plan movements based on the form and lyrics. (You may wish to divide the class into small groups for this activity.)
• Take turns doing their movements with the song.
• Discuss *Think It Through*.

## APPRAISAL

The students should be able to:
1. Sing the solo alone and sing "Cum-ma-la Be-stay" in two parts.
2. Identify the form of "Cum-ma-la Be-stay" as ABA.

307

# MUSIC LIBRARY

**Focus: Contrasting Styles**

## Objectives
To identify elements in Mexican and Native American musical styles
To use accurate diction in languages other than English

## Materials
Recordings: "One-Eyed Ford"
"Guadalajara"
Pronunciation:
"Guadalajara"
"Guadalajara" (performance mix)
Recorders, keyboard, bells or other mallet instruments, large drum (optional)

## Vocabulary
Vocables

## TEACHING THE LESSON

**1. Introduce "One-Eyed Ford."** Have the students:

• Read about the song.
• Listen to "One-Eyed Ford." (Call attention to the repeat sign to aid following the notation.)
• List features of the style. (Native American, English words and vocables, pitch slides, unmetered, unison, strong rhythm, repeated melodic patterns, drum accompaniment)
• Listen to "One-Eyed Ford" again and practice pronouncing the vocables.
• Listen to the song again and find the vocal slides. (measures 1, 2, 7, 11, 12)
• Describe what the singers on the recording did on the slides. (Singers started on the pitch and let the pitch slide down to an indeterminate pitch.)
• Practice the vocal slides.

The song "One-Eyed Ford" often accompanies social dancing at powwows, particularly among the Native American nations of the southern plains of the United States. "One-Eyed Ford" is a type of song known as "49s." These frequently humorous "49s" songs often contain English lyrics mixed with vocables. **Vocables** are sung sounds that are not words. Compare the use of vocables in this song with scat singing.

The *one-eyed Ford* refers to a car with only one light. Many years ago any kind of car was a prized possession. Often the roads were not good and the cars had only one 'eye' because the lights got knocked out.

308

# One-Eyed Ford

CD6:11

Drum: ♫ ♫ ♫ ♫ except during English words

**Key: G♭ pentatonic**   **Range G♭₁–G♭**

Inter-tribal Native American 49 Song

*Repeat song in higher keys*

Solo
we ya ha do we ya ha do we ya ha do we ya ha do

3
ya __ yo __ he ya he ____ ya he ya ho hai ya

5
he ya ha he ya ha do we ya ha we ya ha do we ya ha do

8
ya __ yo __ he ya he ____ ya he ya ho hai ya he ya ha he ya ha do

11
When the dance is o-ver, sweet-heart, I will take you home __ in my one-eyed Ford.

13
he ya he ____ ya he ya ho hai ya he ya ha he ya ha-e

\* Voices overlap

💡 **THINK IT THROUGH:** Some of the pitches in "One-Eyed Ford" slide down. How do the slides affect the character of the piece? Evaluate your success in producing the slides. Recommend ways to improve your performance.

309

## MUSIC LIBRARY

- Discuss the lack of meter signature. (There is no meter signature because the measures do not contain the same number of beats.)
- Find the rhythms that they know. (Students should be able to find eighths, quarters, eighth-two sixteenths, dotted eighth-sixteenth, two sixteenths-eighth. Call attention to the sixteenth-dotted eighth and explain that it is short-long pattern that is the reverse of the dotted eighth-sixteenth that they know.)
- Clap the melodic rhythm.
- Listen to the song and sing the melody softly on the syllable *too*. (The range of the song is good for boys with changing voices. Changed voices should be encouraged to sing in the upper range of their voices. Girls may sing the first line or as much of the song for which they have range.)
- Identify which measure is being sung as you or a student sings one of the measures.
- Sing the song with the vocables and English words.
- Discuss *Think It Through*.

## MORE MUSIC TEACHING

1. Explain that in some Native American music, more than one drummer may play the same large drum simultaneously. Have one or more students play the dotted eighth-sixteenth rhythm of "One-Eyed Ford" on a drum. This rhythm pattern is an approximation of the actual sound. The first note of the pattern is stressed. The beat of the drum is not always the same as the beat of the singing.

2. Have the students improvise a G-pentatonic melody on recorder, keyboard, or bells that may be accompanied by a dotted-rhythm drum ostinato.

## BACKGROUND

A powwow is a Native American social gathering. It is an occasion for reunions and the transmission of values and culture. There are four basic roles in a powwow: the group that sponsors the event; principal officials such as the head singer, head dancers, and announcer; singer/dancers; and spectators. Many different dances may be performed at a powwow. They include open-participation dances for the general public and performance dances which are dance contests. "One-Eyed Ford" is often accompanied by the round dance, a social dance. The round dance is a circle dance in which the dancers often hold hands and side-step to the left.

# MUSIC LIBRARY

**2. Introduce "Guadalajara."** Have the students:
- Read about the song.
- List other songs about cities that they know. (for example, "Chicago," "I Left My Heart in San Francisco," "New York, New York," "I Love Paris")
- Find the lines that have multiple-measure rests. (Line 1, 9, 14. Explain how to count the measures of rest, if needed.)
- Listen to the song.
- List features of the style. (Mexican, in Spanish, major key, key change, repeated melodic and rhythmic patterns, long sustained notes, ⁶/₈ meter, interludes, vocal harmony at end)
- Practice the melody on a neutral syllable. (Add the harmony parts at the end when students are ready.)
- Practice managing their breath to sing the long sustained tones.
- Listen to "Pronunciation: 'Guadalajara'" and practice saying the Spanish words. Work on uniform vowels.
- Sing the song in Spanish. (Give students repeated listenings to aid in the pronunciation and style. Vocally model sections of the song as needed.)
- Sing parts of the song in small groups and have the class evaluate the accuracy of the pronunciation as compared to the recording.
- Identify the dynamics. (*mf*, *f*, *ff*, crescendo)
- Sing the song using the appropriate dynamics.
- Discuss *Think It Through*.

"Guadalajara" (gwäd-ə-lə-här´-ə) was written during the 1930s, a time that has been considered a golden age of Mexican popular music. Radio stations at that time broadcast Mexican music throughout Mexico and into the United States Southwest.

Guadalajara is capital of the state of Jalisco (hə-lis´kō), Mexico. It is a beautiful old city, founded by the Spanish in 1530. The city is an important trading and manufacturing center known for its fine pottery and blown glass. The Spanish lyrics of the song speak of the beauty of Guadalajara. *Colomitos* are green leafy plants that grow in the region of Guadalajara.

CD6:12–13, CD8:4

Piano Accompaniment on page PA 52

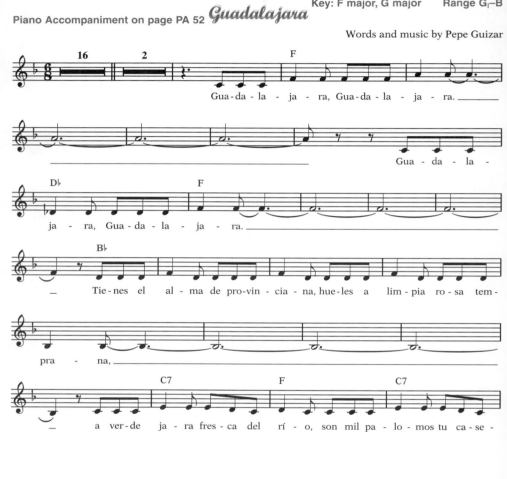

### Guadalajara

Key: F major, G major    Range G₁–B

Words and music by Pepe Guizar

310

---

# EXTENSION

## MORE MUSIC TEACHING IDEAS

1. Call attention to the key changes in "Guadalajara." Explain that the natural in Line 9 cancels out the key signature of F and in Line 14 it goes back to the key of F.
2. Have the students tap the beat and tell when the song feels like it changes from ⁶/₈ to ³/₄. Explain that this rhythmic shifting is part of the style.
3. Have the students play the chords, chord roots, or melody on mallet instruments or keyboard.

## PRONUNCIATION

Guadalajara.
gwä-dä-lä-hä´rä

Tienes el alma de provinciana,
tēeh-nes el äl´mä de prō´vēn-sēä´nä

hueles a limpia rosa temprana,
we´les ä lēm-pē-ä rro´sä tem-prä´nä

a verde jara fresca del río,
ä ver´de hä´rä fres´kä del rrē´ō

son mil palomos tu caserío,
son mēl pä-lō´mōs tōō kä-se-rē´ō

sabes a pura tierra mojada.
sä´bes ä pōō´rä tēeh´rrä mō-hä´dä

Ay colomitos lejanos,
äē kō-lō-mē´tōs le-hä´nōs

Ay ojitos de agua hermanos.
äē ō-hē-tōs de ä´gwä er-mä´nōs

Ay colomitos inolvidables,
äē kō-lō-mē´tōs ē-nol-vē-dä´bles

inolvidables como las tardes
ē-nol-vē-dä´bles kō-mō läs tär´des

en que la lluvia desde la loma
en kä lä yōō´vē-ä des´de lä lō´mä

irnos hacia hasta Zapopan.
ēr´nōs ä´sēä äs´tä sä-pō´pän

rí - o, Gua-da-la - ja - ra, Gua-da-la - ja - ra sa - bes a  pu - ra tie - rra mo -

ja - da. _____

16    2    **G7**
¡Ay! _____    co - lo - mi - tos le -

**C**    **G7**
ja - nos. _____    ¡Ay! _____

**C**
_ o - ji - tos de a-gua her - ma - nos. _____    ¡Ay! co - lo -

**G**    **C6**    **G9**    **C**
mi - tos i - nol - vi - da - bles, i - nol - vi - da - bles co - mo las    tar - des en que la

**G**    **C6**    **G9**    **C**
llu - via des - de la    lo - ma ir - nos ha - ci - a has - ta Za - po - pan. _____

16    **F**    *mf*    freely *cresc.*
¡Gua - da - la -

*mf* **Db**    *cresc.*    **Db7**    *ff* **F**
ja - ra! _____    ¡Gua - da - la - ja - ra!

**THINK IT THROUGH:** Experiment by singing this song at a slower or
faster tempo.  Justify the tempo you think is appropriate.

311

**3. Compare and contrast styles.** Have the
students:
• List similarities and differences between
"One-Eyed Ford" and "Guadalajara."
(Similarities: basically in unison, accompanied, "popular music"; Differences: accompaniment by drum/mariachi, vocables
and English/Spanish, unmetered/ $\frac{6}{8}$, short
song/long song, folk song/composed)
• Perform each song in the appropriate
style.

## APPRAISAL

The students should be able to:
1. Identify stylistic elements in "Guadalajara" and "One-Eyed Ford."
2. Use correct diction in pronouncing
Native American vocables in "One-Eyed
Ford" and Spanish in "Guadalajara."

## TRANSLATION

(The city) Guadalajara has the soul of a
country girl, you smell like an early pure
rose, like a green, fresh rockrose from the
river, you dwell with a thousand little
doves, you taste like pure wet soil.

Ah, distant *colomitos* (plant similar to a
philodendron), Ah, clear springs, my
brothers, Ah, unforgettable *colomitos*, unforgettable like those rainy afternoons in
which we used to go from the hill to
Zapopan.

# MUSIC LIBRARY

**Focus: Voice Ranges**

## Objectives
To identify characteristics of the young voice and the changing voice
To classify voices according to range
To identify soprano, alto, tenor, cambiata

## Materials
Recordings: "America" (in B♭)
"America" (in B♭) (performance mix)
"America" (in G)
"America" (in G) (performance mix)
Mallet instruments, keyboard (optional)

## Vocabulary
treble, soprano, alto, cambiata, tenor

## TEACHING THE LESSON

1. **Teach "America" (in B♭).** Have the students:
• Read about vocal tone color.
• Speak a selected passage one at a time, and have the class describe the quality of sound. For example, big/small, breathy/clear, bright/dark, heavy/light.
• Read about the young voice and discuss the information.
• Listen to "America" (in B♭), focusing on the voices in octaves.
• Sing the song and determine whether they can still sing in the treble range.
• Compare their voices to the voices on the recording. (Adjust the volume on the compact disc channels so the students can hear either the high or low octave alone.)
• Determine whether they are closer to a soprano, alto, or cambiata range.

### Marvelous Changable Voices
Each person has a unique vocal tone color. This tone color enables others to identify a person by hearing just the sound of that person's voice.

### The Young Voice
As a child, each of you had a voice that sounded high. This high voice is considered to be in the **treble** range. Many famous children's choirs from around the world consist of boys and girls singing with unchanged voices in the treble range. One of the most famous choirs is the Vienna Boys' Choir, which has toured throughout the world since its founding in 1496.

• Sing "America" in the key of B♭ and determine whether you can still sing comfortably in the treble range.

## America

Music by Henry Carey
Words by Samuel F. Smith

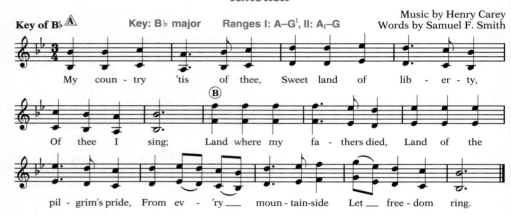

Key of B♭ Ⓐ    Key: B♭ major    Ranges I: A–G¹, II: A₁–G

My coun-try 'tis of thee, Sweet land of lib - er - ty,
Of thee I sing; Land where my fa - thers died, Land of the
pil - grim's pride, From ev - 'ry ___ moun - tain-side Let ___ free - dom ring.

If you sang the B section of "America" comfortably in the upper octave, or high-treble range, you may have a **soprano** (high voice) range. If you sang the B section more comfortably in the lower octave, or lower-treble range, you may have an **alto** (middle voice) range or **cambiata** (changing voice) range.

312

---

# EXTENSION

## MORE MUSIC TEACHING IDEAS
Have the students play the melody of "America" in the key of B♭ in either octave on mallet instruments or keyboard.

## BACKGROUND
### "America"
The melody of "America" is borrowed from the British national anthem "God Save the Queen." After the American Revolution, people wanted to set the United States apart from its British heritage and establish it as a nation in its own right. Many Americans wrote patriotic words to the much-resented British anthem. The words we are familiar with today were written by Samuel Francis Smith for a Boston July 4th celebration in 1831. The words and music were first printed together in 1832, in a collection by music educator Lowell Mason entitled *The Choir*.

### The Changing Voice

As you become older, your voice and body change. During the teenage years, the vocal quality of girls' singing voices will change more than the ability to sing high or low. Girls continue to have treble voices, but they gradually develop either a soprano or an alto range.

Boys' voices change more dramatically than girls' voices. A boy's voice develops a lower range. The rate of change differs from person to person. Some voices change gradually, others change suddenly. When a boy's voice is in the process of changing, the voice is called a cambiata voice. As a boy's voice becomes lower, the voice will develop a tenor, baritone, or bass range.

• Sing "America" to help you determine whether you are an alto or a tenor.

**America**  Key: G major    Ranges I: F♯–E¹, II: F♯₁–E

Piano Accompaniment on page PA 45

Music by Henry Carey
Words by Samuel F. Smith

Key of G

My coun-try 'tis of thee, Sweet land of lib-er-ty,
Of thee I sing; Land where my fa-thers died, Land of the
pil-grim's pride, From ev-'ry __ moun-tain-side Let __ free-dom ring.

If you sang the A section of "America" comfortably in the upper octave, you may have an alto voice.

If you sang the A section more comfortably in the lower octave, you may have a **tenor**, or lower, voice.

313

## MUSIC LIBRARY

• Notice the key signature. (Explain that a key signature with two flats is either the key of B♭ or G minor. The last note can give a hint to which of these keys it is—in this case, it is B♭.)

**2. Teach "America" (in G).** Have the students:
• Read about the changing voice and discuss the information.
• Listen to "America" (in G), focusing on the voices in octaves.
• Sing the song and identify which octave is more comfortable.
• Compare their voices to the voices on the recording. (Adjust the volume on the compact disc channels so the students can hear either the high or low octave alone.)
• Determine whether they are closer to an alto or a tenor range.
• Notice the key signature. (Explain that a key signature with one sharp is either the key of G or E minor. The last note can give a hint to which of these keys it is—in this case, it is G.)

### MORE MUSIC TEACHING IDEAS

Have the students play the melody in the key of G in either octave on mallet instruments or keyboard.

# MUSIC LIBRARY

**3. Identify ranges.** Have the students:
• Sing "America" in both keys to identify the highest and lowest pitch each student can sing.
• Discuss vocal ranges, locating each on the chart.
• Discuss *Think It Through*.
• Determine their present vocal range.
• Form groups according to their vocal range and sing "America," one group at a time in the appropriate key. (Students singing with tension may be singing in the incorrect vocal range.)

## APPRAISAL

The students should be able to:
1. Identify several characteristics of the young voice and the changing voice.
2. Classify their voice according to vocal range.
3. Identify by sound and range: soprano, alto, tenor, and cambiata.

**THINK IT THROUGH:** Compare your vocal range with the singing ranges for young adults shown on the chart. What do you conclude about your vocal range?

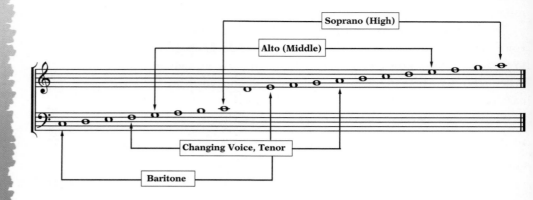

Your voice will continue to change as you become older and more physically mature. As you sing, notice whether you are comfortable as you sing higher and lower. You may be moving into a higher or lower voice range. Enjoy the experience of each new voice!

314

**PREPARING** *to Sing "'60s Medley"*

Sometimes when you sing in the higher or lower part of your vocal range, the quality of sound changes. The ability to maintain the same quality across your vocal range can be developed. This ability allows you to sing with more control, comfort, and beauty of sound.

- Sing this pattern higher and lower to experience your vocal range. What is the highest note of your range? The lowest?

My vo - cal range goes from high to low.

Singing higher is easier if the voice is located, or **placed**, correctly.

- Sing this pattern to help place your voice.

We _____ sing _____ high.

- Sing this passage to prepare to sing "'60s Medley."

Whee, _____ whee, whee, whee, whee.

315

**Focus: Voice Placement, Upper Range**

### Objectives
To develop the ability to place the voice and sing in the upper register
To improve vocal tone quality

### Materials
Recordings: "'60s Medley"
"'60s Medley" (performance mix)

### Vocabulary
Placed

## TEACHING THE LESSON

**1. Introduce "'60s Medley."** Have the students:
- Read about maintaining vocal quality and placement.
- Find the first and second endings and repeat signs in "The Lion Sleeps Tonight." (Call attention to the use of both music notation and lyrics only.)
- Listen to "'60s Medley."
- Identify some of the characteristics of the singing. (high range, light quality, sometimes an artificially high voice known as *falsetto*)
- Sing the medley with the recording, aiming for an even quality of sound and comfortable singing. (Encourage changed and changing voices to sing in their upper range, using falsetto as appropriate or needed.)

# MUSIC LIBRARY

**2. Develop voice placement.** Have the students:

• Listen as you model the first exercise on page 315.

• Sing this example in higher and lower keys to experience as wide a vocal range as possible.

• Identify students who can sing the highest and the lowest.

• Listen as you model the second exercise on page 315.

• Sing this example in higher and lower keys to experience placing the tone in different areas of the vocal range.

• Identify students who place the tone comfortably in the higher vocal range. (Be alert for straining.)

• Discuss placing the tone. (Explain the need for placement in order to sing the higher vocal portions of "'60s Medley." Model these passages as needed.)

• Sing Warm-up 3 to help place the voice throughout the upper portions of their vocal range. (See below. Emphasize breath and evenness and consistency of sound when descending the scale.)

• Listen as you model the third exercise on page 315.

• Sing the example in higher and lower keys to practice placing the tone and singing comfortably. (Stress singing with good placement, breath support, and well-formed, focused vowels. Have students sing individually as well as in groups.)

The four songs contained in "'60s Medley" became popular in the 1960s. CD6:16, CD8:7    Key: G major, A major    Range D–F♯¹

Piano Accompaniment on page PA 57  *'60s Medley*

Adapted from "The Lion Sleeps Tonight," Words and Music by Solomon Linda;
"Big Girls Don't Cry," Words and Music by Bob Crewe and Bob Gaudio;
"Under the Boardwalk," Words and Music by Artie Resnick and Kenny Young;
"In My Room," Words and Music by Brian Wilson and Gary Usher.

316

# EXTENSION

## WARM-UP 3

Noo _____

*Continue sequence to key of B-flat*

Noo _____

Noo _____

## MORE MUSIC TEACHING IDEAS

1. Have the students find the eighth-note triplets in "The Lion Sleeps Tonight." (Lines 2–3. Explain that the first two eighths of the triplet are added together to be a quarter note. This forms the long-short pattern within the beat. The word *simile* means to continue in a similar manner.)

2. Have the students compare the sound of eighth-note triplets in 4/4 to the sound of eighth notes in the 12/8 meter of "In My Room." (They sound the same. Explain that 12/8 is similar to 6/8, except there are four main beats in the measure instead of two.)

3. Find the occurrences of syncopation in "The Lion Sleeps Tonight." (in lines 1, 4, 5, 6)

4. Have the students sing harmony parts to Lines 2 and 3 of "The Lion Sleeps Tonight."

**"Big Girls Don't Cry"**

Big girls don't cry. Big girls don't cry.

Big girls, don't cry, they don't cry.

Big girls, don't cry, Big girls don't cry.

**"Under the Boardwalk"**

Oh, when the sun beats down and burns the tar upon the roof,

And your shoes get so hot, you wish your tired feet were fireproof.

Under the boardwalk, down by the sea, yeah,

On a blanket by the seashore, that's where I'll be.

Under the boardwalk, down by the sea, yeah,

On a blanket by the seashore, that's where I'll be.

**THINK IT THROUGH:** Evaluate the consistency of your vocal quality in all parts of your range. Suggest ways for improvement.

# MUSIC LIBRARY

**3. Teach "'60s Medley."** Have the students:
• Sing "'60s Medley," with and without accompaniment, using the lighter register. (Encourage boys to try falsetto.)
• Discuss what they learned from the third exercise on page 315 that should be applied to "'60s Medley." (Use pure vowels, light quality, even sound; place tone in upper portion of range.)
• Sing the medley in small groups or as individuals and evaluate vocal placement and vowels.
• Discuss *Think It Through*.

## APPRAISAL

The students should be able to:
1. Place their voice and sing comfortably in the upper portion of their vocal range.
2. Use good tone quality as they sing "'60s Medley."

## BACKGROUND

Refer to pages 235–237 for more information about American popular music of the 1960s. Brian Wilson, one of the composers of "In My Room" is one of the Beach Boys.

# MUSIC LIBRARY

**Focus: Diction**

## Objectives
To expand vocal range
To develop confidence in singing through a three-part round
To develop good diction

## Materials
Recordings: "New Year's Round"
"New Year's Round" (performance mix)
Guitar, Autoharp, keyboard, pitched instruments, bells, synthesizer (optional)

## Vocabulary
Diction

## TEACHING THE LESSON

**Teach "New Year's Round."** Have the students:
• Read the page and sing exercise 1, emphasizing evenness of sound.
• Sing exercise 2, emphasizing diction.
• Listen to "New Year's Round," softly patting the half-note beat.
• Find repeated patterns in the song, (mm 1, 3; 5, 7; 9, 10, 11 are the same; mm 2, 4, 8, 12 have the same rhythm.)
• Speak the rhythm of "New Year's Round" in unison and as a round.
• Listen to the song again.
• Practice the melody, aiming for clear diction and correct vocal placement.
• Find the range of the song. (C to high E)
• Sing the song as a three-part round.
• Discuss *Think It Through*.

## APPRAISAL

The students should be able to:
1. Sing a song with a wide vocal range.
2. Sing a three-part round with confidence.
3. Sing a song with good diction.

**PREPARING** *to Sing "New Year's Round"*

"New Year's Round" has a vocal range from low 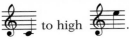 to high .

• Sing this pattern starting on different pitches to expand your vocal range. This exercise will help you perform the high and low passages of "New Year's Round."

Bring the New Year _ in.        Bring the New Year _ in.

**Diction,** or how you pronounce words, is an important aspect of the performance of any choral music.

• Sing the following from "New Year's Round." This exercise will help to develop your diction and enhance your choral performance. Work for pure vowels and clear consonants.

Time    to    ring    the    New    Year    in.

Antonio Caldara, who wrote the "New Year's Round," lived from 1670 to 1736.

### New Year's Round    Key: C major    Range C–E¹

Piano Accompaniment on page PA 60        Music by Antonio Caldara
Words by MMH

Time and tide _ are mov-ing on.    Soon the old _ year will be gone.

Let our joy-ful song _ be-gin!    Time to ring the New Year in!

Sing - ing,    Ring - ing.    Bring _ the New Year in!

**THINK IT THROUGH:** Evaluate your performance. Recommend ways in which the diction can be enhanced.

318

---

# E X T E N S I O N

## MORE MUSIC TEACHING IDEAS

1. Have the students perform the round with one or two on a part and then discuss the level of confidence of the singers, the placement of the voice in measures 9–12, and the balance between the parts.

2. Have the students play the chords on guitar, Autoharp, or keyboard. Encourage them to play the harmony by ear. Have them improvise an appropriate strum rhythm.

3. Have the students play chord roots on pitched instruments.

4. Have the students play one of the lines as an ostinato or play the whole song.

5. Choose various bell sounds to add to the song. Bells as well as varous bell tone colors on a synthesizer could be used.

6. Have the students describe some of the New Year's celebrations they observe. For example, some watch the large ball come down at Times Square to begin the New Year on January 1. Performers dress as dragons or lions to celebrate the Chinese New Year in January or February. The Jewish New Year of Rosh Hashanah in September is a solemn occasion.

7. Have the students compose a round using pitches from the C and G7 chords. Use the harmonic sequence C C C C C C G7 C or C C G7 C. The melody can be made up using pitches from the appropriate chord as well as passing tones.

8. Call attention to the 2/2 meter signature. Explain that it means the same thing as the cut time sign—two beats in a measure with

the half note getting the beat.)

9. Call attention to the slurs. Explain that a slur smoothly connects two different pitches.

"We Shall Overcome" is an American song expressing social concern. This song is an adaptation of an old hymn tune. It came into being in the 1930s at a time when coal miners in West Virginia were struggling for a decent standard of living and for safe conditions in the mines. The song became prominent during the Civil Rights Movement in the 1960s. "We Shall Overcome" has since become identified with struggles against many kinds of oppression.

CD6:18, CD8:9

Key: C major     Range C–D¹

## We Shall Overcome

Piano Accompaniment on page PA 62

American Freedom Song
Words by Zilphia Horton, Frank Hamilton,
Guy Carawan, and Pete Seeger

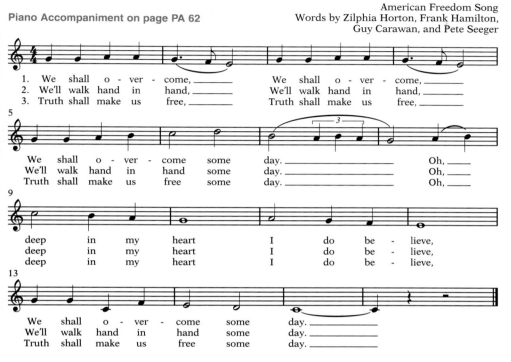

1. We shall o-ver-come, _____ We shall o-ver-come, _____
2. We'll walk hand in hand, _____ We'll walk hand in hand, _____
3. Truth shall make us free, _____ Truth shall make us free, _____

We shall o-ver-come some day. _____ Oh, _____
We'll walk hand in hand some day. _____ Oh, _____
Truth shall make us free some day. _____ Oh, _____

deep in my heart I do be-lieve,
deep in my heart I do be-lieve,
deep in my heart I do be-lieve,

We shall o-ver-come some day. _____
We'll walk hand in hand some day. _____
Truth shall make us free some day. _____

**THINK IT THROUGH:** Choose musical elements to change to show different moods. Describe how your choices reflect the message of this song.

319

# MUSIC LIBRARY

**Focus: Expressive Singing**

## Objectives
To sing a song with expression

## Materials
Recordings: "We Shall Overcome"
"We Shall Overcome" (performance mix)
Copying Master C-1 Sight-Reading Patterns I
Keyboard, recorder, bells (optional)

## TEACHING THE LESSON

**Teach "We Shall Overcome."** Have the students:
• Read about the song.
• Listen to the song and describe the style and lyrics. (unison, repeated melodic patterns, lyrics that speak of social concerns)
• Find the quarter-note triplet in line 2 and explain its meaning. (A *quarter-note triplet* has three quarter notes that fit in the duration of two normal quarter notes.)
• Read the rhythm of the song. (You may wish to use Copying Master C-1 Sight-Reading Patterns I at this time.)
• Sing "We Shall Overcome."
• Identify emotional qualities that should be expressed in their performance of the song (conviction, energy, confidence)
• Discuss how these qualities can be shown musically. (Emphasize important words; pronounce the words clearly to stress the message; use good breath management to keep a strong tone; show appropriate facial expression.)
• Discuss *Think It Through*.
• Sing the song expressively.

## APPRAISAL

The students should be able to sing "We Shall Overcome" with expression.

## MORE MUSIC TEACHING IDEAS

1. Have the students discuss social concerns of today and the deep feelings some people have about them. (for example, pollution, unemployment, health issues, conflicts) List current songs that speak to social issues.
2. Have the students name other freedom songs they know.
3. Have the students take turns singing the song as a solo.
4. Play the melody on keyboard, recorder, or bells. Encourage the students to play the melody by ear.
5. Have the students identify the key of the song. (key of C.)
6. Listen as you sing various phrases using the syllable *loo*, and identify which measures you sang.

# MUSIC LIBRARY

**Focus: Articulation**

**Objectives**
To sing an American folk song
in three parts
To articulate lyrics clearly

**Materials**
Recordings: "Leila"
             "Leila" (performance mix)
Keyboard, bells, recorder (optional)

**Vocabulary**
Articulating

## TEACHING THE LESSON

**Teach "Leila."** Have the students:
• Read the first paragraph on page 320.
• Sing Warm-up 4 to develop pure vowels and good choral tone. (See below.)
• Sing the C-major scale up and down to establish the key.
• Sing the vocal exercise on page 320, working for pure vowels. (Help them to quickly focus the vowels.)
• Read about and discuss articulation.
• Sing the vocal exercise using various consonants instead of "l."
• Locate the melody of the exercise in the song. (measures 3, 4 and 15, 17)
• Find the syncopation in the song and then read the rhythm of the melody using rhythm syllables or words. (Call attention to the repeat signs and first and second endings if needed.)
• Say the words in rhythm, articulating them clearly.
• Listen to the song, following one of the parts. Listen again and follow the other part.
• Sing the Part 1 (melody), concentrating on articulating the words, then learn Part 2 and the solo parts.

## PREPARING *to Sing "Leila"*

The sound of your singing is enhanced when you produce clear, distinct vowels. Vowels provide the "center" of your vocal tone. In singing, vowels are usually held as long as possible and consonants are pronounced quickly.

• Sing a melodic pattern from the North Carolina folk song "Leila." This pattern uses vowel sounds found in the lyrics.

| (L)ay | (l)ay | (l)ay | (l)ay | (l)ay | (l)ay, | (L)ah | (l)ah | (l)ah | (l)ah | (l)ah | (l)ah, |
| (L)oh | (l)oh | (l)oh | (l)oh | (l)oh | (l)oh, | (L)oo | (l)oo | (l)oo | (l)oo | (l)oo | (l)oo, |
| (L)ee | (l)ee | (l)ee | (l)ee | (l)ee | (l)ee | | | | | | |

**Articulating** (speaking or singing clearly and distinctly) crisp, short consonants is important to performing "Leila" in the correct musical style. Many of the words begin with the consonants *l, s, m, t, n*.

• Sing the entire melodic pattern above, combining the vowel with each of the consonants.

---

# EXTENSION

## WARM-UP 4

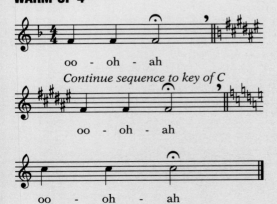

oo - oh - ah

*Continue sequence to key of C*

oo - oh - ah

oo - oh - ah

## MORE MUSIC TEACHING IDEAS

1. Have the students sing silently and follow conducting gestures, breathing at phrase endings of "Leila" to indicate their attention.
2. Have students play all of Part I or only the Group part on keyboard, bells, or recorder.

C major    Range I: C–C¹, II: F₁–C, solo: C–G  *Leila*    CD6:19, CD8:10

Piano Accompaniment on page PA 64

Folk Song from North Carolina

Lei - la, that's shoo my love, Lei - la, that's shoo my love.

*Second time only*

Lei - la, that's shoo     my     love, Lei - la, shoo my love.

*Solo*                                          *Group*

Turn me in a cir - cle now. Shoo, Lei - la, shoo my love,

Shoo,     Lei - la,     shoo my love.

*Solo*                                          *Group*

Turn me in a cir - cle now. Shoo, Lei - la, shoo my love.

Shoo,     Lei - la,     shoo my love.

*Coda*
*Solo*

Turn me in a cir - cle now,     In a cir - cle.     cir - cle now.

I

Lei - la, that's shoo my love, Lei - la, that's shoo my love.  shoo my love.

II

Lei - la, that's shoo     my     love, Lei - la, shoo my love.  shoo my love.

**THINK IT THROUGH:** Apply the principles of good articulation to the song. Appraise your performance. Suggest ways to achieve consistent vowel sounds.

# MUSIC LIBRARY

• Sing the song with all parts with and without accompaniment. (Have different combinations of students sing the song with various numbers of students on a part.)
• Discuss *Think It Through*.

## APPRAISAL

The students should be able to:
1. Sing "Leila," an American folk song from North Carolina in three parts.
2. Articulate the lyrics of "Leila."

321

# MUSIC LIBRARY

**Focus: Singing Chords**

### Objectives
To hear and sing the tonic chord
To develop independent part singing

### Materials
Recordings: "Eagle"
"Eagle" (performance mix)
Bells, keyboard, Autoharp, guitar, pitched instruments (optional)

## TEACHING THE LESSON

**Teach "Eagle."** Have the students:
• Read the page.
• Practice singing the G-major chord in root position and in first and second inversion. (Invite groups of three students to sing the chord. You may wish to do this also with the D7 chord.)
• Listen to the canon, focusing on the sound of the G-major chord in the voices.
• Read the rhythm of the song.
• Sing the melody.
• Sing the song as a three-part canon.
• Sing the canon in slow motion without accompaniment to hear the chords.
• Discuss the meaning of *andantino* and *legato*. (*Andantino* is a tempo that is a little faster than a moderate walking speed. *Legato* means smooth and connected.)

## APPRAISAL

The students should be able to:
1. Hear and sing the tonic chord in G major.
2. Sing a three-part canon with independence.

---

A round is an easy way to sing in harmony. Notice the pitch below each entrance number. These pitches—G, B, D—form a chord and sound good when sung together. The music for this round was composed by Moritz Hauptmann who lived from 1792 to 1868.

CD6:20, CD8:11                    Key: G major     Range D–D¹

Piano Accompaniment on page PA 61

### Eagle

Music by Moritz Hauptmann (adapted)
Words by MMH

Wheel - ing and turn - ing, an ea - gle in flight Will fly a - way, will fly a - way, will soar out of sight.

### PREPARING *to Sing* "Jane, Jane"

"Jane, Jane" is an African American ring game from Mississippi. It is sometimes known as "Three Mockingbirds."

"Jane, Jane" is in **call-and-response** form. The call section, which can be done as a solo, is followed by the response, which is often a word or phrase repeated with the same or similar music. The response in this song is *Jane, Jane*.

• Practice each part of the response.

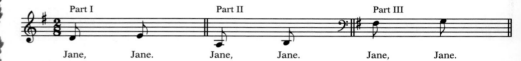

Jane,    Jane.    Jane,    Jane.    Jane,    Jane.

• Practice singing the response with all parts together.

**THINK IT THROUGH:** Describe the vocal qualities that you think are appropriate for this style of song. Decide which qualities you are able to use in your performance.

322

## MORE MUSIC TEACHING IDEAS

1. Have the students accompany the song using G and D7 chords on bells, keyboard, guitar, or Autoharp. Encourage the students to play by ear and to improvise an appropriate rhythm.
2. Have the students play the melody on pitched instruments. Encourage the students to play by ear.

**Piano Accompaniment on page PA 323**

## Jane, Jane

African American Game Song

**Key: E minor**   **Ranges I: D–B, II: A₁–B₁, III: F♯₁–G₁**

323

---

# MUSIC LIBRARY

**Focus: Call and Response**

### Objectives
To develop vocal independence
To sing a call-and-response song

### Materials
Recordings: "Jane, Jane"
    "Jane, Jane" (performance mix)
Pitched instruments (optional)

## TEACHING THE LESSON

**Teach "Jane, Jane."** Have the students:

• Read about "Jane, Jane" on page 322.
• Sing Warm-up 5, focusing on the rhythm pattern and rhythmic singing. (See below.)
• Listen to the song, focusing on the call and response.
• Find the rhythm in the song that sounds the most like the Warm-up 5. (measures 30–31)
• Sing the melody.
• Learn the three-part harmony response. (Have all students learn all parts.)
• Sing the song with all parts.
• Take turns singing the call as a solo.
• Identify the key. (E minor)
• Identify the meter. (2/8 Explain that this means there are two beats in the measure and the eighth note lasts for one beat.)
• Discuss *Think It Through*.
• Sing the song again using the vocal qualities discussed.

## APPRAISAL

The students should be able to:
1. Sing one of three parts with independence.
2. Sing the call and response to "Jane, Jane."

---

## WARM-UP 5

koo - koo - koo - koo - koo

*Continue sequence to key of E minor*

koo-koo-koo-koo-koo

koo - koo - koo - koo - koo

## MORE MUSIC TEACHING IDEAS

1. Have the students create other verses using the same pattern as the song.
2. Have the students play the response on pitched instruments.

# MUSIC LIBRARY

**Focus: Part Singing**

**Objectives**
To sing in three parts

**Materials**
Recordings: "Vive L'amour"
"Vive L'amour"
(performance mix)

## TEACHING THE LESSON

**Teach "Vive L'amour."** Have the students:
• Read page 324 and locate the melody.
• Sing the melody of the song.
• Perform the rhythm of the exercise by tapping the eighth notes in the palm of the hand, clapping the quarter note, and pat-sliding the dotted quarter note tied to the eighth.
• Sing each vocal part of the exercise with pitch syllables, first by itself and then all together.
• Locate the exercise in the song and sing those measures using the words. (the response—measures 3–4 and 7–8)
• Clap the rhythm of the song.
• Listen to the song, singing the response.
• Describe what happens in measures 1–2 and 5–6. (Voices sing the same thing in octaves.)
• Sing the first verse.

**PREPARING** *to Sing "Vive L'amour"*

"Vive L'amour" had its beginning long ago as a college song. The melody in this arrangement moves from part to part. Look at the music and find the melody. Parts I and III have the melody in measures 1 and 2. Part I has the melody in measures 3 and 4. Part II has the melody in measures 9-12, and Part I has it again in the measures 13-16. Can you sing the melody from this information?

• Practice singing the response using pitch syllables.

• Practice singing the parts to the whole song.

Key: B♭ major     Ranges I: D—E♭¹, II: C—E♭, III: D₁—C

### Vive L'amour

Piano Accompaniment on page PA 68

College Song

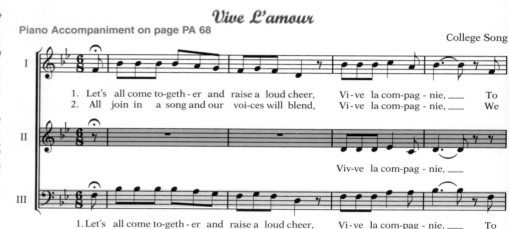

324

# EXTENSION

## MORE MUSIC TEACHING IDEAS

Have the students sing the whole song with pitch syllables or letter names.

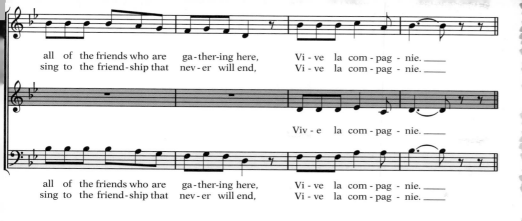

all of the friends who are ga-ther-ing here, Vi - ve la com-pag - nie. _____
sing to the friend-ship that nev-er will end, Vi - ve la com-pag - nie. _____

Viv - e la com-pag - nie. _____

all of the friends who are ga-ther-ing here, Vi - ve la com-pag - nie. _____
sing to the friend-ship that nev-er will end, Vi - ve la com-pag - nie. _____

*Refrain*

Vi - ve l'a - mour, l'a - mour, oh,

Vi - ve la, vi - ve la, vi - ve l'a-mour, Vi - ve la, vi - ve la, vi - ve l'a-mour,

Vi - ve la, vi - ve la, vi - ve l'a-mour, Vi - ve la, vi - ve la, vi - ve l'a-mour,

*ad lib. ending*

Vi - ve l'a-mour, vi - ve l'a mour, vi - ve la com-pag - nie! _____

*ad lib. ending*

Vi - ve l'a-mour, vi - ve l'a mour, vi - ve la com-pag - nie! _____

*ad lib. ending*

Vi - ve l'a-mour, vi - ve l'a mour, vi - ve la com-pag - nie! _____

**THINK IT THROUGH:** Recommend ways the group can maintain the continuity of the melody as it moves from part to part. Assess your performance for the clarity of the melody.

325

# MUSIC LIBRARY

- Listen to the song again.
- Determine the form of the song. (verse and refrain or AB)
- Notice that there are two parts in the treble clef and one part in the bass clef.
- Practice singing each part alone and in combination. (Assign students to each part. Part I: male and female high trebles; Part II: low trebles or cambiatas; Part III: changed voices. Optional baritone notes may be added.)
- Find the fermata and explain its meaning. (The fermata is on the first note and in measure 14.)
- Sing the song with all parts with and without accompaniment. (Have both boys and girls sing measures 1–2 and 5–6 as solos or have small ensembles perform the song to develop independent singing.)
- Discuss how well they maintained vocal parts, balanced parts, and sang accurate pitches.
- Discuss *Think It Through*.

## APPRAISAL

The students should be able to sing "Viva L'amour" in three parts.

# MUSIC LIBRARY

**Focus: Legato Singing**

## Objectives
To develop breath management for legato singing
To perform rounds in minor

## Materials
Recordings: "Wind and Snow"
"Wind and Snow" (performance mix)
"Circles"
"Circles" (performance mix)
Percussion, synthesizer, pitched instruments (optional)

## TEACHING THE LESSON

**1. Introduce "Wind and Snow."** Have the students:
• Read the page, practice the C-minor scale, and sing the exercises.
• Listen to "Wind and Snow" to become familiar with its minor sound.
• Practice managing their breath. (See exercises below.)
• Use breath management to sing each syllable of the examples in a *legato* manner. Sing each example in four-beat, then eight-beat, then sixteen-beat phrases.
• Sing Warm-up 6 to develop breath support and expression. (See below. Tell students to feel the resistance and support for the tone as the "Sss" gives way to singing.)
• Listen to the song again, then sing the melody. (Changed voices might sing down an octave, cambiatas might sing only the words *wind and snow*, and sopranos might omit line 2.)
• Sing the melody, focusing on diction.
• Discuss *Think It Through*, then sing the melody following their choices.
• Sing the song as a three-part round.

**PREPARING** *to Sing "Wind and Snow"*

"Wind and Snow" is a three-part round built on the C-minor scale.

• Sing the C-minor scale and these major and minor examples.

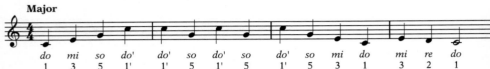

Managing your breath is important for singing "Wind and Snow." This control will help you to sing long phrases.

• Use breath management to sing each syllable of the major and minor examples above in a legato, or connected, manner. Try singing each example in four-beat, then eight-beat, phrases.

### Wind and Snow
Key: C minor    Range G♭–D

Piano Accompaniment on page PA 71
Words and Music by Linda Worsley

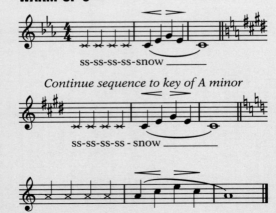

Win-ter, win-ter, ice on the win-dow, Wind and snow, cold and blow-ing,

wind and snow, Can-dles glow-ing, light-ing a win-ter hol-i-day.

Come out of the wind and snow, By the warm fire_____ come and stay.

**THINK IT THROUGH:** Suggest places in the song to breathe. Explain your choices.

326

# EXTENSION

## VOCAL DEVELOPMENT
### Breath Management

| INHALE | EXHALE ON "sss" |
|--------|-----------------|
| 4 counts | 4 counts, then 8, 16, and 32 counts |
| 2 counts | 4 counts, then 8, 16, and 32 counts |
| 1 count | 4 counts, then 8, 16, and 32 counts |

Explain that the control gained by managing their breath will help them to sing long phrases.

## WARM-UP 6

ss-ss-ss-ss-ss-snow _____

*Continue sequence to key of A minor*

ss-ss-ss-ss - snow _____

ss - ss - ss - ss - snow _____

## MORE MUSIC TEACHING IDEAS

1. Have the students determine the range of the "Wind and Snow." (wide range: low G to high D)
2. Have the students choose percussion, synthesizer, vocal, or found sounds to create winter sounds to accompany "Wind and Snow."
3. Have the students play the melody on pitched instruments.
4. Have the students find the repeated musical motive that occurs in each part. *(wind and snow)*
5. Have the students discuss if they achieved vocal balance in the round and work to improve the balance, if needed.

**PREPARING** *to Sing "Circles"*

"Circles" requires sustained, legato singing. Legato singing will highlight the continuous, circular theme of the lyrics.

• Sing this warm-up in the key of D minor and emphasize legato singing.

Sing le - ga - to, sing!
1  2  3  1  2  3  1  2  3  1

Smooth and con - nect - ed, Sing, oh, sing!
1  2  3  1  2  3  1  3  1

• Emphasize the feeling of ¾ meter by singing the count of each pitch in the warm-up. The first beat of each measure is slightly stressed. Notice the ties throughout the song.

Key: D minor     Range A₁ –D¹

*Circles*

Piano Accompaniment on page PA 76

Words and Music by Linda Worsley

I
Round and round_____ in a cir - cle I wan - der,

II
Rings and sat - el - lites_____ spin - ning by. Like a

III
Bright - ly shim - mer - ing wheel in the heav - en, I'm

IV
Turn - ing cir - cles_____ in the sky.

💡 **THINK IT THROUGH:** Assess your performance of the song. Propose ways to achieve a more legato sound.

---

# MUSIC LIBRARY

**2. Introduce "Circles."** Have students:
• Read page 327.
• Sing the legato exercise with words. Work to manage breath, focus vowels, create an even sound and a forward motion.
• Sing the legato exercise with numbers. Hold out the numbers for the duration of the pitch. Stress the first beat of each measure slightly.
• Identify the key signature of one flat as the key signature for D minor as well as for F major. (Remind students that the last note of a song often helps determine which key it is—in this case, it is D minor.)
• Listen to "Circles" and do a body-percussion pattern of clap-snap-snap to feel the ¾ meter.
• Find the ties. (starting in measures 1, 6, 14)
• Sing the melody with and without accompaniment. (Some students might wish to sing down an octave.)
• Determine where to take breaths.
• Sing the melody again, concentrating on breath management, phrasing, and good diction.
• Sing the song as a four-part round.
• Discuss *Think It Through*.
• Sing the round in small ensembles with and without accompaniment and discuss the balance and blend achieved.
• Listen to "Circles" and compare it to "Wind and Snow." (same: rounds, legato, minor, use many quarter notes, same composer; different: number of parts, length, meter, key)
• Discuss the style, tempo, and mood of each piece.

## APPRAISAL

The students should be able to:
1. Use proper breath management for legato singing.
2. Perform three-part and four-part rounds in minor.

---

# MORE MUSIC TEACHING IDEAS

Have the students play one of the lines of "Circles" as an ostinato or play the whole song on pitched instruments.

# MUSIC LIBRARY

**Focus: Countermelody/Descant**

## Objectives
To sing a melody, countermelody, and descant
To develop breath control
To sing expressively a folk song from South Carolina

### Materials
Recordings: "Oh, Watch the Stars"
"Oh, Watch the Stars" (performance mix)
Unpitched percussion, synthesizer (optional)

## TEACHING THE LESSON

**Teach "Oh, Watch the Stars."** Have the students:
• Read about the song and the eighth-note triplet.
• Find the triplets in the song. (on the words *see how they*)
• Find the multiple measures of rest and explain what the symbol means. (lines 1, 4, and 7; the number above the multiple-rest sign tells how many measures of silence there are, the voices rest while the instruments play)
• Listen to the song.
• Find the key change and tell the key the song started in and ended in. (measure 29; key of C, key of D)
• Discover how the arrangement of the song is organized. (melody alone, countermelody alone, then key change with the two parts sung together, descant added)
• Sing Parts I and II, then identify how the two parts are similar or different. (similar in style and rhythm, different in pitch)

# E X T E N S I O N

## MORE MUSIC TEACHING IDEAS

1. Have the students add shimmering "starry" sounds to the song using unpitched percussion, found sounds, or synthesizer sounds.
2. Have the students practice small ensemble work by singing the song as a trio.
3. Have the students discuss how the event of stars coming out might be shown in music, visual arts, poetry, or dance. Explore these ideas by creating their own song, art work, poetry, or dance on this theme.

Sing "Oh, Watch the Stars" expressively. Notice that the melody occurs first and is then followed by the countermelody. Later the countermelody joins the melody and a third part is added.

Notice the eighth-note triplet in the first measure on the words *see how they run.* An eighth-note triplet means there are three sounds within one quarter-note beat:

CD6:25, CD8:16     Key: C major, D major

Piano Accompaniment on page PA 72

Range I: C–D$^I$, II: A$_I$–F#, descant: D–D

*Oh, Watch the Stars*

South Carolina Folk Song

328

**THINK IT THROUGH:** Experiment with various tempos, dynamics, and ways to emphasize the words. Choose an expressive combination to use in your performance. Justify your choices.

329

# MUSIC LIBRARY

• Sing Parts I and II together. (Emphasize legato, focused vowels, and breath management.)
• Sing the two parts together in small ensembles or as a duet.
• Learn the descant and add it to the song. (Select a few treble voices for the descant.)
• Sing the three parts together.
• Discuss ways of make the music expressive. (for example, use dynamics to get louder as the melody goes up and softer as it goes down; sing in a legato manner)
• Discuss *Think It Through*, then try out their choices.
• Discuss whether the class achieved balance, good diction, legato, focused vowels, and breath management as they sang. Suggest improvements and sing the song again.

## APPRAISAL

The students should be able to:
1. Sing a melody, countermelody, and descant.
2. Sing a song using breath control.
3. Sing the folk song "Oh, Watch the Stars" with expression.

# MUSIC LIBRARY

**Focus: Combining Voices, Instruments, and Movement**

**Objectives**
To perform four-part choral music
To perform a processional step from Cameroon
To perform a percussion accompaniment

**Materials**
Recordings: "Oh, Come Sing a Song"
"Oh, Come Sing a Song" (performance mix)
Claves, calabash, double bells, congas; optional—African percussion or other percussion, mallet instruments, keyboards, MIDI equipment, sequencer

## TEACHING THE LESSON

**1. Introduce choral singing.** Have the students:
• Read and discuss the information regarding singing in a chorus. (Relate this information to singing experiences students have had and the expectations for choral groups they are in.)
• Discuss how choral singing is different from solo or small-ensemble singing. (In choral singing, singers need to watch conductor, blend and balance parts, and standardize diction.)
**2. Introduce "Oh, Come Sing a Song" and the processional step.** Have the students:
• Read about the song.
• Listen to the song.
• Practice the processional step and do it with the recording.
**3. Teach "Oh, Come Sing a Song."** Have the students:
• Learn each of the four melodies by rote. (Model parts as needed. Parts III and IV might be sung by cambiatas or changed voices. The parts are flexible and may be sung by various combinations of voices.)

# Choral Anthology

Singing in a chorus or other group provides an opportunity to develop excellent skills in diction, breath control, reading music, and other aspects of musicianship. As you acquire these skills, you can move on to more challenging material. This material may include more vocal parts, other languages, and different meters, dynamics, and styles.

**PREPARING** *to Sing "Oh, Come Sing a Song"*
"Oh, Come Sing a Song" is a processional melody from Cameroon, a country in West Africa. The original words were French, one of the official languages of that country. The procession was traditionally done on special Sundays.

• Perform this processional step as you listen to the song.

The processional step is done on the beat using this pattern:

Right foot (rest on left)
| | |
|---|---|
| Beat 1 | Out-tap |
| Beat 2 | In-tap |
| Beat 3 | Back-tap |
| Beat 4 | Step forward |

Repeat the pattern starting on the left foot.

• Add these percussion parts after you have learned the song. Follow the order shown.

Two measure introduction: claves
Add Vocal Part I and continue claves
Add Vocal Part II and calabash
Add Vocal Part III and bells
Add Vocal Part IV and congas
330    Repeat as appropriate.

---

## WARM-UP 7

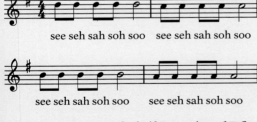

see seh sah soh soo    see seh sah soh soo

see seh sah soh soo    see seh sah soh soo

*Continue sequence by half step to key of E-flat*

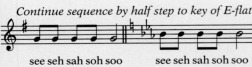

see seh sah soh soo    see seh sah soh soo

see seh sah soh soo    see seh sah soh soo

see seh sah soh soo    see seh sah soh soo

## MORE MUSIC TEACHING IDEAS

1. Have the students create and notate other percussion parts for "Oh, Come Sing a Song." Create a conversation between the instruments.
2. Have the students play the four vocal parts on mallet instruments or keyboards.
3. Have the students investigate African percussion sounds on MIDI equipment and create percussion ostinatos on sequencing equipment.
4. Have the students investigate other African percussion instruments and report their findings to the class.
5. Have the students create another processional step for "Oh, Come Sing a Song."
6. Have the students sing the song with pitch syllables, numbers, or letters.

## Oh, Come Sing a Song

Piano Accompaniment on page PA 77

Key: C major    Range I: C–A, II: E–C¹, III: G₁–F, IV: F–C¹

Traditional Cameroon Processional Melody
Words by M.J., Arranged by MMH

I: Oh, come sing a song, __ sing a joy-ful song ev-'ry-bod-y!

II: Oh, sing a song, sing a joy-ful song ev-'ry-bod-y!

III: Oh, come sing a song, __ sing a joy-ful song ev-'ry-bod-y!

IV: Oh, sing a song, _____ ev-'ry-bod-y!

Sing a joy-ful song __ ev-'ry-bod-y! Sing a joy-ful song __ ev-'ry-bod-y!

Sing a joy-ful song __ ev-'ry-bod-y! Sing a joy-ful song __ ev-'ry-bod-y!

Sing a joy-ful song __ ev-'ry-bod-y! Sing a joy-ful song __ ev-'ry-bod-y!

Sing, sing a song __ ev-'ry-bod-y! Sing, _____ ev-'ry-bod-y!

**THINK IT THROUGH:** What other percussion instruments or rhythm patterns might work well with this song? Why?

331

## MUSIC LIBRARY

- Sing Warm-Up 7 to help focus vowel sounds. (See below.)
- Read each of the four melodies, focusing on vowel sounds. (Students should focus on the shape of the mouth and the position of the tongue to help shape each vowel sound.)
- Sing each melody in sections, small groups, or as individuals, focusing on vowel sounds.
- Perform the melodies in different two-part and three-part combinations, then perform all four parts together.
- Perform all four melodies simultaneously as some students do the processional step. (Determine a pathway for the procession as well as whether students should move in single file or by twos or threes.)

**4. Teach the percussion parts.** Have the students:
- Practice the percussion parts and then perform them in different two-part and three-part combinations before performing all four parts together. (Emphasize maintaining a steady beat. Explain that a *calabash* is a type of gourd with rattles on the outside.)
- Follow the performance order of the song, layering instruments and voices until all are performing. Do the processional step as the music is performed.
- Discuss *Think It Through*.

### APPRAISAL

The students should be able to:
1. Perform "Oh, Come Sing a Song" in four parts.
2. Perform a processional step with "Oh, Come Sing a Song."
3. Perform a percussion accompaniment to a Cameroon processional.

### CURRICULM CONNECTION: SOCIAL STUDIES

Cameroon, a nation located in west-central Africa, is about the size of Colorado and Utah combined. The official languages are French and English. The several hundred ethnic groups living in Cameroon form two main groups. To the north are the Sudanic peoples, who are predominantly semi-nomadic herders. To the south and west are the Bantu peoples, who are mostly farmers and businessmen. The economy is based on agriculture. Cassava (a bushy shrub with edible roots, from which tapioca is made); grain—corn, millet, sorghum; fruit—banana and plantain; and taro (the tuber of which is eaten like a potato) are the main food crops.

### CURRICULUM CONNECTION: ART

The African thumb piano, also known as the sanza, kalimba, or mbira, is often played for relaxation and recreation.
A thumb piano can be made using the following materials:
6" × 6" block of 3/4" thick wood
6" cross stick, wide enough to insert screws
1/4" dowel or 2 craft sticks
8 craft sticks
3 screws (screwdriver)
With the screws, loosely attach the cross stick about 1 1/2" down the block of wood. Place the craft sticks in parallel lines under the cross stick. Tighten the screws so that the cross stick almost touches the craft sticks. Push the dowel under the craft sticks as far toward the cross stick as it will

go. Play the thumb piano by plucking the craft-stick prongs with the thumbs. Tune it by sliding the craft sticks forward or backward. Create a thumb piano accompaniment to "Oh, Come Sing a Song."

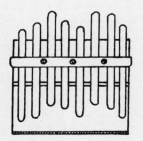

## MUSIC LIBRARY

**Focus: Minor**

**Objectives**
To sing a two-part song in minor
To identify accidentals, slurs, ties, fermata

**Materials**
Recordings:   "Bashana Haba-a"
"Pronunciation:
'Bashana Haba-a'"
"Bashana Haba-a"
(performance mix)

### TEACHING THE LESSON

**1. Introduce Warm-up 8.** Have the students:
• Read about "Bashana Haba-a."
• Perform Warm-Up 8 to help develop vowel focus and to produce a unified vocal tone quality. (See below.)
**2 Introduce minor.** Have the students:
• Read about minor.
• Sing the A♭-major scale beginning on *do* (1) and the relative F-minor scale beginning on *la* (6). Discuss the difference in sound between major and minor.
• Sing Warm-up 8 in major and minor, emphasizing the difference in sound.
**3. Establish the key of F minor for "Bashana Haba-a."** Have the students:
• Sing the two-measure pattern to establish the tonal center for F minor.
• Sing the third exercise (two phrases from "Bashana Haba-a") using pitch syllables or numbers.
• Find the phrases in the song that are used in the third exercise. (Part I, measures 8–10 and 16–18; Part II, measures 10–13 and 18–21)
**4. Introduce "Bashana Haba-a."** Have the students:
• Find the repeat signs and endings in the song. (in the last two lines)

---

The melody of "Bashana Haba-a" was written in 1969 by Nurit Hirsh, a songwriter who has lived in the United States and Israel. The song is about hope and looking forward to good things in the year to come.

**CD7:2–3, CD8:**

**PREPARING** *to Sing "Bashana Haba-a"*
"Bashana Haba-a" uses the pitches from a minor scale as well as a few altered pitches. A minor scale uses the same scale tones as the major scale it is related to. The difference is the scale tone, or tonal center, on which the scale begins. In a major scale, *do* is the tonal center. The related minor scale begins on the tonal center of *la*.

• Sing the A♭-major scale. Then sing the F-minor scale. Listen carefully to the difference.

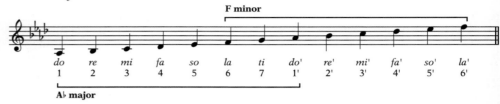

• Sing this pattern to help clarify the F-minor tonal center.

• Sing these phrases from "Bashana Haba-a." This song is in the key of F minor.

Key: F minor

Range I: C–D♭¹, II: D♭–B♭

*Bashana Haba-a*

Piano Accompaniment on page PA 78

Music by Nurit Hirsh
Words by Ehud Manor
Arranged by V. Pasternak

---

## E X T E N S I O N

### WARM-UP 8

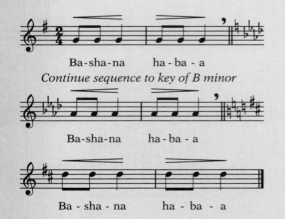

Ba-sha-na    ha-ba-a
*Continue sequence to key of B minor*

Ba-sha-na    ha-ba-a

Ba-sha-na    ha-ba-a

### TRANSLATION

A loose translation of the song follows:
In the year to come, as I sit on my porch and count the birds flying around,
I will see children playing;
running between houses and in the fields.
You will see, you will see how good it will be in the year to come.

### PRONUNCIATION

Bashana haba-a
bä-shä-nä hä-bä-ä

néshév al hamir peset
ne-shev al hä-mēr peh-set

v'nis por tsiporim nod'dot
vih-nēs poor tsē-po-rēm no-dih-dot

y'ladim b'chuf sha y'sachaku
yih-lä-dēm bih-hhuf-shä yih-sä-hhä-kōō

to feset bén habayit l'vén hasadot
to fe-set ben hä-bä-yēt lih-vehn hä-sä-dot

od tire kama tov yiye
o tēr-ā kä-mä tov yih-yeh

shév al ha- mir- pe- set v' nis põr tsi- po-
ba- sha- na ha- ba- a ba- sha- na

rim nõ- d'- dot _____ y'- la- dim b'- chuf-
ha- ba- a _____ ba- sha- na

sha y'- sa- cha- ku to- fe- set bén ha-
ha- ba- a ba- sha- na ha- ba- a

ba- yit l'- vén ha- sa- dõt _____ õd tir-
ba- sha- na ha- ba- a _____ õd tir-

e õd tir- e ka- ma tõv yi- ye ba- sha- na ba- sha-
e õd tir- e ka- ma tõv yi- ye ba- sha- na ba- sha-

na ha- ba- a õd tir- na ha- ba- a.
na ha- ba- a õd tir- na ha- ba- a.

💡 **THINK IT THROUGH:** What aspects of your perfomance were successful? Why? How might you improve diction and breath management?

333

# MUSIC LIBRARY

- Listen to "Bashana Haba-a" and determine which part sings the melody. (Part I sings the melody.)
- Find the fermata and explain its meaning. (The fermata is on the last note. The note is lengthened.)
- Find ties and slurs and explain the difference. (A *tie* creates a longer sound by connecting two notes of the same pitch; a *slur* smoothly connects different pitches.)

**5. Teach "Bashana Haba-a."** Have the students:

- Locate the accidentals and explain their meaning. (The natural sign applied to a flatted note removes the flat, raising the pitch a half step.)
- Sing the melody (Part I) using the syllable *loo*. (Emphasize an even quality of sound throughout the vocal range and sustained singing on the breath.)
- Sing Part II in the same manner.
- Sing Parts I and II together with and without the recording using the syllable *loo*. (Emphasize part singing and even tone quality.)
- Listen to "Pronunciation: 'Bashana Haba-a.'"
- Practice speaking, then singing the Hebrew words. (See *Pronunciation* below.)
- Sing the song in Hebrew, in two parts.
- Sing again in small groups and/or duets.
- Sing the song with the accompaniment. (Emphasize an even tone, balance, two-part singing, diction, and posture.)
- Discuss *Think It Through*.

## APPRAISAL

The students should be able to:

1. Sing "Bashana Haba-a," a two-part song in minor.
2. Identify and locate the accidentals, slurs, ties, and fermata in "Bashana Haba-a."

## MORE MUSIC TEACHING IDEAS

1. Have the students silently sing "Bashana Haba-a," following conducting gestures. Students should breathe at the ends of phrases to show that they are keeping their place.
2. Discuss and describe ways to show expression in "Bashana Haba-a" and try them out.
3. Have the students create an eight-measure melody in minor in $\frac{2}{4}$ using eighth notes, quarter notes, half notes, and rests. The melody should begin and end on *la*. Invent or choose a method of notation and notate the melody. Teach the method of notation to another student and have that student read the melody.

# MUSIC LIBRARY

**Focus: Rhythm**

## Objectives

To read eighth notes, quarter notes, half notes, and eighth rests

To sing expressively by observing tempo and dynamic markings

## Materials

Recordings: "After the Rain"
"After the Rain"
(performance mix)

## TEACHING THE LESSON

**1. Introduce rhythmic patterns.** Have the students:

• Read and perform each of the rhythmic patterns on page 334. (Emphasize independence, rhythmic accuracy, and maintaining a steady beat.)

• Read and perform the rhythmic pattern of each line of the two-part example, using the appropriate motions.

• Form two groups and perform the two-part example.

---

**PREPARING** *to Sing "After the Rain"*

These exercises will help you prepare the rhythm of "After the Rain."

• Count each beat aloud as you clap each quarter note.

• Count each beat aloud. Clap each quarter note and use a pat-slide motion for the half notes.

• Count each beat aloud. Use a pat-slide motion for the half notes and tap the eighth notes on the palm of your hand.

• Make a palms-up gesture for the eighth rests in the following example, using the same gestures as before for the notes.

"After the Rain" has many repeated rhythmic patterns, including some from the example above.

• Perform each line of the following example separately. Then combine the two lines.

334

---

E X T E N S I O N

## MORE MUSIC TEACHING IDEAS

1. Have the students sing "After the Rain" silently and follow conducting gestures, breathing at the ends of phrases to indicate their attention.

2. Determine the keys in "After the Rain." (C major and D major)

3. Have the students compose a short piece based on sounds found in nature (such as the sound of gentle rain, a thunderstorm, or a waterfall, or the sounds of bird calls) using nontraditional instrumentation, found sounds, or electronic media. Give the piece a descriptive title and perform the piece for the class. Student might notate the piece using traditional or nontraditional notation.

## CURRICULUM CONNECTION: ART

Have the students compare examples of artistic expression dealing with similar subject matter, such as rain. For example, "After the Rain," the painting *Flood* on page 199, storms represented in Beethoven's Sixth Symphony, Rossini's *William Tell* Overture, and Grofé's *Grand Canyon* Suite.

Have the students create a work of art based on some aspect of weather. This work might take the form of music, visual arts, dance, poetry, drama, or a combination of the arts. Analyze, describe, and interpret how students' works conveyed the images or emotions of the subject.

## After the Rain

**Piano Accompaniment on page PA 81**

Words and music by Allan Robert Petker

Af-ter the rain, __ af-ter the rain, __ af-ter the rain, _____ The streets are

washed, the path is clear, what was un - seen _____ can now ap - pear. What was un -

heard _____ now all will hear, _____ af-ter the rain, af - ter the rain. Af - ter the

rain, af - ter the rain, af - ter the rain, af-ter the rain. Af-ter the
rain, _____ rain, _____ rain, _____ Af-ter the

rain, _____ rain, _____ rain, _____ af-ter the rain.
rain, af-ter the rain, af-ter the rain, af-ter the rain.

Copyright © 1989 by Hinshaw Music, Inc.
Used by permission

**Key: C major, D major**   **Range I: B♭–E♭, II:A♭–C'**

335

## MUSIC LIBRARY

**2. Introduce "After the Rain."** Have the students:
• Examine the score and locate the rhythms that they performed in the two-part example. (Measures 32–36 are the same; variations appear elsewhere.)
• Follow the score and listen to "After the Rain" to determine which part sings the melody. (The melody moves between the parts.)
• Listen to the song while following Part I. (Call attention to the *unison* and *divisi* areas as well as the multiple-measure rests.)
• Listen to the song while following Part II.
• Determine the form. (introduction, three verses, coda)

# MUSIC LIBRARY

**3. Teach "After the Rain."** Have the students:
- Practice singing Parts I and II, reading as much as possible.
- Discuss places to breathe. (during the rests, after punctuation marks)
- Find the dynamic markings and discuss their meaning. (*p*, *pp*, *mf*, *mp*, cresc., decresc.)
- Find all of the tempo markings and discuss their meaning. (*Andante*—walking speed, *rit.*, *a tempo*, fermata, *rubato*—flexible tempo)
- Sing the parts separately and then together, following the dynamics and tempos in the score. (Put together the parts of each verse slowly, emphasizing the accurate reading of rhythms.)
- Sing each part individually and in small groups.
- Learn the optional part on the next to the last line.
- Review the meaning of *accidental* and find the accidentals in the song.
- Discuss *Think It Through*.
- Sing the song, expressing the mood of the song. (Emphasize an even sound and balance.)

336

**THINK IT THROUGH:** What do you like best after it rains? Which phrases in the song are most like your thoughts? What musical characteristics does the composer use to relate to the idea of falling rain? How can you express the mood of the song?

337

# MUSIC LIBRARY

## APPRAISAL

The students should be able to:
1. Read the rhythms in "After the Rain."
2. Sing "After the Rain" expressively, observing the tempo and dynamic markings.

# MUSIC LIBRARY

**Focus:** $\frac{6}{8}$ Rhythms

## Objectives
To read rhythms in $\frac{6}{8}$ meter
To perform partner songs

## Materials
Recordings: "Night of Stars/Silent Night"
"Night of Stars/Silent Night"
(performance mix)
Autoharp, guitar, keyboard, or bells
(optional)

## TEACHING THE LESSON

**1. Introduce "Silent Night."** Have the students:
• Sing "Silent Night," following the score. (Encourage sustained breath management throughout each vocal line. Emphasize support for high and low tones in the vocal range.)

**2. Introduce partner songs.** Have the students:
• Read about the songs.
• Identify the part in "Night of Stars/Silent Night" that is the partner song to "Silent Night." (Part I)
• Compare and contrast the notation of the two songs. (Part I contains more eighth rests and is a little longer than Part II. Part II has more dotted rhythms and slurs. The melodies contrast.)
• Define and find the first, second, and third endings.

**3. Introduce $\frac{6}{8}$ rhythms.** Have the students:
• Read about note values and $\frac{6}{8}$ meter.
• Clap rhythm lines 1 and 2. (Emphasize rhythmic accuracy.)
• Speak the words and clap the rhythmic pattern from "Night of Stars."
• Find this pattern in the song. (Part I—measures 15–20 and 15, 24–28)

"Night of Stars/Silent Night" are partner songs. Partner songs are songs that can be sung at the same time to create harmony. The composer combined her melody "Night of Stars" with the famous Christmas carol "Silent Night." "Silent Night" was originally in German and titled "Stille Nacht, Heilige Nacht." It was written on Christmas Eve in 1818 by Franz Gruber, an Austrian organist and composer, and Josef Mohr, a clergyman.

**PREPARING** *to Sing "Night of Stars/Silent Night"*
"Night of Stars" uses various combinations of quarter notes and eighth notes. It also uses dotted quarter notes and dotted half notes.
In $\frac{6}{8}$ meter

• Clap these rhythms to prepare for reading "Night of Stars."

• Clap this rhythm as you say the words. Then find the pattern in "Night of Stars."

Hope and love and peace. Night of stars, night of peace, Night of hope and love and peace.

"Silent Night" uses another dotted pattern:
This dotted eighth-sixteenth-eighth pattern starts with a long sound followed by a short sound. Find this pattern in the song.

**THINK IT THROUGH:** Determine where you successfully maintained a legato line. Suggest ways to express the beauty of the night through your performance.

---

# EXTENSION

## MORE MUSIC TEACHING IDEAS

1. Have the students name other partner songs they know (for example, the songs in "American Quodlibet").
2. Have the students accompany "Night of Stars/Silent Night" on Autoharp, guitar, keyboard, or bells (B♭, E♭, F7 chords) by ear. Create a strum rhythm to use. Transpose the accompaniment to other keys such as C or G.
3. Have some students hum (or *ooh*) a chordal accompaniment as others sing "Night of Stars/Silent Night." For the chords B♭, E♭, and F7, the top part might sing B♭ B♭ A, the middle part might sing F G F, and the bottom part might sing D E♭ C. This accompaniment can be done by ear or taught.

4. Explain that a *cadence* signals the end of a composition, section, or phrase. One of the most commonly used cadences is the chord progression V–I. Have the students find cadences in the song.

## BACKGROUND

The famous carol "Stille Nacht" ("Silent Night") was composed in 1818 in Obernorf, Germany. Father Josef Mohr (1792–1848) was serving as an assistant priest in the Church of St. Nicholas in Obernorf. Franz Grüber (1787–1863) was the village schoolmaster and church organist. When Mohr received word that the church organ was not functioning, he decided to write his own Christmas hymn in order to have music for the special

Christmas Eve Mass. Mohr took the words to Grüber, who set them to music. The hymn was completed in time for the service, and Mohr and Grüber sang the new hymn to the accompaniment of Grüber's guitar. It is reported that a few days later the organ repairman came to the church and obtained a copy of the song. Through his influence the carol spread throughout the entire Tyrol region. The song's popularity spread throughout Germany and Austria and around the world. The most widely sung translation from German to English, made by John F. Young, was first printed in 1863. The song has been translated into the major languages of the world and remains a favorite Christmas song.

## Night of Stars/Silent Night

CD7:5, CD8:20

Words and Music by Linda Worsley
Music by Franz Gruber
Words by Josef Mohr

ano Accompaniment on page PA 88

Key: B♭      Range I: C–D′, II: B♭′–E♭′

1., 3. Night of won-der, night of stars, one bright-er star a-

2., 3. Si - lent night, ho - ly night, All is calm,

bove. Lis - ten now to an - gels sing-ing. Hear the joy - ful

all is bright 'round yon vir - gin moth-er and child. Ho - ly in-fant so

mes - sage ring-ing: Peace, peace to all ___ man-kind, Hope and love and

ten - der and mild, Sleep in heav-en-ly peace, ___ Sleep ___ in heav-en-ly

peace. Night of stars, night of peace, Night of hope and love and

peace. peace. Night of stars, night of

peace. ___ peace. ___ Sleep in heav - en-ly

peace, Night of hope and love and peace. ___ Peace. ___

peace, ___ Sleep ___ in heav-en-ly peace. ___ Peace. ___

339

# MUSIC LIBRARY

- Read about the dotted eighth-sixteenth-eighth pattern ( ) and find examples in the song. (Part II—measures 5, 6, 9, 10, 11, 12, 13, 15, 25, and 27.)

**4. Teach "Night of Stars/Silent Night."** Have the students:

- Read and sing Part I and Part II, performing accurate dotted rhythms and unified vowel sounds. (Call attention to the multiple measures of rest. Encourage students to be aware of the shape of the mouth and the position of the tongue in shaping each vowel.)
- Perform Part I and Part II in sections, small groups, and as individuals. (Have all students experience both parts.)
- Look at the third ending and describe what happens. (Part I has the same notes as the first ending. Part II repeats the last phrase of the song. The song ends with a four-part chord.)
- Sing both parts together. (Add the four-part ending when students are ready. Either part may be sung by male and/or female voices.)
- Listen as part of the class sings the partner songs together. Then discuss how successful they were at singing parts, maintaining balance, sustaining focused vowels, and maintaining an even tone quality.
- Sing the songs, following you or a student conductor.
- Discuss *Think It Through* and sing the song incorporating their suggestions.

## APPRAISAL

The students should be able to:
1. Read and perform $\frac{6}{8}$ rhythmic patterns, including the dotted eighth-sixteenth-eighth pattern, in "Night of Stars/Silent Night."
2. Sing the partner songs "Night of Stars" and "Silent Night" together.

## CURRICULUM CONNECTION: LANGUAGE ARTS

You may wish to have the students sing "Silent Night" in German.

Stille Nacht! Heilige Nacht!
shti'le näcкнt hī'li-ge näкнt

Alles schläft, einsam wacht
äl'les shläft īn'säm väкнt

Nur das traute hochheilige Paar,
noor däs trou'te hōкн-hī'li-ge pär

Holder Knabe im lockigen Haar,
hôl'der knä'be im lok'ē-gen här

Schlaf in Himmlischer Ruh. (2 times)
shläf in him'lish-ər roo

## MORE MUSIC TEACHING IDEAS

Have the students evaluate the quality and effectiveness of their performance of "Night of Stars/Silent Night" by answering these questions.

1. Do facial expressions and musical expressions reflect the sentiment?
2. Diction through consonants conveys meaning. Articulation enables diction. Are the words intelligible when sung? Do they seem to flow naturally?
3. Is the intake of breath more audible than some of the notes or words?
4. Does the sound of the group project across the room or does the sound not carry well?
5. Is the ensemble precise? Does everyone work together closely?

# MUSIC LIBRARY

**Focus: Round**

## Objectives

To perform an extended round expressively with good articulation
To read ♩. ♪

## Materials

Recordings: "America, My Homeland"
"America, My Homeland"
(performance mix)
Bells, keyboard, percussion (optional)

## TEACHING THE LESSON

**Teach "America My Homeland."** Have the students:

• Read about the song.
• Read and clap the rhythm of the song, concentrating on accuracy of ♩. ♪
• Listen to the song and identify its form. (round)
• Sing the melody.
• Discuss where to breathe, and then sing the melody, breathing in those places. (Emphasize breath management and phrasing.)
• Notice that many words begin with consonants. Then practice saying and singing the words, using uniform and clear consonants.
• Find where the round parts begin and note similarities in the parts. (lines 1, 3, 5; same length and chords, similar rhythms)
• Sing the three-part round, with emphasis on shaping the melody and expressing the meaning of the lyrics.
• Discuss *Think It Through.*

## APPRAISAL

The students should be able to:

1. Sing "America, My Homeland" expressively with good articulation.
2. Read the rhythm, including ♩. ♪ in "America, My Homeland."

People all over the world express love for their country and homeland through song. The three-part round "America, My Homeland" describes the beauty of the United States.

CD7:6, CD8:21

Key: F major     Range C–D♭

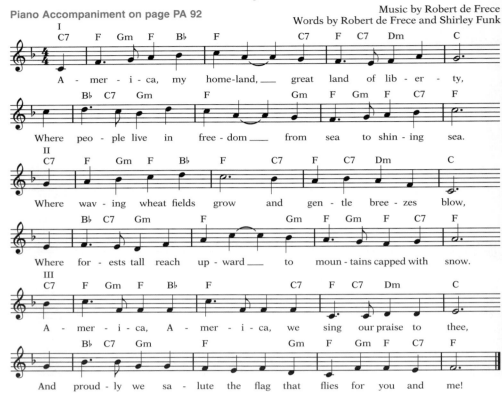

*America, My Homeland*

Piano Accompaniment on page PA 92

Music by Robert de Frece
Words by Robert de Frece and Shirley Funk

THINK IT THROUGH: What songs do you know from other countries that are patriotic or express love for homeland? Compare them with songs about the United States. What elements of the music and text are the same? Different?

340

---

# EXTENSION

## MORE MUSIC TEACHING IDEAS

1. Have the students play the chords or chord roots on bells or keyboards. This accompaniment can be simplified by playing only on the downbeats.
2. Have the students create percussion ostinatos to enhance the song.
3. Have the students identify the instruments in the recorded accompaniment. (brass)
4. Have the students sing the song using pitch syllables, numbers, or letters.
5. Have the students name and perform other rounds they know. (for example, "Row, Row, Row Your Boat" and "Are You Sleeping?")
6. Listen as small groups sing the round. Evaluate the use of breath to sing through

phrases and the part balance.
7. Have the students identify the key. (F major)

## VOCAL DEVELOPMENT

Confidence is a state of mind. Confidence appears to exude from those who know what to do and have an awareness of what they are doing. Discuss the effect of confidence in terms of its contribution to an effective choral performance. Singers can appear confident even when they are not. They can stand with correct singing posture and reflect the mood of the song by showing appropriate facial expression. Their eyes should focus on the conductor, or if there is no conductor, they can look just above the heads of the audience.

The singers should be proud of what

they or their group has learned to do. Compare individuals or small groups as they intentionally adopt a confident appearance or a sloppy, slouching, fearful, unfocused appearance as they sing.

## CURRICULUM CONNECTION: SOCIAL STUDIES

Compile a collection of songs that express a love for country. These might include national anthems, patriotic songs, and songs about certain countries. The songs might be gathered from songbooks and recordings or from relatives, neighbors, or the students themselves. The students might sing the songs, compare them, or use them as a springboard to find out more information about the song or the country.

The words to "Autumn Vesper" were written by Emily Brontë. Emily and her sisters, Charlotte and Anne, were novelists and poets. They lived on the lonely moors of Yorkshire, England. Emily is best known for her novel *Wuthering Heights*.

"Autumn Vesper" includes references to the moors. A *wold* is an upland area of open country or a hilly region; a *tell* is a hill or mound; a *dell* is a secluded hollow or small valley usually covered with trees or turf. *Vesper* refers to the evening.

The tempo changes in "Autumn Vesper." A *ritardando* means to slow down. A *tempo* means to return to the original tempo.

- Find the tempo changes in the song.

Key: D major    Range I: D–D¹, II: B₁–D¹, III: B₁–D¹

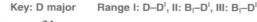

### Autumn Vesper

Piano Accompaniment on page PA 93

Music and additional words by
Audrey Snyder
Words by Emily Brontë

---

## MUSIC LIBRARY

**Focus: Expressive Singing**

### Objectives
To sing a part song expressively
To identify and observe dynamics, breath marks, fermatas, and tempo indications

### Materials
Recordings: "Autumn Vesper"
"Autumn Vesper"
(performance mix)
Copying Master C-2 Sight-Reading Patterns II (optional)

### TEACHING THE LESSON

**1. Introduce expressive singing.** Have the students:
- Read and discuss the information on "Autumn Vesper."
- Find the tempo markings in the song. (metronome marking at the beginning; *ritardando* in measures 2, 6, 8, 16, 24, 33, 37, 41, 42; *a tempo* in measures 2, 7, 10, 18, 27, 42)
- Find and define other markings in the score that indicate how to perform the song expressively. (Dynamics, breath marks, and fermatas occur. Remind students that breath marks look like large commas above the staff.)
- Read the lyrics. Then discuss and describe how to make them expressive.
- Read the lyrics aloud—exploring tempos, dynamics, fermatas, and inflections of words that contribute to an expressive performance.

---

## MORE MUSIC TEACHING IDEAS

Have the students read "Autumn Vesper" with pitch syllables, numbers, or letter names. (You may wish to use Copying Master C-2 for sight-reading patterns.)

## VOCAL DEVELOPMENT

Expressive singing means that the singer interprets the words with sounds to convey an idea to the audience. That idea—whether happiness, sadness, enthusiasm, or a patriotic spirit—is the heart of the song. Have the students read the lyrics and reflect on their meaning. Have them note the breath marks and breathe between musical phrases. Singers should take breaths as silently as possible.

# MUSIC LIBRARY

**2. Introduce "Autumn Vesper."** Have the students:

• Listen to "Autumn Vesper" and determine if the expressive ideas they explored are present.

• Perform Warm-up 9 to help emphasize breathing, legato singing, and unified vowels throughout the vocal range. (See below.)

**3. Teach "Autumn Vesper."** Have the students:

• Form three groups. (Male and female treble voices may be assigned randomly to Parts I, II, and III. Call attention to the *unison* and *divisi* parts. Part II is written in cue notes and is optional.)

• Identify the key of the song. (D major)

• Sing the D-major scale to establish the key.

• Read and sing their assigned part as they listen to measures 2–18 of the recording. (Emphasize singing unison sections with pitch accuracy, legato articulation, and choral blend.)

• Practice on each part separately, following the tempos, dynamics, and breath marks.

• Combine the parts. (Emphasize independent part singing, legato line, and vocal balance.)

• Perform measures 1–18 with different tempos, dynamic levels, and articulations (staccato, marcato, legato). Decide which choices best fit the lyrics.

• Sing measures 1–18 in small ensembles. (Emphasize expressiveness, vocal blend, and accuracy of part singing.)

• Read their assigned part as they listen to measures 19–27 of the recording.

• Practice each part separately, following the tempos, dynamics, and breath marks.

• Combine the parts. (Emphasize independent part singing, legato line, and balance.)

342

# EXTENSION

**WARM-UP 9**

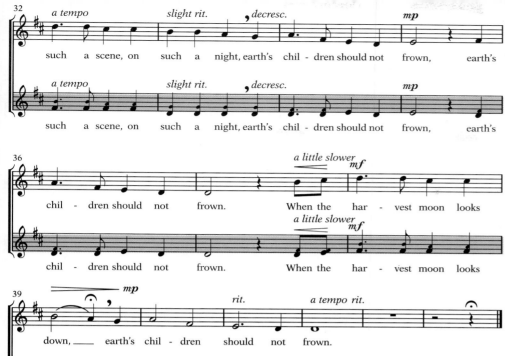

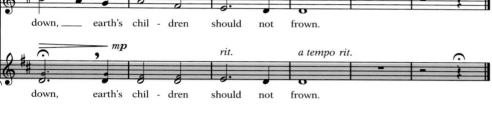

💡 **THINK IT THROUGH:** Assess how your performance reflects the tempo changes. How would the expression of the song be different if there were no tempo changes in this song?

## MUSIC LIBRARY

• Perform measures 19–27 with different tempos, dynamic levels, and articulations (staccato, marcato, legato). Decide which choices best fit the lyrics.
• Sing measures 19–27 in small ensembles.
• Compare measures 28–37 to the first part of the song. (They are similar.)
• Read "Autumn Vesper" all the way through.
• Practice each part separately in measures 28–37.
**4. Perform "Autumn Vesper."** Have the students:
• Sing the three parts together expressively, observing tempos, dynamics, breath marks, and fermatas. (Challenge the students to maintain an even tone quality, sustain vowel sounds, shape phrases, and balance vocal parts.)
• Discuss *Think It Through*.

### APPRAISAL

The students should be able to:
1. Sing "Autumn Vesper" expressively.
2. Identify and observe dynamics, breath marks, fermatas, and tempo indications.

# MUSIC LIBRARY

**Objectives**
To identify steps, skips, and leaps in treble and bass clefs
To identify syncopation

**Materials**
Recordings: "Ring the Bells"
"Ring the Bells"
(performance mix)
Bells such as hand bells, tone chimes, or resonator bells, claves (optional)

## TEACHING THE LESSON

**1. Introduce steps, skips, and leaps.**
Have the students:
• Read and discuss the information on steps, skips, and leaps.
• Sing examples 1–3, listening for the sound of steps, skips, and leaps.
• Sing up and down the D-major scale in example 4 using pitch syllables or numbers to establish the key and to hear steps.
• Sing example 5 using pitch syllables or numbers and identify the steps, skips, and leaps.
• Sing intervals created by pointing to different pitches on the scale. (Place the scale on the board and point, or have a student point, to the pitches.)
**2. Introduce "Ring the Bells."** Have the students:
• Read example 6 using pitch syllables or numbers. (Model the line and review pitches in the bass clef as needed.)
• Identify and sing the steps, skips, and leaps in example 6. (many steps, 1 leap, and 1 skip)
• Find example 6 in "Ring the Bells." (It is in Part III at letters C and E. Letters F and G are similar.)
• Read Part III as they listen to the recording. (Emphasize accuracy of pitch and rhythm, breathing, and sustained vowels.)

## PREPARING to Sing "Ring the Bells"
Pitches in melodies move by step, skip, or leap.

• Sing these exercises to experience steps, skips, and leaps.

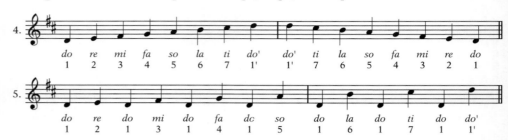

This pattern is found in "Ring the Bells." Sing it with pitch syllables. Does it contain steps? Skips? Leaps? Which are harder to sing with a good tone?

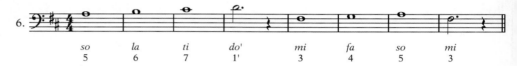

• Find the pattern above in "Ring the Bells." Which vocal part uses this pattern? baritone

• Play this part on chimes, hand bells, or resonator bells. Begin playing at rehearsal letters B, C, E, F, and G.

• Play this pattern on claves for 16 measures, starting at letter B. Then play it for 28 measures, starting at letter E.

---

# EXTENSION

## MORE MUSIC TEACHING IDEAS

1. Have the students compose and notate a two-measure or four-measure melody in D major comprised of only steps (or skips or leaps). Play or sing these melodies and discuss which were the easiest to perform. Discuss drawbacks or advantages of using only one kind of interval. Then have the students compose a melody using steps, skips, and leaps. Play the melodies and discuss how they differed from the melodies using a single interval.
2. Have the students identify the measures in "Ring the Bells" that are homophonic and polyphonic. (See page 19.)
3. Have the students exchange vocal parts to hear how the parts sound in different octaves. Discuss the resulting sounds. Did

the result sound better, just as good as, or worse than what was written?
4. Explain that a *sequence* is the repetition (in one part) of a short musical phrase at another pitch level, usually a step above or a step below. Have the students find the sequences in Part I, starting at letter F. Play the sequence on bells with the song.
5. Have the students take melodic dictation. Start with a two-measure or four-measure melody that moves stepwise and uses simple rhythms. Include other intervals and more complex rhythms when the students are ready.

**Ring the Bells**

CD7:8, CD8:23

Words by Jane Foster Knox
Music by Mark Wilson

**A** I
*mf*

All the bells of Christ-mas, _ Ring-ing loud and clear,

Sing their joy-ful tid-ings _ For ea-ger peo-ple to hear.

**B** I, & II
*mp*

Ring the bells _ so mer-ri-ly, _ Sound a car-ol to say,

*mf*

"Peace and joy _ to all the earth _ On this Christ-mas Day!" Oh,

**C** I, & II

Ring the bells _ so mer-ri-ly; _ Let their mu-sic re-lay.

Part III

Al - le - lu - ia!

Peace and joy _ to all the earth _ On this Christ-mas Day!

Al - le - lu - ia!

Key: D major    Range I: B₁–D¹, II: B₁–B, III: D₁–D

**MUSIC LIBRARY**

**3. Teach "Ring the Bells."** Have the students:
• Find examples of syncopation in the song. ( ♪♩♪; ♩. ♪♪; ♪♪♪; ♪♫♩ )
• Practice clapping the syncopated patterns.
• Listen to "Ring the Bells" and follow their assigned part. (Part I: trebles; Part II: trebles and/or cambiatas; Part III: changed voices and cambiatas as appropriate.)
• Sing their part softly with the recording. (Focus on accuracy of pitch and rhythm.)
• Practice Parts I, II, and III separately for the first verse (measures 1–29), emphasizing pitch and rhythmic accuracy. (Note when the parts are in unison.)
• Practice Parts I, II, and III separately for measures 50–69. (Call attention to where the parts are in unison.)
• Read the musical notation of the second verse (measures 30–49). (This section has familiar melodic patterns.)
• Sing the song in small ensembles, emphasizing pitch accuracy and confident part singing.

345

# MUSIC LIBRARY

**4. Perform "Ring the Bells."** Have the students:
- Sing the song with all three parts.
- Identify the dynamics. (*p, mp, f, mf* )
- Listen as small ensembles perform the song using the dynamics and then discuss the performances.
- Sing the song again, incorporating the suggestions.
- Practice the bell and claves parts.
- Discuss *Think It Through.*
- Sing the song in three parts with the instrumental parts.

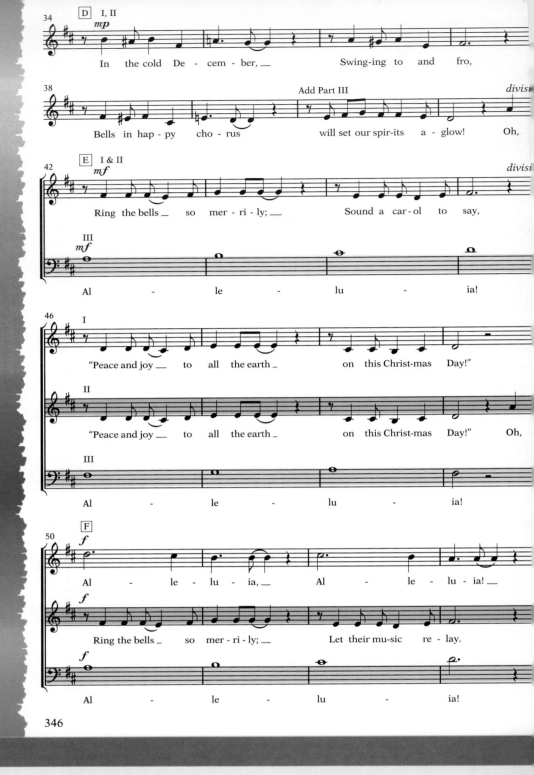

346

**THINK IT THROUGH:** How does the knowledge of steps, skips, and leaps help you to remember the pattern of the bell part?

347

## APPRAISAL

The students should be able to:
1. Identify and refine their skills in reading steps, skips, and leaps in treble and bass clefs.
2. Identify and read syncopation in "Ring the Bells."

# MUSIC LIBRARY

**Focus: Articulating Consonants**

## Objectives
To sing a canon with rhythmic precision
To articulate consonants clearly

## Materials
Recordings: "Morning Light"
"Morning Light"
(performance mix)
Bell tree, suspended cymbal, synthesizer, sequencer (optional)

## TEACHING THE LESSON

**1. Prepare to sing "Morning Light."**
Have the students:
• Read about the song.
• Read and discuss the information on consonants and on rhythmic precision.
• Identify which consonants are shaped by the tongue (*n, t, d, l, c* ) and which by the lips (*w, m, b, f, v*).
• Speak the lyrics that start with consonants, aiming for uniform and clear sounds and precise attacks. (*Now, we, to, the,* and so on)
• Read and perform the rhythm of the three examples with body percussion, by speaking, and by singing. (Review note values as needed. Emphasize steady beat, crisp articulation of consonants, and focused vowels. Model the examples as needed.)

The melody of "Morning Light" was written by Georg Philipp Telemann, a German composer who lived from 1681 to 1767. Telemann wrote in the baroque style, the same style that the composers Bach and Handel used.

### PREPARING *to Sing "Morning Light"*

Rhythmic precision is important when performing "Morning Light." By clearly articulating the consonants you can help make the rhythm precise. Use clear consonants, pure vowel sounds, and accurate rhythms to make the words of the song understandable and rhythmically precise.

The sound of a consonant may be shaped by the lips or the tongue. Say each of the following consonants and decide which are shaped by the tongue and which by the lips: *n, w, t, d, s, r, m, g, b, c, f, v, l.*

• Speak the words in "Morning Light" that start with consonants.

• Perform the rhythm of each of the following examples by patting the quarter notes, clapping the eighth notes, and tapping the sixteenth notes on the back of your hand.

1. Moon and stars have gone, and the hor - i - zon is bright. Our _ wor-ry and care,

2. Now we a-wak-en _ to the _ dawn-ing, _see the _ ris-ing of the morn - ing,

3. They van - ish in the splen-dor of the morn - ing light.

• Speak the words of the above examples in rhythm. Then sing the examples, using good diction.

• Learn the complete melody. Then sing the song as a three-part canon. Be sure the voices end together as written.

## MORE MUSIC TEACHING IDEAS

1. Have the students experiment with adding instrumental sounds to represent the morning light. (shimmering sounds, a bell tree, a suspended cymbal, or synthesizer sounds) Evaluate whether the instrument enhanced the song or not and suggest changes as needed.
2. Record the canon on a sequencer using appropriate baroque instrumental sounds such as violin, viola, cello, bass, recorder, flute, or oboe. Then change the instrumental sounds to contemporary tone colors such as various synth sounds, electric guitar, or saxophone. Discuss the musical effect and compare it to the baroque sounds. Suggest other tone color combinations and try them.

3. Have the students accompany the canon with the following chordal pattern: G G Am D7.
4. Have the students compose their own three-measure, three-part canon. The chordal pattern for each measure can be G G Am D7. Each part enters after one measure. The melody can be made up of chord tones as well as passing tones. Words might be added. Perform the canon by singing or playing.
5. Have the students compare the role and status of baroque musicians with those of present-day musicians. This comparison might be extended to other periods of music and to the musicians of various countries.

## BACKGROUND

The baroque period of music lasted approximately from 1600 to 1750. Many forms were developed during the baroque period including the opera, cantata, oratorio, fugue, concerto, overture, and dance suite. Basic concepts of baroque music included improvisation and ornamentation. The thoroughbass technique used in the baroque period led to a texture of melody and bass with improvised harmony between. The harmony was created from the special notational symbols in the bass part. Often the music had a steady tempo and the rhythm pushed the music on. Important composers during this time were J. S. Bach, G. P. Telemann, G. F. Handel, and A. Corelli.

## Morning Light

**Key: G major**    **Range C–E¹**

CD7:9, CD8:24

Music by Georg Philipp Telemann
Arr. M.J., Words by MMH

Piano Accompaniment on page PA 106

Now we a-wak-en — to the — dawn-ing, — see the — ris-ing of the morn-

ing, Moon and stars have gone, and the hor-i-zon is

bright. Our — wor-ry and care, the dark-est fears ____ of the night,

They fly a-way, they dis-ap-pear and all our cares are out of

⊕ *Part III to Coda*    ⊕ *Part II to Coda*    ⊕ *Part I to Coda*

sight. They van-ish in the splen-dor of the morn-ing light.

⊕ *Coda*

light. They dis-ap-pear in the

splen-dor of the morn-ing light.

sight. They van-ish in the splen-dor of the morn-ing

splen-dor ____ of morn-ing light.

They dis-ap-pear in ____ morn-ing light.

light. the morn-ing light.

🔆 **THINK IT THROUGH:** Which rhythms did you perform accurately?
Suggest ways to achieve more rhythmic precision.

349

## MUSIC LIBRARY

**2. Teach the melody of "Morning Light."** Have the students:
- Examine the score and determine the form. (three-part canon with coda)
- Sing up and down the G-major scale using pitch syllables or numbers to establish the key.
- Listen to "Morning Light." (Call attention to where each part moves to the coda.)
- Sing the melody of the canon. (Emphasize good diction and precise rhythms. Cambiatas may need to change octaves at times.)
- Perform the melody of the canon in sections, small ensembles, and individually.

**3. Teach "Morning Light" as a canon.** Have the students:
- Form three equal groups and softly sing their part as they listen to the song. (Assign a balance of girls and boys to each part.)
- Practice Parts I, II, and III of the coda.
- Sing the coda in three parts.
- Sing "Morning Light" as a two-part and then a three-part round.
- Perform the canon in small groups, then discuss the level of confidence demonstrated by the singers, the rhythmic accuracy, and the articulation and precision of consonants.

**4. Perform "Morning Light."** Have the students:
- Sing the song as a three-part canon with the coda.
- Discuss *Think It Through* and try out their suggestions.

### APPRAISAL

The students should be able to:
1. Sing "Morning Light" with rhythmic precision.
2. Articulate the consonants in "Morning Light" clearly.

## BIOGRAPHY

Georg Philipp Telemann (1681–1767) was a German composer of the baroque period. He taught himself music, learning to play violin and keyboard instruments. Telemann entered the University of Leipzig as a law student but became involved in music instead. He took the post of director of the Leipzig Opera. Later he was the concertmaster and then kapellmeister in Eisenach where he became a friend of J. S. Bach. When Telemann lived in Hamburg, he was music director for several churches there as well as for the Hamburg Opera. Telemann wrote a large quantity of both sacred and secular music including oratorios, cantatas, operas, concertos, sonatas, and overtures.

# MUSIC LIBRARY

**Focus:** $\frac{6}{8}$ rhythms

## Objectives
To read rhythms in $\frac{6}{8}$
To perform chanted sounds in a Japanese song
To perform a rhythmic ostinato
To identify and observe staccato and accent

## Materials
Recordings: "Jōban Tanko Bushi"
Pronunciation: "Jōban Tanko Bushi"
"Jōban Tanko Bushi" (performance mix)
Tight drums, woodblock, guitar, keyboard, bells or other melodic instruments (optional)

## TEACHING THE LESSON

**1. Introduce "Jōban Tanko Bushi."** Have the students:
• Read about the song.
• Count "1-2-3-4-5-6" in a repeated steady pattern, tapping beats 1 and 4 in the palm of their hand. (Use the same tempo as "Jōban Tanko Bushi.")
• Listen to "Jōban Tanko Bushi" as they tap and silently count the six beats in each measure. Describe what they heard. (chanting, singing, clapping, different quality of vocal and instrumental sounds)
• Listen again, focusing on the vocal rendition of the shamisen (*tō, tō*) and the high-pitched chant. (Have students identify the shamisen part by touching a finger to their chin and identify the chanting by touching their thumb and index finger together imitating a moving mouth.)

"Jōban Tanko Bushi" is a traditional work song of the miners of Ibaragi Prefecture in Japan. The words are in an old Ibaragi dialect as well as standard Japanese. They cheerfully invite you to visit the mine.

The piece starts with a rhythm ostinato. After the ostinato is established, a vocal rendition of the shamisen (three-stringed instrument) part occurs (*tō, tō...*). The sung melody enters at measure 17. Punctuating the melody is a high-pitched chant called *ka-ke-go-e* or "chipmunk chant." These words have no meaning but serve as an encouragement to the singers.

**PREPARING** *to Sing "Jōban Tanko Bushi"*

• Clap the following lines to develop your ability to perform the rhythm ostinato. Speak the numbers as you clap each rhythm.

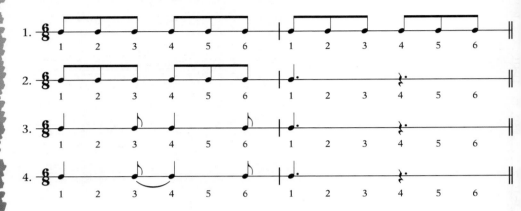

• Find the rhythm of line 4 in "Jōban Tanko Bushi."

"Jōban Tanko Bushi" includes both chanting and singing. The X-shaped notes indicate chanted sounds at the approximate pitch level shown.

• Practice each of these chanted parts.

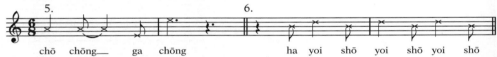

 **THINK IT THROUGH:** What other work songs do you know? How do their moods compare with the mood of "Jōban Tanko Bushi"?

350

---

## PRONUNCIATION

cho chong ga chong
chō chōng gä chōng

to
tō

ha yoi sho
hä yō ē shō

1. Ha asa mo hayo kara yo kantera sagete-nai hä ä-sä mō hä-yō kä-rä yō kän-teh-rä sä-geh-teh-näē

Konai mawari mo yo donto nushi no tame nai
kō-näē mä-wä-rē mō yō dōn-tō nōō-shē nō tä-meh näē

2. Ha ora ga tanko ni yo ichido wa gozare-nai hä ō-rä gä tän-kō nē yō ē-chē-dō wä gō-zä-reh-näē

Giri to ninjo no yo donto hana ga sakunai gē-rē tō nēn-jō nō yō dōn-tō hä-nä gä sä-kōō-näē

("r" has a short roll. The result is almost like a "d.")

## TRANSLATION

1. Every day from early morning I carry my lantern to this area to work hard for the mine owner.
2. I would like you to come, once, to visit the mine. We have a lot of warmth that blooms like a flower among us.

*Nai* and *yo* are similar to "ya know" in English.

## Jōban Tanko Bushi

Key: yō scale    Range I: B♭–D¹, II: B♭–D¹

*Pay attention to relative pitches as indicated.*

Japanese Folk Song
Arr. by Wendy B. Stuart

Chant: chō  chōng ___  ga  chōng          chō  chōng ___  ga  chōng

II

chō  chōng ___  ga  chōng          chō  chōng ___  ga  chōng

*Clap ostinato throughout by Part II or both parts.*

tō  tō  tō  tō  tō  tō  tō  tō  tō  tō  tō  tō  tō  tō  tō  tō

*Clap and/or percussion such as tight drums and/or woodblocks throughout*

*divisi*

tō  tō  tō  tō  tō  tō  tō  tō  tō  tō  tō

I

1. ha _____ a - sa  mo
2. ha _____ o - ra  ga

II

tō  tō  tō  tō  tō  1. ha _____ a - sa  mo
2. ha _____ o - ra  ga

ha - yo ka - ra  yo _____ ka - n - te - ra _____ sa - ge - te
ta - n - ko ___ ni  yo _____ i - chi - do  wa _____ go - za - re

ha - yo ka - ra  yo _____ ka - n - te - ra
ta - n - ko ___ ni  yo _____ i - chi - do  wa _____

351

# MUSIC LIBRARY

**2. Teach the ostinato.** Have the students:
• Clap the rhythms of examples 1–4 as they speak the numbers. (You may wish to review note values in ⁶⁄₈ at this time.)
• Perform each rhythm in sections, small groups, or individually.
• Examine the score and identify which rhythm example is the clapped ostinato. (It is Rhythm 4, beginning in measure 5.)
• Listen to the song and perform the ostinato by clapping or playing woodblocks and/or tight drums.

**3. Teach the chanting parts.** Have the students:
• Read and speak chant examples 5 and 6 using the syllable *tah*.
• Describe pitch changes in the examples. (Example 1 starts at a medium pitch, then goes from low to high. Example 2 alternates between a lower pitch and higher pitch.)
• Speak the chant examples, emphasizing pitch changes. (Model the examples as needed.)
• Listen to "Pronunciation: 'Jōban Tanko Bushi.'"
• Practice the pronunciation for the words in these two examples.
• Listen and perform the chanted parts with the recording.

## BACKGROUND

Japan is, after the United States, the world's largest market for recorded music. The Japanese like all kinds of rock and contemporary popular music, as well as world music and Japanese music.

"Jōban Tanko Bushi" is a *minyō*. Minyō is a centuries old, highly conservative style of Japanese folk song that remains popular today. Traditional minyō instruments include the *shamisen* (similar to a three-stringed banjo), the *shakuhachi* (bamboo flute), and *taiko* (huge barrel drum). *Ka-ke-go-e* ("chipmunk chant") parts are typical in Japanese folk music.

"Jōban Tanko Bushi" is from the Ibaragi Prefecture, northeast of Tokyo. Mining is not an important economic activity for Japan. Its mineral resources are sparse except for limestone and bituminous coal. Almost all other ores are imported.

### MORE MUSIC TEACHING IDEAS

1. Have the students play the shamisen part (*tō, tō*) on guitar or electronic keyboard set for a shamisen or other plucked-string sound.
2. Perform "Jōban Tanko Bushi" in small ensembles. Discuss and make suggestions for improvement and refinement.
3. Have the students create a new two-measure ostinato to accompany "Jōban Tanko Bushi."
4. Have the students create and perform an 8-measure or 16-measure melody in ⁶⁄₈ using the pitches of "Jōban Tanko Bushi."

The pitches are G B♭ C D F. The tonal center is G. Tell the students that these pitches form the Japanese Yō scale.
5. Have the students discuss familiar uses of chanting, such as football chant, Gregorian chant, nursery rhyme or childhood game chants, and rap. Compose and notate a four-measure chant in ⁶⁄₈ on the subject of work.
6. Have the students investigate, build, and play various kinds of scales including: major, minor, chromatic, whole tone, pentatonic, blues, and the Japanese yō scale.

# MUSIC LIBRARY

**4. Teach the verses of "Jōban Tanko Bushi."** Have the students:

• Listen to the song again, singing Part I softly on the syllable *too* in measures 17–32.

• Look at measures 18 and 42 and find the sixteenth-note triplet. (Explain that a *sixteenth-note triplet* has three sixteenths in the space of one eighth note.)

• Compare Part II with Part I in measures 17–32. (The sung parts are almost the same.)

• Read Part II from measures 9 to 32 on the syllable *too*, emphasizing pitch and rhythmic accuracy.

• Sing both Parts I and II separately, then together up to measure 32.

• Listen to "Pronunciation: 'Jōban Tanko Bushi.'"

• Practice pronouncing the Japanese words and sing each part using words.

• Perform measures 1–32 with the ostinato, chanting, and two vocal parts.

• Practice speaking, then singing the words to Verse 2.

• Compare the words of Verse 3 (measures 41–56) to Verses 1 and 2. (The words of Verses 1 and 3 are the same.)

**5. Teach the "shamisen" part.** Have the students:

• Listen to the song, singing the vocal rendition of the shamisen part (*tō, tō*)—Part II measures 9–16, 61–65.

• Compare Part I measures 33–40 to Part II measures 9–16. (They are the same.)

• Describe what happens in Part II, measures 33–40, then sing the part. (A one-measure pattern repeats.)

• Identify and define the articulation marks in Part II, measures 41–56, then sing the part. (*Accent* means to stress the note or make it a bit louder. A *staccato dot* means to detach that note and make it shorter.)

352

yo _____ ka - n te - ra _____ sa - ge - te nai ha yoi shō

tō tō tō tō tō tō tō tō tō tō tō tō tō tō _____

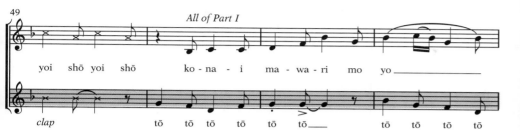

yoi shō yoi shō ko - na - i ma - wa - ri mo yo _____

clap       tō tō tō tō tō tō _____ tō tō tō tō

don - to nu - shi _____ no ta - me nai ha yoi shō yoi shō yoi shō

tō tō _____ tō tō tō tō tō tō tō tō tō

tō tō tō tō tō tō tō tō tō tō tō tō tō tō tō tō

Chant: chō chōng _ ga chōng      chō chōng _ ga chōng

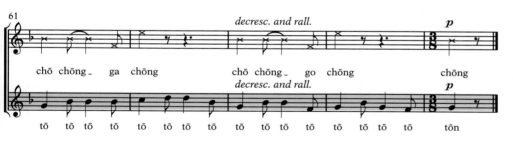

decresc. and rall.    **p**

chō chōng _ ga chōng     chō chōng _ go chōng     chōng
decresc. and rall.    **p**

tō tō tō tō tō tō tō tō tō tō tō tō tō tō tō tō tōn

353

## MUSIC LIBRARY

**6. Perform "Jōban Tanko Bushi. Have the students:**
- Sing all of Parts I and II separately.
- Practice various segments of the song in two parts, then sing the whole song.
- Review the ostinato.
- Perform the complete song with the ostinato. (A small group of students may perform the ostinato.)
- Discuss *Think It Through* and perform the song to show the mood.

### APPRAISAL

The students should be able to:
1. Read the $\frac{6}{8}$ rhythms in "Jōban Tanko Bushi."
2. Perform chanted sounds in "Jōban Tanko Bushi."
3. Perform a rhythmic ostinato by clapping or playing percussion with "Jōban Tanko Bushi."
4. Identify and observe staccato and accent in "Jōban Tanko Bushi."

# MUSIC LIBRARY

**Focus: Phrasing**

## Objectives
To read rhythms in a two-part composition
To read the slur and tie
To sing phrases expressively, using breath management

## Materials
Recordings: "Where Go the Boats?"
"Where Go the Boats?" (performance mix)
Keyboards or mallet instruments (optional)

## TEACHING THE LESSON

**Teach "Where Go the Boats?"** Have the students:
• Read about Robert Louis Stevenson.
• Listen to "Where Go the Boats?" and determine which part has the melody. (Part I)
• Describe how Part II is similar to Part I. (Many rhythms are the same.)
• Read and clap the rhythm of Part II. (Review note values and ties as needed.)
• Sing up and down the C-major scale to establish the key.
• Read and softly sing the harmony (Part II) with the recording, focusing on pitch and rhythmic accuracy. (Review the meaning of the slur as needed.)
• Read and clap the rhythm of Part I.
• Read and softly sing the melody (Part I) with the recording. (Emphasize an even quality of sound throughout the vocal range and sustained singing on the breath.)

The words to "Where Go the Boats?" were written by Robert Louis Stevenson. Stevenson was a Scottish novelist, essayist, and poet who lived from 1850 to 1894. As a young person he loved adventure and travel as well as reading. He is known for his adventure stories, such as *Treasure Island*.

CD7:12, CD8:26        Key: C major        Range I: B♭–E♭¹, II: A♭–C¹

## MORE MUSIC TEACHING IDEAS

1. Have the students sing silently and follow conducting gestures, breathing at the ends of phrases to indicate their attention.
2. Have the students play one or both parts on keyboards or mallet instruments.
3. Have the students create either a new melody for the lyrics of "Where Go the Boats?" or a new set of lyrics for the existing melody.
4. Have the students find or create a short poem, then create and notate a melody for it. Sing the new composition.

## BACKGROUND

"Where Go the Boats?" is a poem by Robert Louis Stevenson. It is part of the famous collection of his poems called A *Child's Garden of Verses*.

way          down the  val - ley,      a - way   down the hill.  A -
way,    a -  way,      a -   way   down the hill.  A -

way          down the  riv - er,        a ___  hun - dred miles or  more,
way,    a -  way,      a        hun - dred miles or  more,

*mf*                — *mp*
Oth - er        lit - tle  chil - dren     shall   bring   my  boats  a -

*mf*                — *mp*
Oth - er  lit - tle       chil - dren     shall   bring   my  boats  a -

     — *p*        *poco rit.*
shore,          shall   bring   my  boats  a - shore. _____

     — *p*        *poco rit.*
shore, ____     shall   bring   my  boats  a - shore. _____

**THINK IT THROUGH:** Suggest ways of phrasing that might produce a smooth, lyrical sound. Evaluate your performance and make further recommendations.

# MUSIC LIBRARY

- Determine the rhyme scheme of the lyrics. (*aa bb cc ddd*)
- Examine the lyrics and the melody and determine if all the phrases are the same length. (No, most phrases are two measures long, but the phrases that start at measures 19 and 31 are four measures long.)
- Determine the best places to breathe for emphasizing the phrases. (at the punctuation)
- Practice singing phrases in "Where Go the Boats?" by singing Parts I and II separately as well as together. (Emphasize managing breath to equalize the sound in phrases of different lengths.)
- Sing Parts I and II together with the accompaniment. (Emphasize phrasing through breath management and balanced two-part singing.)
- Perform in small ensembles and as duets.
- Refine the parts by observing the dynamics, ritardando, and fermata.
- Discuss *Think It Through* and sing the song using the recommendations.

### APPRAISAL

The students should be able to:
1. Identify and read note values in "Where Go the Boats?"
2. Read the slur and tie in "Where Go the Boats?"
3. Show increasing ability to sing expressively by managing their breath in two-measure and four-measure phrases.

355

# MUSIC LIBRARY

**Focus: Reading Treble and Bass Clef**

## Objectives
To sing with breath management and energy
To place vowels correctly
To read in treble and bass clefs, using letter names

## Materials
Recordings: "With Songs of Rejoicing"
  "With Songs of Rejoicing" (performance mix)
Copying Master C-3 Sight-Reading Patterns III (optional)
Pitched instruments

## TEACHING THE LESSON

**1. Introduce "With Songs of Rejoicing."**
Have the students:
• Read about the song.
• Identify the key of the first pattern (B♭) and sing up and down the B♭-major scale to establish the key.
• Identify and explain the meter in the first pattern. (6/4 There are six beats in a measure and the quarter note is one beat long.)
• Perform the rhythm of the arpeggiated pattern, then sing the pattern.
• Sing example 1 and then 2 using pitch syllables or numbers. Clap and pat the rhythms if needed for rhythmic accuracy.
• Examine the score of "With Songs of Rejoicing" and find and sing the measures that are the same as examples 1 and 2. (example 1: Part I, measures 4–6, 13–14, 30–31, 37–38; example 2: Part II, same measures)

"With Songs of Rejoicing" is from the cantata *Denn du wirst meine Seele*. A *cantata* is a vocal piece consisting of a number of movements such as arias, recitatives, duets, and choruses. This cantata was composed to be sung in church.

The Bach family in Germany produced a number of musicians and composers during two centuries. For a long time historians thought *Denn du wirst meine Seele* was written by Johann Sebastian Bach. The cantata was later discovered to be written by Johann Ludwig Bach, a distant relative of J. S. Bach who lived around the same time.

During the baroque period of music, from approximately 1600 to 1750, composers often ornamented music by using many notes sung to a single word. Look for this type of ornamentation in "With Songs of Rejoicing."

**PREPARING** *to Sing "With Songs of Rejoicing"*

• Perform the rhythm below by patting the quarter notes and pat-sliding the half note. Stress Beats 1 and 4.

| do | mi | so | mi | do | so | mi | do | so | do |
|----|----|----|----|----|----|----|----|----|----|
| 1  | 3  | 5  | 3  | 1  | 5  | 3  | 1  | 5  | 1  |

• Sing the melody above, which outlines the tonic chord of B♭ major. Use pitch syllables or numbers.

Many repeated melodic patterns can be found in both parts of "With Songs of Rejoicing."

• Sing each of the following patterns on pitch syllables or numbers. Find each pattern and repetition of the pattern in either Part I or Part II of the song.

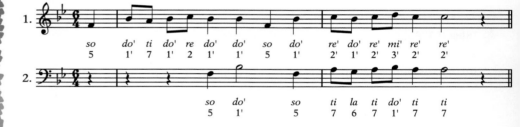

1.
| so | do' | ti | do' | re | do' | do' | so | do' | re' | do' | re' | mi' | re' | re' |
|----|-----|----|----|----|-----|-----|----|-----|-----|-----|-----|-----|-----|-----|
| 5  | 1'  | 7  | 1' | 2  | 1'  | 1'  | 5  | 1'  | 2'  | 1'  | 2'  | 3'  | 2'  | 2'  |

2.
| so | do' | so | ti | la | ti | do' | ti | ti |
|----|-----|----|----|----|----|-----|----|----|
| 5  | 1'  | 5  | 7  | 6  | 7  | 1'  | 7  | 7  |

356

## WARM-UP 10

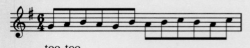

too too. . .

*Continue sequence by half step to key of B-flat*

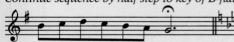

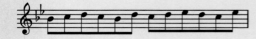

The word *joy* is important in this composition. Bach ornaments the word by having it sung for over two measures on many different pitches.

CD7:13, CD8:27

- Sing the follow excerpt using pitch syllables or numbers. Then sing it using the words. Use breath support and vowel placement to draw attention to the ornamented word *joy*.

re' ti do' la so   la so la   ti la ti do' ti la so   la so la   ti la ti do' ti la so
2'  7  1'  6  5    6  5  6    7  6  7 1'  7  6  5       6  5  6    7  6  7 1'  7  6  5

Break forth in-to joy! _____

**Key: B♭    Range I: B♭₁–D¹, II: C₁–E♭**

## With Songs of Rejoicing

from the cantata *Denn du wirst meine Seele*

Music by Johann Ludwig Bach
Words from Psalm 98 (adapted)
Arranged by Hal Hopson and adapted by MMH

**Piano Accompaniment on page PA 113**

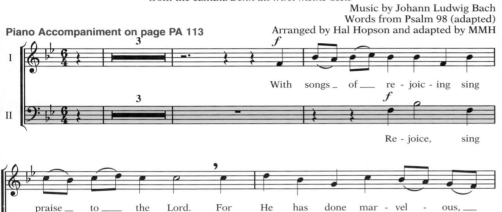

I: With songs_ of _ re-joic-ing sing
II: Re-joice, sing

praise _ to _ the Lord. For He has done mar-vel-ous, _
praise _ to _ the Lord, For He has done, has done

357

**2. Teach "With Songs of Rejoicing."** Have the students:
- Listen to "With Songs of Rejoicing," softly singing as they follow their part. (Part I should be treble voices; Part II should be cambiatas and changed voices. Call attention to the multiple measures of rest.)
- Discuss what they heard. (steady tempo, repeated sections, often one word with many notes, baroque style, and so on)
- Read about and discuss the information on ornamentation, a characteristic of the baroque style.
- Read the ornamentation example using pitch syllables or numbers, and then words. (Model the line as needed.)
- Sing Warm-Up 10 (below) to assist in developing rhythmic and vocal energy for performing the ornamented passages in "With Songs of Rejoicing." (Explain that rhythmic energy is a characteristic of baroque music.)

### BACKGROUND
#### "With Songs of Rejoicing"

The melody of "With Songs of Rejoicing" is from Kantate Nr. 15 *Denn du wirst meine Seele nicht in der Hölle lassen* BWV 15. The title of the cantata means "For you will not leave my soul in hell." The original German words were on an Easter text. They spoke of rejoicing in the defeat of sin and of deliverance and redemption by the Savior. The original piece was a soprano aria accompanied by two violins, viola, and continuo.

### BIOGRAPHY

**Johann Ludwig Bach** (1677–1731) was a German composer of the famous Bach family. J. L. Bach and J. S. Bach were both born in the city of Eisenach in what is now central Germany. J. L. Bach worked as a court musician at Meiningen. He also held posts as Kantor and court Kapellmeister. Most of his instrumental works have been lost. J. S. Bach preserved and performed many of J. L. Bach's cantatas. Kantate Nr. 15 *Denn du wirst meine Seele nicht in der Hölle lassen* BWV 15 was thought to be an early work by Johann Sebastian Bach, but later was found to be by Johann Ludwig Bach. (For information on the baroque period, see *Teacher's Edition*, page 348.)

# MUSIC LIBRARY

- Practice Parts II and I separately for the first A section (measures 1–17), focusing on pitch and rhythmic accuracy.
- Identify the letter names of the pitches in the treble and bass clefs, then sing parts of the song with letter names.
- Find the accidentals, tell which part has them, and tell the meaning of an accidental. (Part II has them. An accidental on a note alters the pitch of that letter throughout the remainder of that measure. The natural in measure 9 raises the E♭ to E♮. The flat in measure 25 lowers the A to an A♭.)
- Discuss the need for breath management in the song and find the breath marks.
- Sing Parts I and II together for measures 1–17.
- Perform the first A section in small ensembles and as duets.

358

---

## MORE MUSIC TEACHING IDEAS

1. Have the students practice sight reading in treble and bass clefs. Use examples from the book or have the students compose and notate examples for each other to read. (You may wish to use Copying Master C-3 Sight-Reading Patterns III at this time.)

2. Have the students perform "With Songs of Rejoicing" as a unison male or female chorus, omitting the bass clef harmony and singing the melody in the appropriate octave.

3. Have the students compose a four-measure or eight-measure melody in $\frac{6}{4}$ in the key of B♭ or the key of their choice.

4. Have the students find examples of baroque art, architecture, and music. Compare the ornamented, exuberant, energetic music of the baroque period with art and architecture. (See harpsichord, page 92; seventeenth century guitar, page 214; "Little Fugue in G Minor" by J. S. Bach, pages 187 and 150; "Morning Light" by G. P. Telemann, page 349.)

5. Have the students identify the instruments heard in "With Songs of Rejoicing." (string orchestra, oboe)

praise    es  the lyre and the trum-pet em-ploy.

The

The

floods  clap  their hands and the   hills sing for joy!

seas  with  their roar-ing speak praise to His name. With

The    seas    speak  praise  to  His  name.

songs  of  re-joic-ing sing praise  to  the Lord:  for

Re-  joice,  sing  praise  to  the Lord;  for

He  has  done mar-vel-ous,  mar-vel-ous things! Break

He    has  done, has  done  mar-vel-ous things!

## MUSIC LIBRARY

• Sing Parts II and I separately and together for the B section (measures 18–29), the next A section (measures 30–38), and the coda (measures 39–46).
• Compare the B section with the A sections. (The B section is softer and has a thinner vocal texture than the A sections.)
• Review and refine individual musical sections as needed. (Emphasize ornamentation, vocal placement, pitch and rhythmic accuracy, and energy)
• Perform the song in small ensembles. Discuss and make suggestions for improvement and refinement.
• Discuss *Think It Through*, then sing the song incorporating their suggestions.

359

## VOCAL DEVELOPMENT

Discuss what to do when performance mistakes happen. Performers should not convey their mistakes to the audience. Many times the audience will not know that a mistake has been made unless the performer calls attention to it. If a mistake is made, the singer should concentrate on keeping his or her place and continue with the music. Keep the flow of the song going. Avoid letting down the appearance of confidence by making a face or other distracting movement and, above all, don't keep thinking about the mistake!

Nervousness during a performance is common in beginners as well as seasoned performers. Knowing the music well, remembering to breathe, and showing confidence will help control nervousness. When standing, try bending the knees a bit, rolling the shoulders back, and tipping the head back slightly or raising the head to allow easier air passage.

# MUSIC LIBRARY

## APPRAISAL

The students should be able to:

1. Sing "With Songs of Rejoicing" with good breath management and energy.

2. Place vowels correctly in "With Songs of Rejoicing" to enhance diction and vocal tone.

3. Read segments of "With Songs of Rejoicing" in treble and bass clefs using letter names.

**THINK IT THROUGH:** Determine how well you maintained breath support and good vowel placement. Recommend ways to express the energy of this song.

360

Sugar cane, a leading crop of the West Indies, is grown chiefly on large plantations. Other important products of the West Indies mentioned in "Down, Down, Down" include molasses (a syrup made from sugar cane), cocoa beans, and bananas. "Down, Down, Down" is sung from the workers' point of view. They work hard and want their pay.

**PREPARING** *to Sing "Down, Down, Down"*

"Down, Down, Down" has various melodic patterns. Some of them move in an upward melodic direction, some move downward, and others move in both directions.

- Read and perform the following melodic patterns to help prepare you for reading and performing "Down, Down, Down." Then find the patterns in the song.

💡 **THINK IT THROUGH:** Appraise your use of dynamics and articulation in conveying the mood of the song. Which musical characteristics would you change to have greater contrast?

# MUSIC LIBRARY

**Focus: Melodic Direction**

**Objectives**
To identify melodic direction in a work song from the West Indies
To identify and perform accent, heavy accent, and staccato
To perform dynamics

**Materials**
Recordings: "Down, Down, Down"
"Down, Down, Down" (performance mix)
Copying Master C-4 Sight-Reading Patterns IV (optional)
Maracas, claves, güiro, cowbell, bongos, congas, pitched instruments (optional)

## TEACHING THE LESSON

**1. Introduce "Down, Down, Down."**
Have the students:
- Read and discuss the information about the song.
- Sing up and down the C-major scale to establish the key.
- Sing melodic patterns 1 and 2 using the syllable *doo*, pitch syllables, or numbers. (Have sections, small groups, or individuals perform. Emphasize accuracy of pitch and rhythm.)
- Examine each melodic pattern and describe its general direction.
- Sing up and down the F-major scale to establish the new key.
- Sing melodic patterns 3–6 using the syllable *doo*, pitch syllables, or numbers.
- Examine each melodic pattern and describe its general direction.

## MORE MUSIC TEACHING IDEAS

1. Have the students practice sight reading using examples from the book or examples they have created and notated. (You may wish to use Copying Master C-4 Sight-Reading Patterns IV at this time.)
2. Have the students play the vocal ostinatos on pitched instruments.
3. Have the students create, notate, and perform two-measure rhythm ostinatos to use with "Down, Down, Down." Use appropriate instruments such as maracas, claves, güiro, cowbell, bongos, and/or congas.
4. Compare "Down, Down, Down" with other work songs, such as "Jōban Tanko Bushi," page 351, for similarities and differences. Discuss the elements in each song that are associated with a specific culture.
5. Discuss why there is a key change in "Down, Down, Down." (probably to make it more interesting)

## MOVEMENT

Create a dance for "Down, Down, Down." Use elements of rhythm and form to give the dance structure. Make decisions about the step, hand movements, pathway, formation, and direction to be used.
You may use this idea as a starting point:
Form a double circle.
**Measures 1–30:** step-touch pattern moving counterclockwise
**Measures 31–46:** stand still, raising and lowering arms, basically following the dynamics
**Measures 47–54:** inside circle faces in and outside circle faces out. Do a repeated pattern of three steps forward and touch alternating with three steps backward and touch.
**Measures 55–77:** step-touch pattern moving clockwise
**Measures 78–86:** stand still, raising and lowering arms, following the dynamics
**Measures 86–93:** step-touch pattern, inside circle moving clockwise, outside circle moving counterclockwise
**Measures 94–end:** inside circle faces in and outside circle faces out. Do a repeated pattern of three steps forward and touch alternating with three steps backward and touch.

# MUSIC LIBRARY

- Examine the score to "Down, Down, Down" and find each melodic pattern on page 361. (Pattern 1: shown in measures 5–6, 7–8, 29–30 but the ostinato continues from measure 5 to 30; Pattern 2: measures 21–26; Pattern 3: measures 86–89; Pattern 4: measures 67–72; Pattern 5: measures 90–93; Pattern 6: measures 49–54, 94–101)
- Sing each melodic pattern using words. (Model the patterns as needed.)

2. Teach "Down, Down, Down." Have the students:

- Listen to "Down, Down, Down," softly singing each melodic pattern as it appears.
- Listen to the song again and discuss what they heard. (steady tempo, syncopation, ostinato, two-part singing, various kinds of articulation and dynamics, key change)
- Relate the melodic direction of example 6 to the lyrics. (The direction matches the words.)
- Look at the Part II ostinato starting in measure 5, identify and define the type of articulation, then sing the ostinato up to measure 30 with the recording. (An *accent* means to stress or emphasize the note.)
- Find and define the articulations in the Part I melody of the first section (measures 1–30). (Accent and staccato are used. *Staccato* means to shorten the note.)
- Sing Part I up to measure 30 focusing on pitch and rhythmic accuracy and correct articulations.
- Sing Parts I and II together up to measure 30.
- Perform the first section in small ensembles and as duets.
- Practice Parts I and II of the second section (measures 31–46) separately, then combine them. (Note that the parts are in thirds and move in parallel motion for most of this section.)

## CURRICULUM CONNECTION: SOCIAL STUDIES

The West Indies are islands that span southeastward from Florida to the coast of Venezuela. They are tropical islands and enjoy sunshine all year round. This constant sun provides the perfect climate for growing sweet potatoes, yams, bananas, citrus fruits, coffee, cassava (manioc), corn, beans, and some tobacco. Sugarcane is a primary crop on many of these islands. From December, when the leaves turn an ashen-silver, until April there is work for all. Afterwards, many simply await the next year's harvest.

## BACKGROUND

Sugarcane is a giant grass that grows in warm, moist regions such as the West Indies. Stalks are cut by hand or by machine and quickly sent to the factory to be processed into sugar. There the cane is chopped and crushed. The extracted juice is refined by a variety of processes. The water is then evaporated in several stages. A centrifuge extracts the dark molasses from the sugar crystals. Further refining is done to produce different grades of sugar including white granulated sugar, soft brown sugar, powdered sugar, liquid sugars, and syrups.

All the day, _____ live long day, _____ The co-coa bean _ we bring, The co-coa bean _ we

All the day, _____ live long day, _____ Ba-nan-a too, _ we bring, Ba-nan-a too, _ we

✾ (Down, down, down.) down.)

bring, The co-coa bean _ we bring, We bring down! _____

bring, Ba-nan-a too, _ we bring, We bring down! _____

Pay me, pay me my mon-ey! Pay me, pay me my mon-ey!

I heard the cap-tain say, _ We sail to-mor-row, I heard the

Mor - row, We sail to-mor-row, Mor -

cap-tain say, _ We sail to-mor - row.

row, We sail to-mor - row. Down, down, down.

*Keep repeating, gradually fade out*

Down, down, down. Down, down, down. Down, down, down.

*One voice shouts:* **"Pay me my money!"**

Down, down, down. Down, down, down. Down, down, down.

363

# MUSIC LIBRARY

- Perform the first and second sections.
- Compare measures 9–38 with measures 55–85. (They are basically the same except for the key.)
- Identify the two keys used in the song. (C major and F major)
- Find the heavy accents. (Measures 68, 70, and 72 each include a *heavy accent*, which means to stress the note as well as to make it as short as possible.)
- Compare measures 86–89 to measures 90–93. (They are almost the same.)
- Read each part of the remainder of "Down, Down, Down" separately, then combine parts. (Call attention to the contrary motion of the two parts in the last line.)
- Sing the whole song concentrating on correct articulations and dynamics. (Review dynamic symbols as needed.)
- Review and refine individual musical sections as needed.
- Perform in small ensembles. Discuss and make suggestions for improvement and refinement, then apply the suggestions to the song.
- Discuss *Think It Through* and apply their suggestions to the song.

## APPRAISAL

The students should be able to:

1. Identify upward and downward melodic direction in "Down, Down, Down."
2. Identify and perform accent, heavy accent, and staccato in "Down, Down, Down."
3. Perform dynamics in "Down, Down, Down."

# MUSIC LIBRARY

**Focus: Balance and Blend**

**Objectives**
To develop choral balance and blend
To sing a patriotic song expressively

**Materials**
Recordings: "One Great Nation"
"One Great Nation" (performance mix)

## TEACHING THE LESSON

**1. Introduce the text to "One Great Nation."** Have the students:
• Read and discuss the information on the background of the lyrics.
• Define and discuss the concept of liberty and discuss *Think It Through*. (*Liberty* is the quality or state of being free, the power of choice, and the enjoyment of certain rights and privileges.)
• Read the lyrics and suggest ways to express the meaning of the lyrics. (Show appropriate facial expression; use good posture and good diction; follow dynamic marks; emphasize important words to get the message across, sing through phrases.)
• Compare words spoken by an eloquent, powerful actor with the same words spoken by someone who speaks in an uninspired fashion. (One student might speak the lyrics or a sentence in an expressive, meaningful way and also in a purposeless, monotone way. Have the students contrast the results.)
• Practice speaking the lyrics expressively.

The words to "One Great Nation" were inspired by Abraham Lincoln's Gettysburg Address. Lincoln gave the speech in 1863 at Gettysburg, Pennsylvania. This speech was part of the dedication of a national cemetery there. Lincoln's message tells of the founding of the United States of America on principles of liberty and equality. It resolves that this nation shall have a new birth of freedom.

💡 **THINK IT THROUGH:** Imagine what the United States would be like if it did not have all the liberty it has now. What would be different? Suggest how your singing can convey the meaning of the words in "One Great Nation."

**PREPARING** *to Sing* "One Great Nation"
Part singing creates a richness of sound that cannot be obtained with unison singing. The ending section of "One Great Nation" is sung in three parts in a very sustained and connected manner.

• Sing Part III with pitch syllables.

• Sing Part II with pitch syllables. Then sing Parts II and III together.

• Sing Part I with pitch syllables. Then combine all three parts.

• Sing the three parts using the words. Combine the sound of your part with each of the other parts to create choral balance and blend.

364

## MORE MUSIC TEACHING IDEAS

1. Have the students develop a multimedia presentation using "One Great Nation" as a theme. The presentation might include a slide show of artwork or photographs illustrating the song as the song is played; a movement activity or procession to the song, perhaps using flags and banners; or a dramatic reading of the Gettysburg Address.
2. Have the students develop a patriotic program to present in class or as a concert. The program could include poetry written by the students or found from other sources, banners, art work, other patriotic songs such as "America," "America, My Homeland," "The Star-Spangled Banner," and "When Johnny Comes Marching Home."
3. Have the class write several sentences which convey different emotions. Have three students read each sentence, each student expressing a different emotion. Discuss which expression worked the most effectively with the sentence.

*One Great Nation*

CD7:15, CD8:29

y: C major, E♭ major    Range I: C–F¹, II: C–D¹, III: F₁–E♭    Words and Music by Stephen L. Lawrence

Words inspired by Lincoln's Gettysburg Address

**With intensity** ♩ = ca. 80–88

## MUSIC LIBRARY

**2. Introduce the ending of "One Great Nation."** Have the students:

• Listen to "One Great Nation" following their assigned part. (Call attention to the first and second endings. Parts may be assigned as follows—Part I: trebles, Part II: trebles and high-range cambiatas, and Part III: low-range cambiatas and changed voices.)

• Sing up and down the E♭-major scale to establish the key and read about singing in parts, page 364.

• Sing each part notated on page 364, using pitch syllables or numbers. Begin with Part III, then add Part II, and finally combine all three parts. (Emphasize expressive singing in rehearsal as well as in performance.)

• Define choral balance and blend. (See page 304 for information on *balance* and page 200 for *blend*. *Blend* is the combination of voices or parts so that the sound becomes uniform.)

• Sing the three parts with words, aiming for choral balance and blend. Begin with Part III, add Part II and Part I.

• Locate the ending in the score. (page 368)

• Listen to "One Great Nation" and sing the ending.

**3. Teach "One Great Nation."** Have the students:

• Listen to "One Great Nation," singing their parts softly, sight reading as much as possible. (Review rhythms and pitches as needed to aid sight reading.)

• Read and sing measures 1–29 with the recording. Work on Parts I, II, and III separately, as needed. (Emphasize pitch and rhythmic accuracy. Use vocal modeling to assist.)

365

- Find the accidentals and explain their meaning. (They are in measures 18–22. The *sharp* raises the pitch of a note and the following notes in the measure with the same letter name by a half step. The *natural* in measure 19 is a reminder to sing the note without the previous sharp.)
- Find and identify the dynamics. (*mf* and *f*, *decrescendo*)
- Sing measures 1–29 in three parts, aiming for choral blend and balance.

366

- Read and sing measures 30–49 with the recording. Work on Parts I, II, and III separately, as needed.
- Describe what happens in measure 32. (There is a key change from C major to E♭ major.)
- Find and identify the dynamics ( *f*, *cresc.*, *ff* ) and accidentals. (measures 36–40, 48)
- Sing in small ensembles, developing balance and blend among parts.
- Sing "One Great Nation" in three parts with attention to phrasing. (You may wish to have segments of the song sung as solos.)

### APPRAISAL

The students should be able to:
1. Sing "One Great Nation" with choral balance and blend.
2. Sing "One Great Nation" expressively.

367

# MUSIC LIBRARY

"Sing We and Chant It" is a madrigal from the Renaissance period of music. **A madrigal** is a choral piece that is often polyphonic and is usually sung without instrumental accompaniment. "Sing We and Chant It" was written in 1595 by Thomas Morley, an English composer. Madrigals written in England often had a definite mood of either merriment or melancholy. Notice the rhymes and the use of the *Fa la las*.

## Sing We and Chant It

Piano Accompaniment on page PA 134

Music by Thomas Morley
Words by Michael Drayton
Arranged by MMH

369

---

# MUSIC LIBRARY

**Focus:** $\frac{3}{4}$ **Meter**

**Objectives**
To read rhythms in $\frac{3}{4}$ meter
To identify steps, skips, and leaps

**Materials**
Recordings: "Sing We and Chant It"
"Sing We and Chant It" (performance mix)

**Vocabulary**
Madrigal

## TEACHING THE LESSON

**1. Introduce "Sing We and Chant It."** Have the students:
• Read and discuss the information on "Sing We and Chant It" and madrigals.
**2. Teach "Sing We and Chant It."** Have the students:
• Say "1-2-3" steadily, while tapping on beat 1 in the palm of their hand. (Use a tempo that is the same as that of "Sing We and Chant It.")
• Listen to "Sing We and Chant It" as they tap and silently count "1-2-3." Describe and discuss what they heard. (steady beat, measure felt in one rather than three, rhythmic vitality, repeated *fa la la*, part singing, crisp diction, madrigal, rhyming words)
• Listen to the song while following their part. (Parts I and II: trebles, Part III: altos and cambiatas, and Part IV: changed voices)
• Identify where the song was polyphonic and where it was homophonic. (The *fa, la, la* sections are polyphonic. The verses are homophonic.)

## MORE MUSIC TEACHING IDEAS

1. Have the students list and discuss styles of music that are primarily a cappella. Examples include barbershop quartets, Sweet Adelines, madrigals, motets, shape-note singing, doo-wop, Gregorian chant, cantors, and Christmas caroling.
2. Discuss the use of music for entertainment during the Renaissance versus the present time. During the Renaissance, families or friends might entertain themselves singing madrigals or playing instrumental music. Today people may entertain themselves by listening to recordings, radio, television, and concerts, or by making their own music.

## THE COMPOSER

**Thomas Morely** lived from 1557 to 1602. He was an English composer and a great master of the madrigal. He was also an organist and master of the choristers in several cathedrals. Morely edited, arranged, translated, and published his own and other composers' music. He even served as a spy for the government of Queen Elizabeth I.

# MUSIC LIBRARY

- Speak the words of their part softly and in rhythm with the recording. (Emphasize music reading, rhythmic accuracy, and staccato articulation.)
- Read the rhythm of the song, one part at a time. (Review note values as needed.)
- Listen to the song again while following their part, then identify the steps, skips, and leaps in their part. Determine the kinds of interval used in each part. (Parts I and II move primarily by step. Parts III and IV include more skips and leaps but also include stepwise passages.)
- Sing Warm-Up 11 to develop tonal focus, diction, and rhythmic energy for "Sing We and Chant It." (See below.)
- Sing up and down the G-major scale to establish the key.
- Identify the key of the song. (G major)
- Sing Part IV of the first section (measures 1–8) of "Sing We and Chant It." (Emphasize accuracy of pitch and rhythm.)
- Sing Part III. (Have students who are assigned to Parts III and I sing Part III for now.)
- Sing Parts IV and III together. (Begin with students assigned to Part IV and II singing Part IV. Repeat, adding students assigned to Parts III and I singing Part III.)
- Sing Part II (only those assigned to Part II).
- Sing Parts IV, III, and II together. Begin with Part IV alone. Repeat, adding students assigned to Parts III and I singing Part III. Repeat, adding Part II.
- Sing Part I (only those assigned to Part I).
- Sing all four parts together. Begin with Part IV. Repeat, adding Part III. Repeat, singing Parts IV, III, and II. Repeat, singing all four parts.
- Sing the first section in four parts, refining parts and noting balance, blend, diction, and breath management.

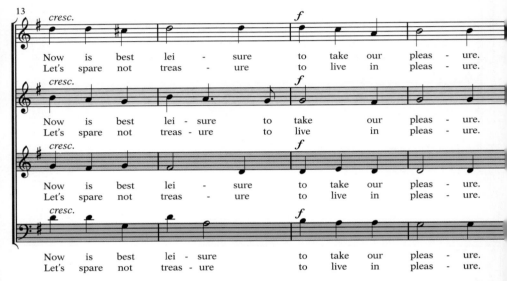

370

**WARM-UP 11**

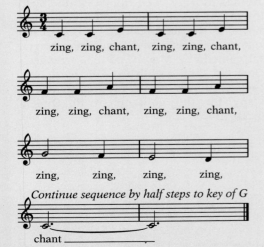

zing, zing, chant, zing, zing, chant,

zing, zing, chant, zing, zing, chant,

zing, zing, zing, zing,

*Continue sequence by half steps to key of G*

chant _____

💡 **THINK IT THROUGH:** Determine which parts of "Sing We and Chant It" you articulated well. What suggestions for improvement can you give for performing the rest of the piece?

## MUSIC LIBRARY

- Sing the second section of "Sing We and Chant It" (measures 9–24) following the procedure for the first section.
- Find the accidentals. (measures 9, 11, 13)
- Sing passages and vocal parts in small ensembles and in different combinations of parts.
- Sing the entire song, a cappella if possible. (Call attention to the order: first half of Verse 1 and repeat, second half of Verse 1 and repeat, first half of Verse 2 and repeat, then second half of Verse 2 and repeat.)

### APPRAISAL

The students should be able to:
1. Read simple $\frac{3}{4}$ rhythmic patterns in "Sing We and Chant It."
2. Identify steps, skips, and leaps in "Sing We and Chant It."

371

# MUSIC LIBRARY

**Focus: Reading in ²⁄₂ meter**

**Objectives**
To read rhythms in ²⁄₂ meter
To blend and balance three vocal parts

**Materials**
Recordings: "Listen to the Music"
"Listen to the Music" (performance mix)
Percussion instruments (optional)

## TEACHING THE LESSON

**1. Introduce "Listen to the Music."**
Have the students:
• Read and discuss the information on ²⁄₂ meter.
• Sing up and down the G-major scale to establish the key.
• Look at the example and identify the key. (G major)
• Sing the rhythm of the example using the syllable *ta*. Start with Part III, then do Part II, and then finally do Part I. When the rhythm is secure, add the pitches, then combine parts. (Parts can be assigned as follows: Part III, changed voices; Part II, trebles and cambiatas; Part I, trebles. Model parts to show rhythmic accuracy.)
• Read and perform the example in sections, small groups, and as trios, emphasizing pitch and rhythmic accuracy and steady beat.

## MORE MUSIC TEACHING IDEAS

1. Have the students create and notate four-measure rhythmic patterns in ²⁄₂ and play them on unpitched percussion instruments.
2. Have the students perform "Listen to the Music" as a percussion ensemble. They can choose a different tone color for each vocal part—for example, claves, drum, güiro. Then have them play the parts without the vocal parts or other accompaniment.

**PREPARING** *to Sing "Listen to the Music"*

In ²⁄₂ meter:

    **o** = two beats

    𝅗𝅥. = one and a half beats

    𝅗𝅥 = one beat

    ♩ = a half beat

    ♪ = a quarter of a beat

• Sing the rhythm of each line of this portion of "Listen to the Music" using the syllable *ta* for each note. Sing the rhythm using the first pitch of each line. Then sing using all the pitches. Establish a strong half-note beat by tapping your toe. This movement will help to maintain rhythmic accuracy.

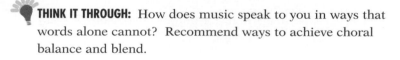

• Learn Part III of "Listen to the Music." Then add Parts II and I, one at a time, to strengthen your three-part singing.

**THINK IT THROUGH:** How does music speak to you in ways that words alone cannot? Recommend ways to achieve choral balance and blend.

# Listen to the Music

Piano Accompaniment on page PA 144

CD7:17, CD8:31

Words and Music by
Ed Robertson

1. Day af - ter day _____ in a trou - bled
2. Learn - ing to live _____ in a trou - bled

1. Find - ing your way _____ in a trou - bled world,
2. Learn - ing to give _____ in a trou - bled world,

world, _____
world, _____

What to do, where to
There are rea - sons to

There's a place to turn _____ when it seems so hope - less.
When you hear a song, _____ then the world seems bright - er.

turn, how to live. _____ Lis - ten to the
hope and to sing. _____

Hear it all a - round you. Hear the

mu - sic ring - ing in the air.

Lis - ten to the mu - sic ring - ing. Lis - ten to the voic - es

Key: G major    Range I: E–E¹, II: C–C¹, III: D₁–G₁

## MUSIC LIBRARY

**2. Teach "Listen to the Music."** Have the students:
• Find the multiple measures of rest, repeat signs, and first and second endings in the score. (Review their meanings as needed.)
• Listen to "Listen to the Music," following their parts.
• Read Part III of the song. (Model the parts as needed.)
• Read Part II of the song. Then sing Parts III and II together with attention to pitch and rhythmic accuracy.
• Read Part I of the song. Then sing Parts III, II, and I together in various combinations.
• Identify the texture of the song. (polyphonic)
• Sing in small ensembles. Discuss the performances in terms of blend and balance.
• Sing "Listen to the Music" in three parts. (Emphasize expression and focus on an even quality of sound throughout each vocal range.)
• Discuss *Think It Through* and incorporate their suggestions into the performance of the song. Evaluate the resulting performance.

373

# MUSIC LIBRARY

## APPRAISAL

The students should be able to:

1. Read and perform $\frac{2}{2}$ rhythms in "Listen to the Music."

2. Achieve blend and balance among the three vocal parts in "Listen to the Music."

Let it speak to you.

mu - sic; Let it speak to you.

Lis - ten to the mu - sic ring; Let it speak to you.

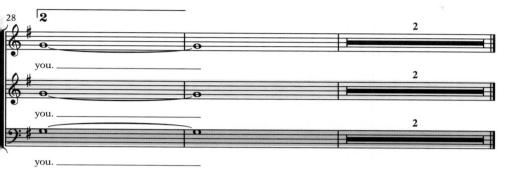

you.

you.

you.

375

MUSIC LIBRARY

# MUSIC LIBRARY

**Focus: Gospel style**

## Objectives

To sing music in gospel style
To identify and perform homophonic music
To identify melodic and rhythmic repetition

## Materials

Recordings: "The Promised Land"
"The Promised Land"
(performance mix)
Percussion (optional)

## TEACHING THE LESSON

**1. Introduce "The Promised Land."**
Have the students:
• Read about gospel style.
• Clap the rhythm of measures 9–13. (Review note values as needed.)
• Form two groups—one group claps the example and the other group snaps on the rests.
• Speak the words of those measures in rhythm with and without the finger snaps. (Emphasize crisp diction, precise rhythm, and clean vocal attacks and releases.)
• Listen to the melody (Part 1) of measures 9–13. (Model this part, calling attention to the pulse on the second pitch of the word *land*.)
• Clap the rhythm and snap on the rests as they listen to the melody in measures 9–13.
• Sing the Db-major scale to establish the key. (Remind students of how to determine the key and help them identify the key of the example.)
• Sing measures 9–13 of Part 1 with a crisp rhythm, putting a slight emphasis or pulse on the second pitch of *land*.

Musical style results when certain musical elements are used in a consistent manner. Often subtle qualities of style are not easily shown in music notation. These qualities can be learned by listening to good performances in those styles.

"The Promised Land" is in a gospel style. The gospel style developed from African American Protestant sacred singing in the twentieth century. To perform "The Promised Land" in this style, you need to use short crisp diction and strong word accents, as well as to pay attention to the rests.

• Clap the rhythm of measures 9–13, adding finger snaps during the rests.

• Speak the words and add a finger snap for each rest. Speak the words without doing the finger snaps. Keep your diction crisp.

• Sing measures 9–13 of Part I with crisp diction. Use your breath and diction to emphasize the rhythm of the melody.

**THINK IT THROUGH:** "The Promised Land" says that joy, peace, and love will be found in the "promised land." What other values are important to you? Propose a new verse using some of these values. Evaluate how well your performance of "The Promised Land" reflected the gospel style.

Key: Db major  Range I: F–Db¹, II: Db–Bb, III: Ab–F, IV: Db₁–Bb₁

## The Promised Land

Piano Accompaniment on page PA 137

Words and music by
Fernando G. Allen

Come and go ____ with me ____ to the pro - mised land. _

376

# EXTENSION

## MORE MUSIC TEACHING IDEAS

Have the students create and add a percussion part to the song.

## BACKGROUND

Gospel music is a form of demonstrative religious music that developed in African American Protestant churches in the twentieth century. In this style, vocalists may sing, shout, hum, whisper, or cry. Songs are embellished by adding syncopation, altering pitches, adding glissandos, and improvising. Fragments of the song may be extended by a soloist who improvises comments alternating with a group that sings a repeated phrase. Spontaneous or choreographed dancing, foot stamping, and hand clapping may occur. Accompanying instruments often include piano, Hammond organ, guitar, bass, drums, and tambourine.

Gospel music evolved from hymns, spirituals, blues, barbershop singing, ragtime, pop, country and western, and jazz. Gospel music in turn became the one of the roots of rhythm and blues (which then led to rock and roll) and of soul (which was a secularized gospel style). These secular forms in turn influenced later gospel music.

Some gospel musicians include Mahalia Jackson, Rosetta Tharpe, the Dixie Hummingbirds, the Mighty Clouds of Joy, and James Cleveland. Today gospel music is performed in concert halls for entertainment purposes as well as in church services for religious purposes.

There'll be joy, \_\_\_ there'll be peace, \_\_ there'll be love. \_\_

There'll be joy, \_\_\_ there'll be peace, \_\_ there'll be love. \_\_

There'll be joy, \_\_\_ there'll be peace, \_\_ there'll be love. \_\_

**9** *Verse*

The joy there will give you strength, \_ in that land, \_\_ in that land. \_

The joy there will give you strength, \_ in that land, \_\_ in that land. \_

The joy there will give you strength, \_ in that land, \_\_ in that land. \_

**13**

_____ The peace there will give you rest, \_\_ in that land, \_ in that land. \_

_____ The peace there will give you rest, \_\_ in that land, \_ in that land. \_

_____ The peace there will give you rest, \_\_ in that land, \_ in that land. \_

377

# MUSIC LIBRARY

**2. Teach the refrain of "The Promised Land."** Have the students:

• Find the *D.C.* at the end of measure 25 and explain its meaning. (*D.C.* stands for *da capo* and means to go back to the beginning.)

• Listen to "The Promised Land" while following their assigned part. (Parts I and II: male and female trebles, Part III: altos and cambiatas, Part IV: changed voices)

• Determine whether the vocal parts are close together or far apart and whether they are homophonic or polyphonic. (The parts, especially the top three parts, are close together. The music is homophonic.)

• Find places where the notes are pulsed. (The *pulses*, marked by lines over the notes, indicate glottal stops to separate and emphasize pitches. They occur on some of the words *land* and *love*.)

• Listen to the song, noticing the accidentals in their part.

• Sing Part IV of the refrain. (All parts should sing Part IV. Call attention to the repeated pitches.)

• Sing Part III of the refrain. (Students assigned to Parts III and I should sing.)

• Sing Parts IV and III of the refrain together. (Students assigned to Parts IV and II should sing Part IV and students assigned to Parts III and I should sing Part III.)

• Sing Part II of the refrain. (Students assigned to Part II should sing.)

• Sing Parts IV, III, and II together. (Begin with Part IV alone. Repeat, adding Part III, sung by students assigned to Parts III and I. Then repeat, adding Part II.)

• Sing Part I of the refrain. (Only students assigned to this part should sing.)

• Sing the refrain in four parts.

• Sing the refrain as quartets or in small groups.

# MUSIC LIBRARY

- Discuss the rhythmic and melodic repetition in the refrain. (Remind the students to look and listen for repetition to aid them in learning their parts.)

**3. Teach the verse and ending.** Have the students:

- Find examples of repetition in the verse and discuss whether the verse should be easy to learn or not. (It has a lot of repetition and should be easy.)
- Practice the parts in the verse in the same manner as the refrain.
- Compare the ending of the song (measures 26 to the end) with the refrain and the verse. (The end is similar to the refrain and uses repetition.)
- Practice the parts in the ending in the same manner as the refrain.
- Find the fermatas and explain what they mean. (A *fermata* on a note means to hold that note longer.)
- Practice adding the sections of the song together.
- Sing "The Promised Land" in four parts. (Emphasize stylistic elements of gospel music and a rhythmic feel.)
- Discuss *Think It Through*.
- Discuss musical elements that can be changed to enhance their performance and make it more expressive. (dynamics, articulation, use of solos, small or large groups, tempo)
- Sing the song with attention to an expressive gospel sound.

There'll be joy,___ there'll be peace,___ there'll be love.___

There'll be joy,___ there'll be peace,___ there'll be love.___

There'll be joy,___ there'll be peace,___ there'll be love.___

There'll be joy,___ there'll be peace,___ there'll be love.___

There'll be joy,___ there'll be peace,___ there'll be love.___

There'll be joy,___ there'll be peace,___ there'll be love.___

There'll be joy,___ there'll be peace, there'll be love.

(love.)

There'll be joy,___ there'll be peace, there'll be love.

There'll be joy,___ there'll be peace, there'll be love.

379

## MUSIC LIBRARY

### APPRAISAL

The students should be able to:

1. Sing "The Promised Land" in gospel style.

2. Identify and perform four-part homophonic music.

3. Identify and use repetition to help them learn "The Promised Land."

Michael Praetorius 1571–1621
Thomas Weelkes 1576–1623

## 1600

1620 Mayflower lands at Plymouth Rock
1643 Louis XIV becomes king of France at age

Jean Baptiste Lully 1632–1687
Johann Pachelbel 1653–1706
Henry Purcell 1659–1695
Antonio Vivaldi 1678–1741
Johann Sebastian Bach 1685–1750
George Frederick Handel 1685–1759

1666 Newton discovers Law of Gravity

## 1700

1707 United Kingdom of Great Britian formed

Franz Joseph Haydn 1732–1809
John Stafford Smith 1750–1836
Wolfgang Amadeus Mozart 1756–1791
Ludwig van Beethoven 1770–1827

1769 James Watt patents his steam engine
1775 American Revolution (ended 1783)
1776 American Declaration of Independence
1787 American Constitutional Convention
1788 John Fitch invents steamboat
1789 French Revolution; George Washington
first president of United States
1791 Bill of Rights
1793 Eli Whitney invents the cotton gin

Franz Schubert 1797–1828

## 1800

1803 Louisiana Purchase
1804 Napoleon crowned emperor; Lewis and
Clark expedition
1807 Robert Fulton builds first commercial
steamboat; London streets lighted by gas

Fanny Mendelssohn Hensel 1805–1847

Felix Mendelssohn 1809–1847
Frédéric Chopin 1810–1849
Robert Schumann 1810–1856
Richard Wagner 1813–1883

1812 War of 1812
1815 Napoleon defeated in Battle of Waterloo
1819 First steamship crosses Atlantic
1825 Opening of the Erie Canal
1825 First public railroad opened in England
1838 Daguerre takes first photographs

1825

Johannes Brahms 1833–1897
Georges Bizet 1838–1875
Modest Mussorgsky 1839–1881
Peter Ilyich Tchaikovsky 1840–1893
Edvard Grieg 1843–1907
Nicolai Rimsky-Korsakov 1844–1908

1844 First telegraph message transmitted
1846 First use of ether as an anesthetic
1848 California Gold Rush; first Women's
Rights Convention

1850

John Philip Sousa 1854–1932
Cécile Chaminade 1857–1944
Giacomo Puccini 1858–1924
Claude Debussy 1862–1918

1860 Lincoln elected president;
Civil War (ended 1865)

380

|  |  |
|---|---|
| | **1863** Gettysburg Address; Emancipation Proclamation |
| | **1865** Abraham Lincoln assassinated |
| **Scott Joplin** 1868–1917 | **1869** First American transcontinental railroad; opening of Suez Canal |
| **James Weldon Johnson** 1871–1938 | |
| **Ralph Vaughan Williams** 1872–1958 | |
| **.C. (William Christopher) Handy** 1873–1958 | |
| **Arnold Schoenberg** 1874–1951 | |
| **Charles Ives** 1874–1954 | |
| **Robert Frost** 1874–1963 — 1875 | **1876** Alexander Graham Bell invents telephone |
| | **1877** Thomas Edison invents the phonograph |
| | **1879** Edison invents improved incandescent electric light bulb |
| **Igor Stravinsky** 1882–1971 | **1885** Louis Pasteur develops milk "pasteurization" |
| **Ferdinand ("Jelly Roll") Morton** 1885–1941 | **1886** Statue of Liberty unveiled in New York Harbor |
| **Gertrude ("Ma") Rainey** 1886–1939 | |
| **Ernst Toch** 1887–1964 | **1889** Completion of Eiffel Tower in France |
| **T.S. (Thomas Stearns) Eliot** 1888–1965 | |
| **Sergei Prokofiev** 1891–1953 | |
| **Bessie Smith** 1894–1937 | **1895** Wilhelm Roentgen discovers X-rays |
| **William Grant Still** 1895–1978 | **1898** Spanish-American War |
| **George Gershwin** 1898–1937 | |
| **Duke Ellington** 1899–1974 | |
| **1900** | |
| **Louis Armstrong** 1900–1971 | **1901** Guglielmo Marconi transmits wireless telegraph signals across Atlantic |
| **Harry Partch** 1901–1974 | **1902** Pierre and Marie Curie discover radium |
| **Langston Hughes** 1902–1967 | **1903** Wilbur and Orville Wright make first successful airplane flight |
| **Ogden Nash** 1902–1971 | **1904** First sound moving picture |
| | **1905** Albert Einstein offers Theory of Relativity |
| **Harold Arlen** 1905–1986 | **1906** San Francisco earthquake and fire |
| | **1908** Model T Ford produced |
| | **1909** Robert Peary and Matthew Henson reach North Pole |
| **Milt Hinton** 1910– | **1910** Discovery of the South Pole; discovery of protons and electrons |
| | **1912** Titanic disaster |
| **John Cage** 1912–1992 | |
| **Morton Gould** 1913–1996 | **1914** Opening of the Panama Canal; World War I (ended 1918) |
| **Benjamin Britten** 1913–1976 | |
| **Lester Flatt** 1914–1979 | |
| **Milton Babbitt** 1916– | |
| **Eve Merriam** 1916– | **1917** Russian Revolution |
| **Lou Harrison** 1917– | |
| **Leonard Bernstein** 1918–1990 | **1920** First commercial radio broadcast; suffrage (19th Amendment) |
| **Dave Brubeck** 1920– | |
| **Katsutoshi Nagasawa** 1923– | |
| **Earl Scruggs** 1924– | |
| **Paul Desmond** 1924–1977 | **1927** Charles Lindbergh's flight across the Atlantic; first television transmission |
| **Pierre Boulez** 1925– — 1925 | **1928** Sir Alexander Fleming discovers penicillin |
| **Burt Bacharach** 1928– | **1929** New York stock market crash; beginning of worldwide depression |
| **Claude Bolling** 1930– | |

381

Stephen Sondheim 1930–
Shel Silverstein 1932–
Isao Tomita 1932–
John Williams 1932–
Krzysztof Penderecki 1933–
Terry Riley 1935–
Philip Glass 1937–
Leo Brouwer 1939–
Trevor Nunn 1940–
Bob Dylan 1941–
David Fanshawe 1942–
George Harrison 1943–
Vangelis 1943–
James C. Pankow 1947–
Elton John 1947–
Andrew Lloyd Webber 1948–
Stephen Schwartz 1948–
Stevie Nicks 1948–
Billy Joel 1949–

## 1950

Peter Gabriel 1950–
Bernie Taupin 1950–
Dewey Bunnell 1952–
Bruce Hornsby 1954–

Gloria Estefan 1957–

1975

1932 Franklin D. Roosevelt elected president

1933 Nazi Revolution in Germany

1939 World War II (ended 1945)

1950 Korean War (ended 1953); Vietnam War
(ended 1975)

1954 First polio vaccine developed by
Jonas E. Salk
1957 Launching of Sputnik, first earth satellite
1961 First successful manned orbital space flig
1962 Cuban missile crisis
1963 President John F. Kennedy assassinated
1965 First "walk" outside spaceship by
an astronaut
1968 Martin Luther King, Jr., and Robert F.
Kennedy assassinated
1969 First men land on the moon
1971 Voting age lowered to 18 years

1976 U.S. celebrates its bicentennial on July 4
Viking I and II landers set down on Mars
1981 Sandra Day O'Connor becomes first
woman appointed to the Supreme Court;
first reusable spacecraft, space shuttle
Columbia, travels into space and
returns to earth
1983 Sally Ride becomes the first American
woman to travel in space
1984 First mechanical heart implanted in
a human
1985 Worldwide Live Aid concert to benefit
famine victims in Ethiopia
1986 Statue of Liberty centennial celebration
1987 Voyager makes first nonstop flight aroun
the world without refueling
1990 Germany reunited; dissolving of the Sovi
Union; spacecraft Magellan maps Venus

382

# GLOSSARY

**accelerando** a gradual increase in the speed of the beat, **145**

**accent (>)** a stress or emphasis on any given musical tone or chord, **3**

**alto** middle voice, **312**

**American musical theater** an American art form combining drama and music, **15**

**articulating** speaking or singing clearly and distinctly, **320**

**a tempo** return to the original speed of the beat, **68**

**atonal music** music without a strong tonal center, **135**

**augmentation** expanding the duration of a note, usually to twice its value, **67**

**bar line** a vertical line on the staff marking off a measure, **17**

**blend** the sound of individual tone colors merging together, **200**

**blues scale** an eight-pitch scale in which the third, fifth, and seventh notes are lower than those of the major scale, **127**

**brass family** musical wind instruments made of brass or other metal, including the trumpet, horn, trombone, and tuba, **28**

**call and response** a form in which the call is often a solo and the response is often a word or phrase repeated with the same or similar music sung by a group, **322**

**cambiata** changing voice, **312**

**chord** three or more pitches sounding together, **80**

**C major scale** eight pitches beginning and ending on C and represented by the white keys of the keyboard, **99**

**conductor** the leader of a choir, band, or orchestra, **187**

**contrast** musical ideas that are new or different from those already heard, **164**

**courante** a dance of the Renaissance period in binary form, **164**

**crescendo** a gradual increase in the loudness of sound, **74**

**diction** how words are pronounced, **318**

**dominant chord** a chord with the fifth pitch of a scale as its root, **123**

**Dorian mode** a scale using all the white keys of the keyboard from D to D, **115**

**dotted note** a note with an added dot; the dot increases the duration of the note by half its value, **66**

**dulcimer** a stringed instrument, on which the player plucks the strings or strikes them with hammers to produce sound, **121**

**duple meter** beats grouped in sets of two, **16**

**dynamics** the varying degrees of softness or loudness of sound, **17**

**eighth note (♪)** a note one eighth as long as the sound of a whole note, **7**

**episode** a section of a fugue in which the subject or main theme is not heard, **152**

**flat (♭)** a symbol indicating that a tone is to be lowered, **117**

**folk rock** a type of popular music combining a strong rock beat with the traditional instruments and style of folk music, **76**

**form** the overall structure and design of a musical composition, **14**

**forte ( *f* )** loud, **17**

383

# GLOSSARY AND INDEXES

**fortissimo** (*ff*) very loud, **116**

**four-chord set** four chords that are repeated in a harmonic progression, found in popular music, **141**

**fugue** a musical composition with imitation of the subject in several different parts, creating polyphonic texture, **148**

**half note** ( ♩ ) a note one half as long as the sound of a whole note, **33**

**half rest** ( ▬ ) an interval of silence lasting as long as a half note, **33**

**homophonic** refers to a melody in the foreground with accompaniment in the background, **19**

**imitation** the repeating of a melody, rhythm, or harmony by another instrument or voice, **148**

**innovation** taking established styles and musical forms and using personal creativity to create something new, **224**

**interval** the musical distance between two pitches, **35**

**jaw harp** a musical instrument made of metal and wood that is held between the teeth and plucked with the fingers, **121**

**jazz** music created by African Americans and based on aspects of the blues and spirituals, **154**

**key tone** the most important tone of the scale, **123**

**legato** smooth and connected, **114**

**madrigal** a choral piece from the Renaissance that is often polyphonic and sung without instrumental accompaniment, **377**

**major scale** eight notes organized according to a pattern that can be represented by the white keys of the keyboard from C to C, **99**

**march** a form of music characterized by a strong steady beat, the use of accents, and repeated and contrasting sections, usually performed by a band, **184**

**measure** a set or grouping of beats between bar lines, **17**

**melodic contour** the upward or downward movement, or shape, of a melody, **94**

**melodic rhythm** the rhythm pattern of the words or melody of a musical composition, **48**

**meter** the grouping of beats within a measure, as shown by the meter signature, **16**

**meter signature** the two numbers on the staff at the beginning of a musical composition that show how many beats are in a measure and what type of note represents the steady beat, **43**

**minor scale** eight pitches organized according to a pattern that is different from the major scale, **105**

**Mixolydian mode** a scale using all the white keys of the keyboard from C to A, plus B♭, or all the white keys from F to F, **117**

**mode** another name for a scale; two modes are the Dorian and the Mixolydian, **115**

**monophonic** refers to a melody without accompaniment, **19**

**multitrack recording** a method of recording music on more than one track, **292**

**natural** (♮) a symbol indicating the removal of a sharp or flat from a particular pitch, **127**

**octave** the musical distance up or down between two pitches of the same name, **99**

**opera** a drama with scenery and costumes, in which all or most of the words are sung to the accompaniment of an orchestra, **75**

**orchestration** the selection of tone colors by a composer for performing a musical composition, **196**

384

**ostinato** a repeated melodic or rhythmic pattern, **103**

**overdubbing** a method of recording where one part is recorded on top of another, **292**

**partner songs** two or more songs that can be performed together to create harmony, **53**

**pentatonic scale** a scale based on five pitches, for example D F G A C, **95**

**percussion family** musical instruments that are struck to produce a sound, including the drum, cymbal, xylophone, tambourine, and piano, **28**

**phrase** a complete musical idea, **45**

**piano** (*p* ) soft, **17**

**placed** referring to the location of the vocal mechanism, **315**

**polyphonic** refers to more than one melody sounding at the same time, **19**

**producer** a person who coordinates a recording to capture the talent and creativity of the performers, **290**

**quarter note** (♩) a note one quarter as long as the sound of a whole note, **2**

**quarter rest** (𝄾) an interval of silence between tones, lasting as long as a quarter note, **2**

**quodlibet** any group of songs that can be performed together, **196**

**ragtime** a style of American popular music having melodies with syncopated rhythms performed over a steady, regular beat, **49**

**range** the pitch distance between the lowest and highest notes of a melody, **33**

**recording engineer** a person who operates the recording equipment in a recording studio, **290**

**register** the general low or high pitch range of a sound, **24**

**Renaissance** the historical period (1450–1600) that saw a rebirth and growth of culture and technology, **164**

**repetition** restating a melody, rhythm, or harmony, **139**

**ritardando** (*rit.* ) a gradual slowing of the beat, **68**

**rondo** a musical form that uses alternating repetitions of the main theme with two or more contrasting sections (ABACA), **173**

**root** the pitch on which a chord is built, **124**

**round** a composition in which a melody is stated, then is repeated exactly by other parts, starting at different times, creating a polyphonic texture, **18**

**score** the written notation of a musical composition, showing all the parts to be played or sung, **190**

**sharp** (♯) a symbol indicating that a tone is to be raised, **105**

**skipwise motion** the motion of a melody containing pitches with skips between them, **35**

**soprano** high voice, **312**

**spirituals** religious songs created by African Americans in the nineteenth and twentieth centuries, **46, 89**

**spoons** used as a percussion instrument when shaken or struck against the body, **121**

**staccato** short and separated, **114**

**staff** a chart of five lines and four spaces on which music is notated, **36**

**steady beat** the underlying beat or pulse, **5**

# GLOSSARY AND INDEXES

# GLOSSARY AND INDEXES

**stepwise motion** the motion of a melody containing pitches that are adjacent to each other, **35**

**storyboard** a picture or sketch of a scene used in planning a music video, **297**

**string family** musical instruments that are made of wood and have strings that are bowed or plucked, including the violin, viola, cello, bass, harp, and guitar, **28**

**subdominant chord** a chord with the fourth pitch of a scale as its root, **123**

**subject** the main musical theme of a fugue, **148**

**suite** a musical composition consisting of a succession of short pieces, **176**

**syncopation** a rhythm pattern that places emphasis on beats that are not normally accented, giving a catchy, uneven sound, **54**

**tempo** the speed of the beat, **43**

**tenor** lower voice, **313**

**ternary form** the structure of a musical composition in three parts with repetition following one contrast (ABA), **31, 171**

**texture** the way in which melody and harmony are combined to create layers of sound, **19**

**theme and variations** a musical form in which the theme is repeated and varied, **159**

**tie** a curved line that combines the duration of two notes of the same pitch. For example, two tied quarter notes sound as long as a half note, **48**

**tonal center** the tonic pitch around which a musical composition or scale is centered, **132**

**tonal music** music having a strong tonal center, **134**

**tone color** the unique sound of an instrument or voice, **21**

**tonic chord** a chord with the first pitch of a scale as its root, **123**

**triple meter** beats grouped in sets of three, **16**

**triplet ( ♩ ♩ ♩ )** three equal notes of the same duration as one quarter note, **82**

**twelve-bar blues** a chord pattern used in the style of American folk music called blues, **129**

**unison** two or more instruments or voices playing or singing the same notes at the same time, **19**

**variation** changing or altering a musical idea, **153**

**vocable** sung sound that is not a word, **309**

**whole note (o)** a note that receives four beats, **7**

**whole rest (–)** an interval of silence lasting as long as a whole note, **7**

**woodwind family** musical wind instruments originally made of wood, that include the flute, oboe, clarinet, bassoon, and saxophone, **28**

386

# CLASSIFIED INDEX

# GLOSSARY AND INDEXES

# GLOSSARY AND INDEXES

# LISTENING SELECTIONS

388

# ALPHABETICAL SONG INDEX

# GLOSSARY AND INDEXES

## African American Music *(See also* Multicultural Music*)*

Bebey, Francis. *African Music: A People's Art.* Chicago: Chicago Review Press, 1975.

Edet, Edna S. *The Griot Sings: Songs from the Black World.* Collected and adapted. New York: Medgar Evers College Press, 1978.

Glass, Paul. *Songs and Stories of Afro-Americans.* New York: Grosset & Dunlap, 1971.

Johnson, James Weldon, and J.R. Johnson, eds. *The Books of American Negro Spirituals.* 2 vols. in 1. Jersey City, N.J.: Da Capo Press, 1977.

Jones, Bessie, and Bess L. Hawes. *Step It Down: Games, Plays, Songs, and Stories from the Afro-American Heritage.* Athens, Ga.: Univ. of Georgia Press, 1987.

Nketia, Joseph H. *The Music of Africa.* New York: W.W. Norton & Co., 1974.

Southern, Eileen. *The Music of Black Americans.* 2d ed. New York: W.W. Norton & Co., 1983.

## Cooperative Learning

Gibbs, Jeanne. *Tribes: A Process for Social Development and Cooperative Learning.* Santa Rosa, Calif.: Center Source Publications, 1987.

Johnson, David W., Robert T. Johnson, and Edythe Johnson Holubec. *Circles of Learning: Cooperation in the Classroom.* Alexandria, Va.: Association for Supervision & Curriculum Development, 1984.

Slavin, Robert E. *Cooperative Learning: Student Teams.* 2d ed. Washington, D.C.: National Education Association, 1987.

## Dalcroze *(See also* Movement*)*

Abramson, Robert M. *Rhythm Games.* New York: Music & Movement Press, 1973.

Aronoff, Frances W. *Move with the Music: Songs and Activities for Young Children, A Teacher-Parent Preparation Workbook Including Keyboard.* New York: Turning Wheel Press, 1982.

Bachmann, Marie-Laure. *Dalcroze Today: An Education Through and into Music.* Oxford: Clarenon Press, Oxford University Press, 1991.

Jaques-Dalcroze, Émile. *Rhythm, Music, and Education.* rev. ed. Translated by Harold F. Rubenstein. London: The Dalcroze Society, 1980.

## Early Childhood Music

Andress, Barbara. *Music Experiences in Early Childhood.* New York: Holt, Rinehart & Winston, 1980.

Aronoff, Frances W. *Music and Young Children: Expanded Edition.* New York: Turning Wheel Press, 1979.

Bayless, Kathleen M., and Marjorie E. Ramsey. *Music: A Way of Life for the Young Child.* 3d ed. Columbus, Ohio: Merrill Publishing Co., 1987.

Birkenshaw, Lois. *Music for Fun, Music for Learning: For Regular and Special Classrooms.* 3d ed. Toronto: Holt, Rinehart & Winston of Canada, 1982.

McDonald, Dorothy C., and Gene M. Simons. *Musical Growth and Development: Birth Through Six.* New York: Schirmer Books, 1989.

Nye, Vernice T. *Music for Young Children.* 3d ed. Dubuque, Iowa: William C. Brown Publisher, 1983.

## Kodály

Choksy, Lois. *The Kodály Context.* Englewood Cliffs, N.J.: Prentice-Hall, 1981.

——. *The Kodály Method: Comprehensive Music Education from Infant to Adult.* 2d ed. Englewood Cliffs, N.J.: Prentice-Hall, 1988.

Daniel, Katina S. *Kodály Approach, Method Book One.* 2d ed. Champaign, Ill.: Mark Foster Music Co., 1979.

——. *Kodály Approach, Method Book Two.* Champaign, Ill.: Mark Foster Music Co., 1986

——. *Kodály Approach, Method Book Three.* Champaign, Ill.: Mark Foster Music Co., 1987.

——. *Kodály Approach, Method Book Two—Song Collection.* Champaign, Ill.: Mark Foster Music Co., 1982.

Szonyi, Erzsébet. *Musical Reading and Writing.* Translated by Lili Halápy. Revised translation by Geoffrey Russell-Smith. 8 vols. London and New York: Boosey & Hawkes Music Publishers, 1973–1979.

## Listening

Copland, Aaron. *What to Listen for in Music.* New York:

McGraw-Hill Book Co., 1988.

Hoffer, Charles R. *The Understanding of Music.* 5th ed. Belmont, Calif.: Wadsworth Publishing Co., 1985.

Miller, Samuel D. "Listening Maps for Musical Tours." *Music Educators Journal 73* (October 1986): 28–31.

## Movement *(See also* Dalcroze*)*

Boorman, Joyce L. *Creative Dance in the First Three Grades.* Toronto: Harcourt Brace Jovanovich, Canada, 1969.

——. *Creative Dance in Grades Four to Six.* Toronto: Harcourt Brace Jovanovich, Canada, 1971.

——. *Dance and Language Experiences with Children.* Toronto: Harcourt Brace Jovanovich, Canada, 1973.

Joyce, Mary. *First Steps in Teaching Creative Dance to Children.* 2d ed. Mountain View, Calif.: Mayfield Publishing Co., 1980.

Weikart, Phyllis. *Teaching Movement and Dance: Intermediate Folk Dance.* Ypsilanti, Mich.: High/Scope Press, 1984.

## Multicultural Music *(See also* African American Music*)*

Anderson, William M. *Teaching Asian Musics in Elementary and Secondary Schools.* rev. ed. Danbury, Conn.: World Music Press, 1986.

Anderson, William M., and Patricia Shehan Campbell. *Multicultural Perspectives in Music Education.* Reston, Va.: Music Educators National Conference, 1989.

Fulton Fowke, Edith, and Richard Johnston. *Folk Songs of Canada.* Waterloo, Ontario, Canada: Waterloo Music Company, 1954.

George, Luvenia A. *Teaching the Music of Six Different Cultures.* rev. ed. Danbury, Conn.: World Music Press, 1988.

Heth, Charlotte, ed. *Native American Dance: Ceremonies and Social Traditions.* Washington, D.C.: National Museum of the American Indian, Smithsonian Institution with Starwood Publishing, Inc., 1992.

Horse Capture, George P. *Powwow.* Cody, Wyo.: Buffalo Bill Historical Center, 1989.

Rhodes, Robert. *Hopi Music and Dance.* Tsaile, Ariz.: Navajo Community College Press, 1977.

Speck, Frank G., Leonard Broom, and Will West Long. *Cherokee Dance and Drama.* Norman, Okla.: University of Oklahoma Press, 1983.

Titon, Jeff Todd, ed. *Worlds of Music: An Introduction to the Music of the World's Peoples. 2nd ed.* New York: Schirmer Books, 1992.

## Orff

Frazee, Jane, and Kent Kreuter. *Discovering ORFF: A Curriculum for Music Teachers.* Valley Forge, Pa.: European American Music Distributors Corp., 1987.

Keetman, Gunild. *Elementaria, First Acquaintance with Orff-Schulwerk.* Valley Forge, Pa.: European American Music Distributors Corp., 1974.

Keller, Wilhelm. *Introduction to Music for Children.* Translated by Susan Kennedy. Valley Forge, Pa.: European American Music Distributors Corp., 1974.

Nash, Grace C., Geraldine W. Jones, Barbara A. Potter, and Patsy S. Smith. *Do It My Way: The Child's Way of Learning.* Sherman Oaks, Calif.: Alfred Publishing Co., 1977.

Orff, Carl, and Gunild Keetman. *Music for Children.* English version adapted from Orff-Schulwerk by Margaret Murray. 5 vols. London: Schott & Co., 1958–1966.

——. *Music for Children.* Canadian (North American) version adapted from Orff-Schulwerk by Doreen Hall and Arnold Walter. 5 vols. London: Schott & Co., 1956.

Regner, Hermann, ed. *Music for Children.* Vol. 2, *Orff-Schulwerk.* Valley Forge, Pa.: European American Music Distributors Corp., 1977.

Shamrock, Mary. "Orff Schulwerk: An Integrated Foundation." *Music Educators Journal 72* (February 1986): 51–55.

## Recorder

King, Carol. *Recorder Roots* (Books I–II). Memphis, Tenn.: Memphis Musicraft Publications, 1978 and 1984.

## Signing

Gadling, Donna C., Pastor Daniel H. Pokorny, and Dr. Lottie L. Riekehof. *Lift Up Your Hands: Inspirational and Patriotic Songs in the Language of Signs.* Washington, D.C.: National Grange, 1975.

Kannapell, Barbara M., and Lillian B. Hamilton. *Songs in*

*Signed English.* Washington, D.C.: Gallaudet College Press, 1973.

Riekehof, Lottie L. *The Joy of Signing.* 2d ed. Springfield, Mo.: Gospel Publishing House, 1987.

Sternberg, Martin. *American Sign Language.* New York: Harper & Row Publishers, 1987.

Weaks, Donna Gadling. *Lift Up Your Hands.* Vol. 2, *Favorite Songs with Sign Language Interpretation.* Washington, D.C.: National Grange, 1980.

## Special Learners

Atterbury, Betty W. *Mainstreaming Exceptional Learners in Music.* Englewood Cliffs, N.J.: Prentice-Hall, 1990.

Cassidy, J.W., and W.L. Sims. "What's In a Name?" *General Music Today* 3 (3–1990). 23–24, 32.

Darrow, Alice-Ann. "Music for the Deaf." *Music Educators Journal* 71 (February 1985): 33–35.

Graham, Richard M., and Alice S. Beer. *Teaching Music to the Exceptional Child: A Handbook for Mainstreaming.* Englewood Cliffs, N.J.: Prentice-Hall, 1980.

Hughes, J.E. "Sing everyone." *General Music Today,* 4 (2–1991), 8–9.

Jellison, J.A. "A Content Analysis of Music Research with Handicapped Children and Youth (1975–1986): Applications in Special Education." In C.K. Furman (ed.), *Effectiveness of Music Therapy Procedures: Documentation in Research and Clinical Practice* (pp. 223–279). Washington, D.C.: National Association for Music Therapy, 1988.

——. "Functional Value as Criterion for Selection and Prioritization of Nonmusic and Music Educational Objectives in Music Therapy." *Music Therapy Perspectives,* 1 (2–1983), 17–22.

——, B.H. Brooks, and A.M. Huck. Structure Small Groups and Music Reinforcement to Facilitate Positive Interactions and Acceptance of Severely Handicapped Students in Regular Music Classrooms." *Journal of Research in Music Education* 39 (1984), 322–333.

——. "Talking About Music: Interviews with Disabled and Nondisabled Children." *Journal of Research in Music Education,* 39 (1991), 322–333.

——. "Writing and Talking About Children with Disabilities. *General Music Today,* 4 (1–1990), 25–26.

Lam, Rita C., and Cecilia Wang. "Integrating Blind and Sighted Through Music." *Music Educators Journal* 68 (April 1982): 44-45.

Pennington, H.D. "Acceptance and Expectations of Disabled Students in Music Classes" *General Music Today* 5 (1–1991), 31.

## Technology

*JVC Video Anthology of World Music and Dance.* Victor Company of Japan and Smithsonian/Folkways Recordings, 1991. Distributed by New England Networks, 61 Prospect Street, Montpelier, Vt. 05602

*MetroGnomes' Music* (MS-DOS, 640K, CGA, or better display, 3.5" or 5.25" drive, hard drive and sound card recommended). Fremont, Calif.: The Learning Co.

*Note Play* (MS-DOS/Windows, MIDI keyboard optional). Available through Educational Resource, Elgin, Ill.

*Piano Works* (MS-DOS, 640K, CGA, or better display, 3.5" or 5.25" floppy drive and hard drive, MIDI interface and keyboard). Bellevue, Wash.: Temporal Acuity Products.

*Soloist* (MS-DOS, 286K, Sound Blaster sound card, microphone). Ibis Software, available through Educational Resource, Elgin, Ill.

## Vocal Development/Choral Music

Bartle, Jean Ashworth. *Lifeline for Children's Choir Directors.* Toronto: Gordon V. Thompson Music, 1988.

Cooksey, John M. *Working with the Adolescent Voice.* St. Louis: Concordia Publishing House, 1992.

Heffernan, Charles W. *Choral Music: Technique and Artistry.* Englewood Cliffs, N.J.: Prentice-Hall, 1982.

May, William V., and Craig Tolin. *Pronunciation Guide for Choral Literature.* Reston, Va.: Music Educators National Conference, 1987.

Rao, Doreen. *Choral Music Experience Education Through Artistry.* Vol. 1, *Artistry in Music Education;* Vol. 2, *The Artist in Every Child;* Vol. 5, *The Young Singing Voice.* New York: Boosey & Hawkes, 1987.

Swears, Linda. *Teaching the Elementary School Chorus.* Englewood Cliffs, N.J.: Prentice-Hall, 1984.

**AB**
creating a visual diagram for, 175
identifying form by using contrasting
   rhythmic patterns, 43
movement patterns in, 166
practicing, 171
by title
   Bashana Haba-a, 332
   Blowin' in the Wind (words only), 264
   Cripple Creek, 42, 165
   Las Flores, 56
   Nine Hundred Miles, 102
   One Great Nation, 365
   Place in the Choir, A, 301
   Praetorius: Courante from *Terpsichore*
      (listening), 164
   Ring the Bells, 345
   Sing Hosanna, 114
   Sing We and Chant It, 369
   Vive L'amour, 324
   Zudio, 73

**ABA**
in art, 169
identifying, 171
listening for repetition and contrast in, 168
practicing, 16
by title
   Cum-ma-la Be-stay, 306
   Guantanamera, 305
   Our World, 170–171
   Rimsky-Korsakov: "Procession of the
      Nobles" (listening), 30
   Shifting Meters, 16
   Stravinsky: "Galop" from Suite No. 2 for
      Small Orchestra (listening), 168
   With Songs of Rejoicing, 357

**Accompaniments.** *See also* Instruments,
Playing; Texture

**Artists.** *See* Biographies

**Background**
African keyboard instruments, 331
African musical concepts, 331
"America," 312
American popular music, 315
audio and audiovisual transmission, 297
baroque, 348
electric guitar, 226
electric keyboards, 230
gospel music, 376
hi-fi and lo-fi, 291
Japan, 351
*Les Misérables*, 13
MIDI controllers, 292
music technology, 286
notation, 333
powwow, 309
"Silent Night," 338
sound systems, 228
sugarcane, 362
synthesizer history, 231
uses of MIDI, 293
Van Halen, 226
"Where Go the Boats?," 354
"With Songs of Rejoicing," 357

**Beat.** *See* Duration/Rhythm

**Bells.** *See* Instruments, Playing

**Biographies.** *See also* Curriculum
   Connections
artists
   Bearden, Romare, 196
   Benton, Thomas Hart, 113
   Bingham, George Caleb, 125
   Calder, Alexander, 138
   Demuth, Charles, 153
   Escher, M. C., 138
   Frankenthaler, Helen, 199
   Gottlieb, Adoph, 188
   Hopper, Edward, 188
   Kandinsky, Wassily, 113
   Monet, Claude, 198
   Picasso, Pablo, 61
   Pollock, Jackson, 135
   Stella, Joseph, 134
   Vasarely, Victor, 153
musicians
   Armstrong, Louis, 251
   Bach, Johann Ludwig, 357
   Bach, Johann Sebastian, 150
   Beethoven, Ludwig van, 97
   Berry, Chuck, 242
   Boulez, Pierre, 135
   Britten, Benjamin, 119
   Estefan, Gloria, 10
   Franklin, Aretha, 284
   Gabriel, Peter, 225
   Gould, Morton, 158
   Grieg, Edvard, 145
   Harrison, George, 109
   Hornsby, Bruce, 287
   Joel, Billy, 224
   Joplin, Scott, 49
   Morely, Thomas, 369
   Mozart, Wolfgang Amadeus, 108
   Nicks, Stevie, 232
   Pachelbel, Johann, 100
   Praetorius, Michael, 165
   Presley, Elvis, 243
   Purcell, Henry, 98
   Riley, Terry, 147
   Rimsky-Korsakov, Nicolai, 31
   Rolontz, Lee, 294
   Schmitt, Al, 291
   Smith, Bessie, 126
   Sousa, John Philip, 187
   Stravinsky, Igor, 169
   Tchaikovsky, Peter Ilyich, 107
   Telemann, Georg Philipp, 348
   Toch, Ernst, 24
   Vangelis, 130
   Vaughan Williams, Ralph, 177
   Williams, John, 84
   Wonder, Stevie, 239
poets
   Eliot, T. S., 23
   Johnson, James Weldon, 47
   Nash, Ogden, 21
   Silverstein, Shel, 21

**Body Percussion.** *See* Creative Activities;
   Ostinatos; Texture

**Canons.** *See* Rounds/Canons

**Careers**
disc jockey, 294
electric guitarist, 227
music business attorney, 284
music critic, 294
music director/program director, 294

personal manager, 284
recording engineer, 290
songwriter/arranger, 287
studio musician, 284
video producer, 296
vocalist, 284

**Choral Music.** *See* Vocal/Choral
   Development

**Chords.** *See* Texture

**Classroom Instruments.** *See* Instruments,
   Playing; Tone Color

**Composers.** *See* Biographies, musicians

**Cooperative Learning**
AB form, practicing, 171
ABA form, practicing, 16, 171
blues composition, creating, 127
folk instruments, exploring, 121
listening map, creating, 177
melodic intervals, exploring, 128
musical heritage, exploring, 46
ostinatos, creating, 146
recording projects, 282
rhythms, reviewing, 72
sharing ideas, 187
syncopation, games using, 88
variations on existing theme, creating, 159
word rhythms, games using, 50

**Creative Activities**
ABA composition, 31
accompaniments, improvising, 17, 115
advertising, 295
arrangement, 288
blues melody, improvising, 129
body percussion, patterns, 18, 52, 84
chant, 351
composition, instrumental, 31, 43, 54, 147,
   167, 175, 188
conversation between instruments, 330
dance, 361
fugue, spoken, 152
guitar strum patterns, 81
melody, 333, 351, 354, 358
melody, improvising, 32, 37, 129, 167, 309
movement for "Cum-ma-la Be-stay," 308
multimedia presentation, 364
multiple-part recording, 293
music video, 297
new version of song, 304
new words, 306, 323
patriotic program, 364
percussion ostinatos, 302, 330, 340, 351
percussion parts, 330, 372, 376
phrases, improvising, 101
poem, 26, 354, 364
processional step, 330
rap, 227
recording, 285
rhythm ostinatos, 304, 351, 361
rhythm patterns, 8, 84, 372
rondo, improvising, 175
round, 318
sight-reading examples, 361
song, art work, poetry, or dance on theme,
   328
song variations, 155, 159
sound composition, 147, 334
thumb piano accompaniment, 331

Grateful acknowledgment is given to the following authors, composers, and publishers. Every effort has been made to trace the ownership of all copyrighted material and to secure the necessary permissions to reprint these selections. In the case of some selections for which acknowledgment is not given, extensive research has failed to locate the copyright holders.

Acum LTD., for *Hine Ma Tov*. Copyright © by Moshe Jacobson. Acum, ISRAEL.

Alfred Publishing Company, Inc., for *One Great Nation* by Stephen L. Lawrence. Copyright MCMXCIII Alfred Publishing Co., Inc. Used with Permission of the Publisher.

Fernando G. Allen for *The Promised Land*. © Copyright 1994 by Fernando G. Allen. All Rights Reserved.

Beckenhorst Press for *Sing Hosanna* by Michael Jothen. © Copyright 1977 by Beckenhorst Press. All rights reserved. Used by permission of the publisher.

Bruce Springsteen Publishing c/o Jon Landau Management for *Born in the U.S.A.* © 1984 ASCAP. All Rights Reserved.

Curtis Brown for the recording of *The Termite*. Used by permission of Curtis Brown Ltd. Copyright 1942 by Ogden Nash. All rights reserved.

Bug Music for *A Place in the Choir* written by Bill Staines. © 1978 MINERAL RIVER MUSIC (BMI) / Administered by BUG. All Rights Reserved. Used by Permission.

Lois Choksy for *Don't Let the Wind* from THE KODÁLY CONTEXT by Lois Choksy. PUBLISHED BY PRENTICE HALL, INC., 1981. USED WITH PERMISSION.

Elva Davilla for *Las Flores* from *CANTARES NAVIDEÑOS* 1961 by Francisco Lopez Cruz. Reprinted by permission.

Robert de Frece and Shirley Funk for *America, My Homeland*. Music by Robert de Frece © 1987. Lyrics by Robert de Frece and Shirley Funk © 1987.

Faber and Faber Ltd. for the Canadian rights for *The Naming of Cats* from OLD POSSUM'S BOOK OF PRACTICAL CATS by T. S. Eliot. Reprinted in Canada by permission of Faber and Faber Ltd.

Fall River Music for *Guantanamera*. Original lyrics and music by José Fernandez Dias, Music adaptation by Julian Orbon and Pete Seeger. Lyric adaptation by Julian Orbon, based on a poem by José Martí. © Copyright 1963, 1965 (renewed) by FALL RIVER MUSIC INC. All Rights Reserved. Used by Permission.

Carl Fischer, Inc. for *With Songs of Rejoicing*, arranged by Hal Hopson. Copyright 1979 by Carl Fischer, Inc., New York. Used by Permission. International Copyright secured.

Foreign Imported Music for *Seal Our Fate*, written by Gloria Estefan. Copyright 1990, 1993 Foreign Imported Productions & Publishing, Inc. (BMI). International Copyright Secured. All Rights Reserved.

Hal Leonard for *Bashana Haba-a*. Original Hebrew version. Lyrics by Ehud Manor. Music by Nurit Hirsh. © 1970 EMI SONGS (ISRAEL) LTD. All Rights Controlled and Administered by EMI BLACKWOOD MUSIC INC. All Rights Reserved. International Copyright Secured. Used by Permission. For *Big Girls Don't Cry*. Words and music by Bob Crewe and Bob Gaudio. © 1962, 1963 (Renewed) CLARIDGE MUSIC COMPANY, A Division of MPL Communications, Inc. All Rights

Reserved. For *Dreams*. Words and music by Stevie Nicks. Copyright © 1977, 1978 Welsh Witch Music. All Rights Administered by Sony Music Publishing, 8 Music Square West, Nashville, TN 37203. International Copyright Secured. All Rights Reserved. For *Our World*. Words by Jane Foster Knox. Music by Lana Walter. Copyright © 1985 by Jenson Publications. International Copyright Secured. All Rights Reserved. For *Under the Boardwalk*. Words and music by Artie Resnick and Kenny Young. Copyright © 1964 by Alley Music Corp. and Trio Music Co., Inc. Copyright Renewed. International Copyright Secured. All Rights Reserved. Used by Permission. For *The Walking Blues*. Words and music by Bob Summers. Copyright © 1982 by Jenson Publications. International Copyright Secured. All Rights Reserved.

Harcourt Brace & Company for the U.S. Rights for *The Naming of Cats* from OLD POSSUM'S BOOK OF PRACTICAL CATS, copyright 1939 by T.S. Eliot and renewed 1967 by Esme Valerie Eliot, reprinted by permission of Harcourt Brace & Company.

HarperCollins Publishers for *Ridiculous Rose* from WHERE THE SIDEWALK ENDS by SHEL SILVERSTEIN. COPYRIGHT © 1974 BY EVIL EYE MUSIC, INC. SELECTION REPRINTED BY PERMISSION of HarperCollins Publishers.

Hinshaw Music for *After the Rain*. Copyright © 1989 by Hinshaw Music, Inc. Used by Permission. For *Go Now in Peace*. Copyright © 1976 by Hinshaw Music, Inc. Used by Permission. For *Ring the Bells*. Copyright © 1977 by Hinshaw Music, Inc. Used by Permission. For *Listen to the Music*. Copyright © 1991 by Hinshaw Music, Inc. Used by Permission.

Irving Music Corp., for *In My Room* © 1964, Renewed 1992, Irving Music Inc. (BMI). All Rights Reserved. International Copyright Secured. Used by Permission.

Little, Brown and Company for *The Termite* from VERSES FROM 1929 ON by Ogden Nash. Copyright 1942 by Ogden Nash. First appeared in THE SATURDAY EVENING POST. By permission of Little, Brown and Company.

Ludlow Music c/o TRO for *We Shall Overcome*. Musical and lyrical adaptation by Zilphia Horton, Frank Hamilton, Guy Carawan and Pete Seeger. Inspired by African American Gospel Singing, members of the Food & Tobacco Workers Union, Charleston, SC, and the southern Civil Rights Movement. TRO © Copyright 1960 (Renewed) and 1963 (Renewed) Ludlow Music, Inc., New York, International Copyright Secured. Made in U.S.A. All Rights Reserved Including Public Performance For Profit. Used by Permission.

Meyers Music for *Rock Around the Clock*. © Renewed 1981 MEYERS MUSIC and CAPANO MUSIC. All Rights Reserved. Used by Permission.

Moose Music for *Colour My World* by James Pankow © 1970 Moose Music/Aurelius Music. All Rights Reserved. International Copyright Secured.

Music Sales Corporation for *Where Go the Boats?* Music by R. Evan Copley. Lyrics by Robert Louis Stevenson. Copyright © 1982 by Shawnee Press, Inc. (ASCAP) International Copyright Secured. All Rights Reserved. Reprinted by Permission.

Terry Philips, Patrick Bradley Music, Inc. for *Cumma-la Be-stay*. Words and music by Donny Burke, Jerry Vance, and Terry Philips. © 1972 by Popdraw Music Corp., New York, NY.

Random House for *The Birch Tree* from A RUSSIAN SONGBOOK by Rose N. Rubin and Michael Stillman, edit. Copyright © 1962 by Rose N. Rubin and Michael Stillman. Reprinted by permission of Random House Inc.

Jerry Silverman for *Jane, Jane*. Originally arranged by Jerry Silverman.

Special Rider Music for *Blowin' In the Wind*. Copyright © 1962 by WARNER BROS. MUSIC, COPYRIGHT RENEWED 1990 BY SPECIAL RIDER MUSIC. All rights reserved. International copyright secured. Reprinted by permission.

Staff Music Publishing Co., Inc. for *Down, Down, Down*. Words and music by Maurice Gardner, STAFF MUSIC PUBLISHING CO. Inc.

Sundance Music for *Circles* by Linda Worsley. Copyright 1986 by Sundance Music. For *Night of Stars/Silent Night*. Music by Franz Gruber and Linda Worsley. Lyrics by Josef Mohr and Linda Worsley. Arranged by Linda Worsley. © Copyright 1994 by Sundance Music. For *Wind and Snow* by Linda Worsley. Copyright Sundance Music.

Viking Penguin for *O Black and Unknown Bards*. Copyright 1917 by James Weldon Johnson, from SAINT PETER RELATES AN INCIDENT by James Weldon Johnson. Used by permission of Viking Penguin, a division of Penguin Books USA Inc.

Warner Bros. Publications for *Autumn Vesper*. Music and additional lyrics Audrey Snyder Brown © 1994 Studio 224. All Rights controlled by Warner Bros. Publications U.S. Inc. All Rights Reserved. Used By Permission. For *Guadalajara*. Spanish words and music by Pepe Guizar. © 1937 (Renewed) Peer International Corporation. All Rights Reserved. Used By Permission. For *The Lion Sleeps Tonight*. New lyric and revised music by George David Weiss, Hugo Peretti and Luigi Creatore. © 1961 Folkways Music Publishers, Inc. © Renewed 1989 by George David Weiss, Luigi Creatore and June Peretti/assigned to Abilene Music, Inc. All Rights Reserved. Used by Permission. For *Trav'ler*. Music by Mark Wilson, words by Jane Foster Knox. © 1988 Studio 224. All Rights controlled by Warner Bros. Publications U.S. Inc. All Rights Reserved. Used by Permission. For *Under the Boardwalk*, by Artie Resnick & Kenny Young © 1964 (Renewed) Trio Music Co., Inc. and Alley Music Corp. WARNER BROS. PUBLICATIONS U.S. INC., Miami, FL 33014

Weekly Reader Corporation for *Foul Shot*. Special permission granted by **READ**® magazine, copyrighted © 1962, renewed 1989, and published by Weekly Reader Corporation. All Rights Reserved.

World Music Press for *Jōban Tanko Bushi*. © 1994 World Music Press, P.O. Box 2565 Danbury, CT 06813.

Some line drawings of musical instruments reprinted by permission of Harvard University Press from NEW HARVARD DICTIONARY OF MUSIC by Don M. Randel. Copyright 1987 by the President and Fellows of Harvard College.

# SPECIAL CONTRIBUTORS

**Consultant Writers**

**Dr. Betty Atterbury**
*Mainstreaming*
Gorham, Maine

**Alex Campbell**
*Choral Music*
Lakewood, Colorado

**Mary Frances Early**
*African American Music*
Atlanta, Georgia

**Dr. JaFran Jones**
*Ethnomusicology*
Toledo, Ohio

**Consultants and Contributing Writers**

**Dr. Clifford Alper**
Towson, Maryland

**Dr. James Anthony**
Towson, Maryland

**Teri Burdette**
Rockville, Maryland

**Glenn Cashman**
Baltimore, Maryland

**Gregory Clouspy**
Reisterstown, Maryland

**Marilyn Copeland Davidson**
Bergenfield, New Jersey

**Ruth Landis Drucker**
Baltimore, Maryland

**Dr. Robert A. Duke**
Austin, Texas

**Nancy E. Ferguson**
Tucson, Arizona

**Donna Brink Fox**
Rochester, New York

**Larry Harms**
Los Angeles, California

**Bernard Hynson, Jr.**
Baltimore, Maryland

**Dr. Judith A. Jellison**
Austin, Texas

**Tom Kosmala**
Pittsburgh, Pennsylvania

**Gilbert Meerdter**
New Windsor, Maryland

**Carl J. Nygard, Jr.**
Fleetwood, Pennsylvania

**Belle Ortiz**
San Antonio, Texas

**Jane Pippart-Brown**
Lancaster, Pennsylvania

**Edwin J. Schupman, Jr.,**
of ORBIS Associates
Spokane, Washington

**Dr. Susan Snyder**
Norwalk, Connecticut

**Cynthia Stephens**
Ellicott City, Maryland

**Mollie G. Tower**
Austin, Texas

**José A. Villarrubia**
Towson, Maryland

**Michael Yockel**
Miami, Florida